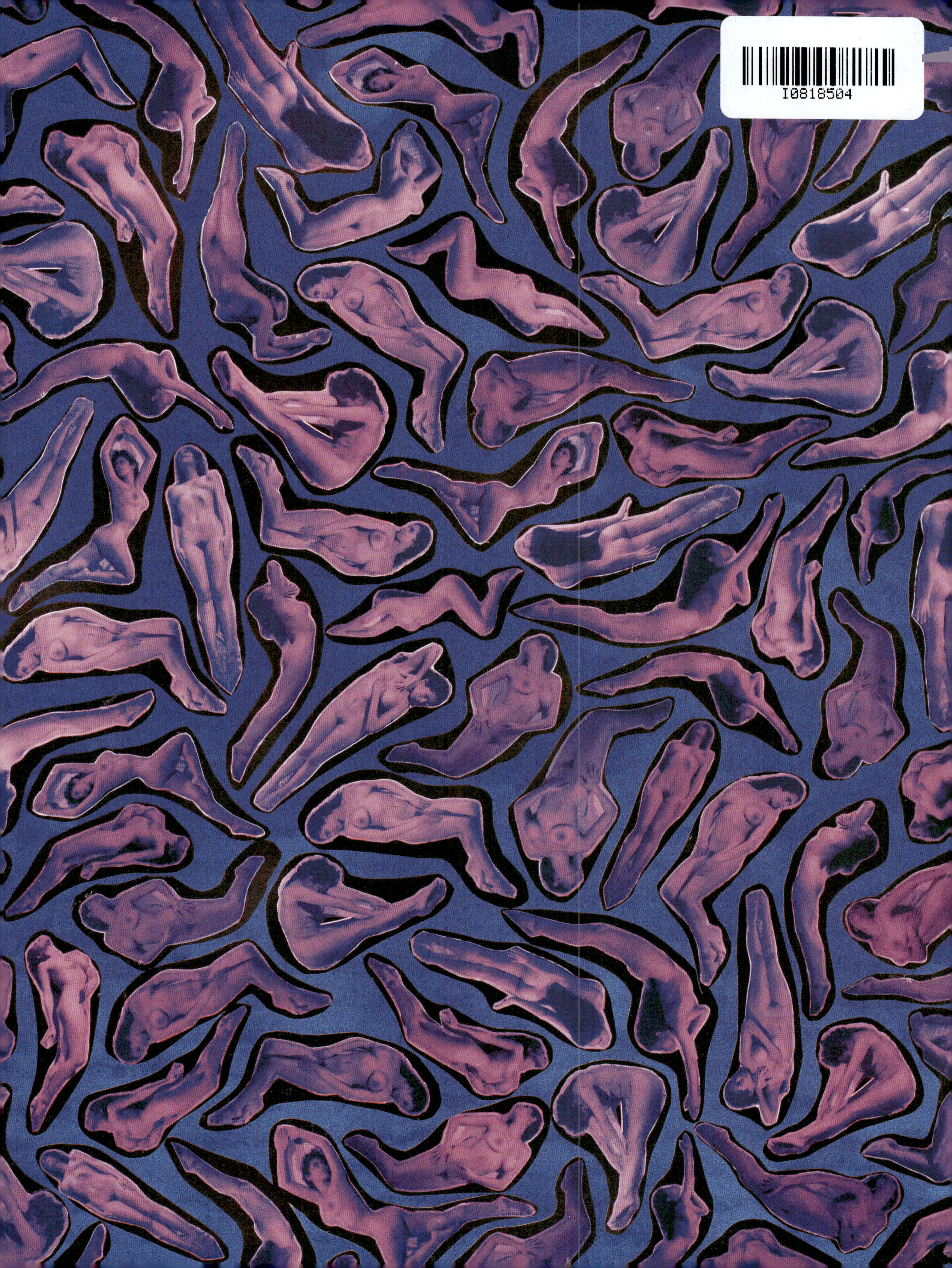
I0818504

explaining

LaChapelle 88

everything.

a struggle for truth

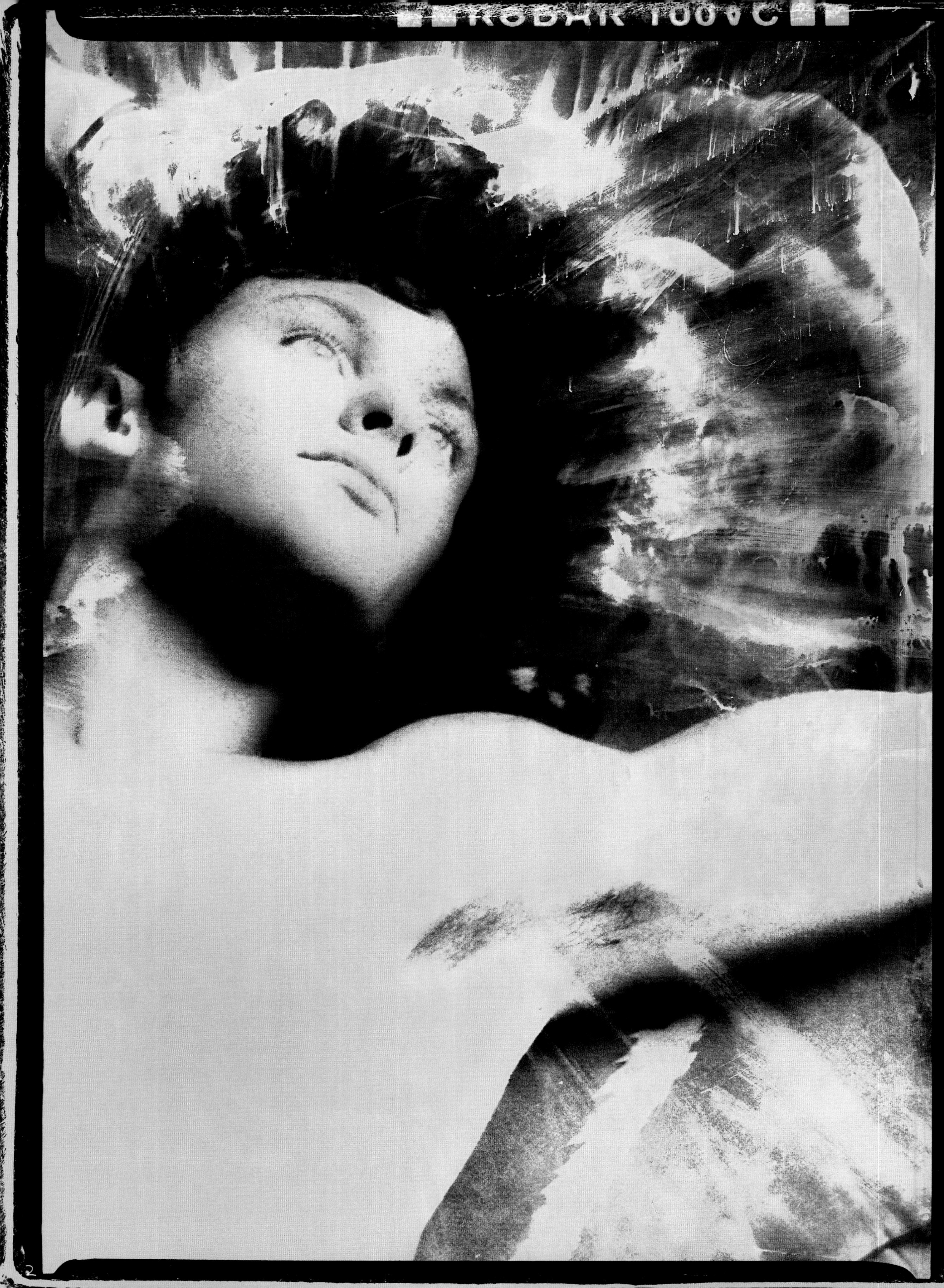

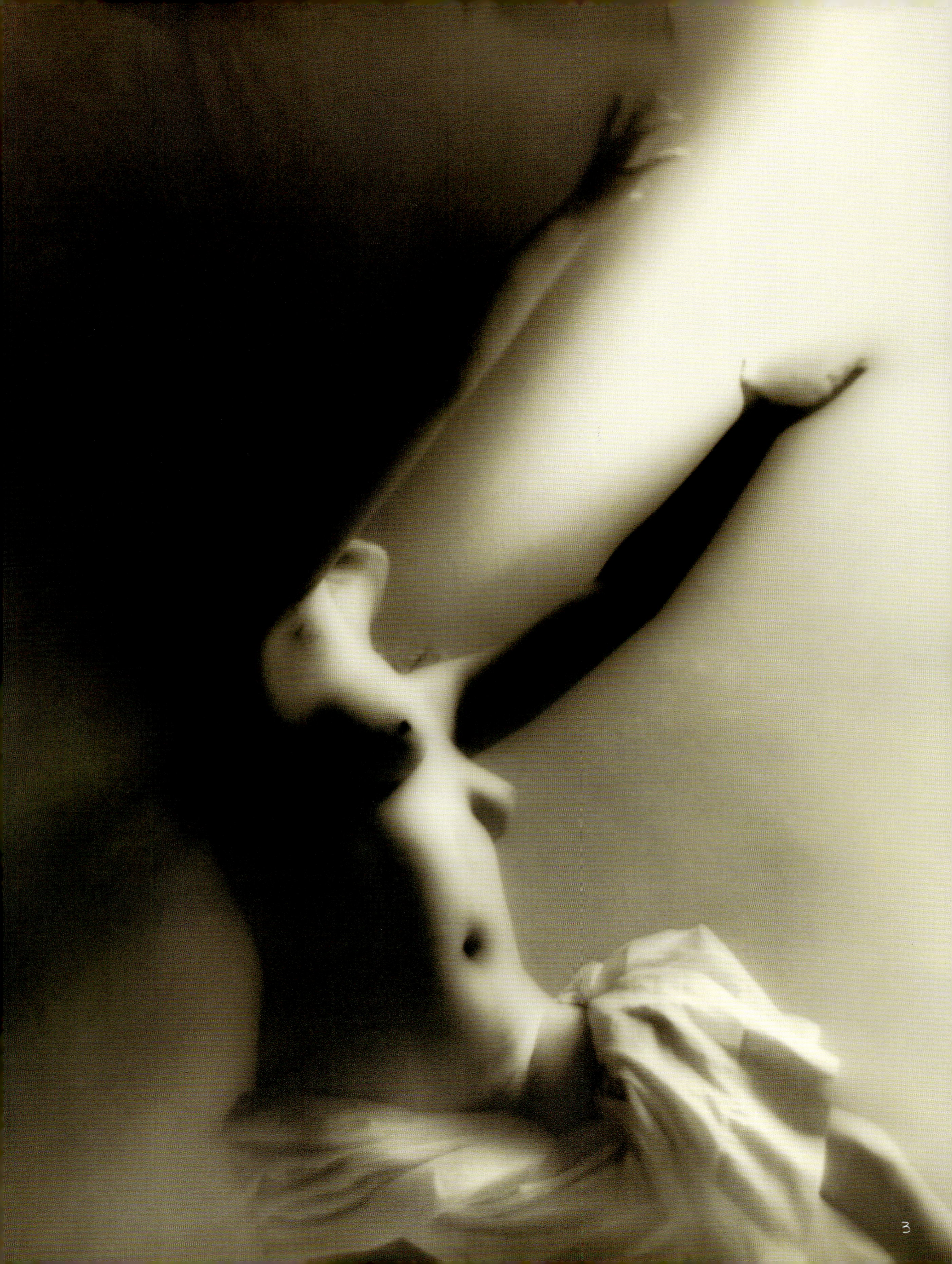

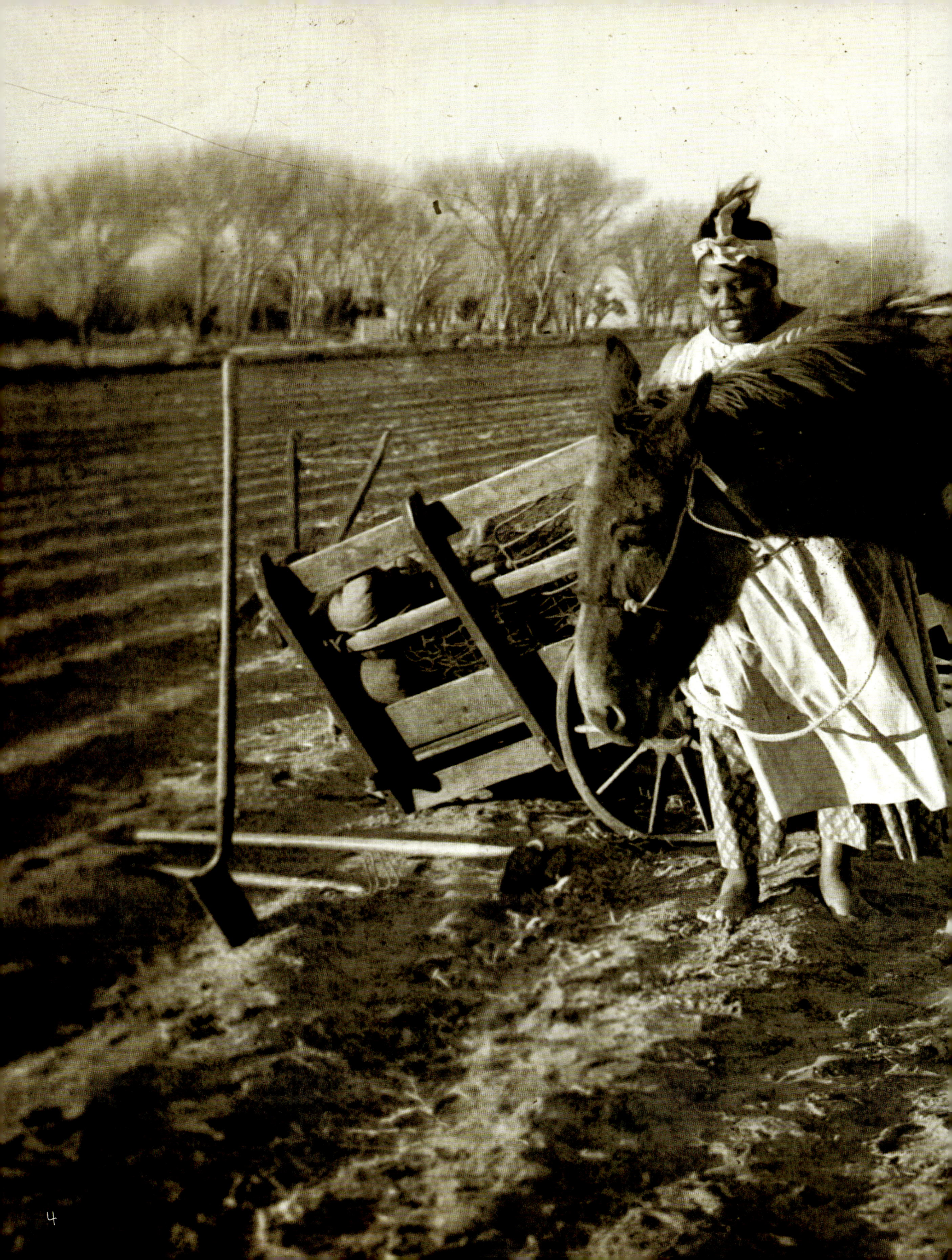

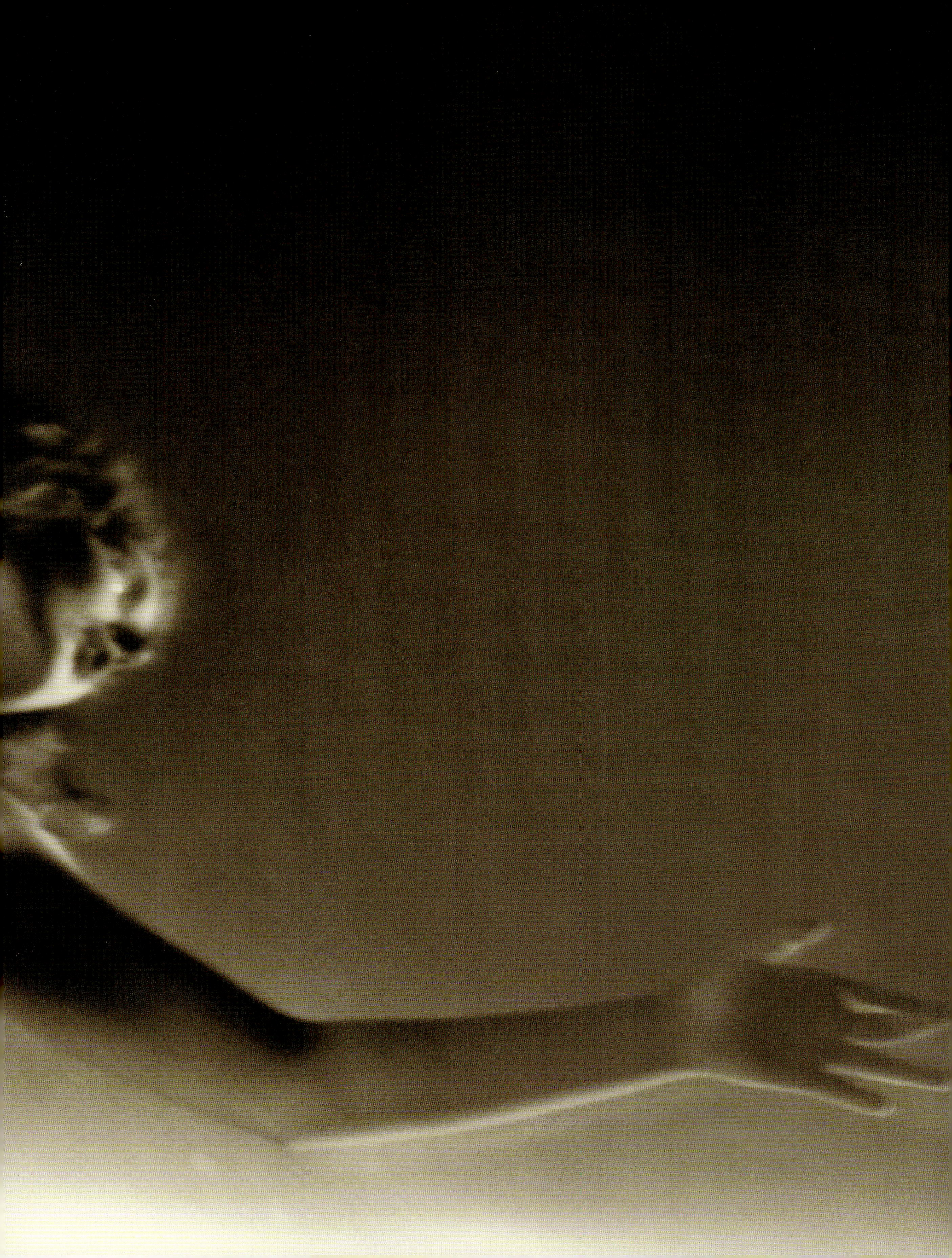

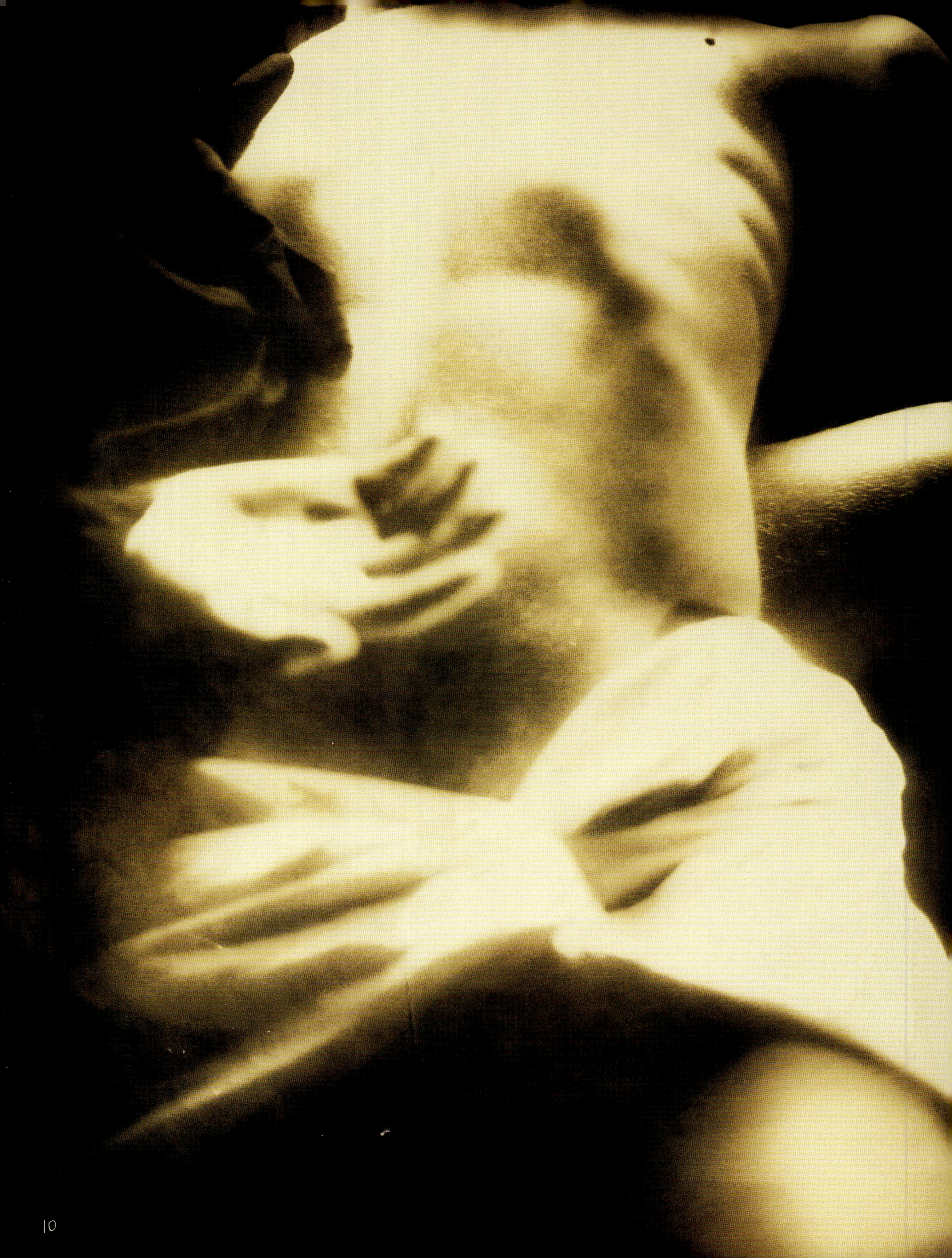

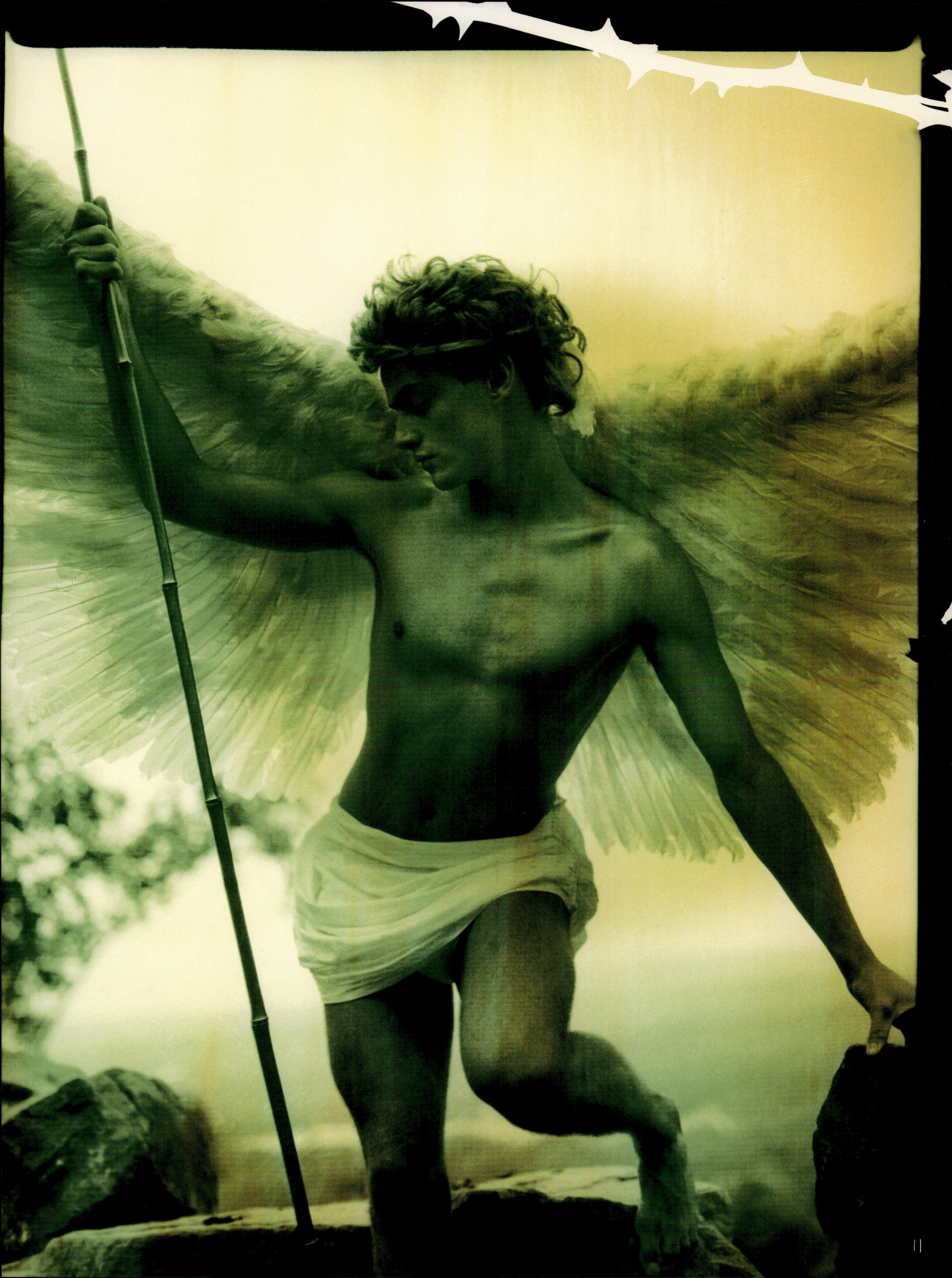

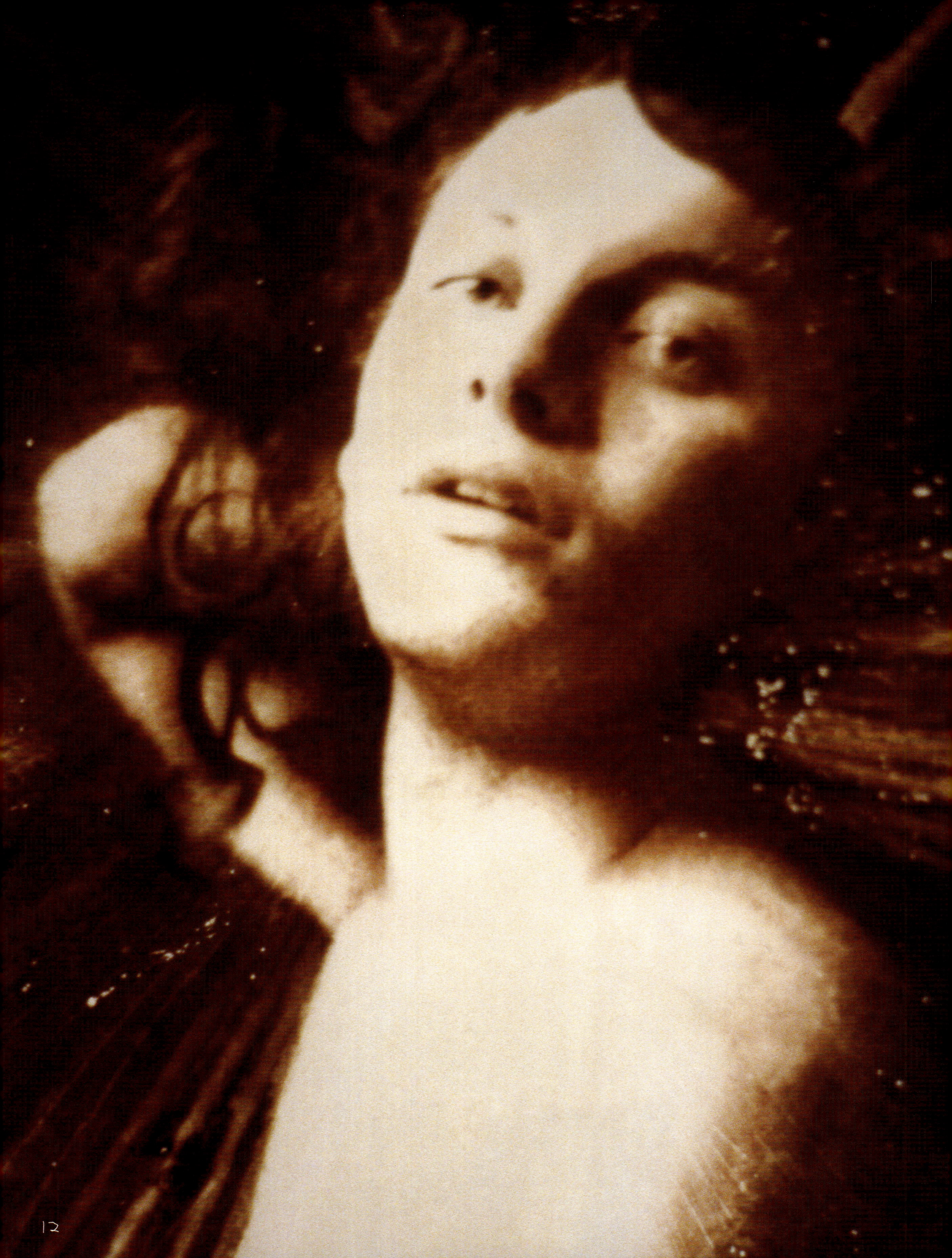

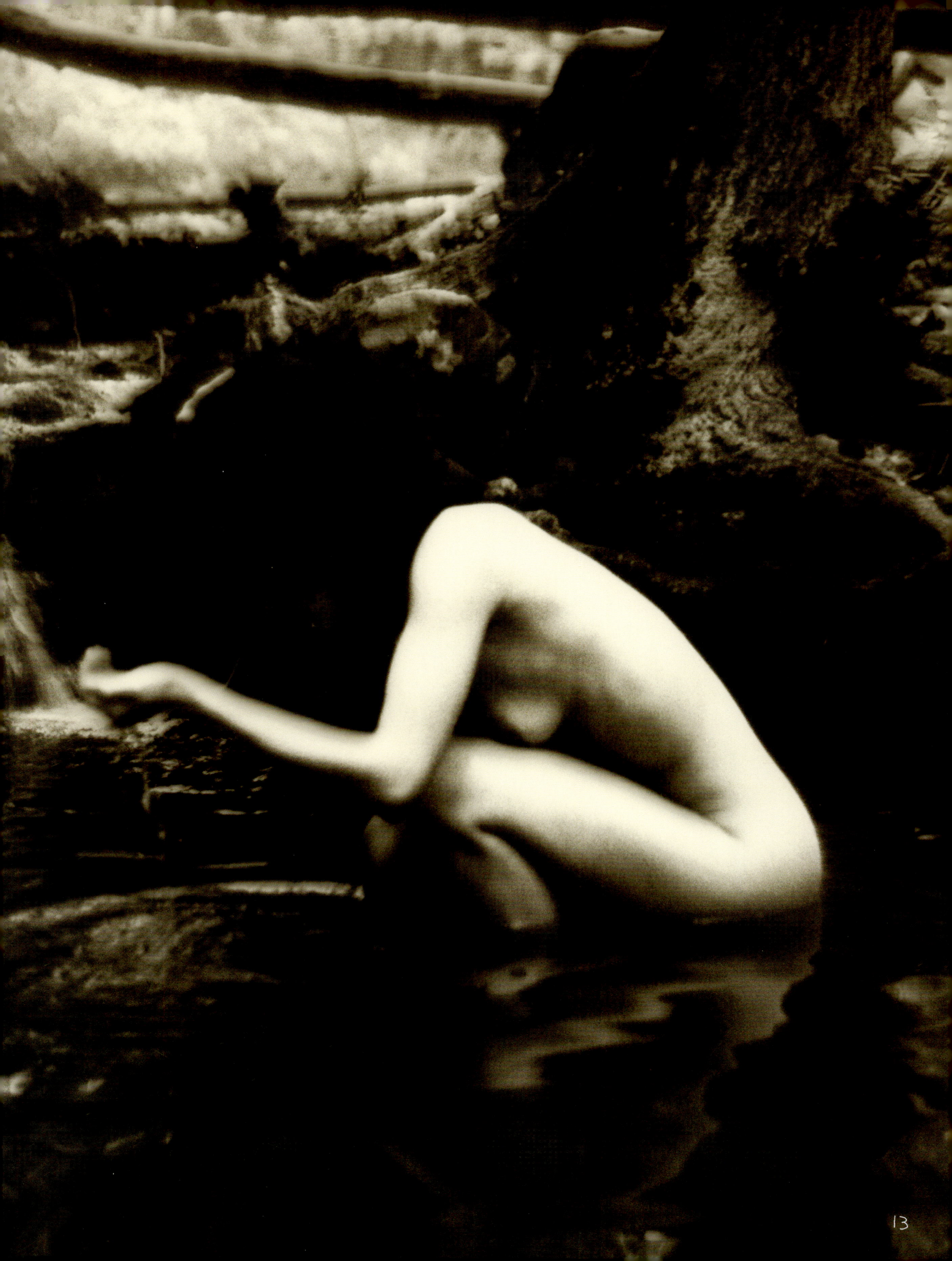

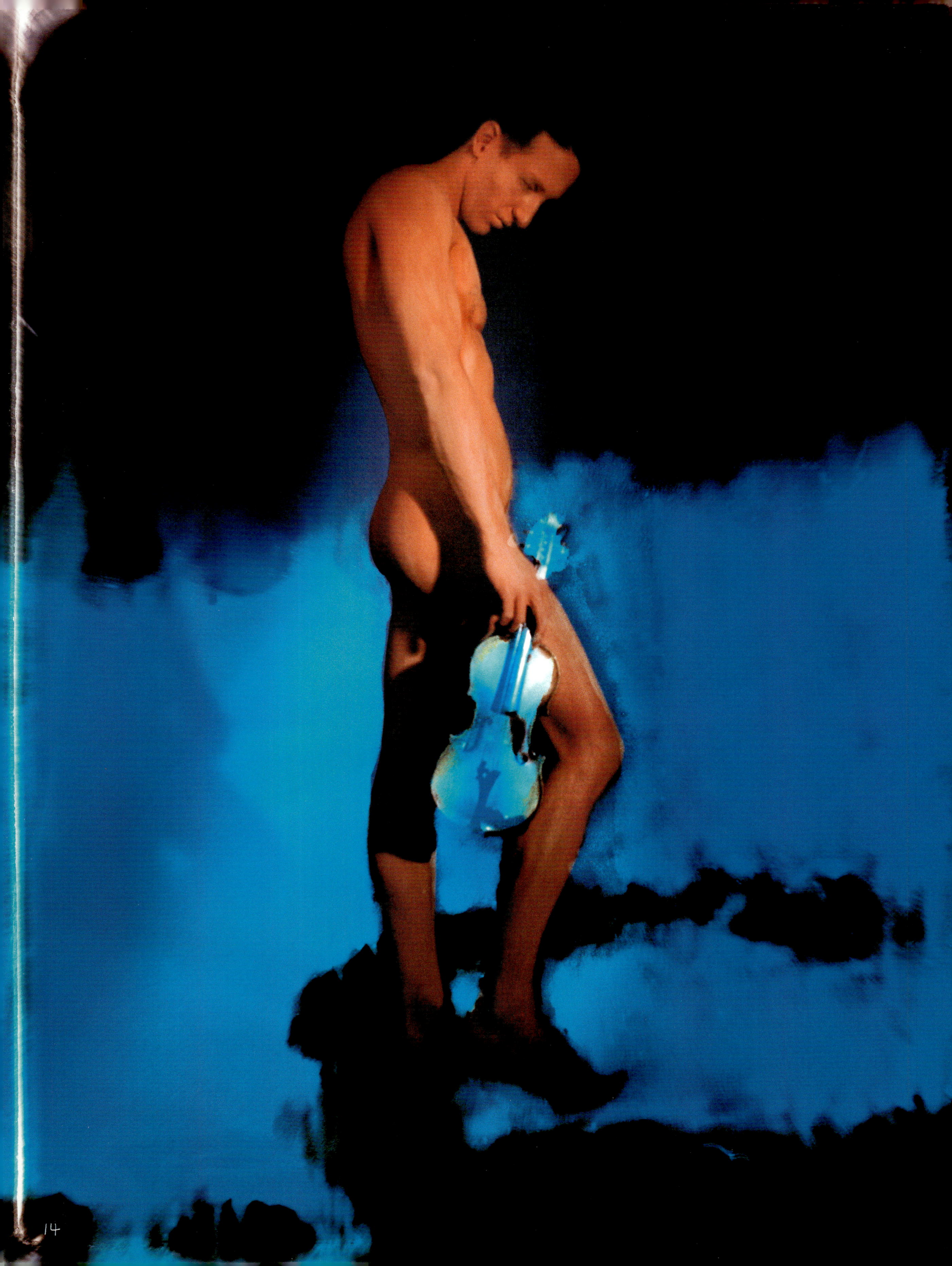

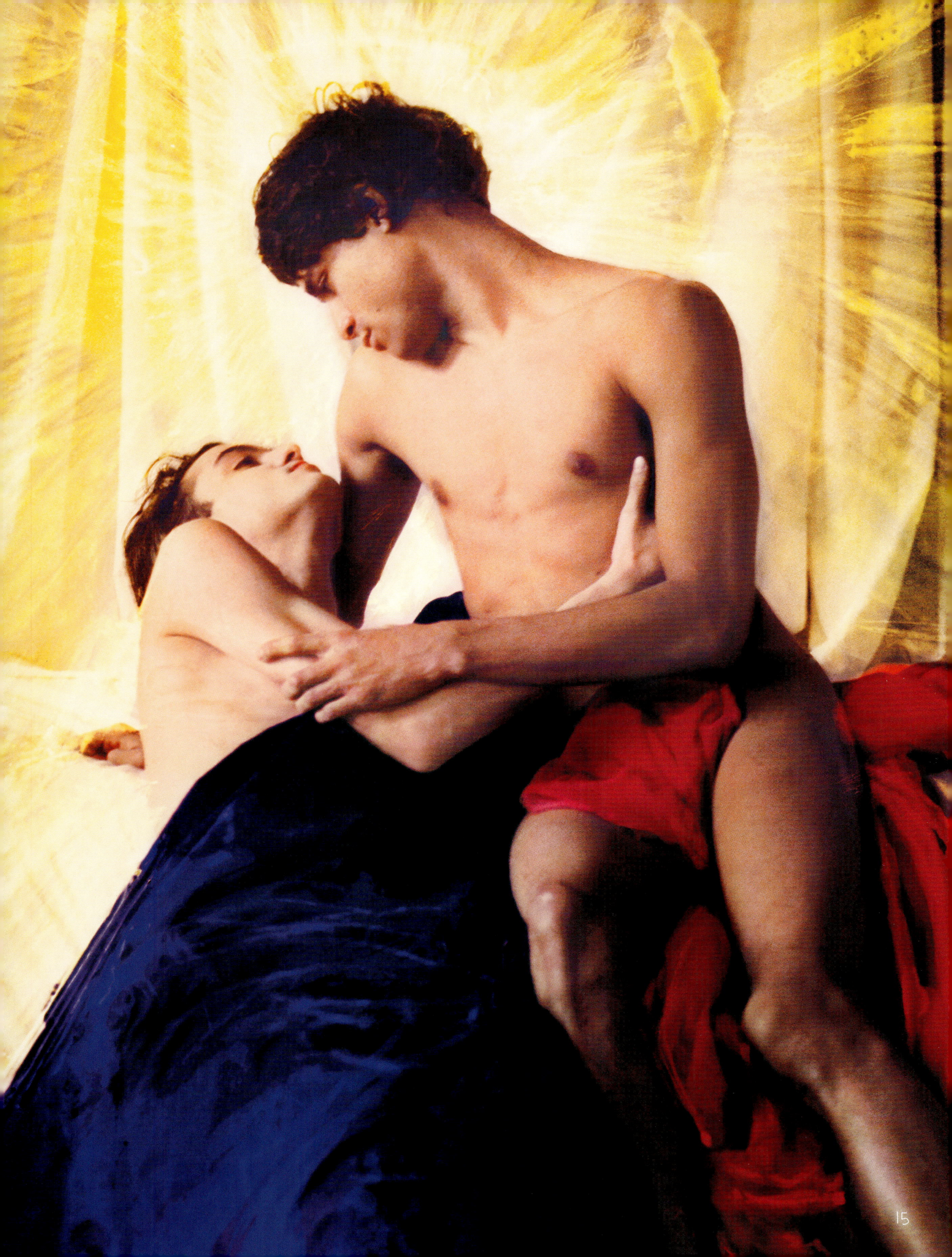

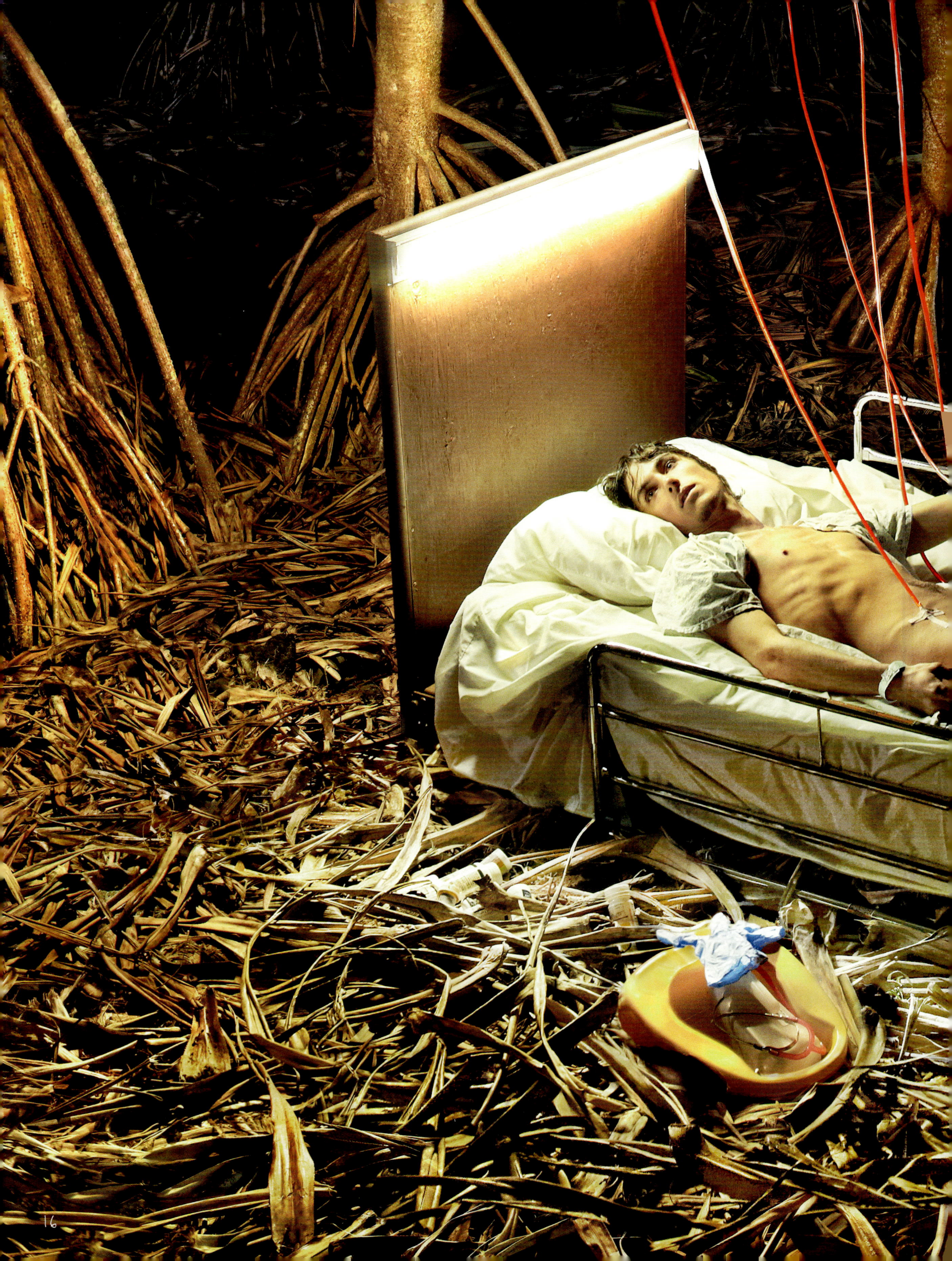

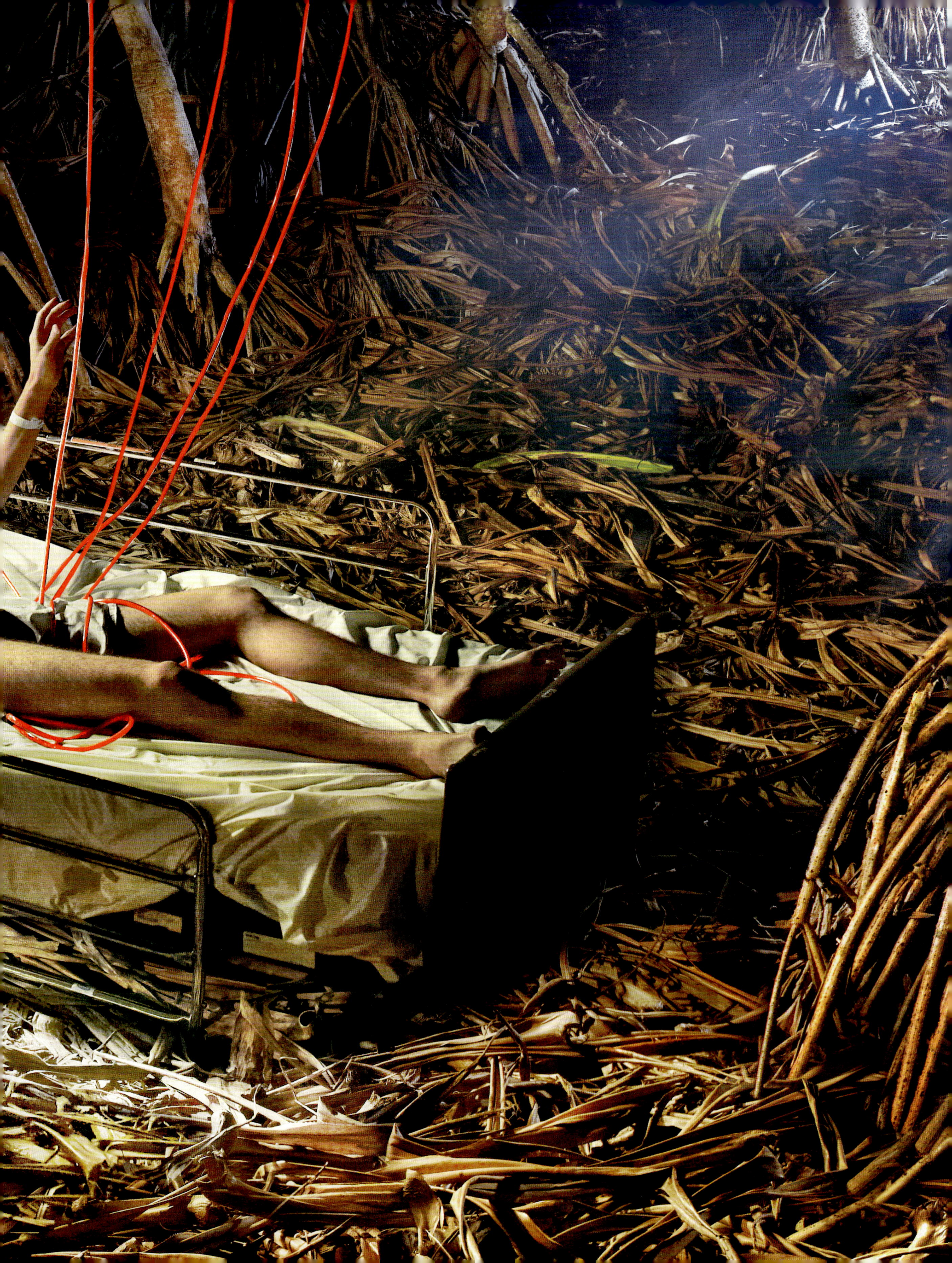

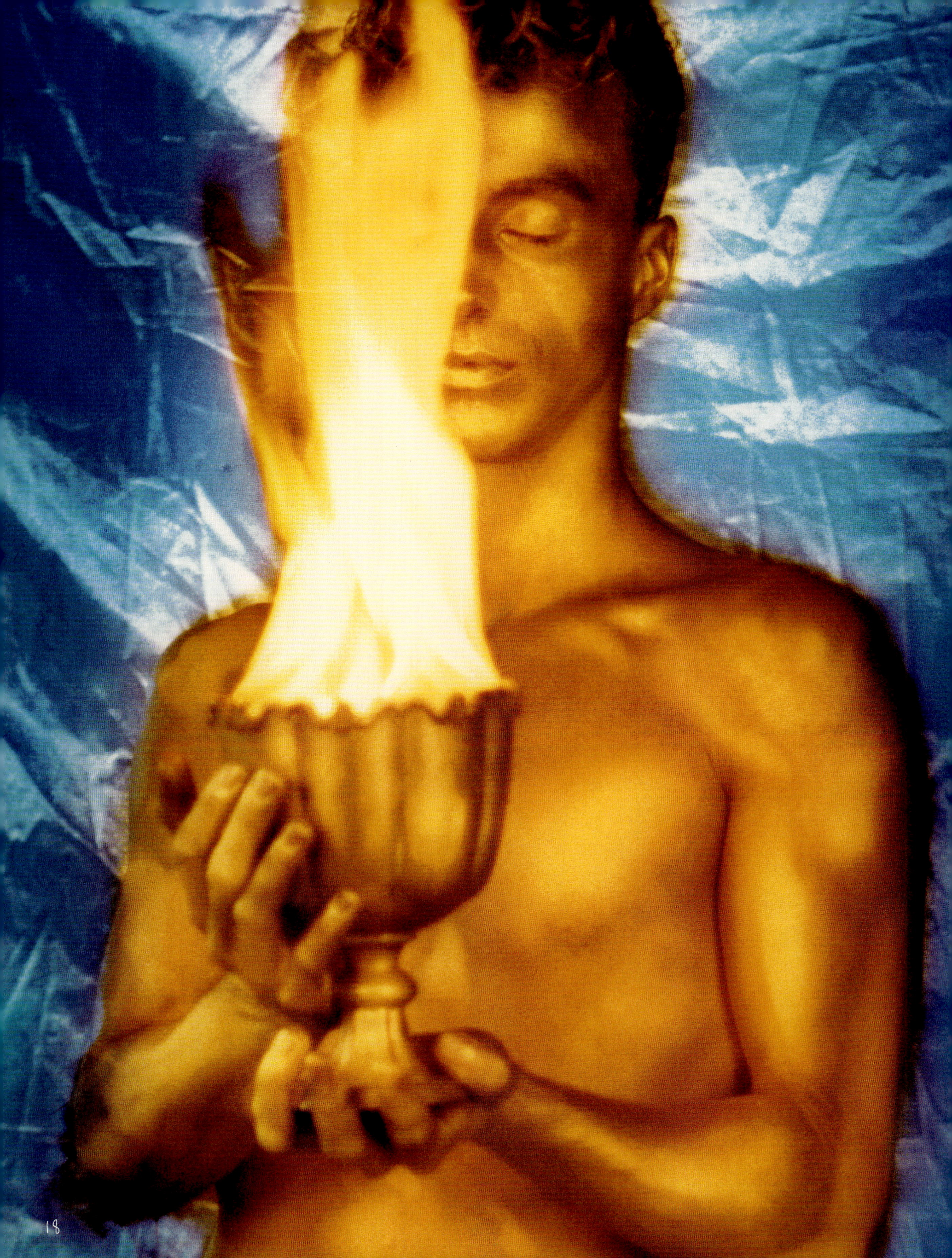

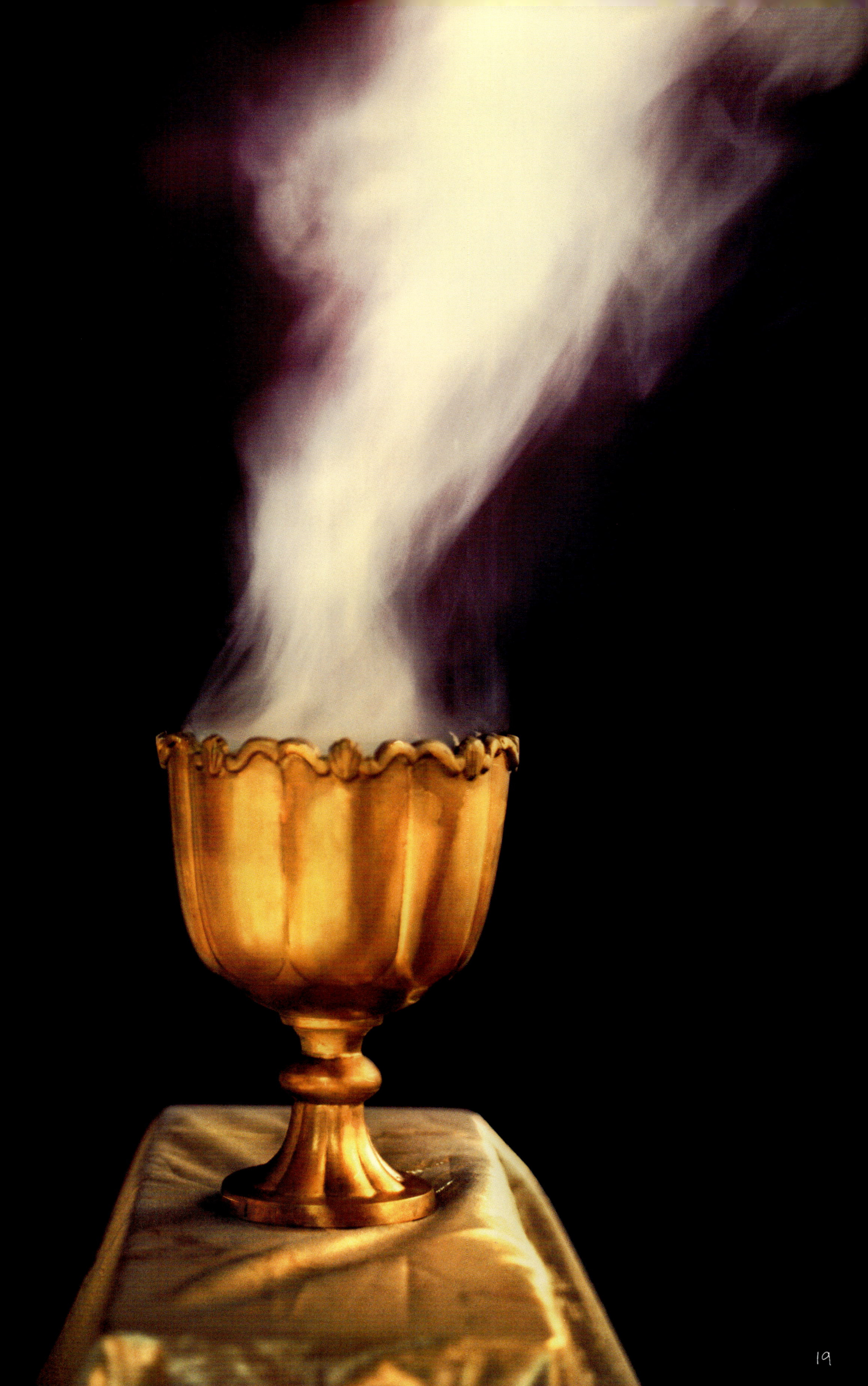

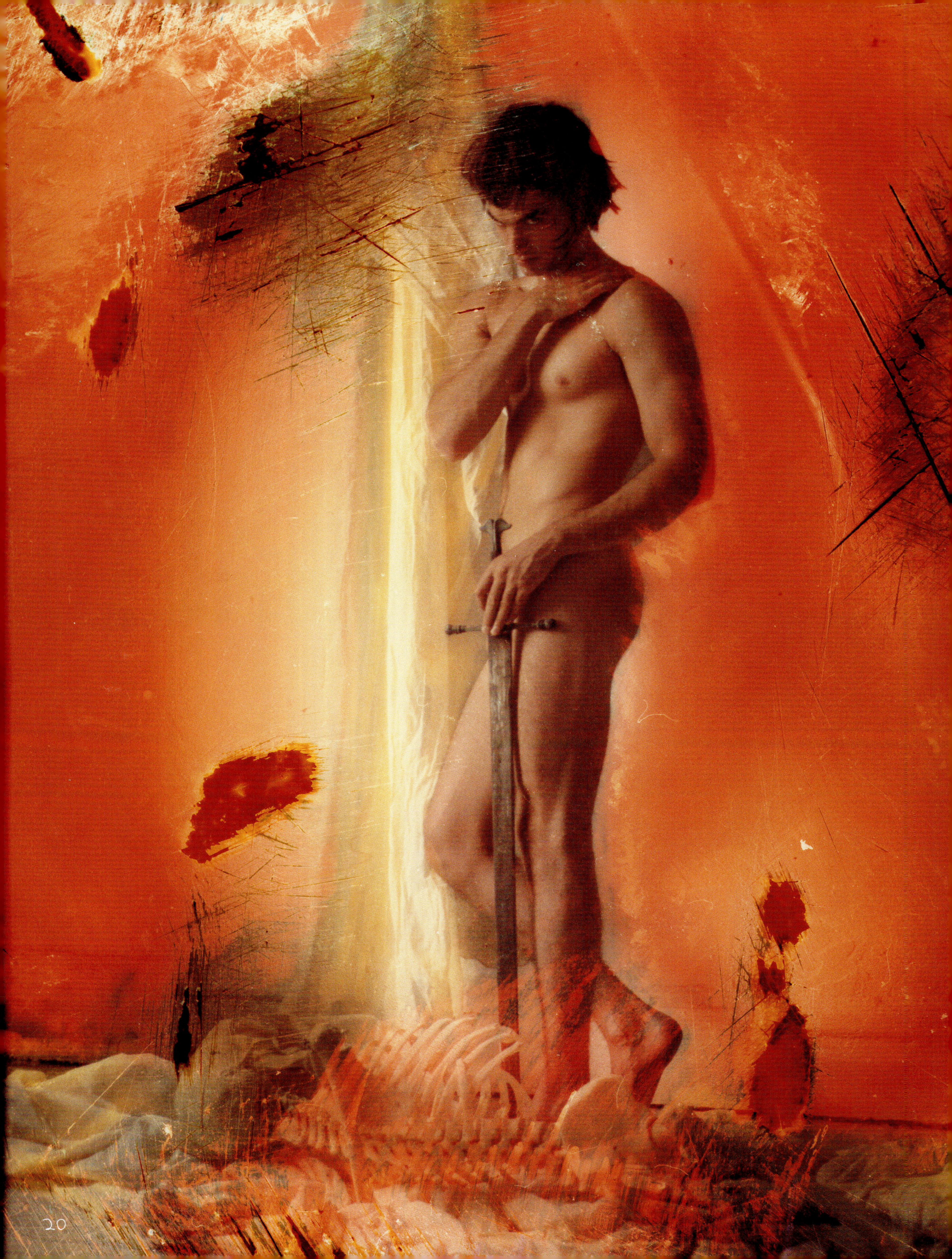

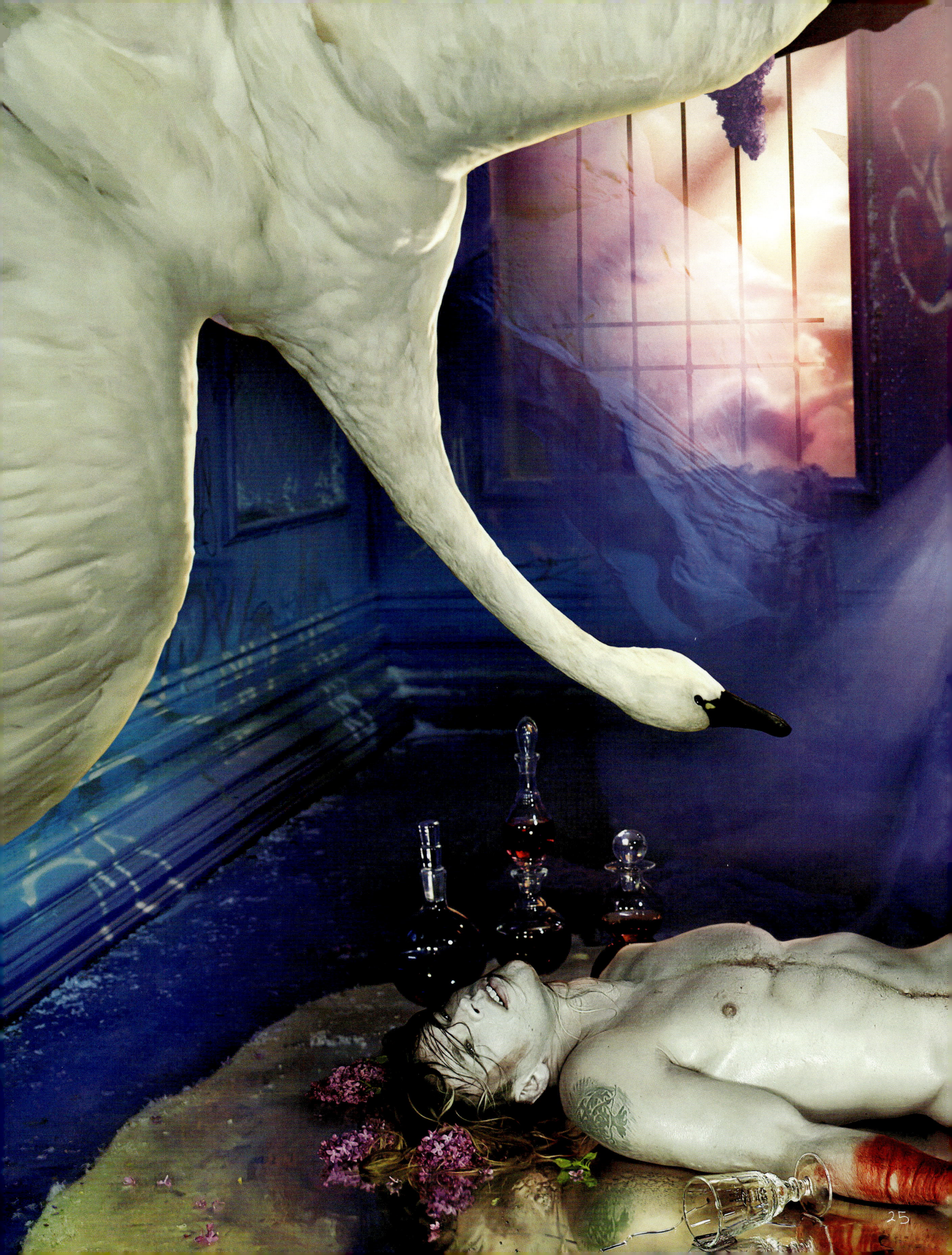

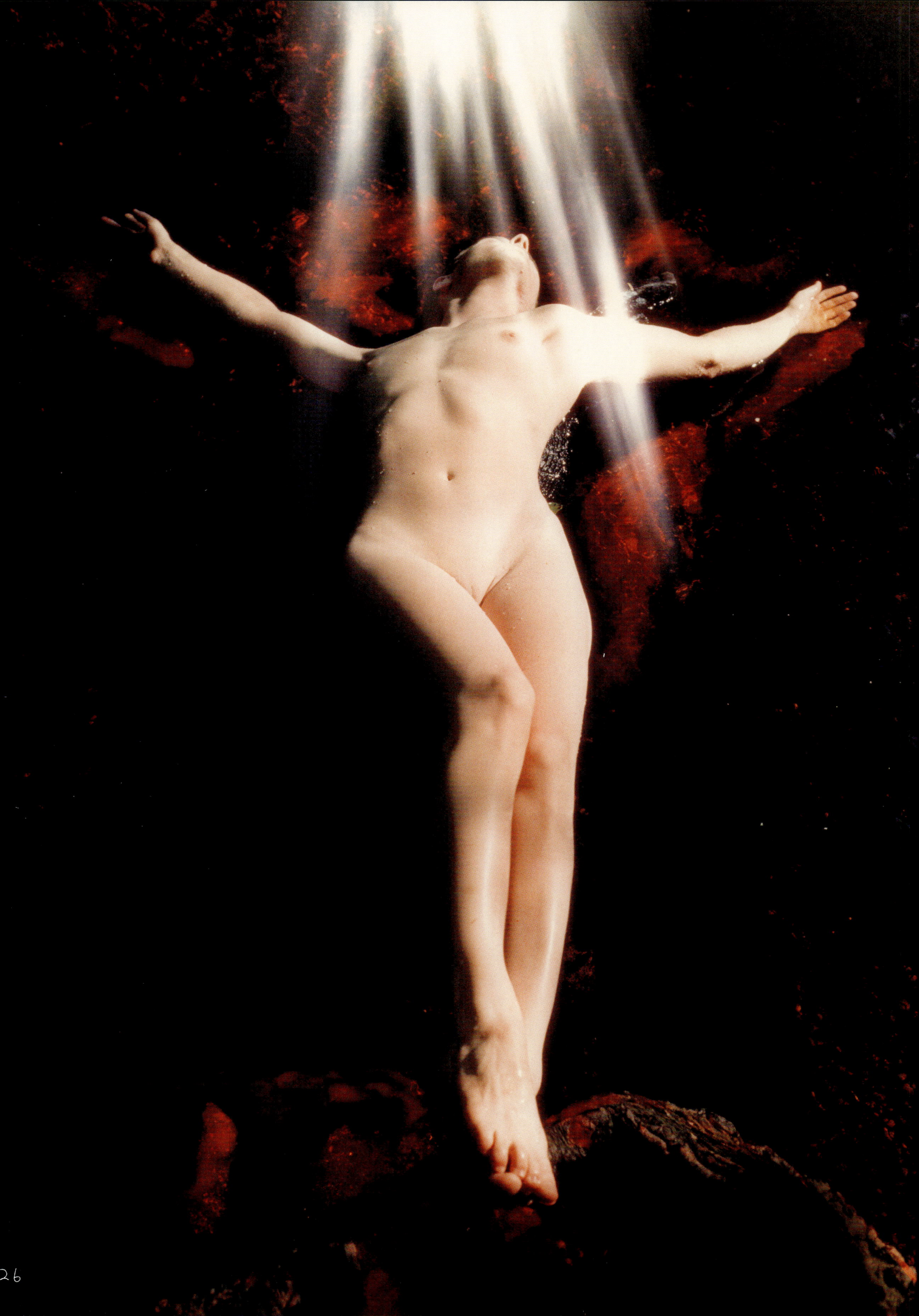

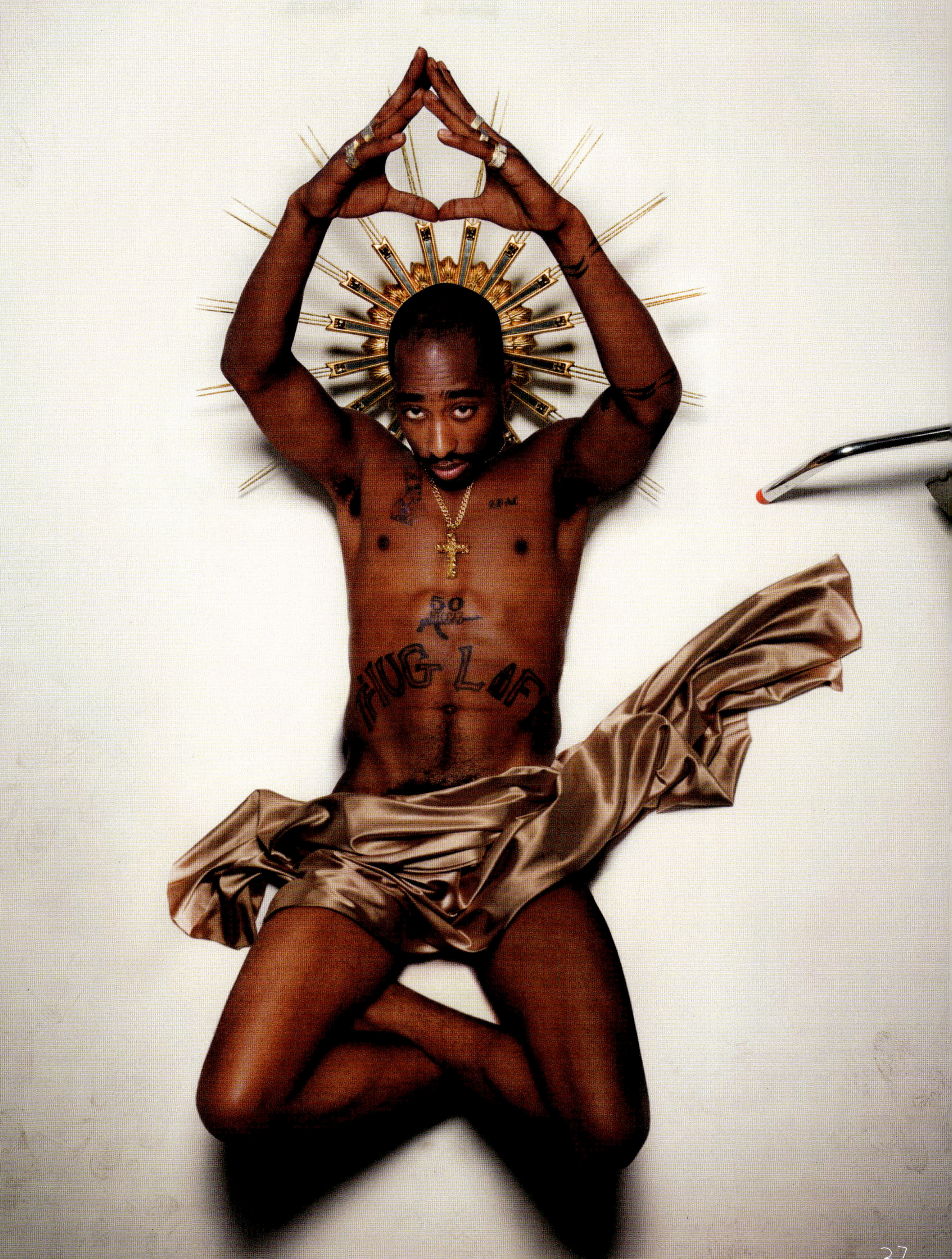

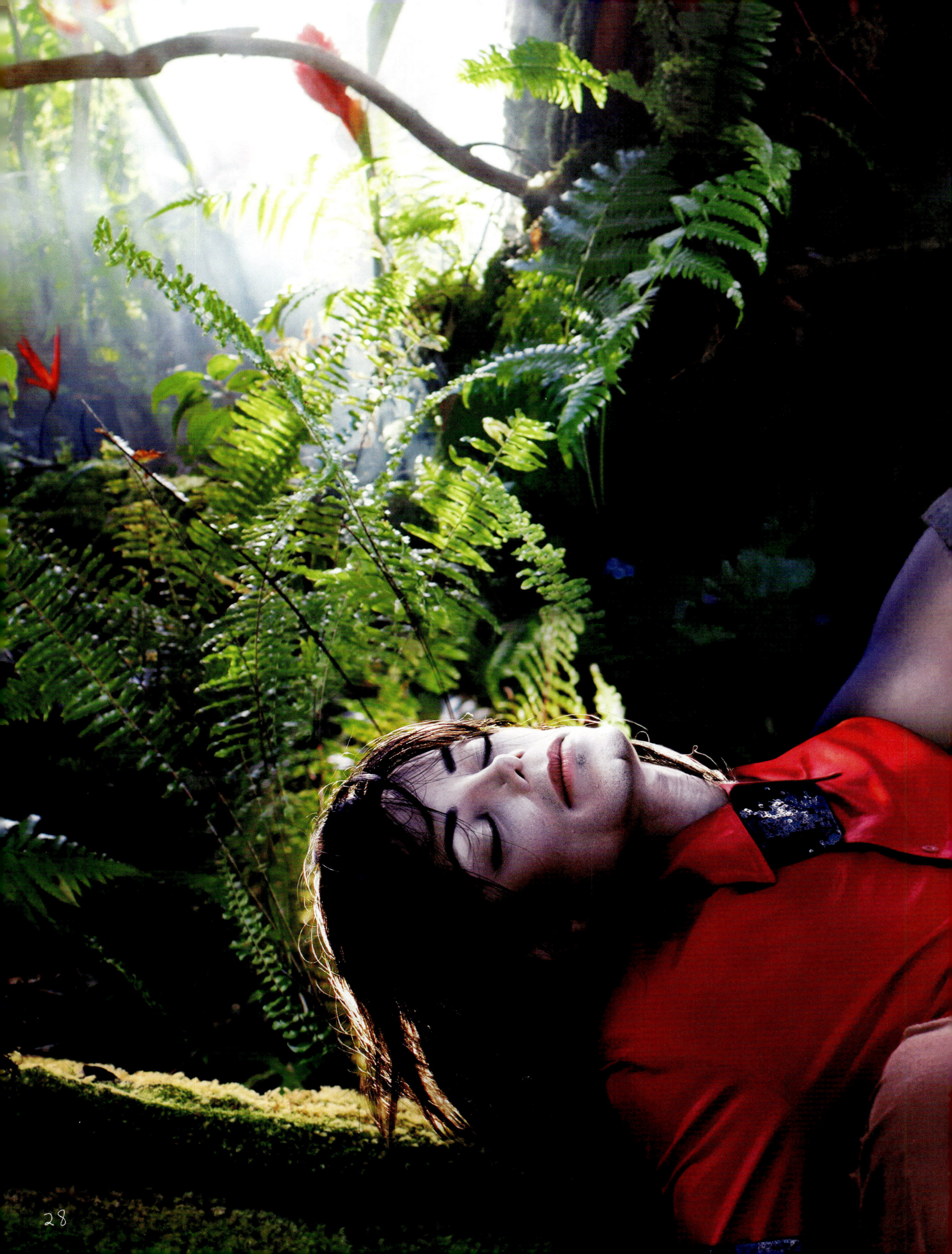

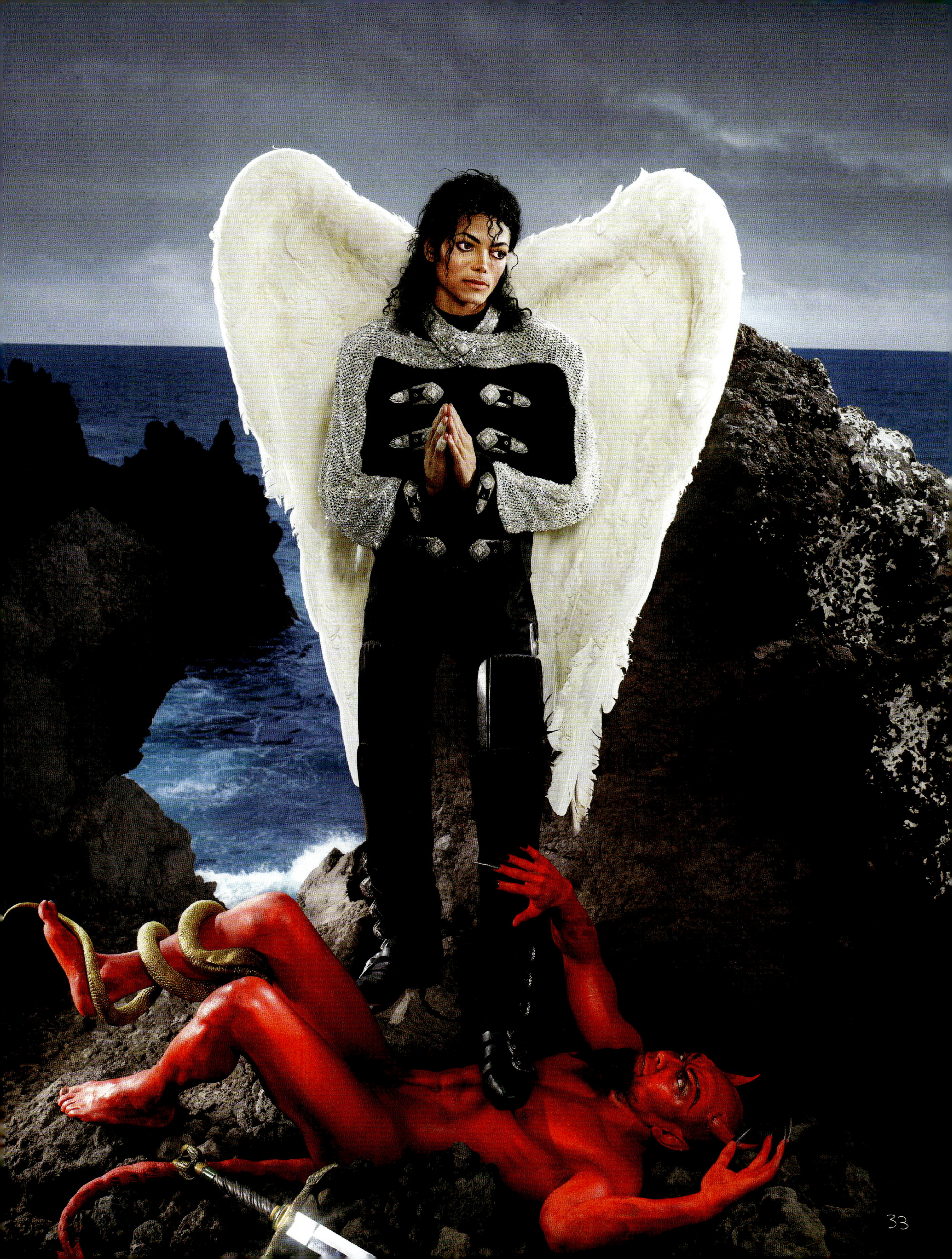

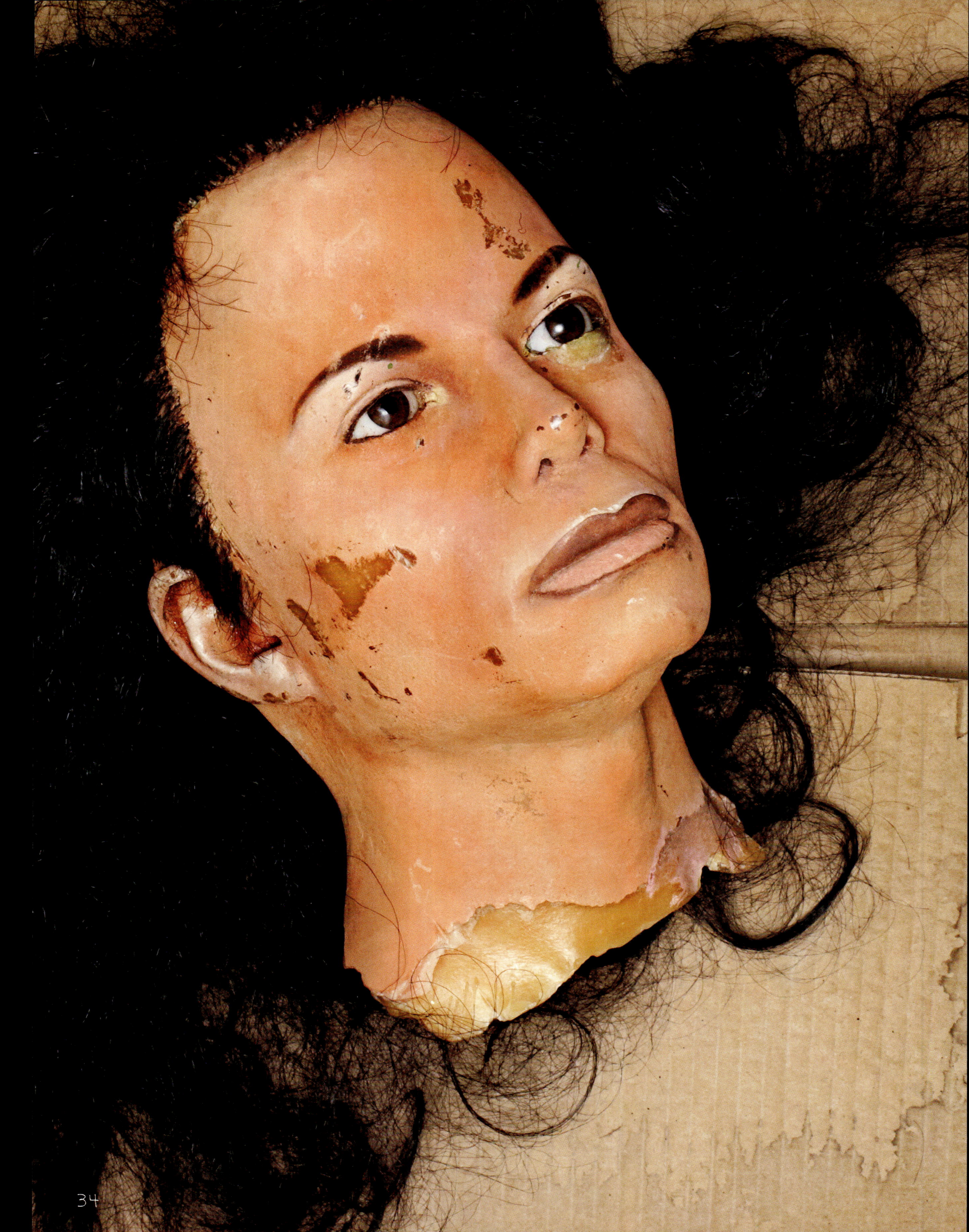

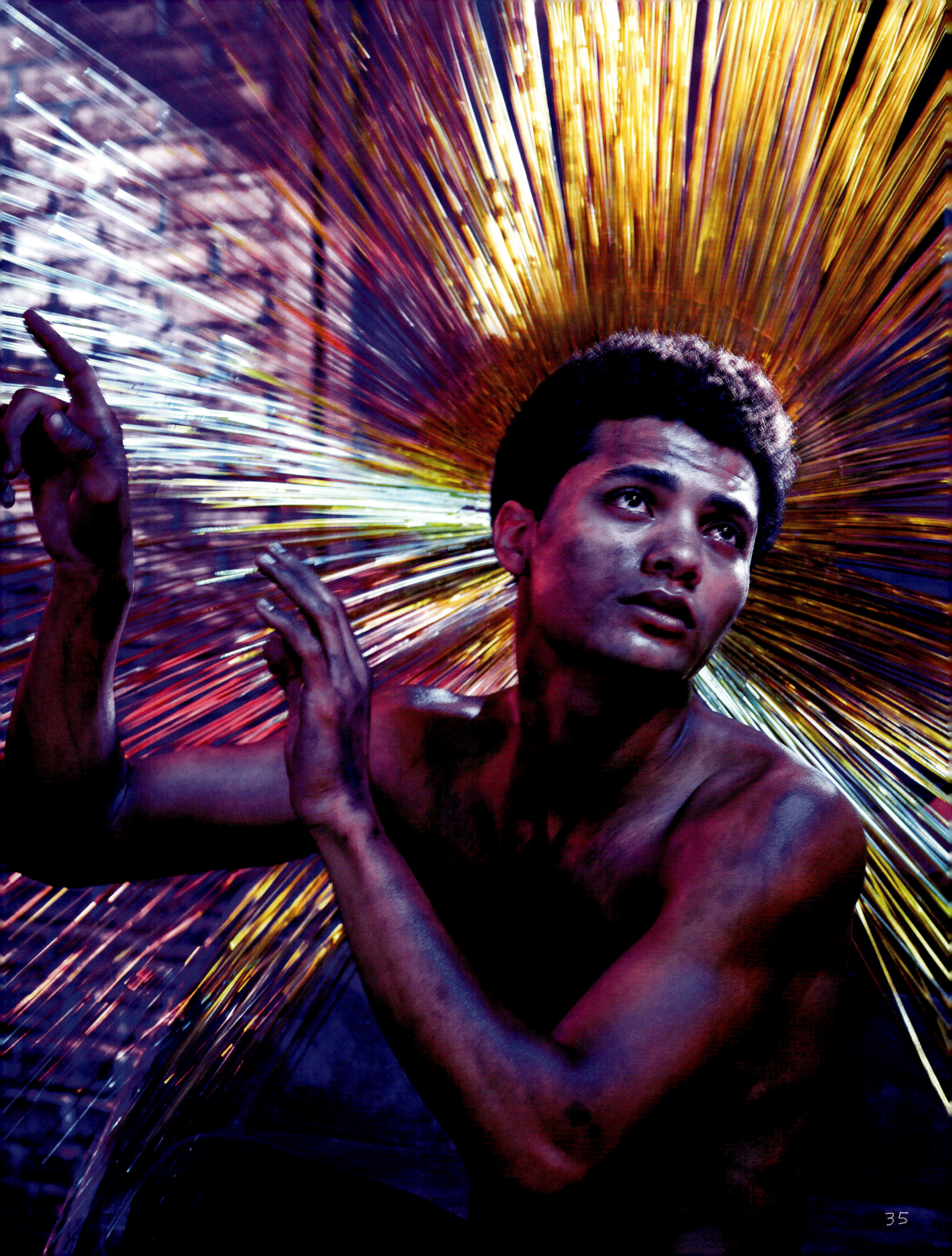

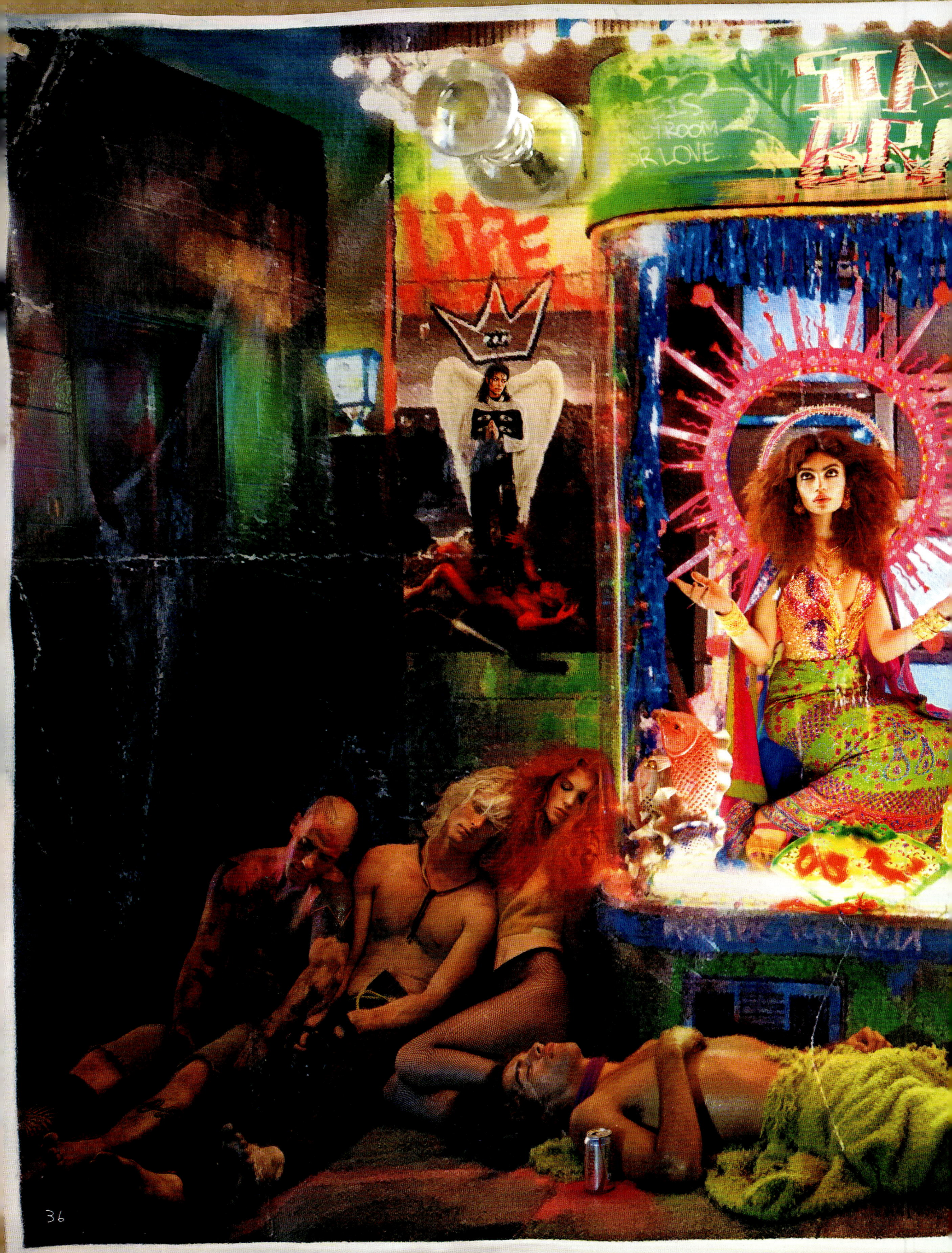
LIFE

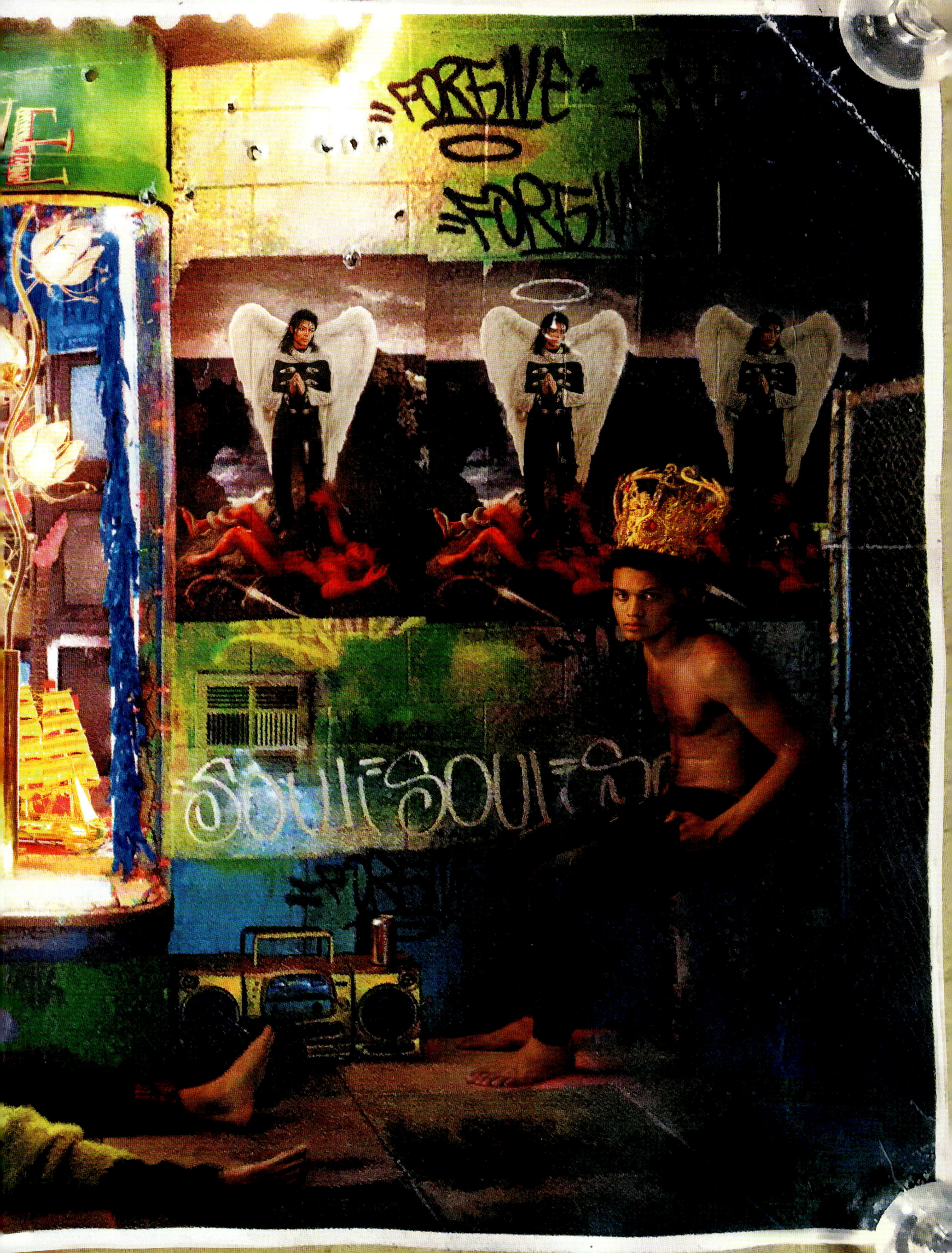
FORGIVE
SOUL SOUL

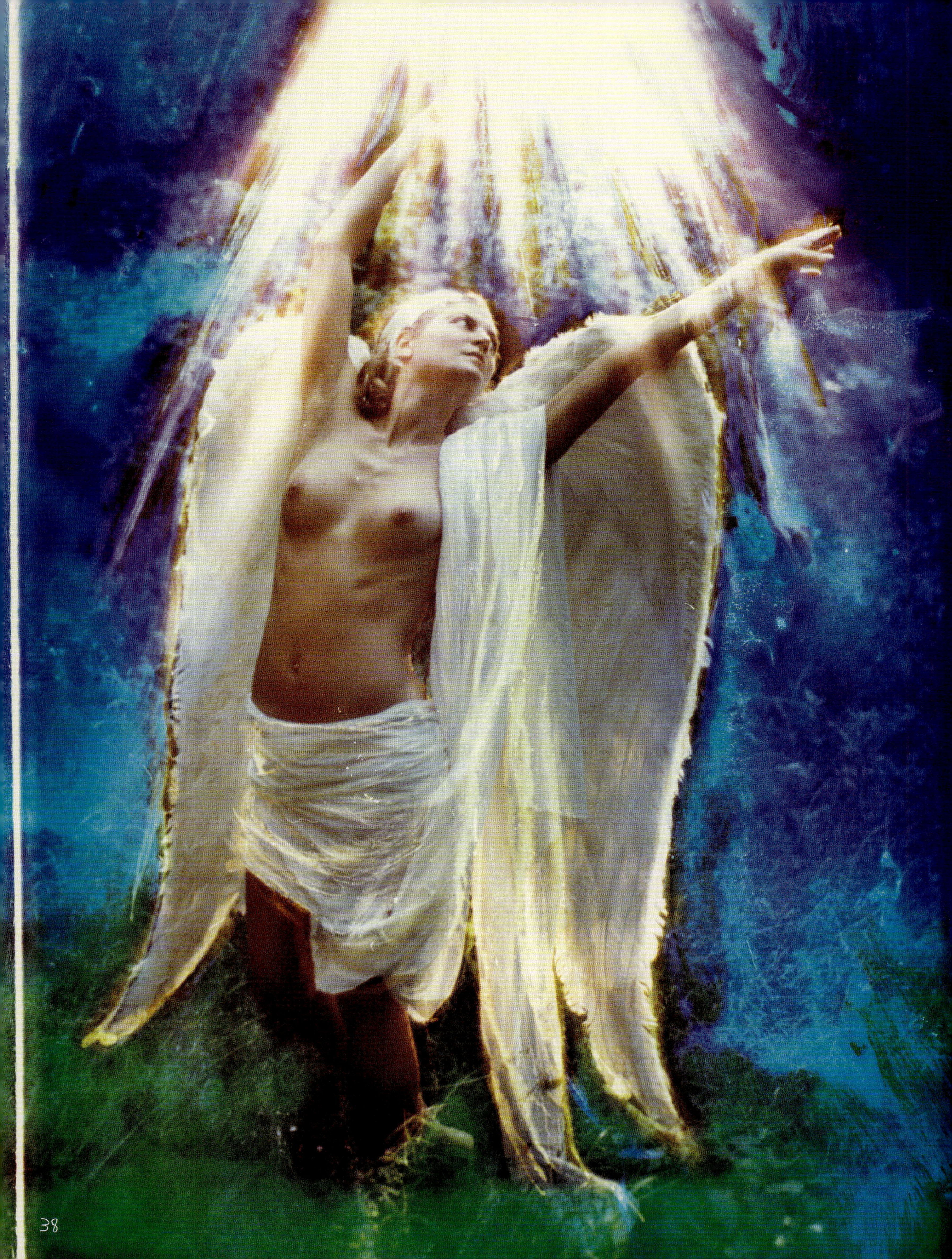

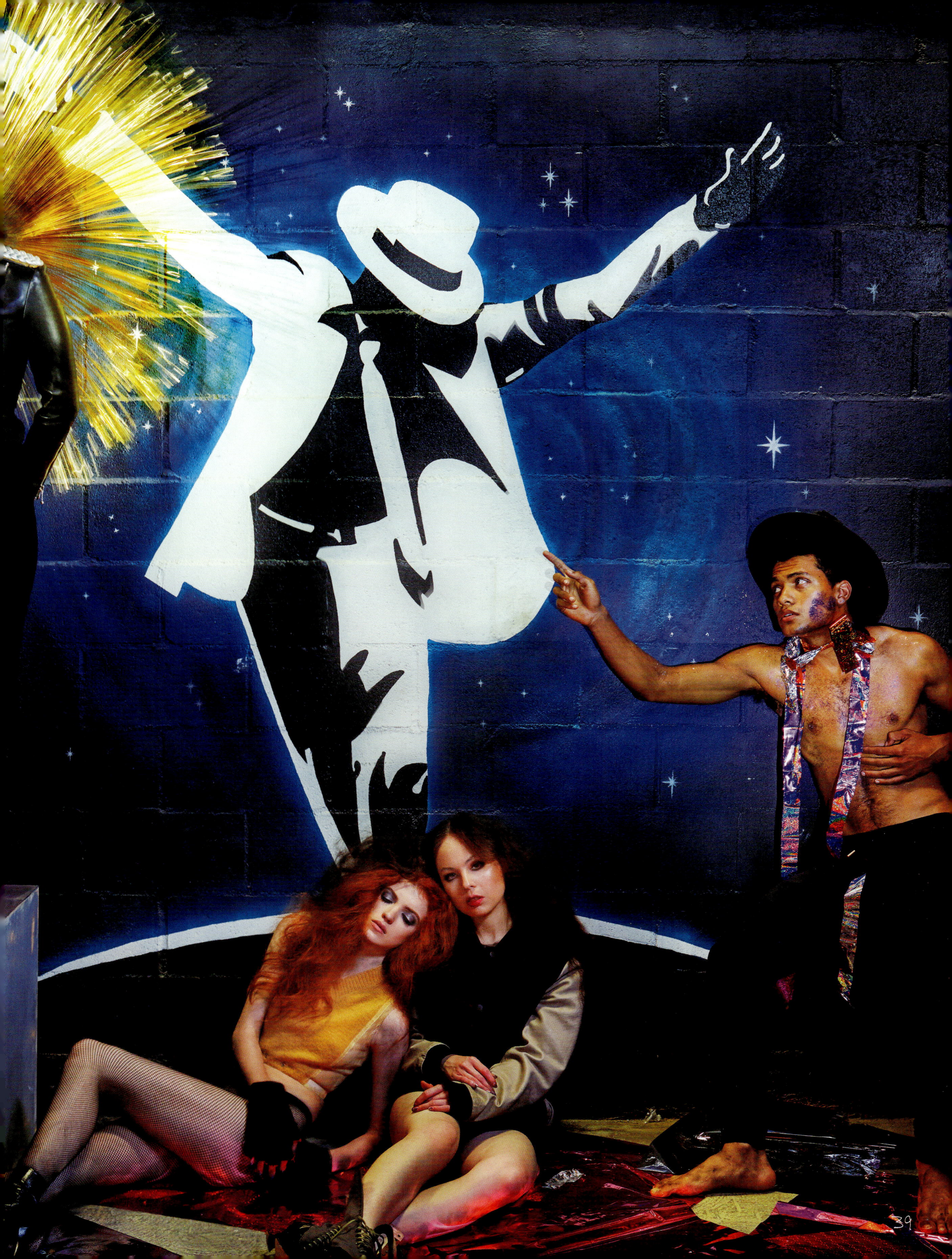

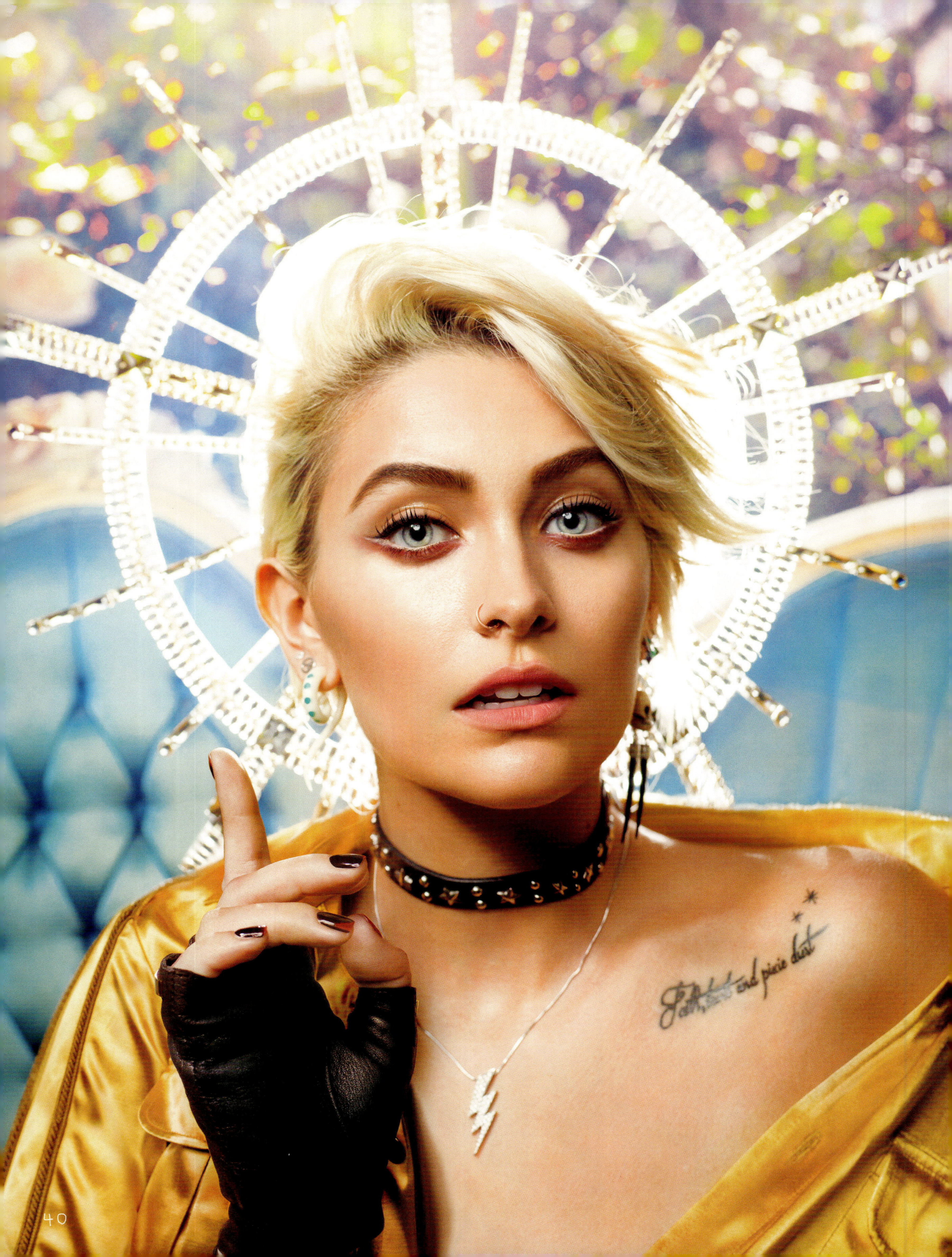

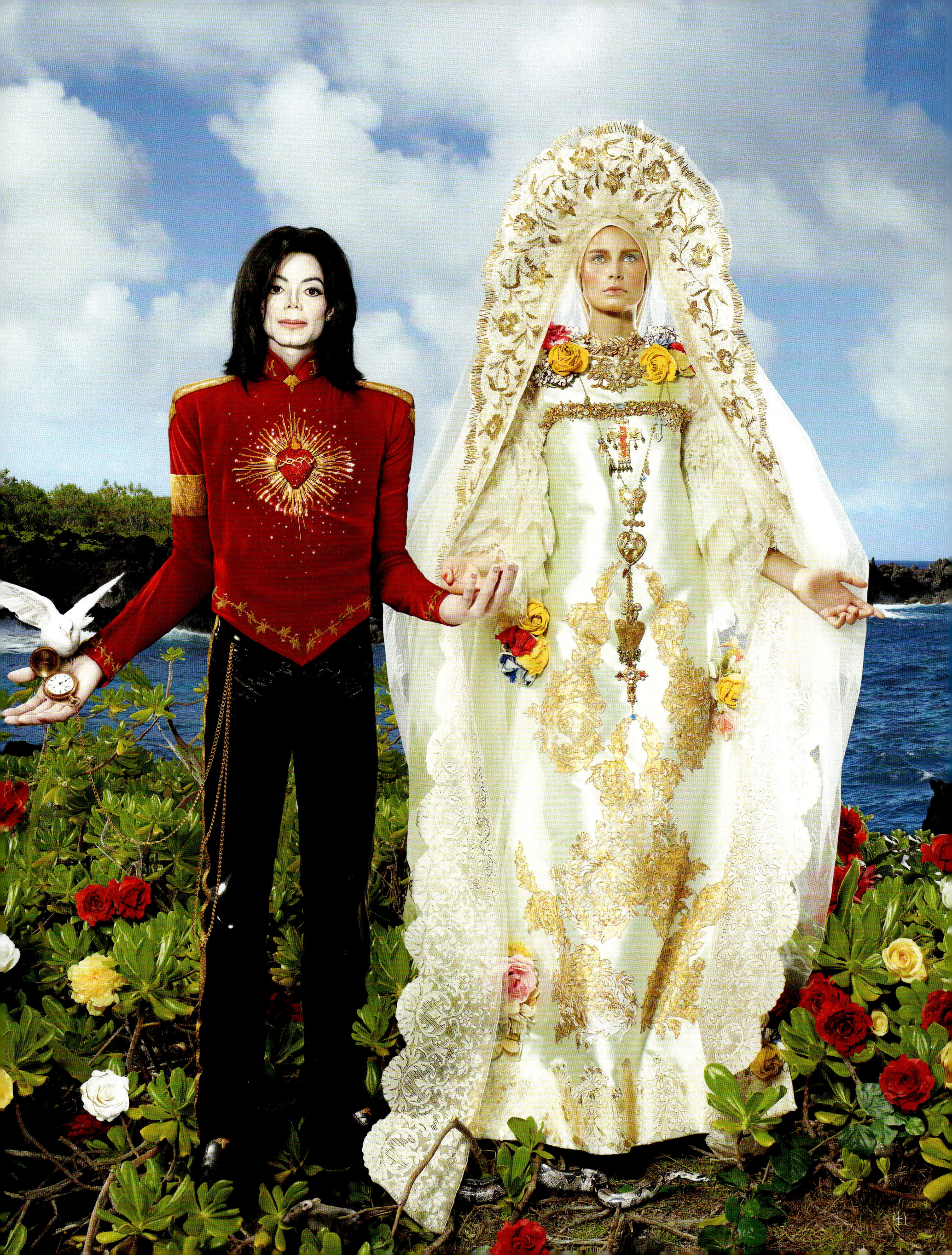

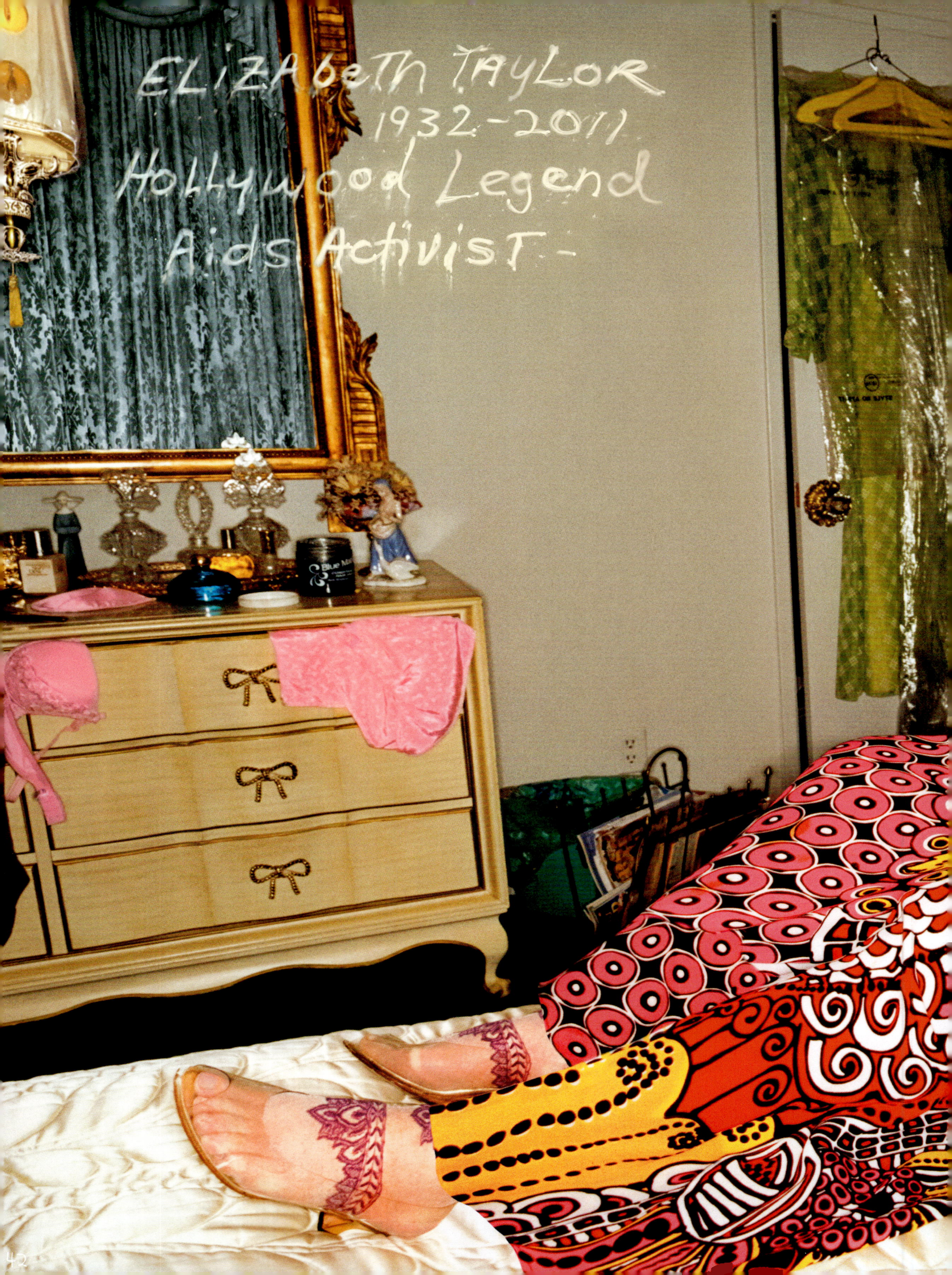
ELIZAbeth TAyLoR
1932-2011
Hollywood Legend
Aids Activist -

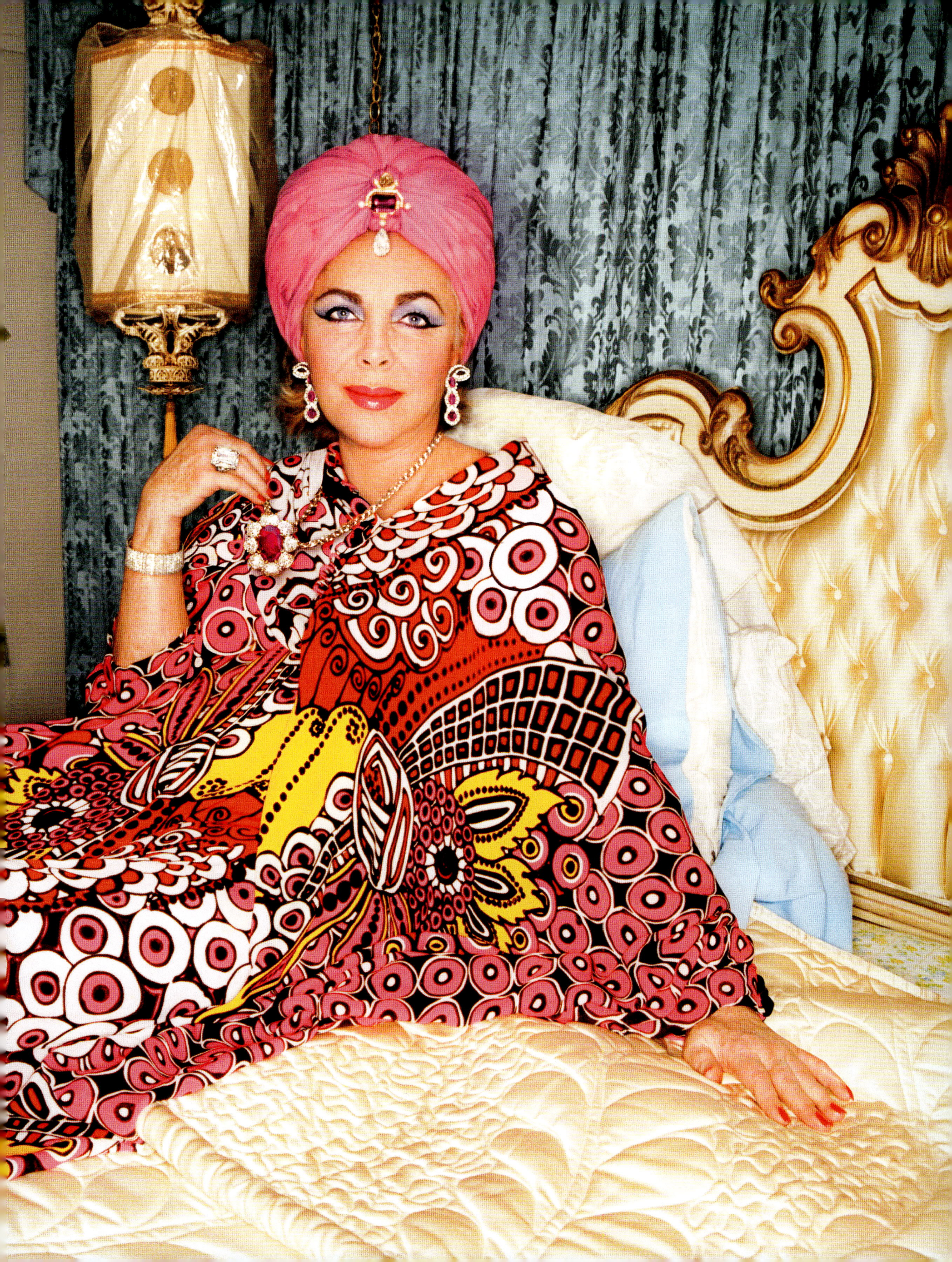

Helen Helen

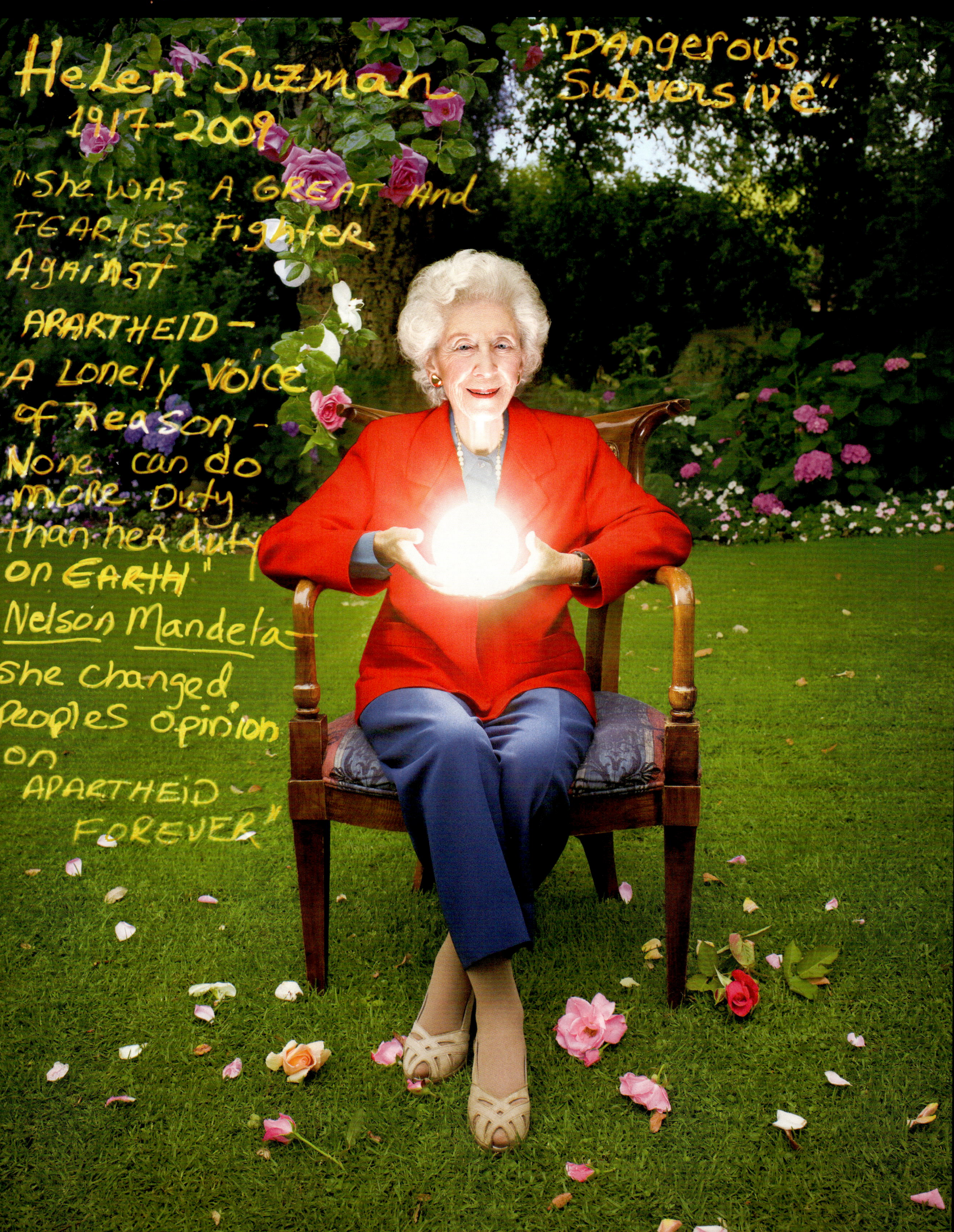

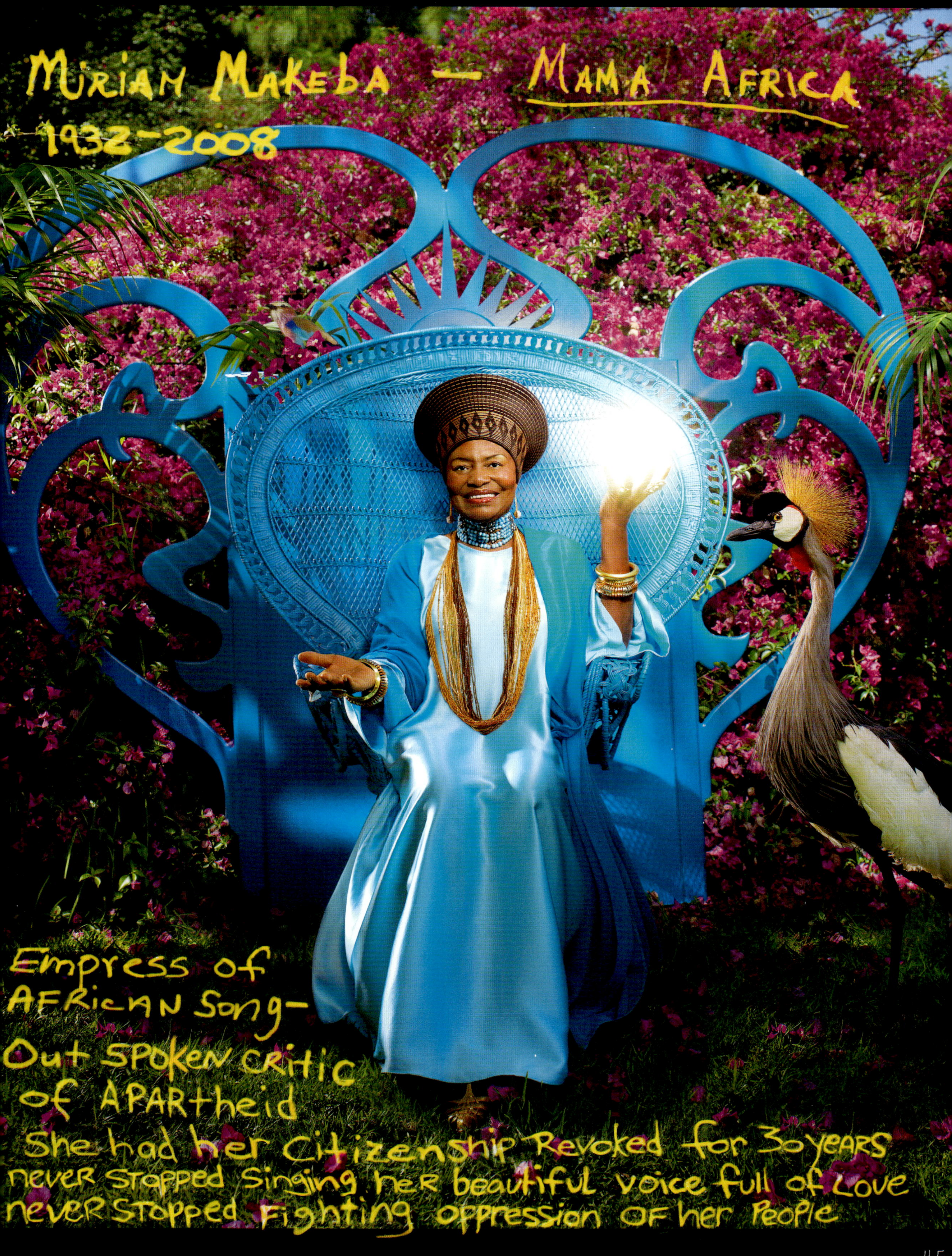
MIRIAM MAKEBA — MAMA AFRICA
1932–2008
Empress of AFRICAN Song–
Out SPOKEN CRitic of APARtheid
She had her Citizenship Revoked for 30 YEARS
never STopped Singing her beautiful voice full of Love
never STopped Fighting oppression OF her People

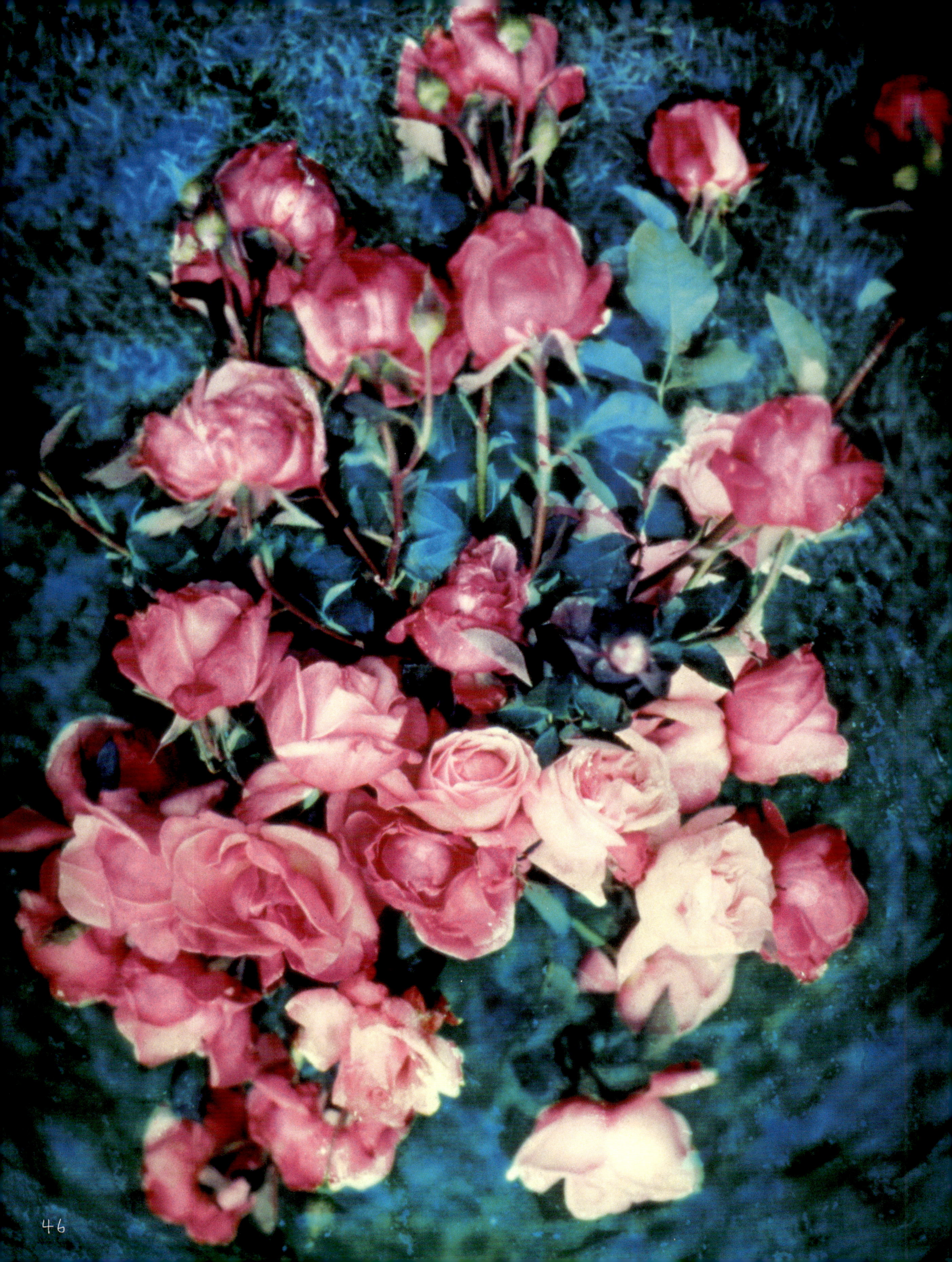

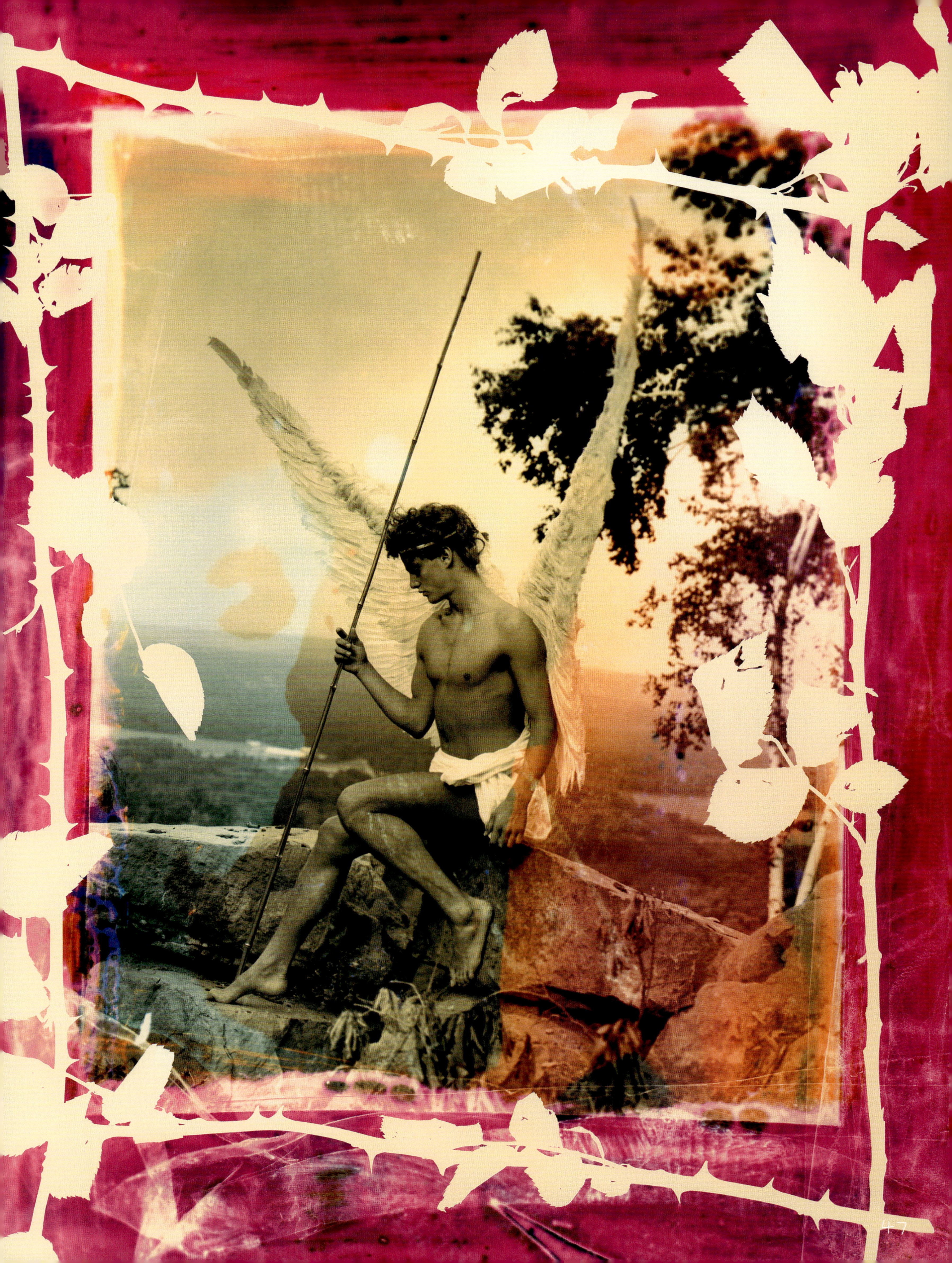

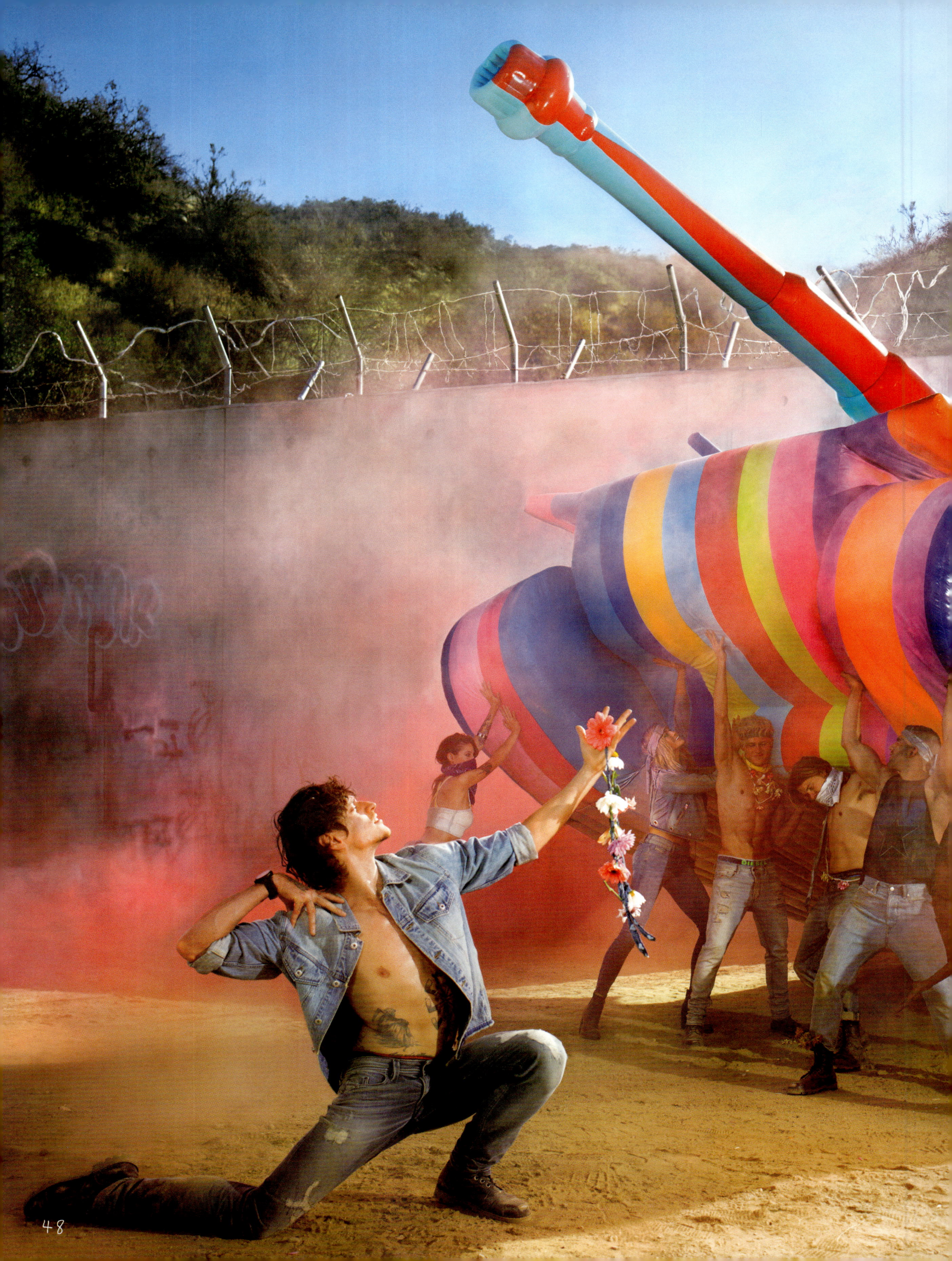

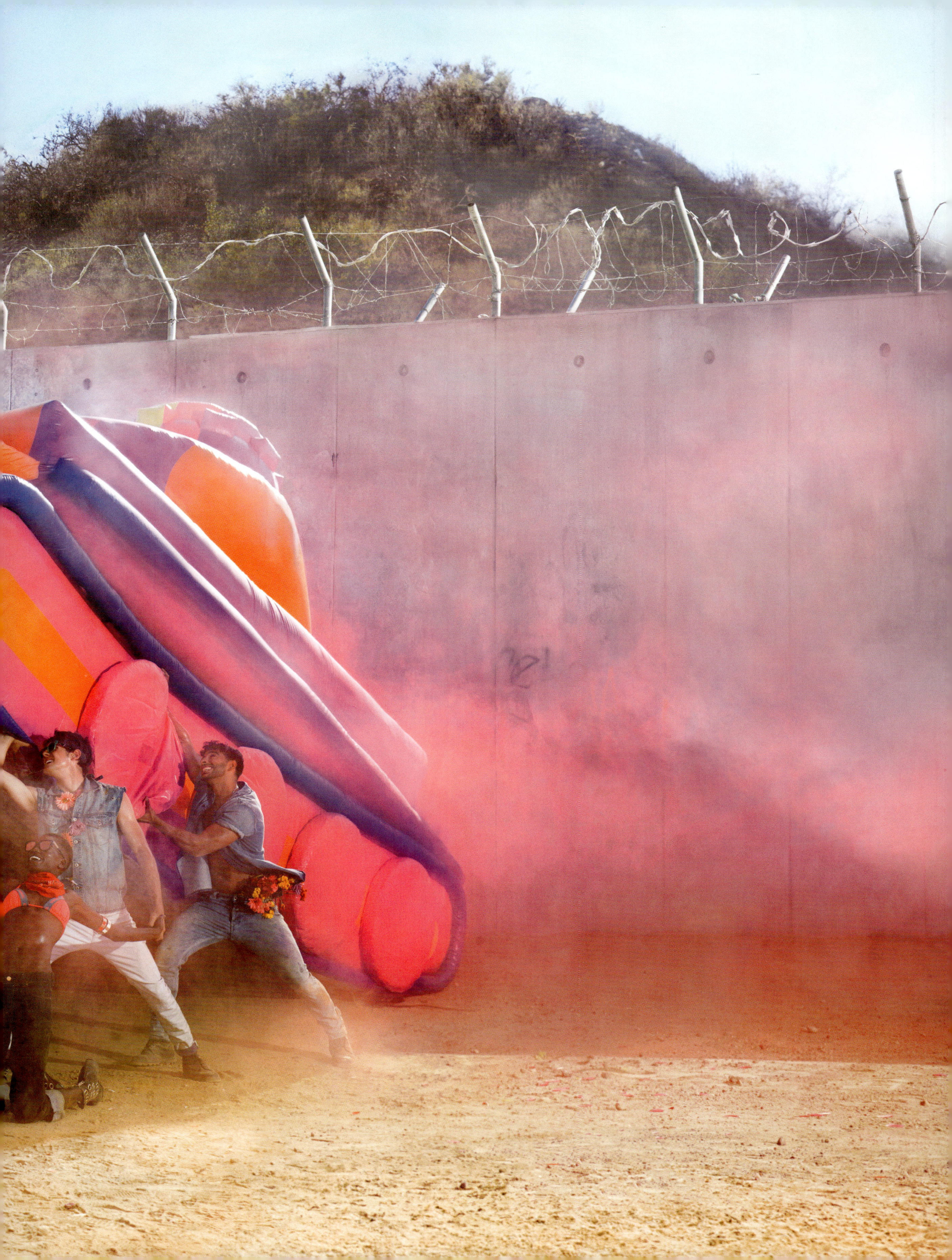

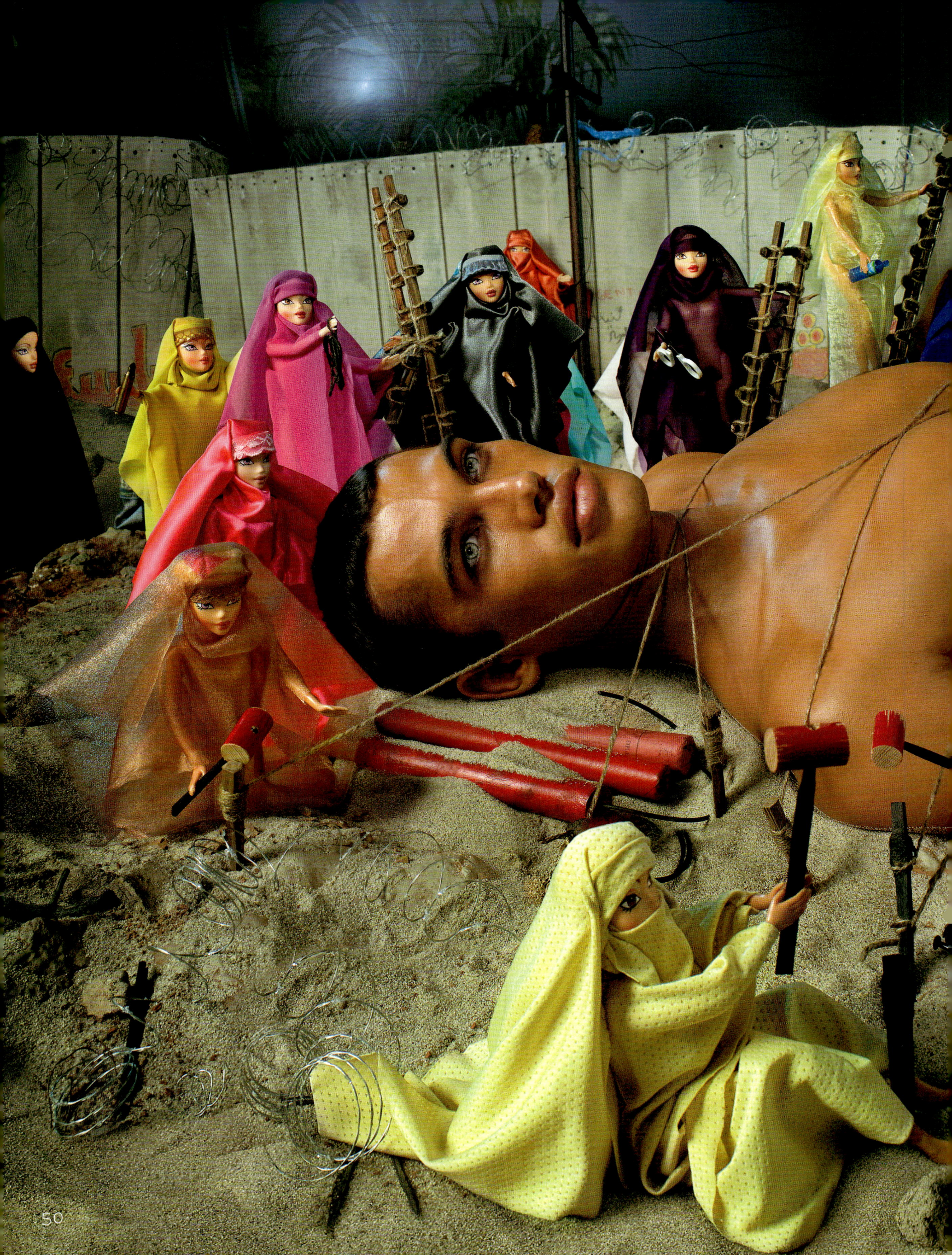

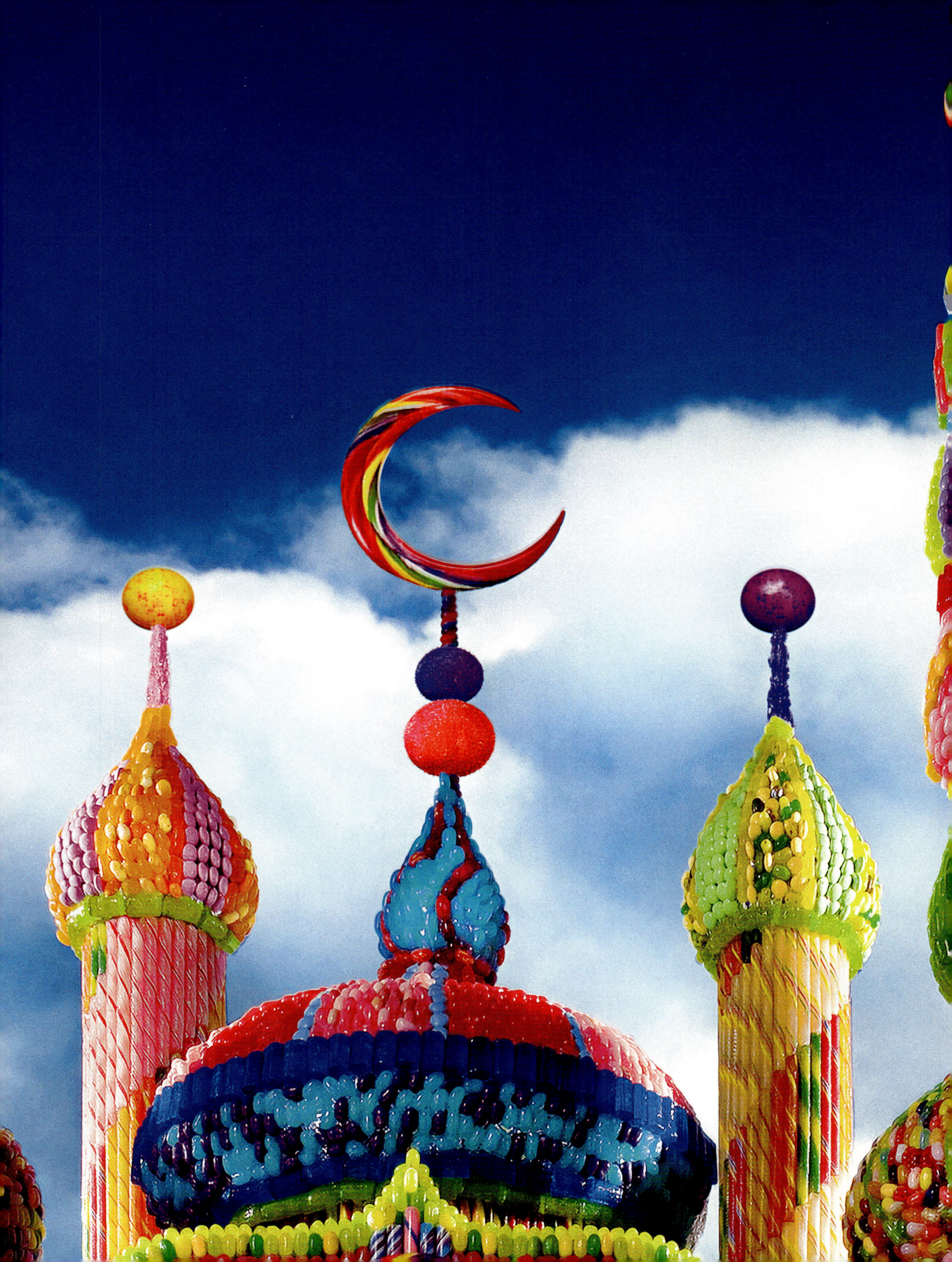

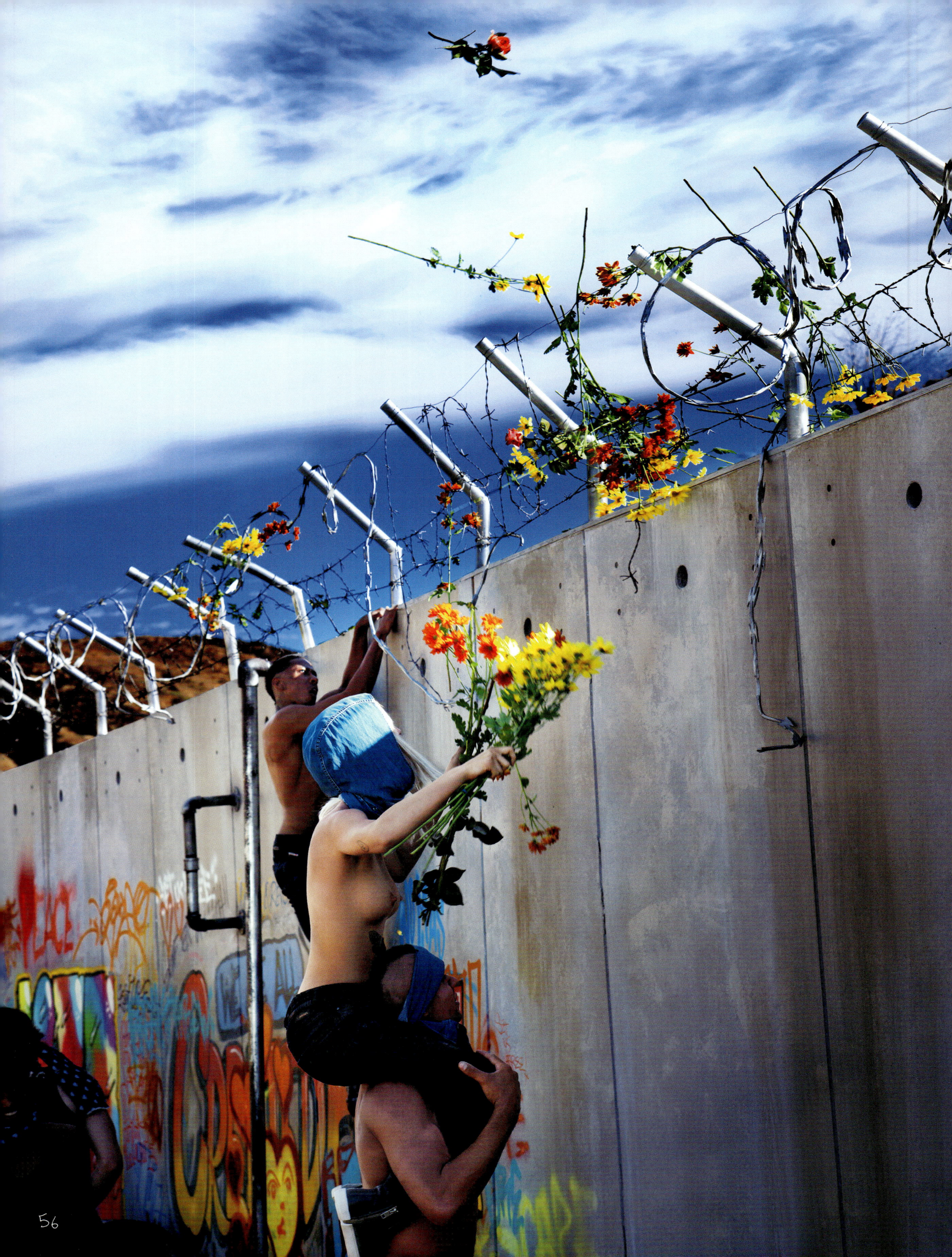

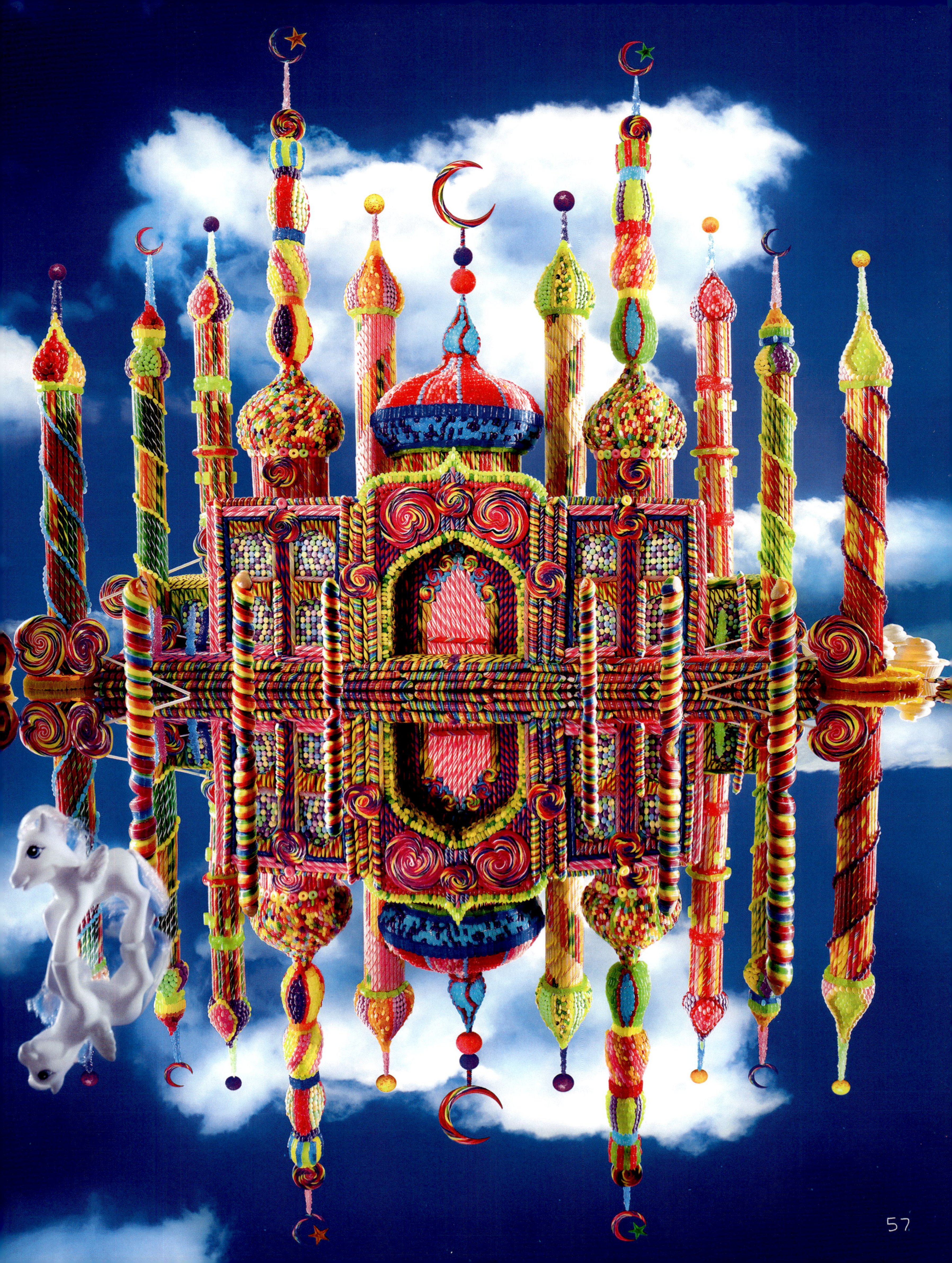

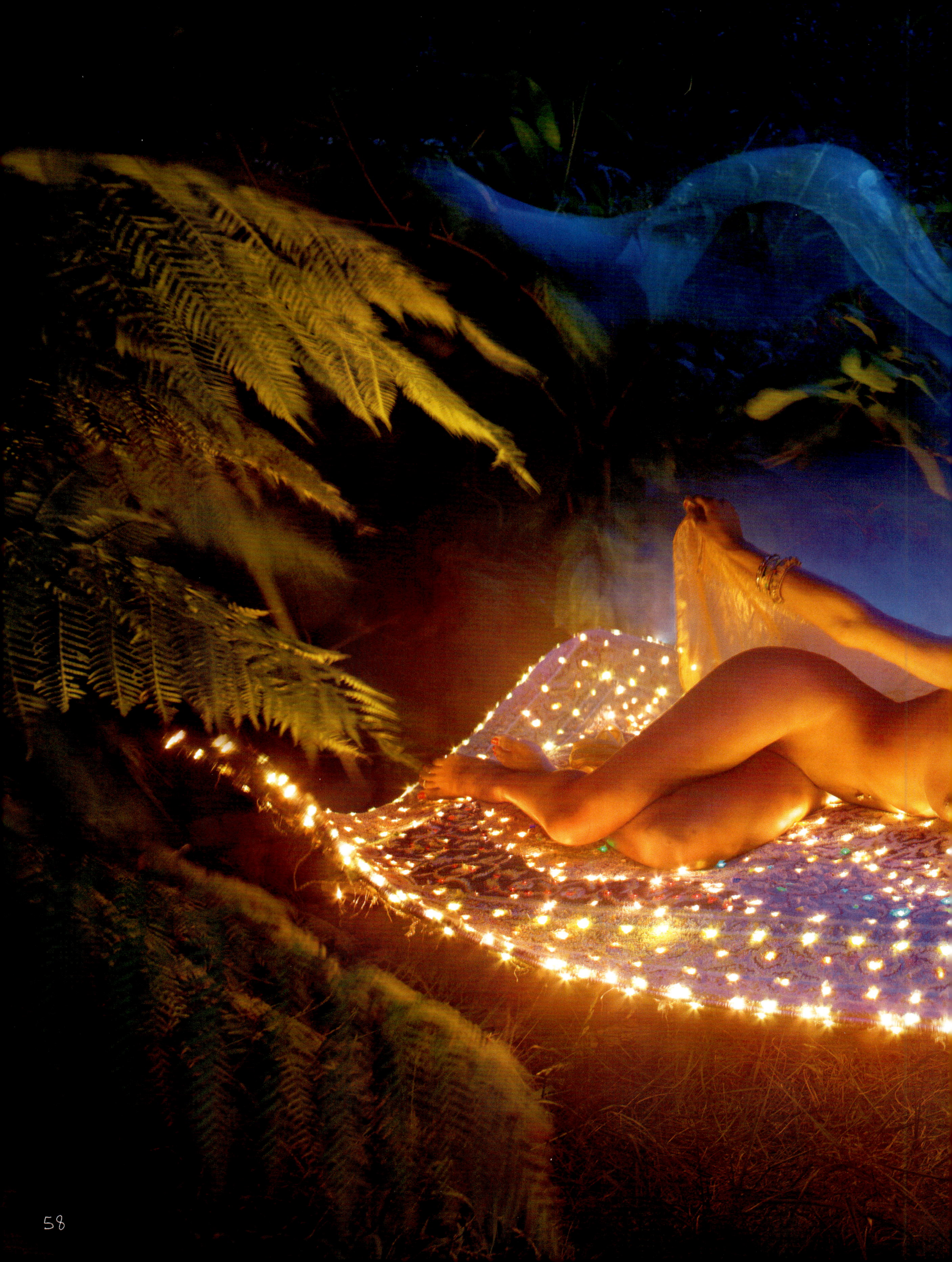

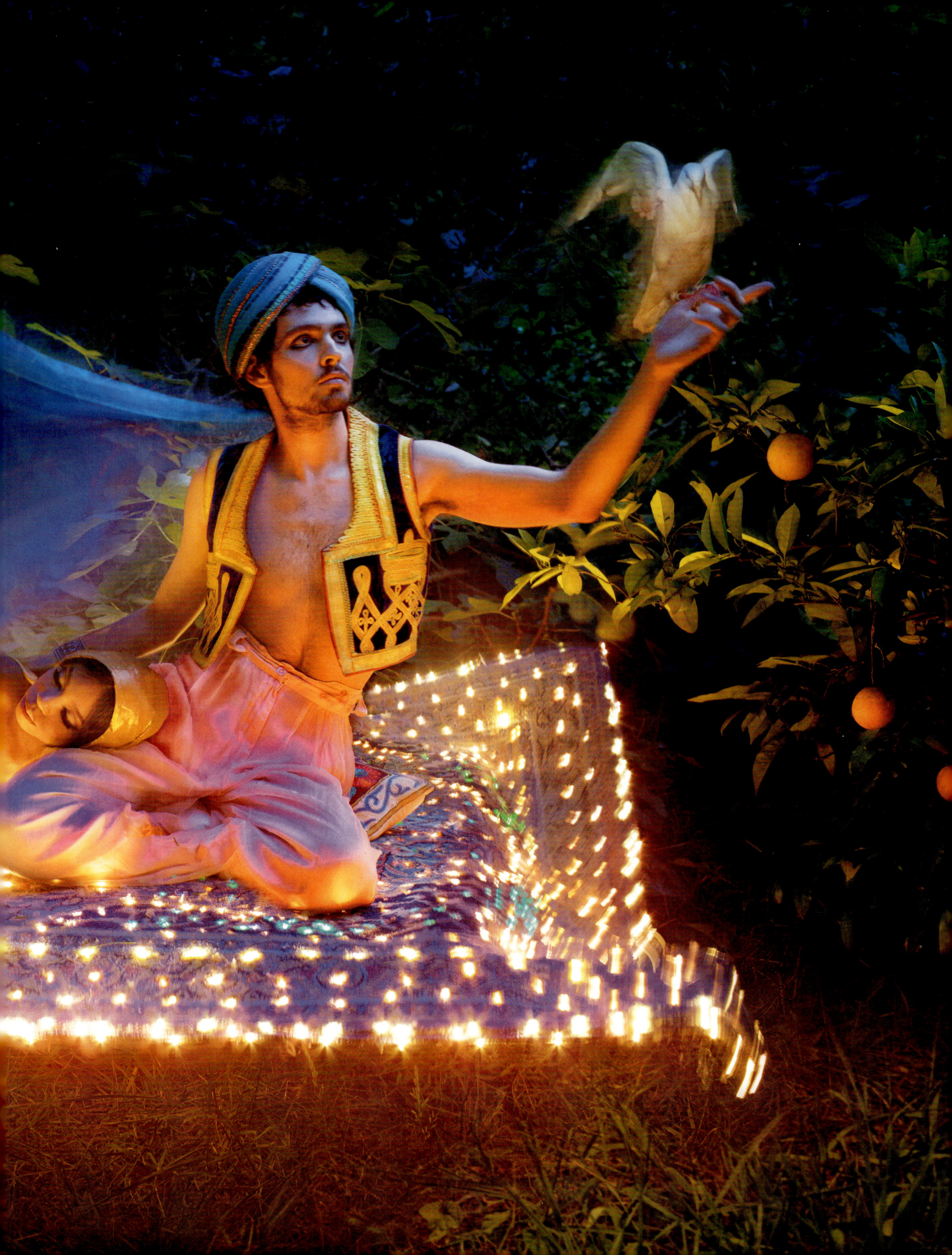

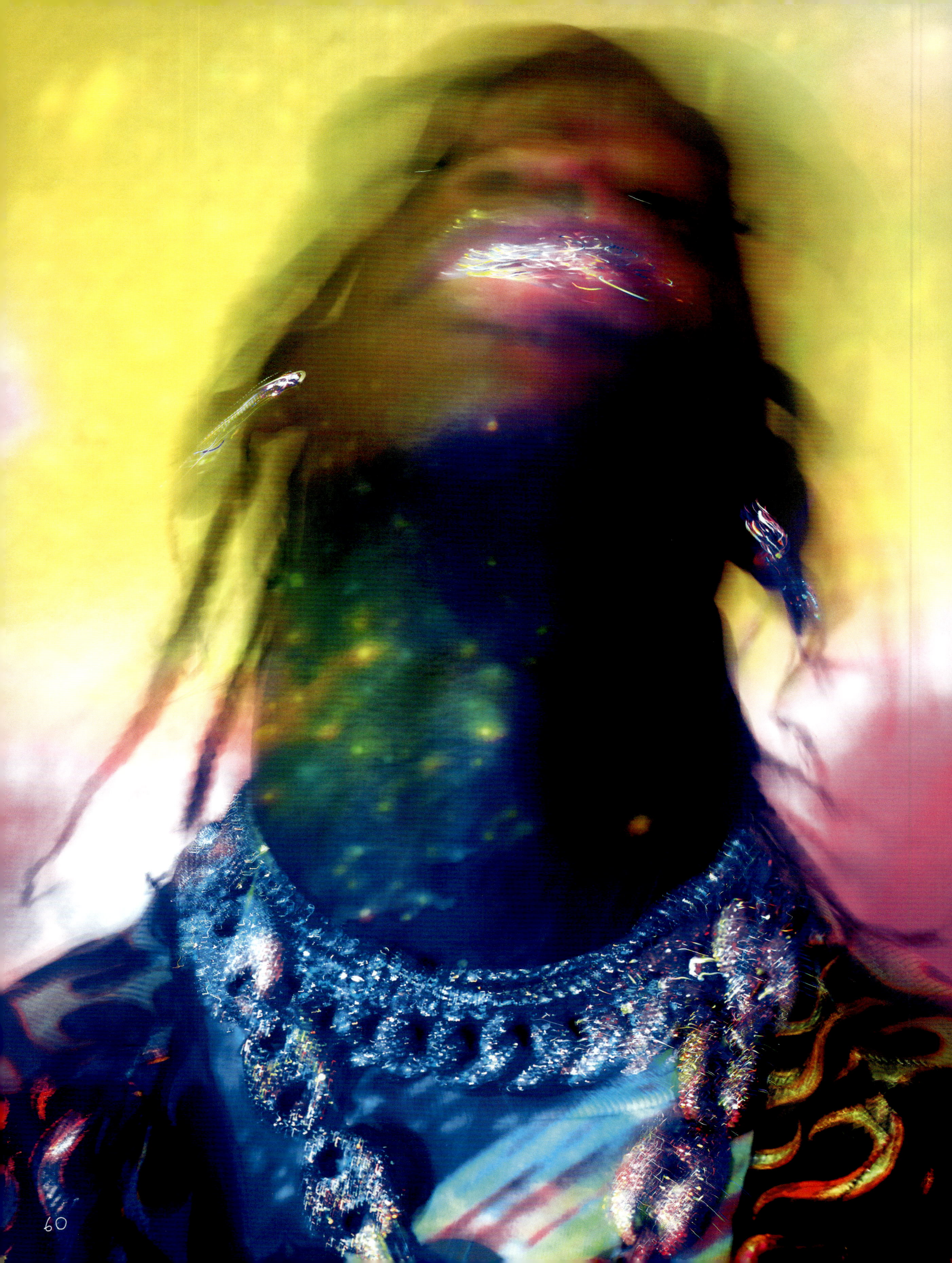

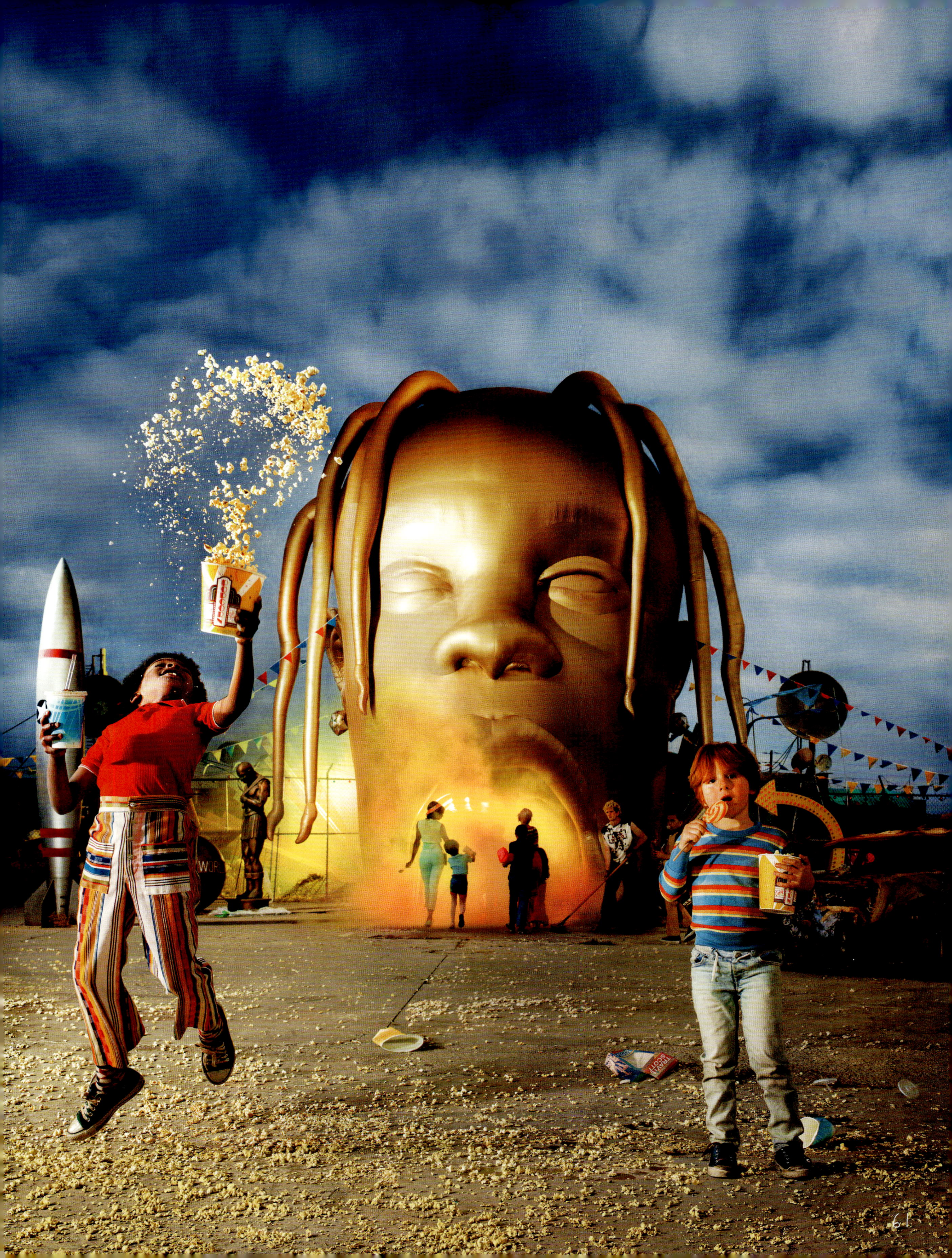

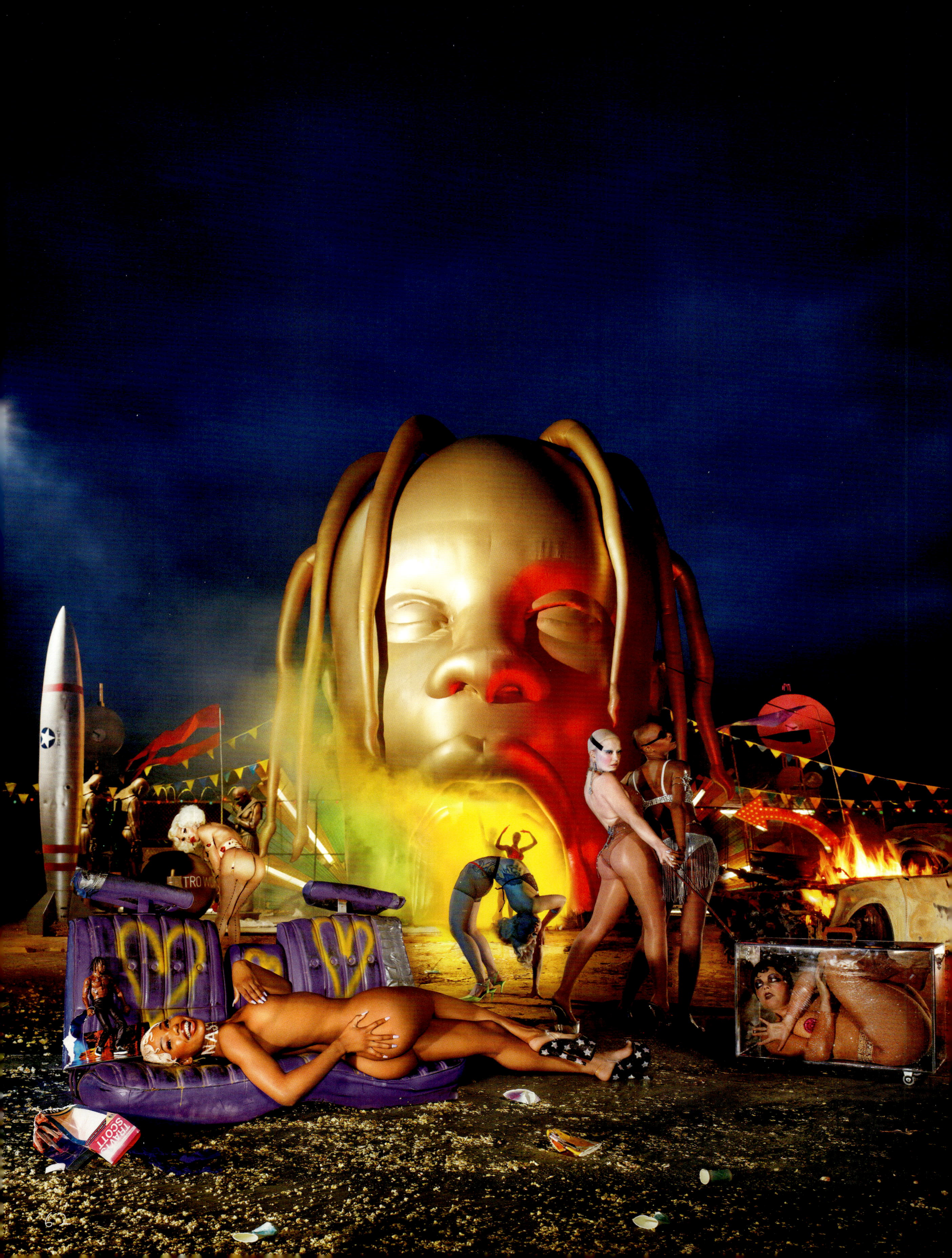
TRAVIS
SCOTT

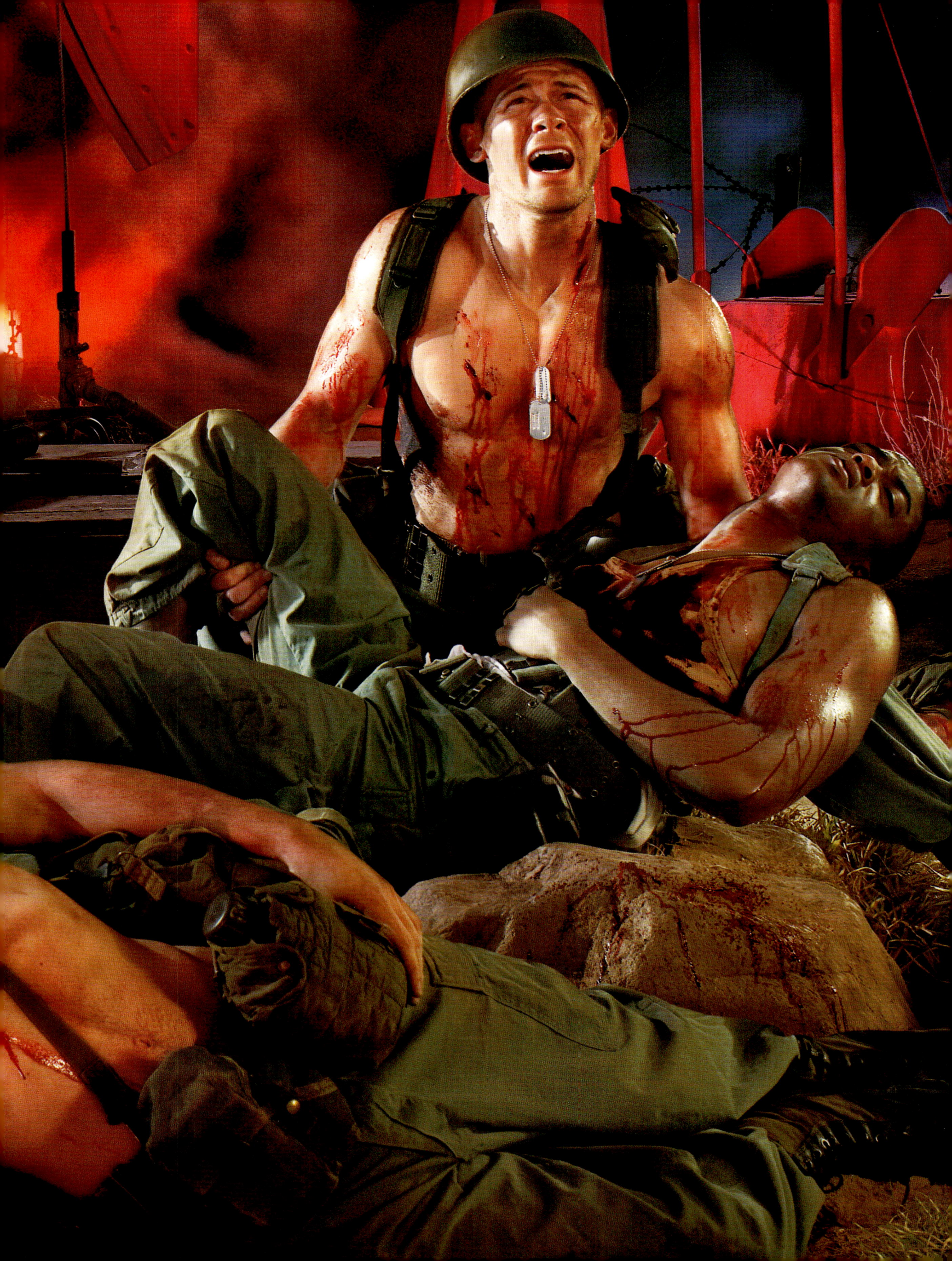

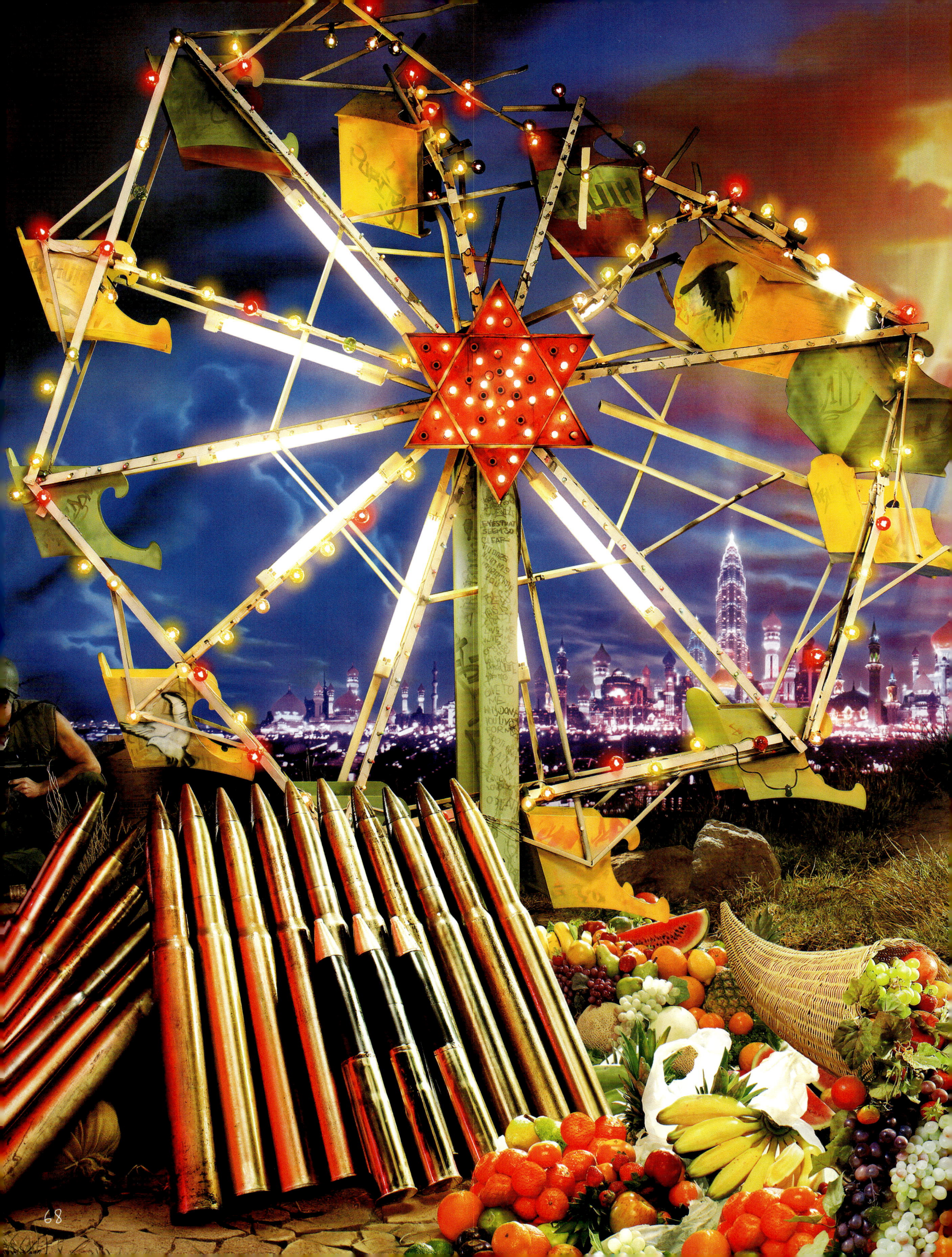

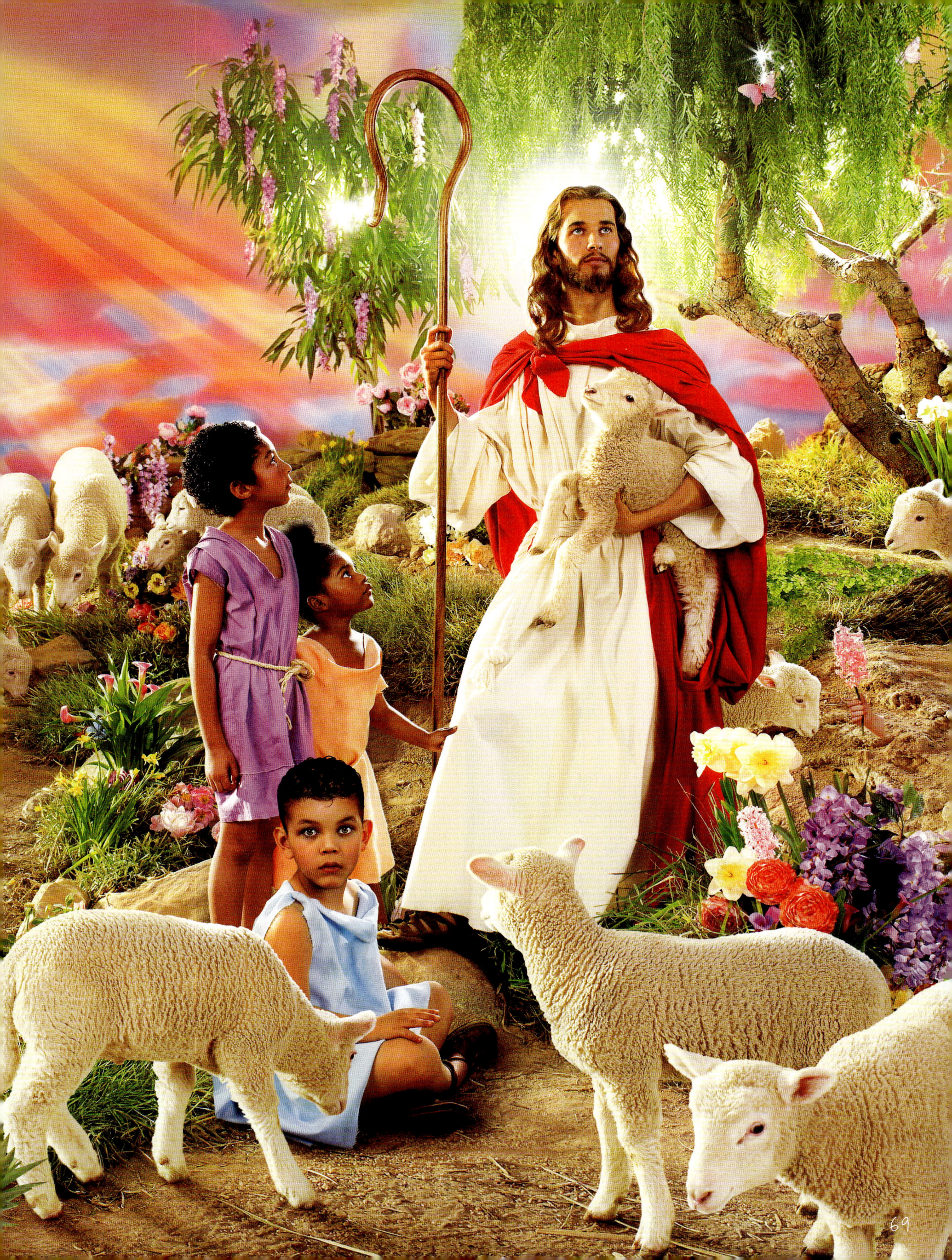

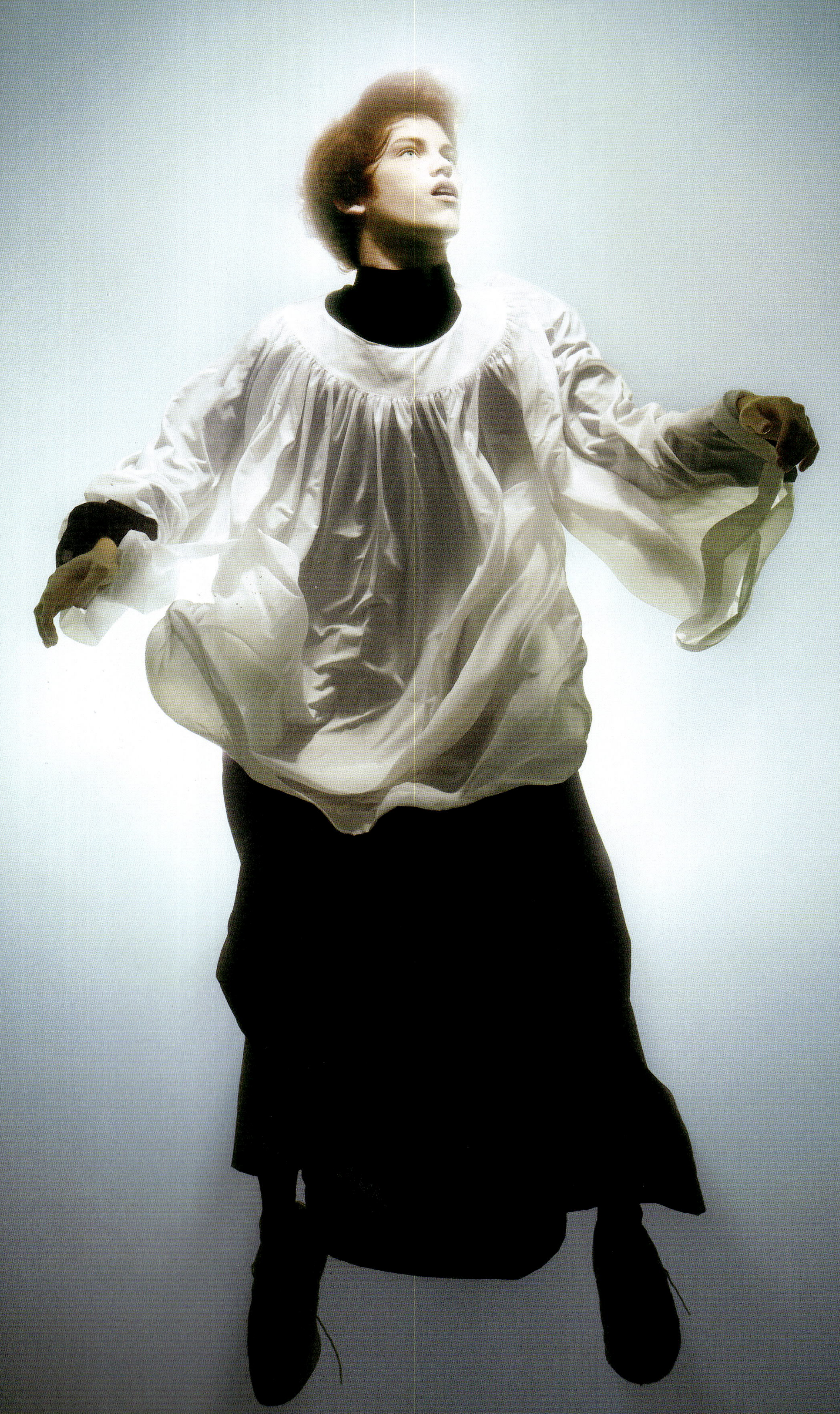

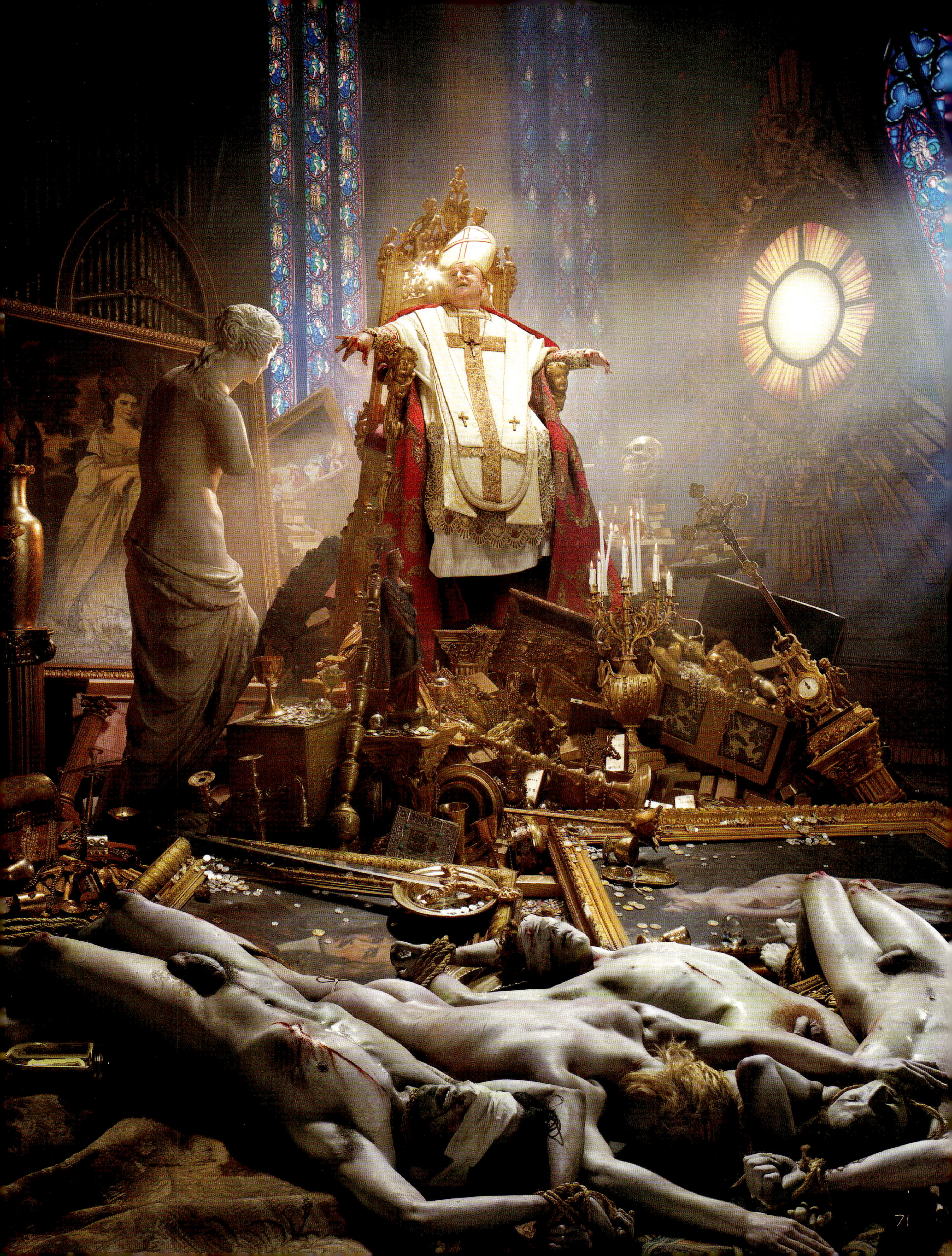

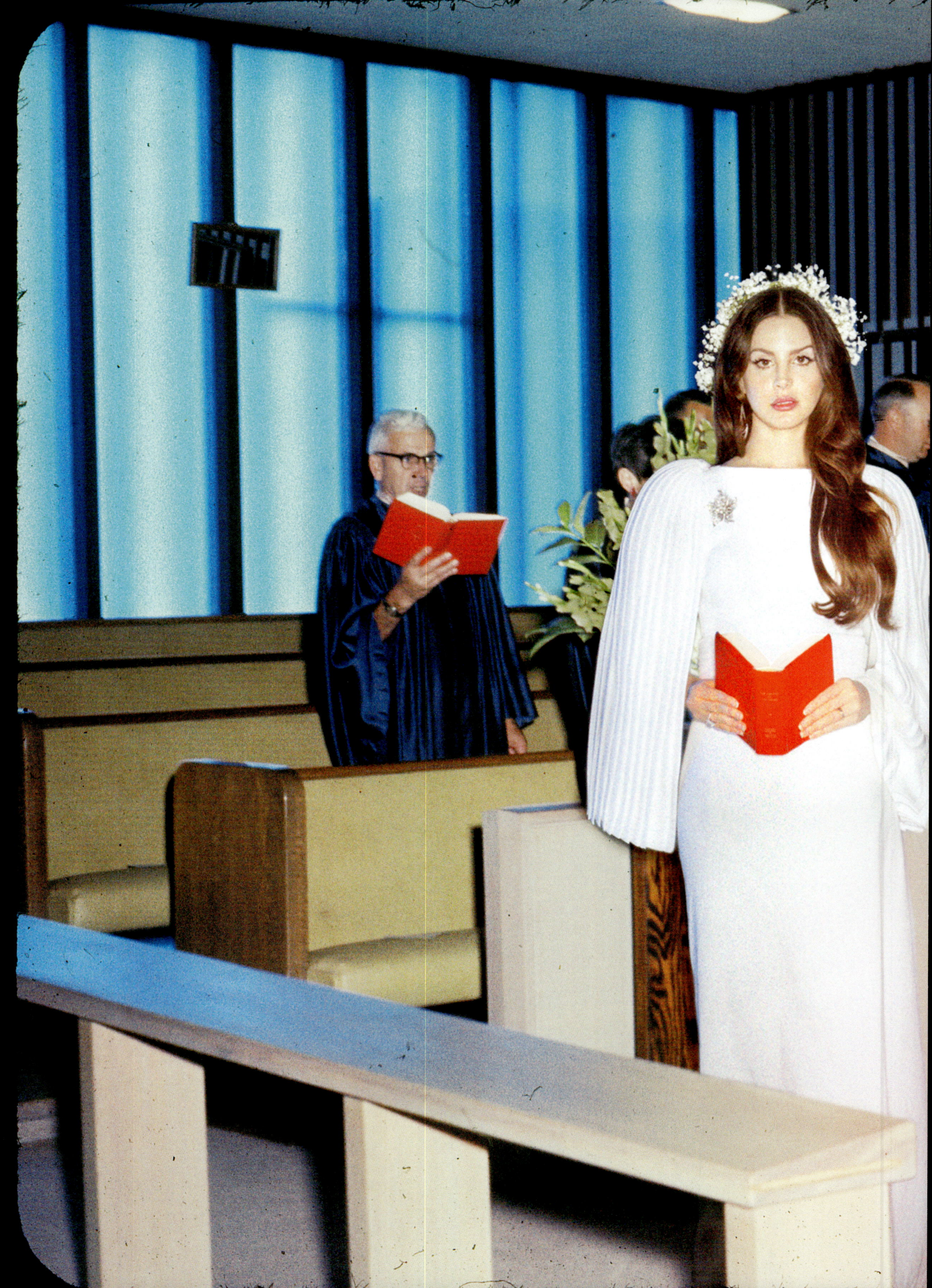

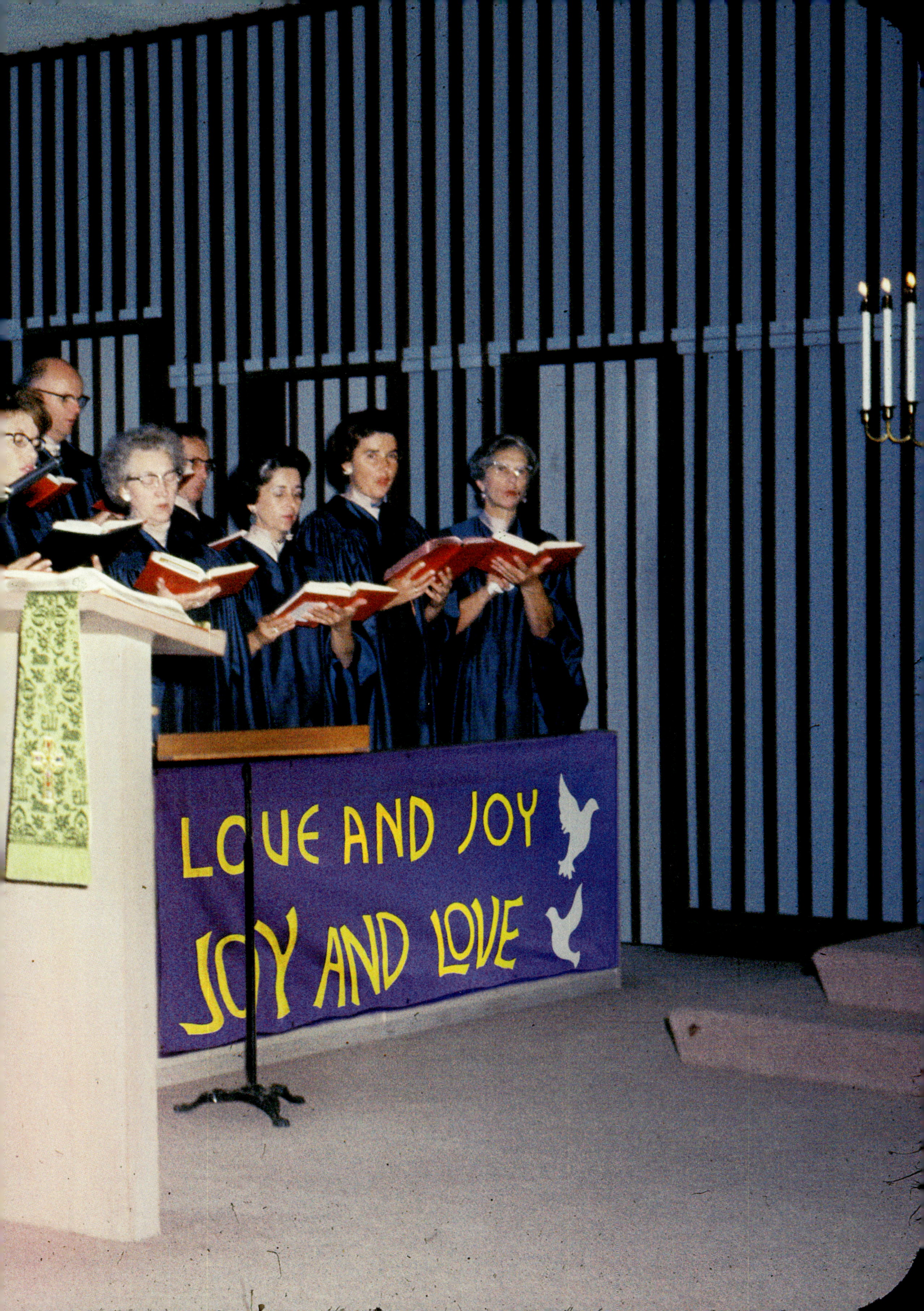
LOVE AND JOY
JOY AND LOVE

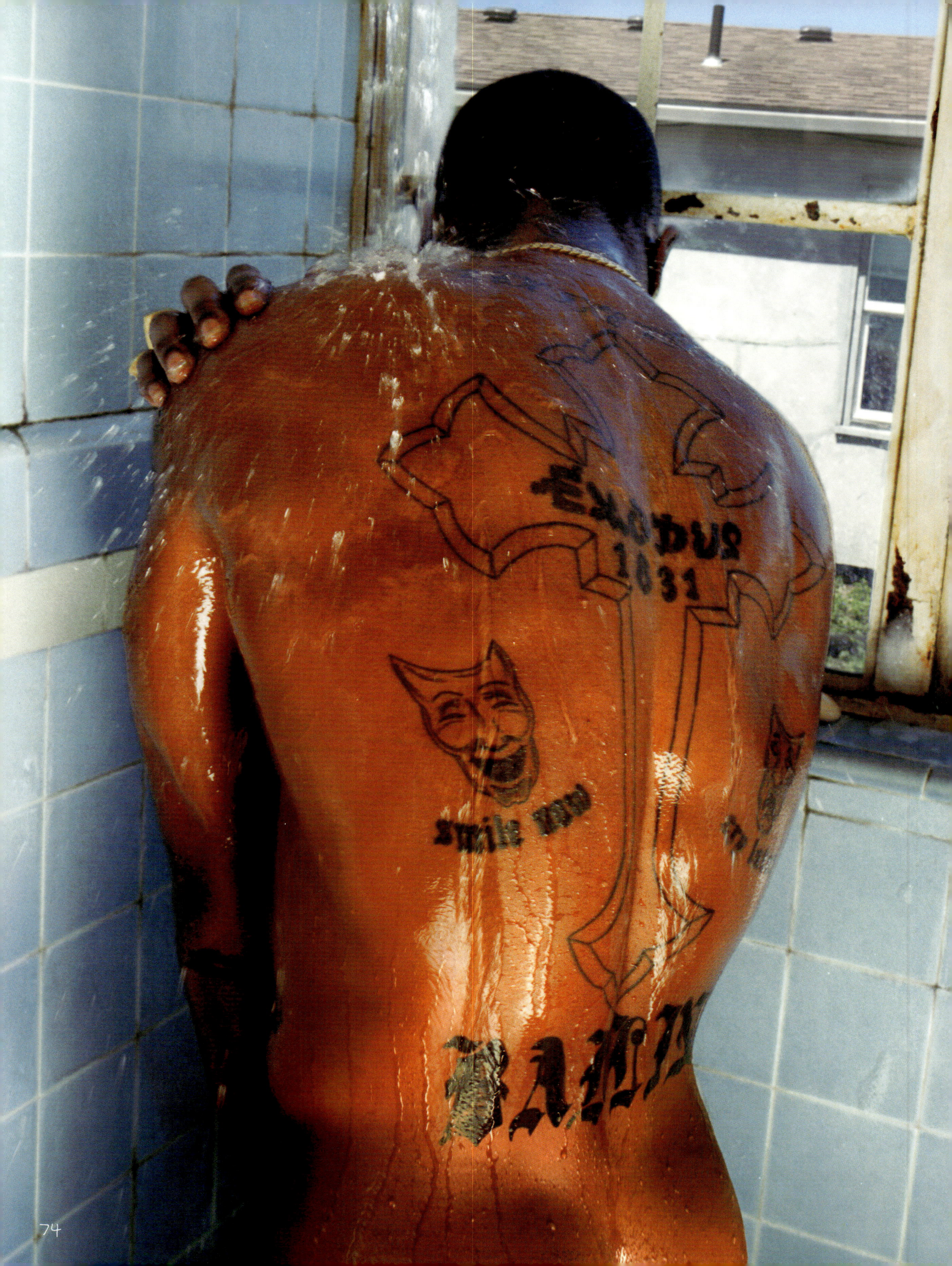
EXODUS
1031
smile now

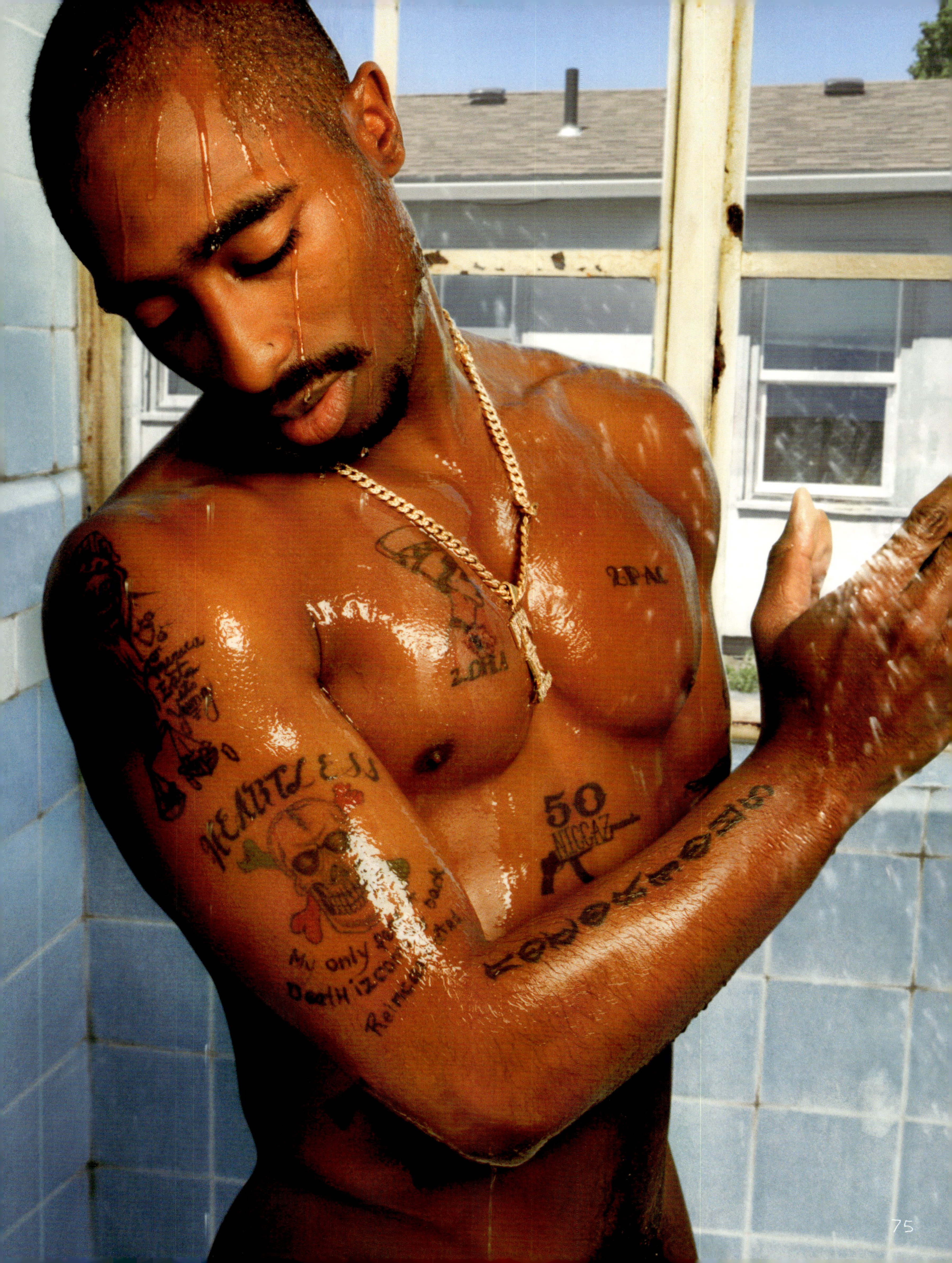
2PAC
HEARTLESS
50
NIGGAZ

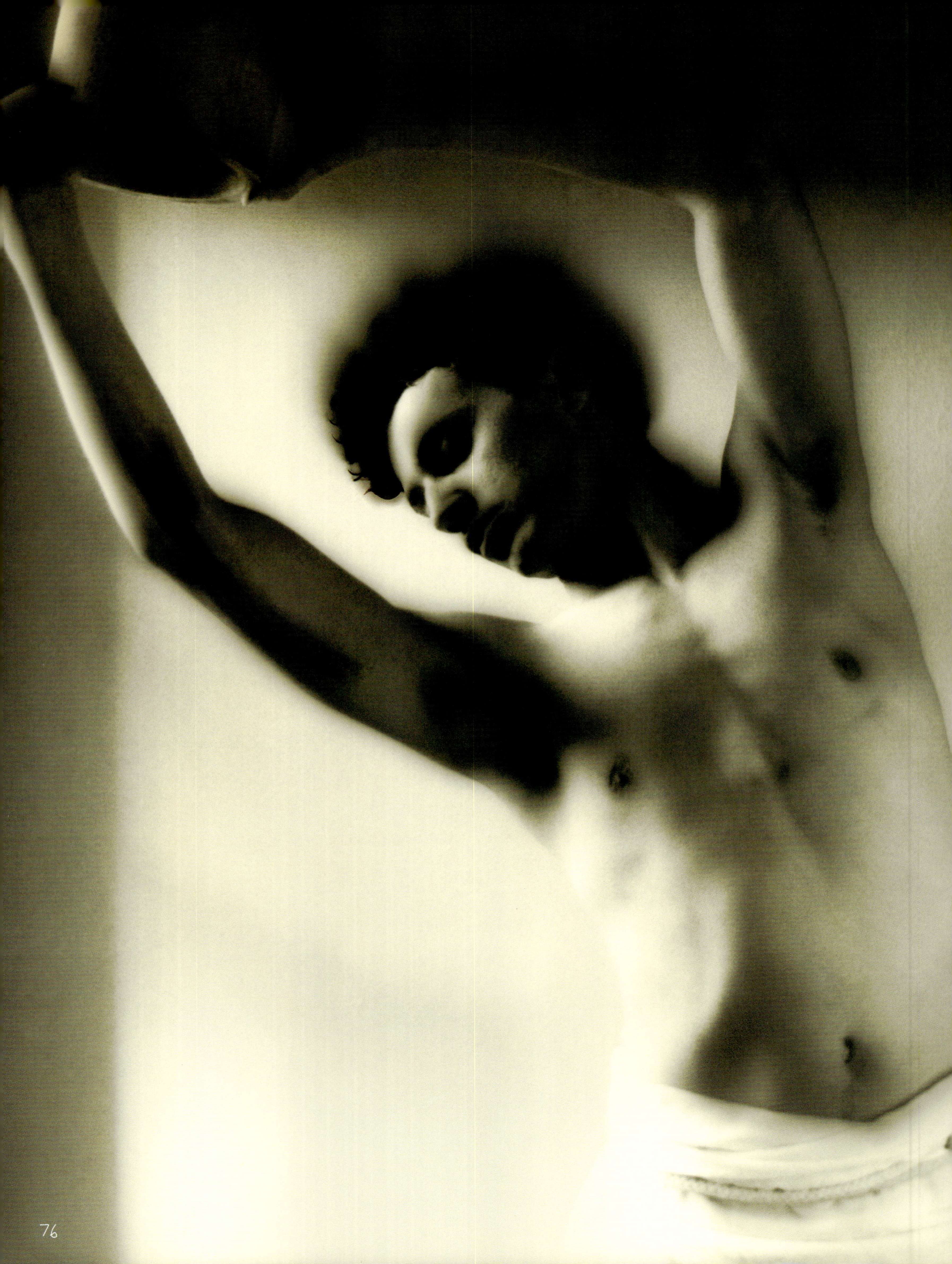

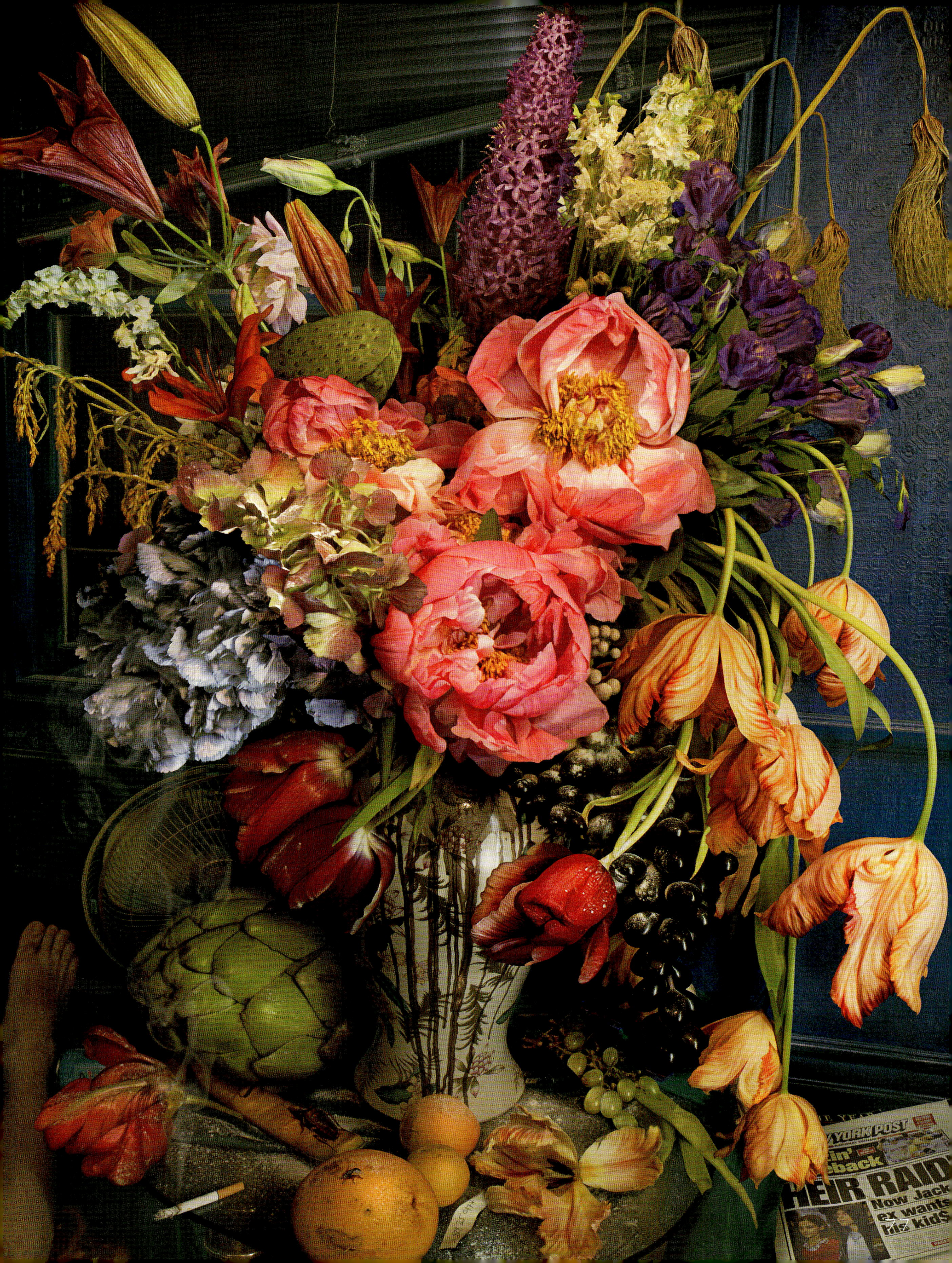
YORK POST
HEIR RAID
Now Jack
ex wants
his kids

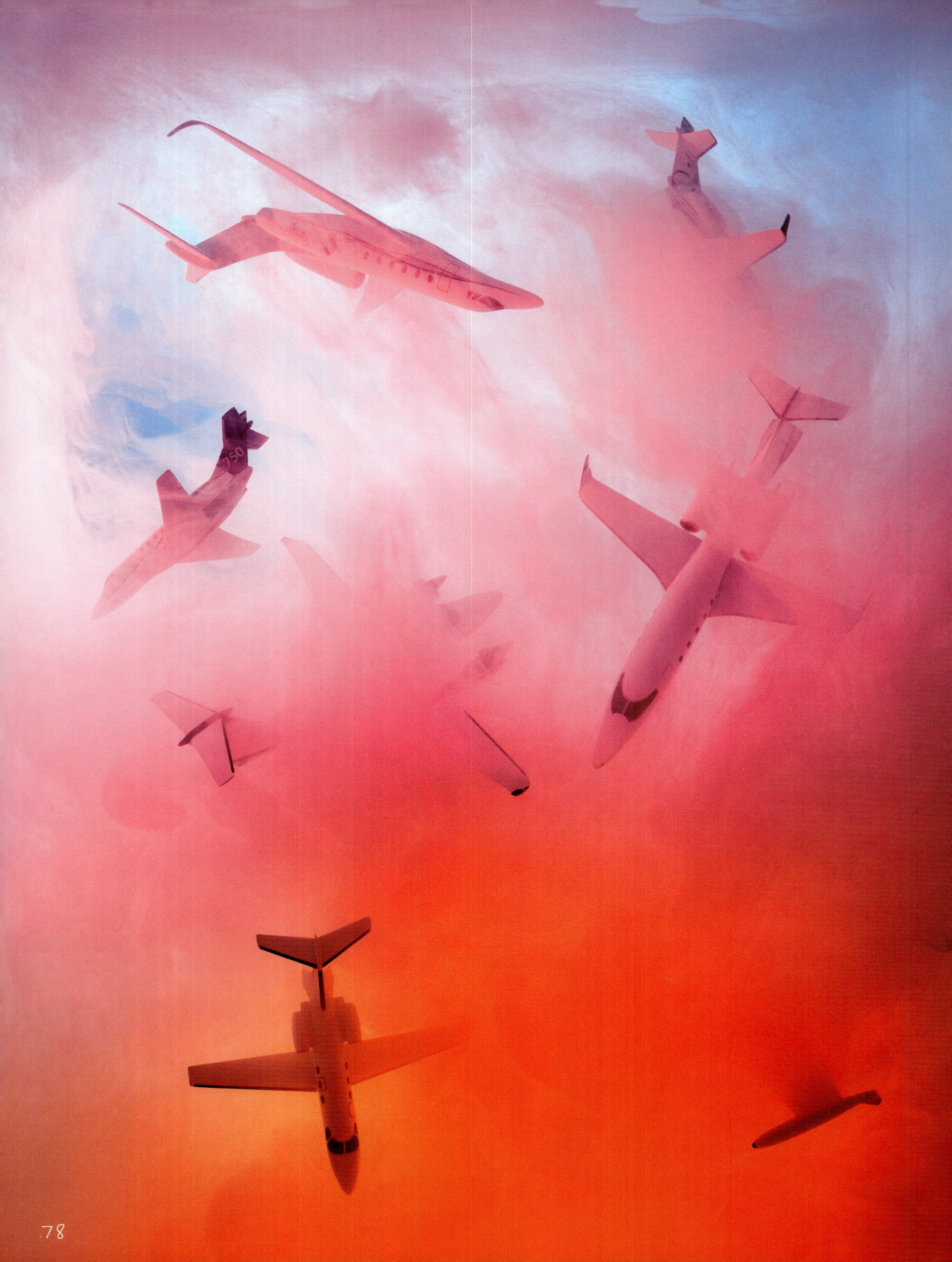

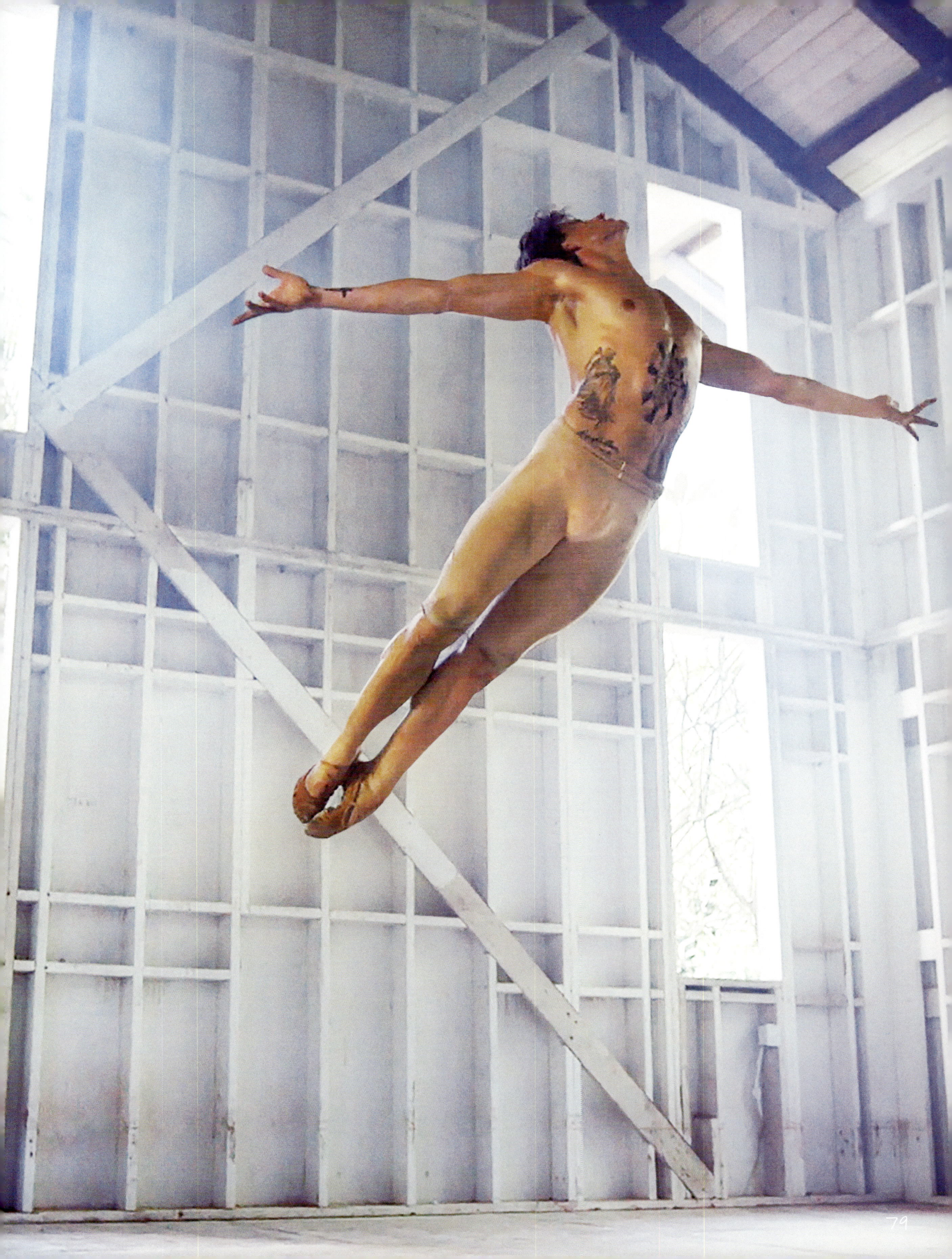

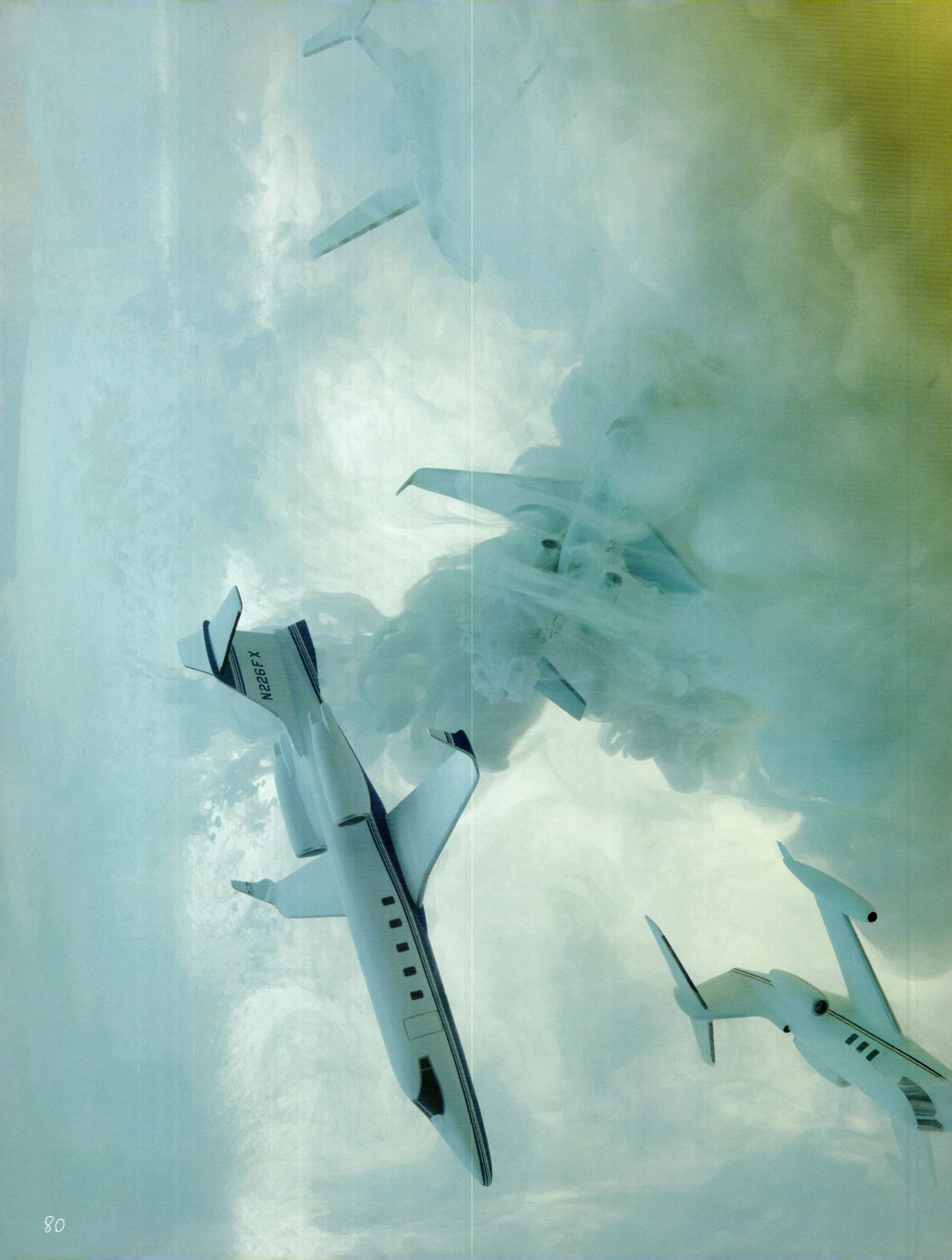
N226FX

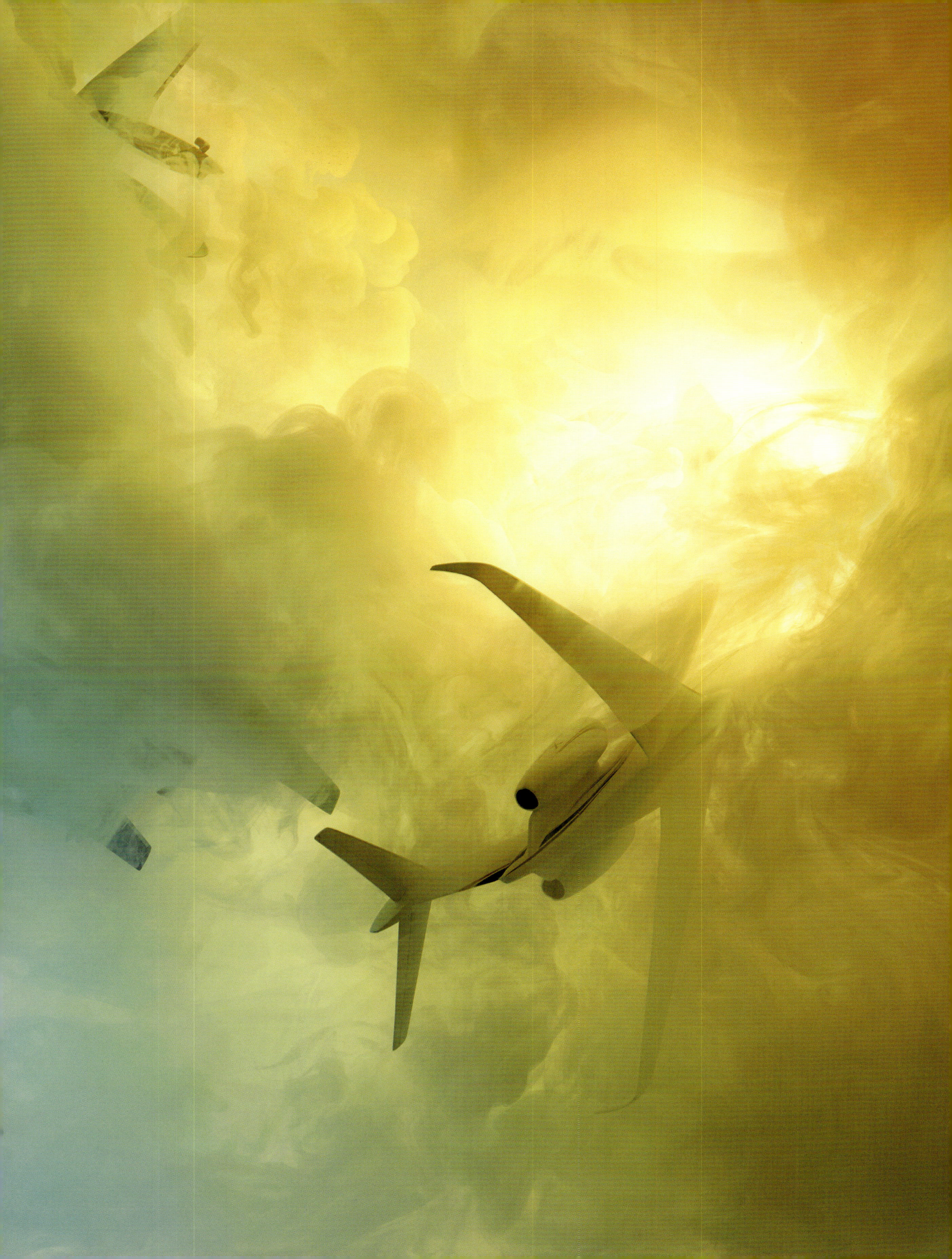

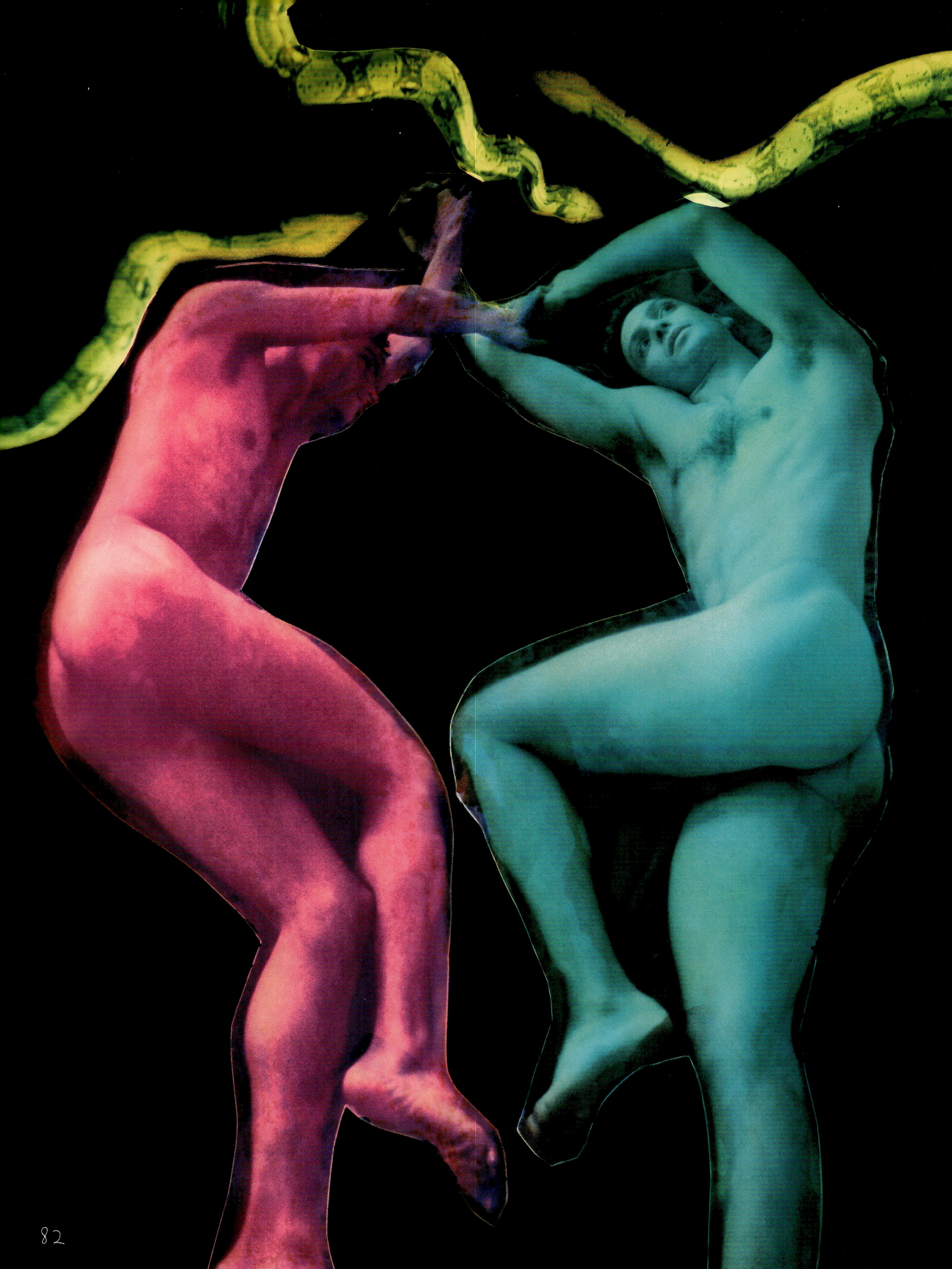

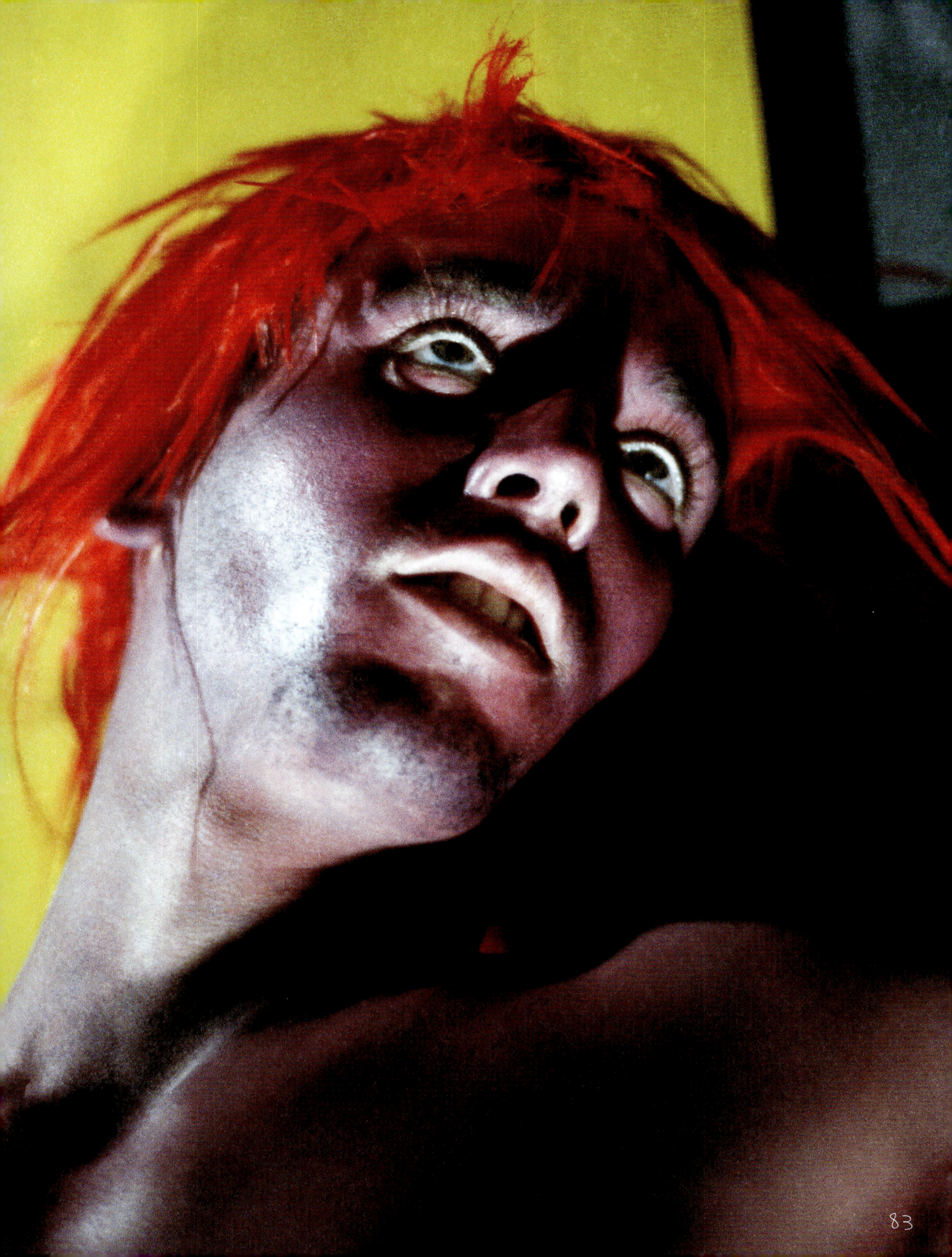

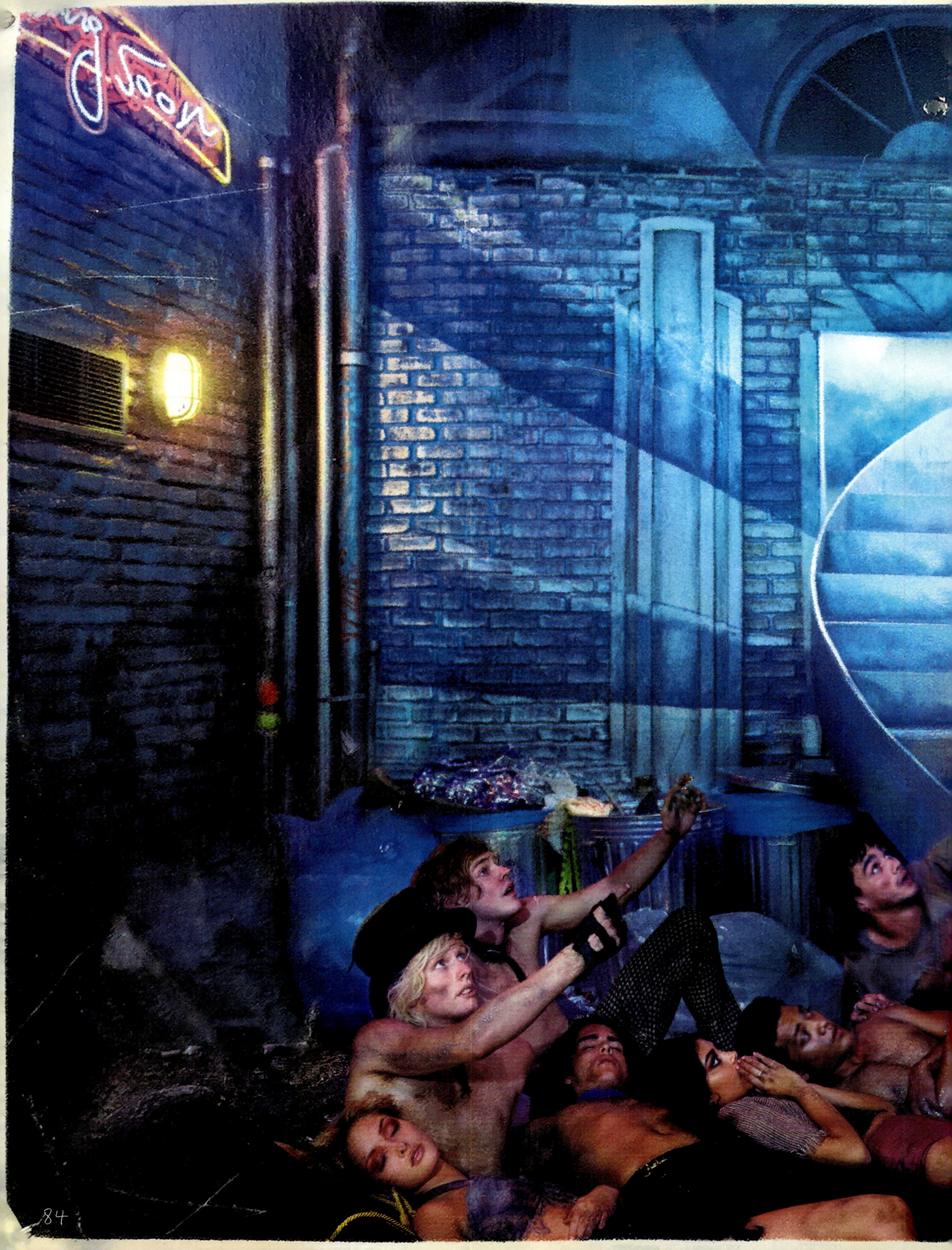

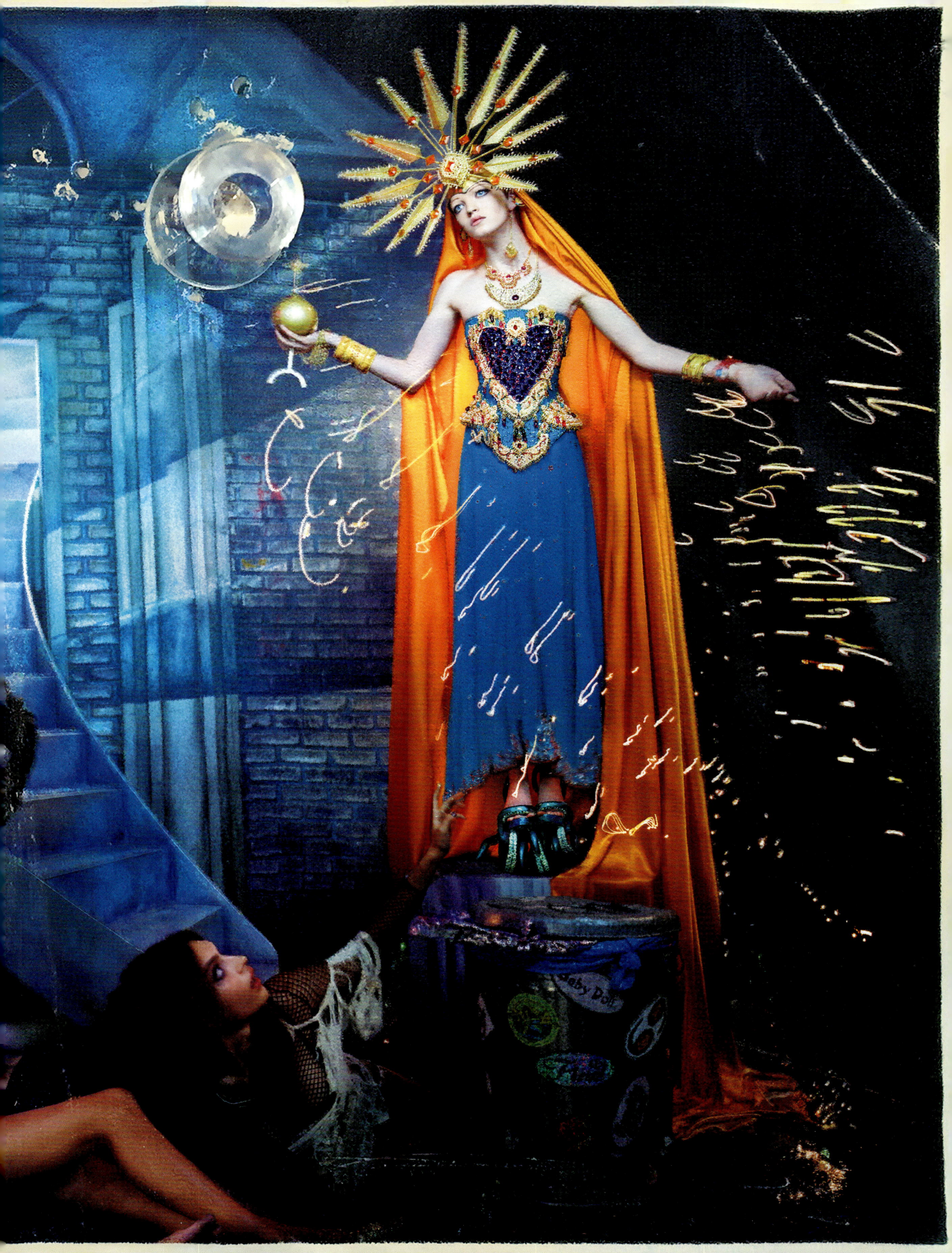

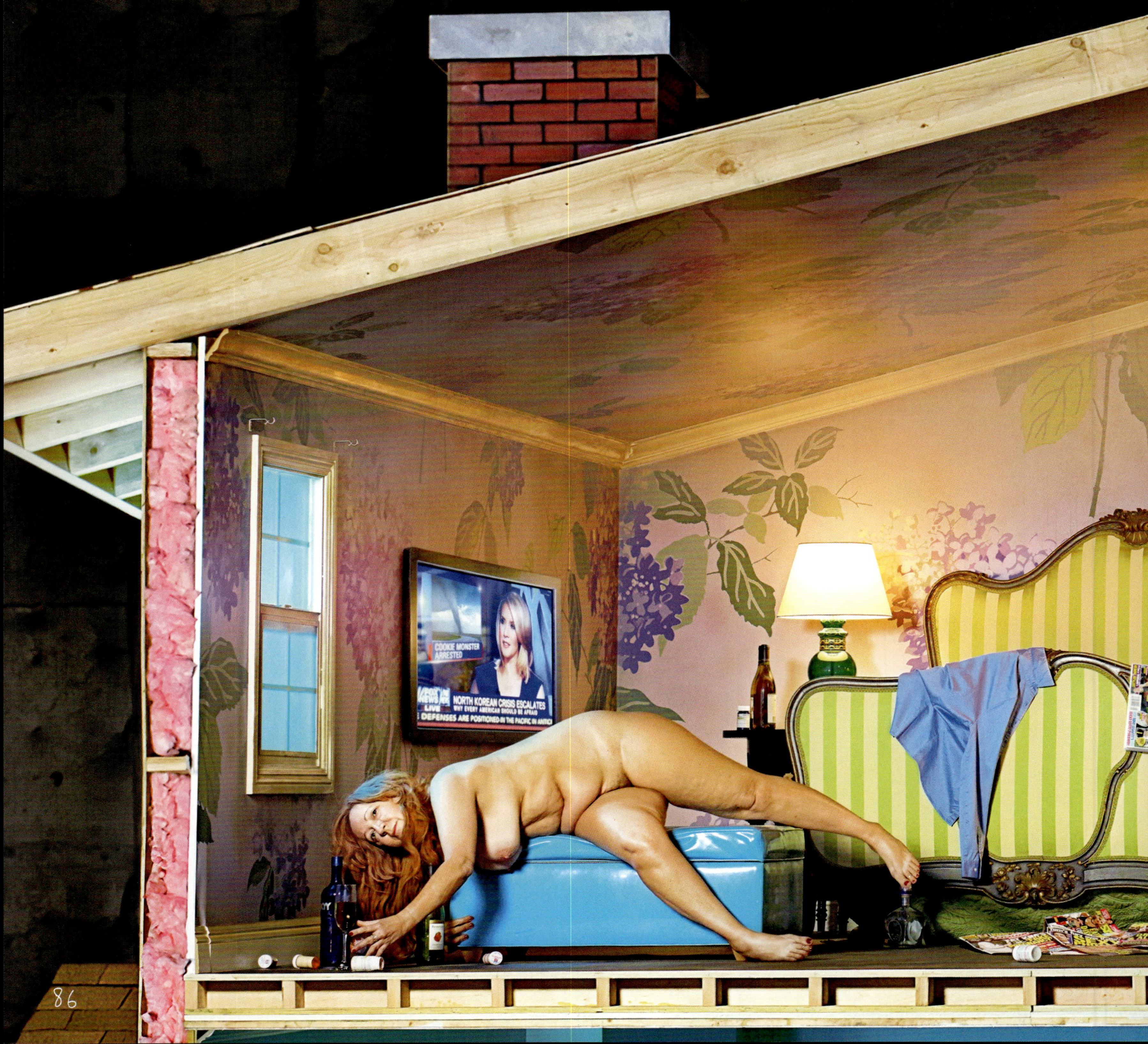
COOKIE MONSTER
ARRESTED
NEWS
LIVE
NORTH KOREAN CRISIS ESCALATES
WHY EVERY AMERICAN SHOULD BE AFRAID
DEFENSES ARE POSITIONED IN THE PACIFIC IN ANTICI

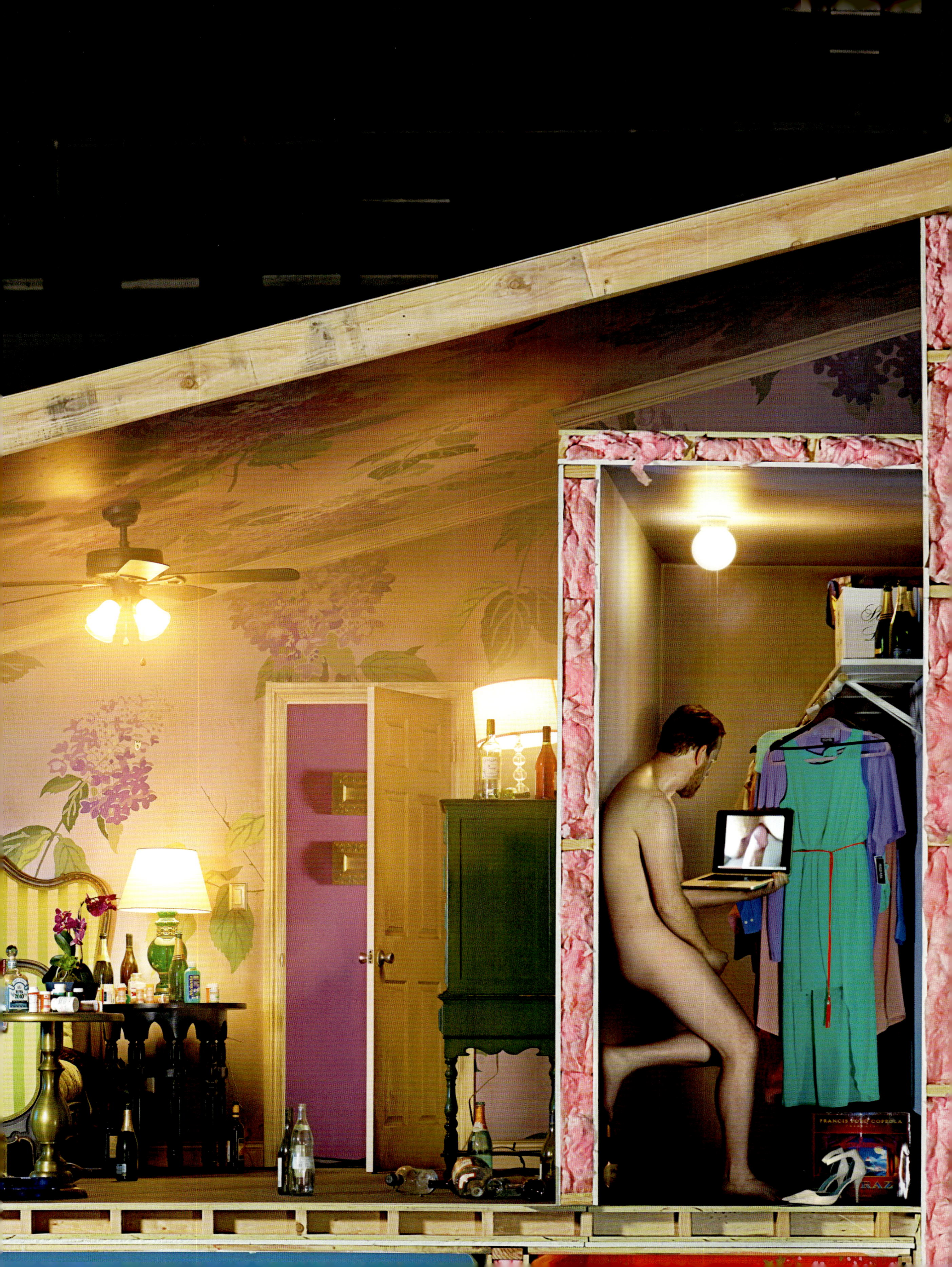

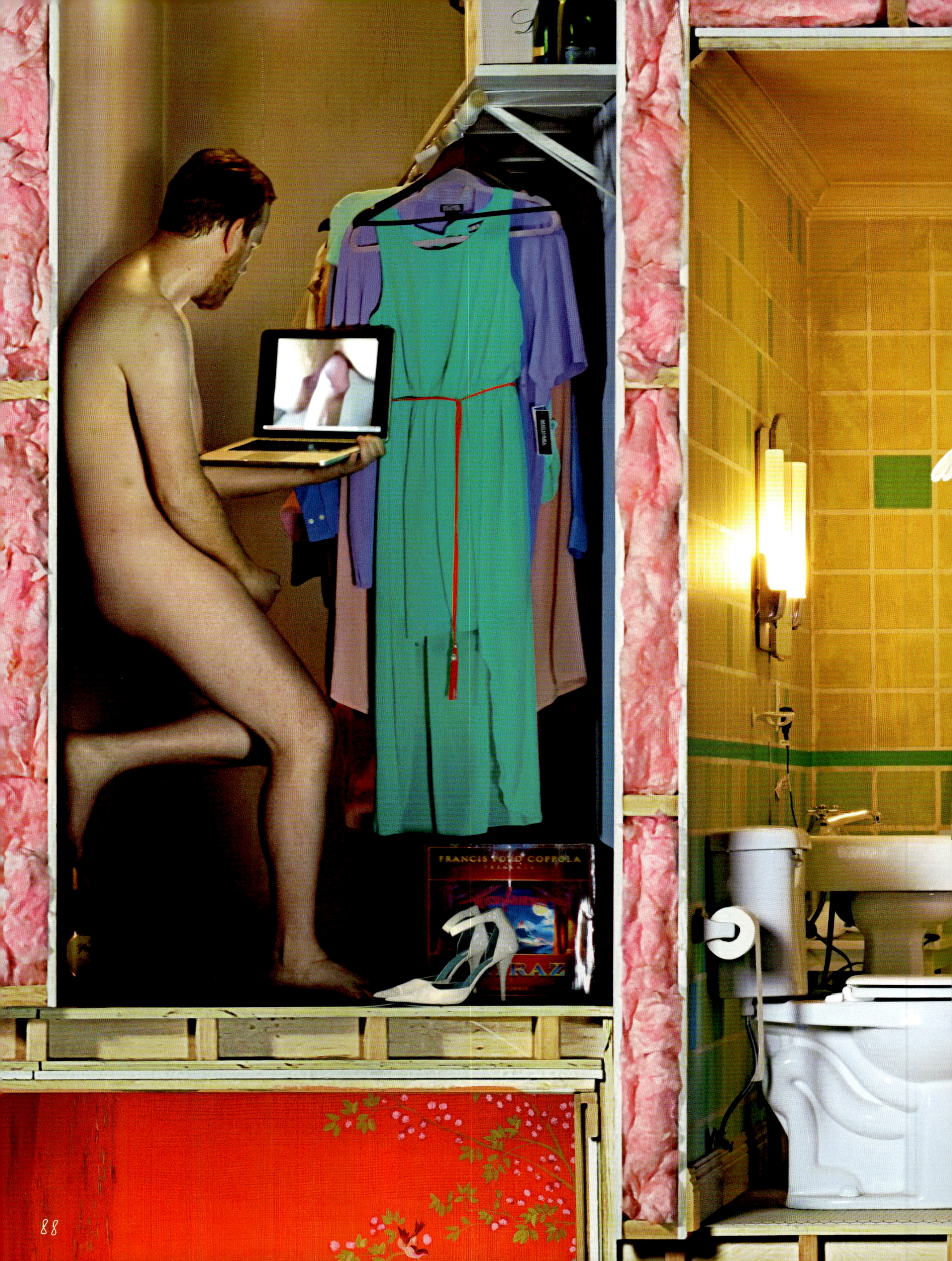

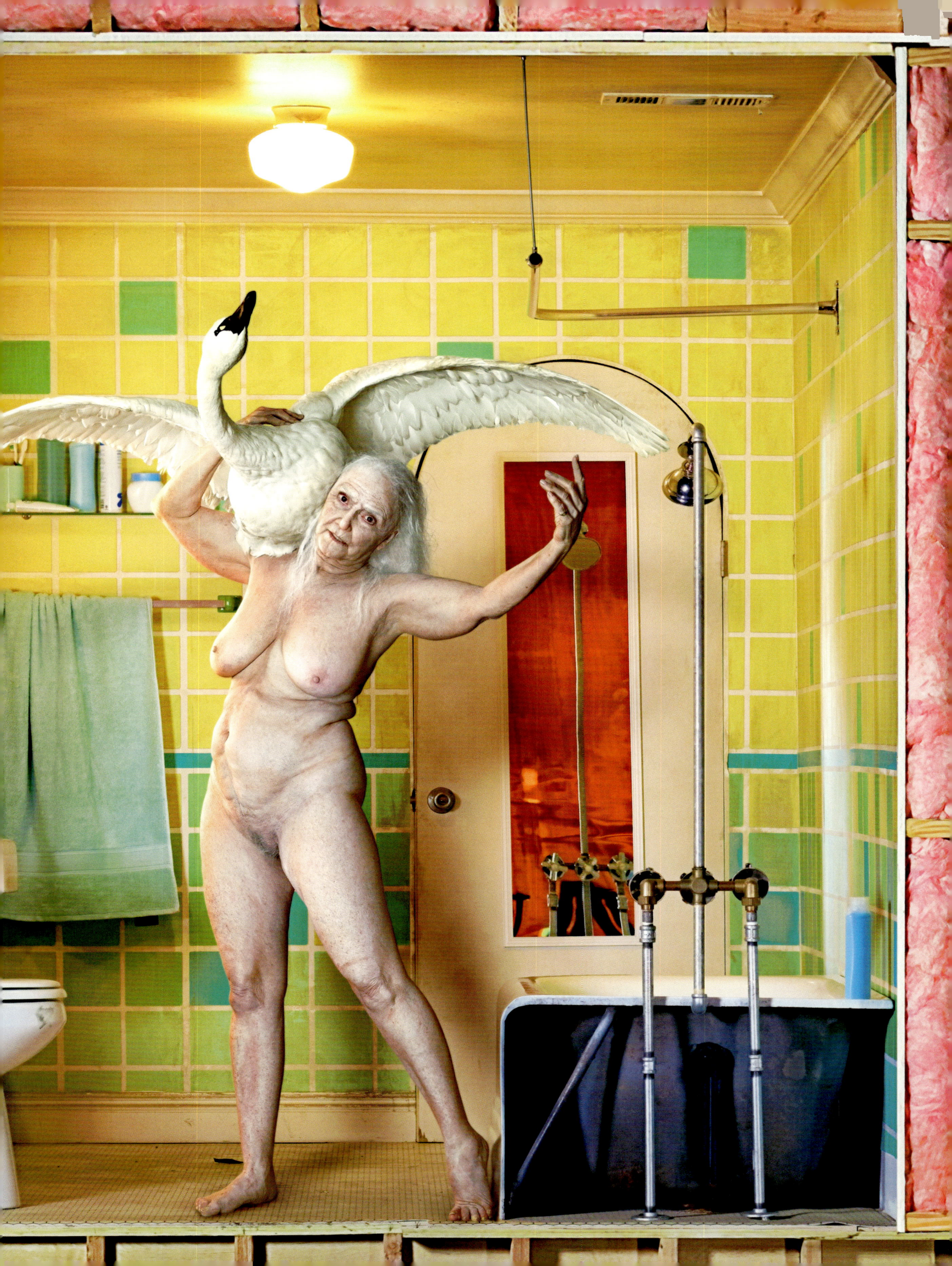

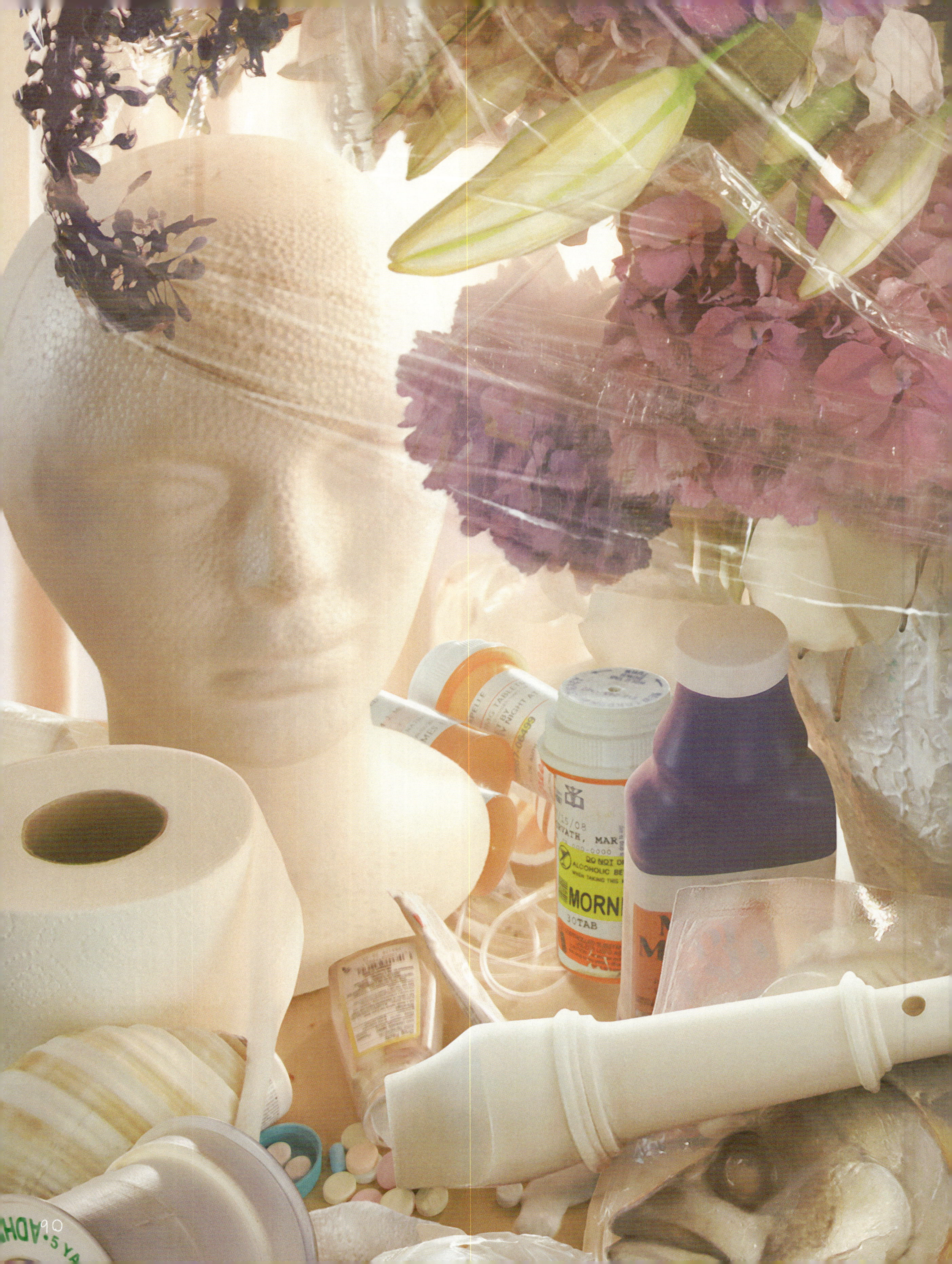
MORN
30TAB

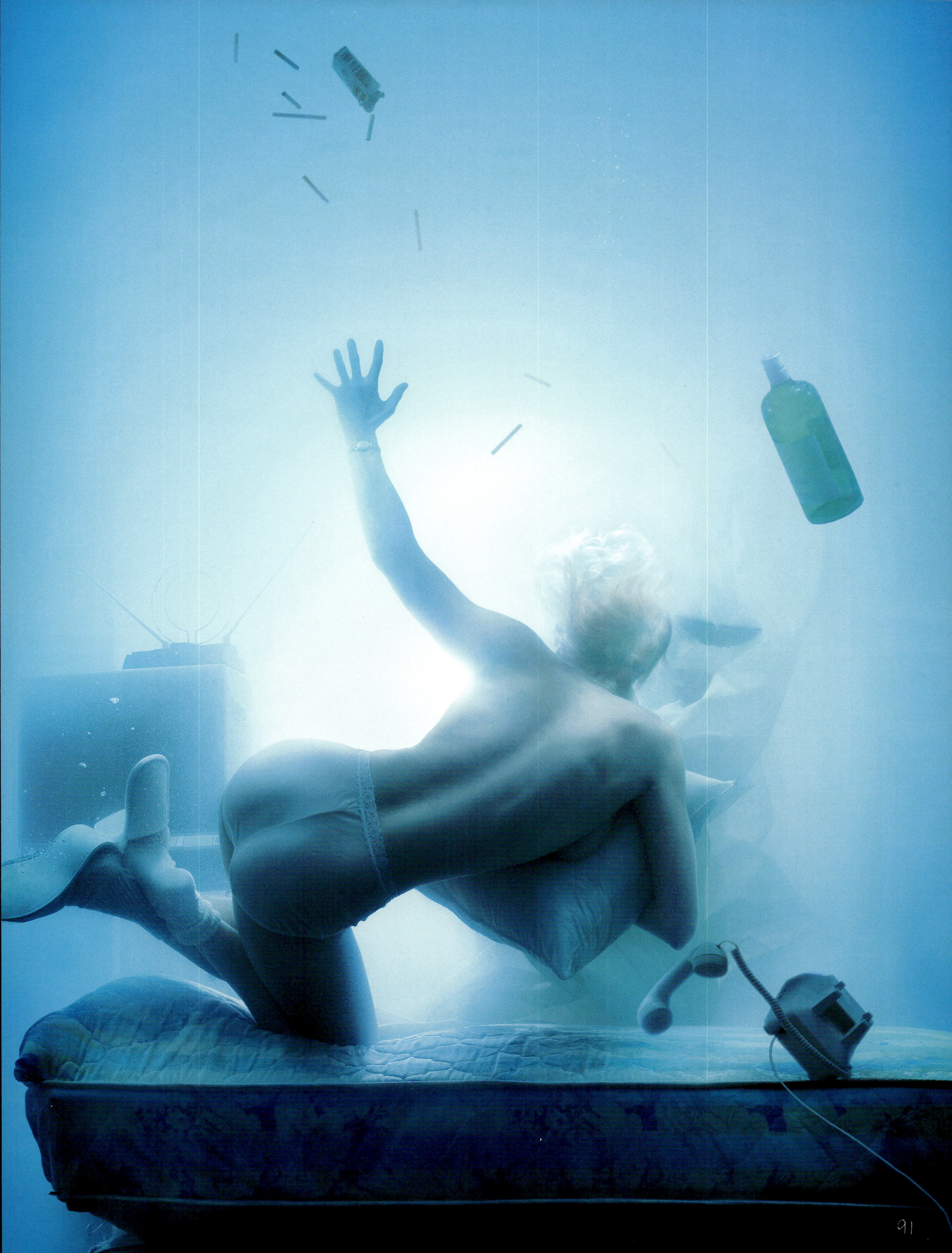

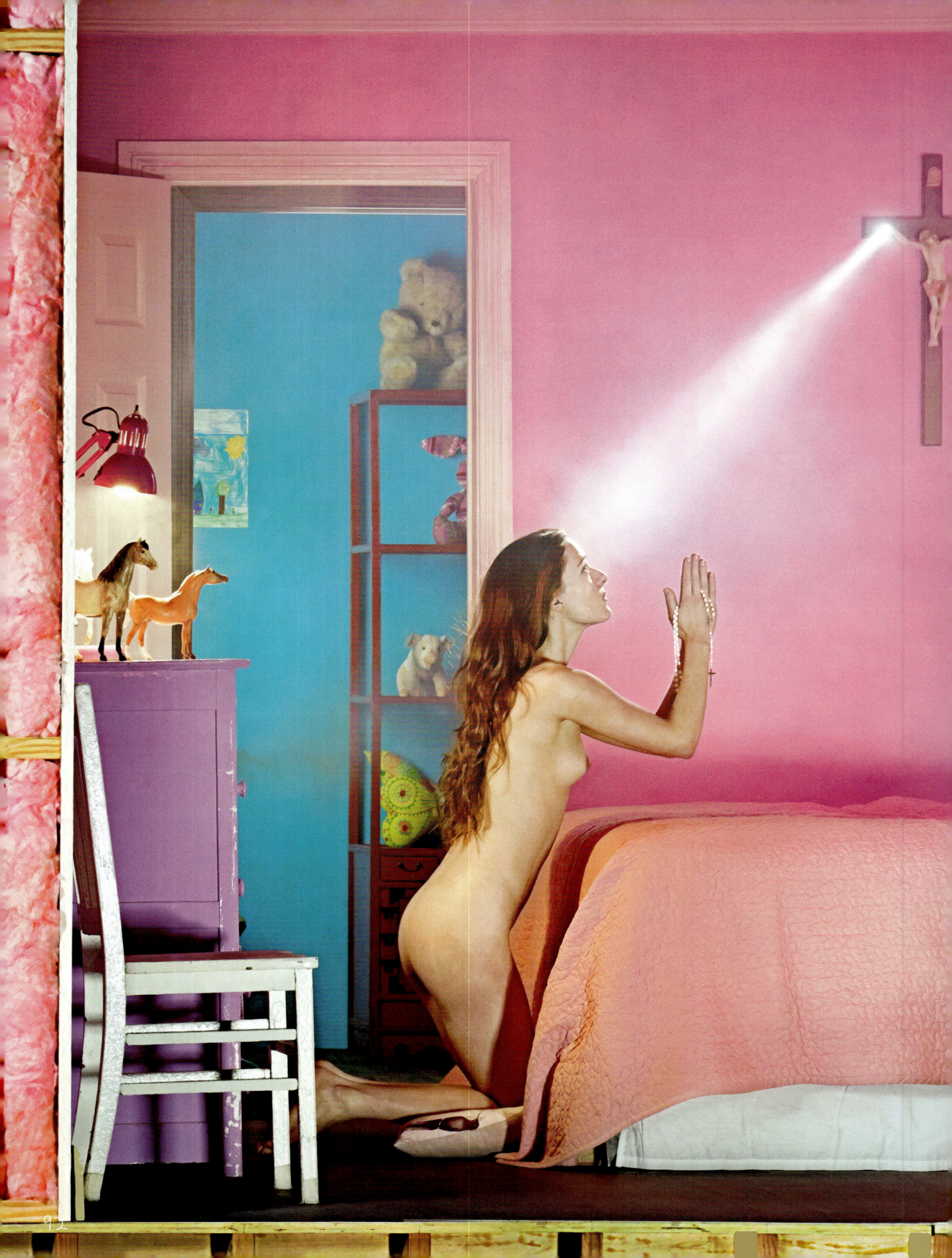

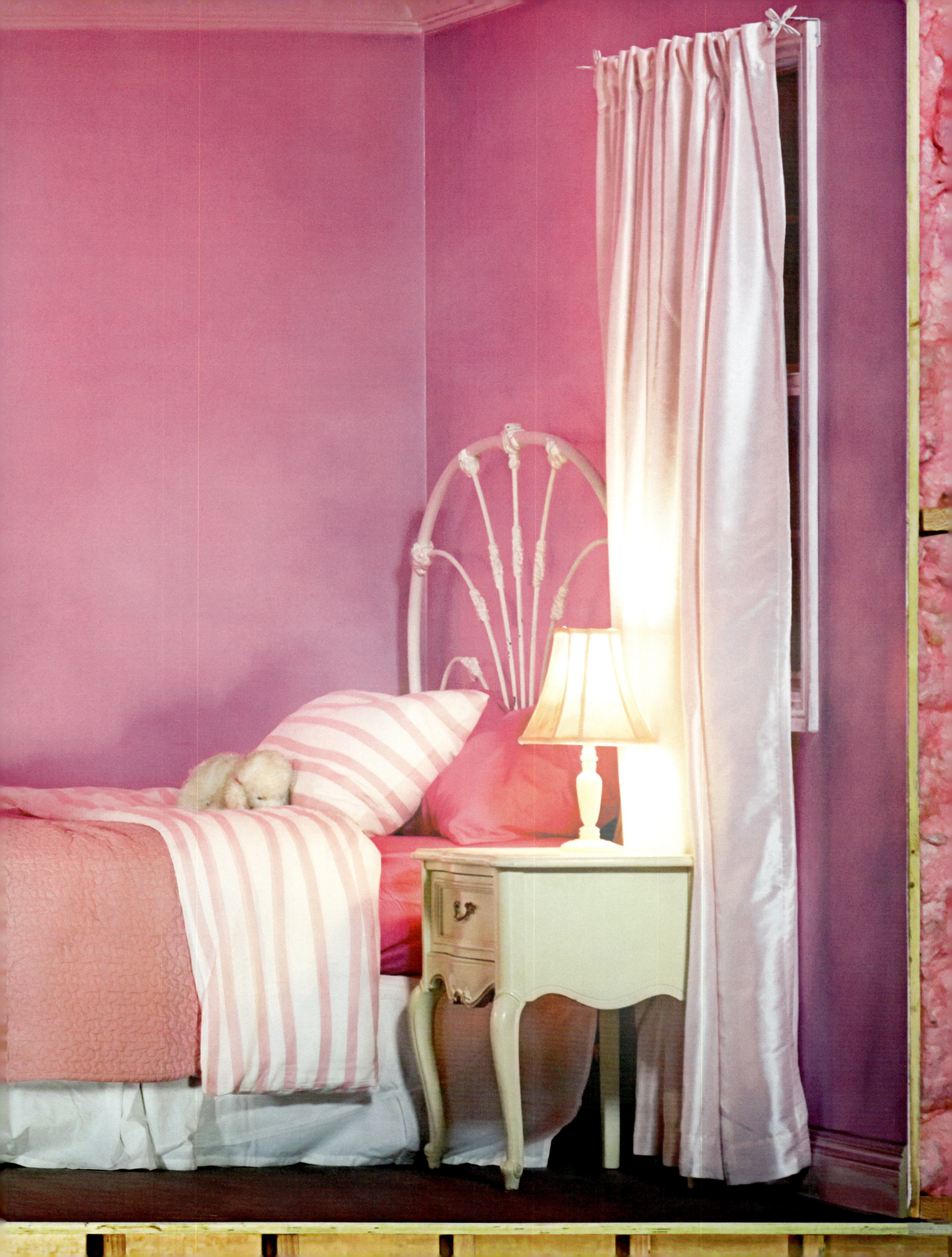

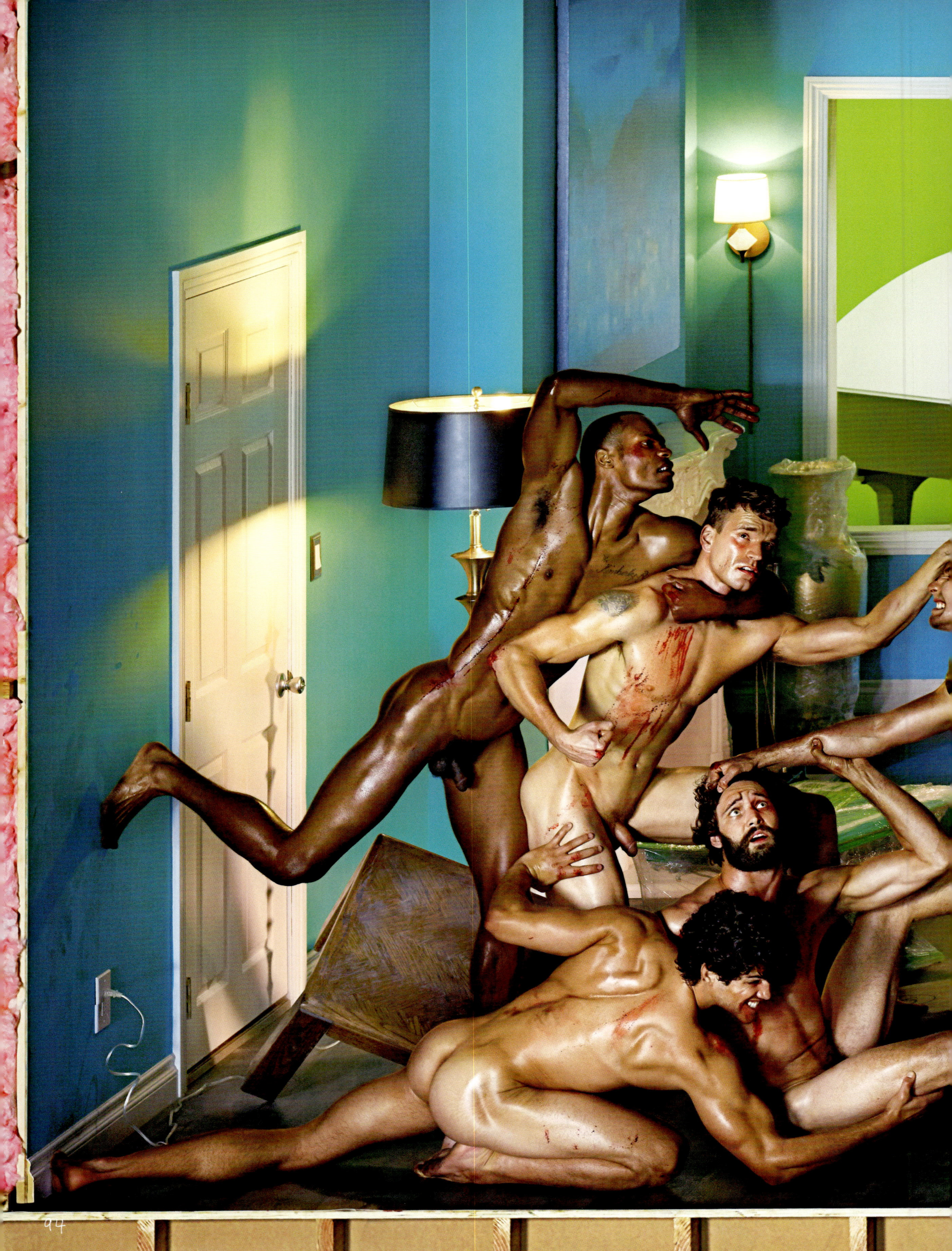

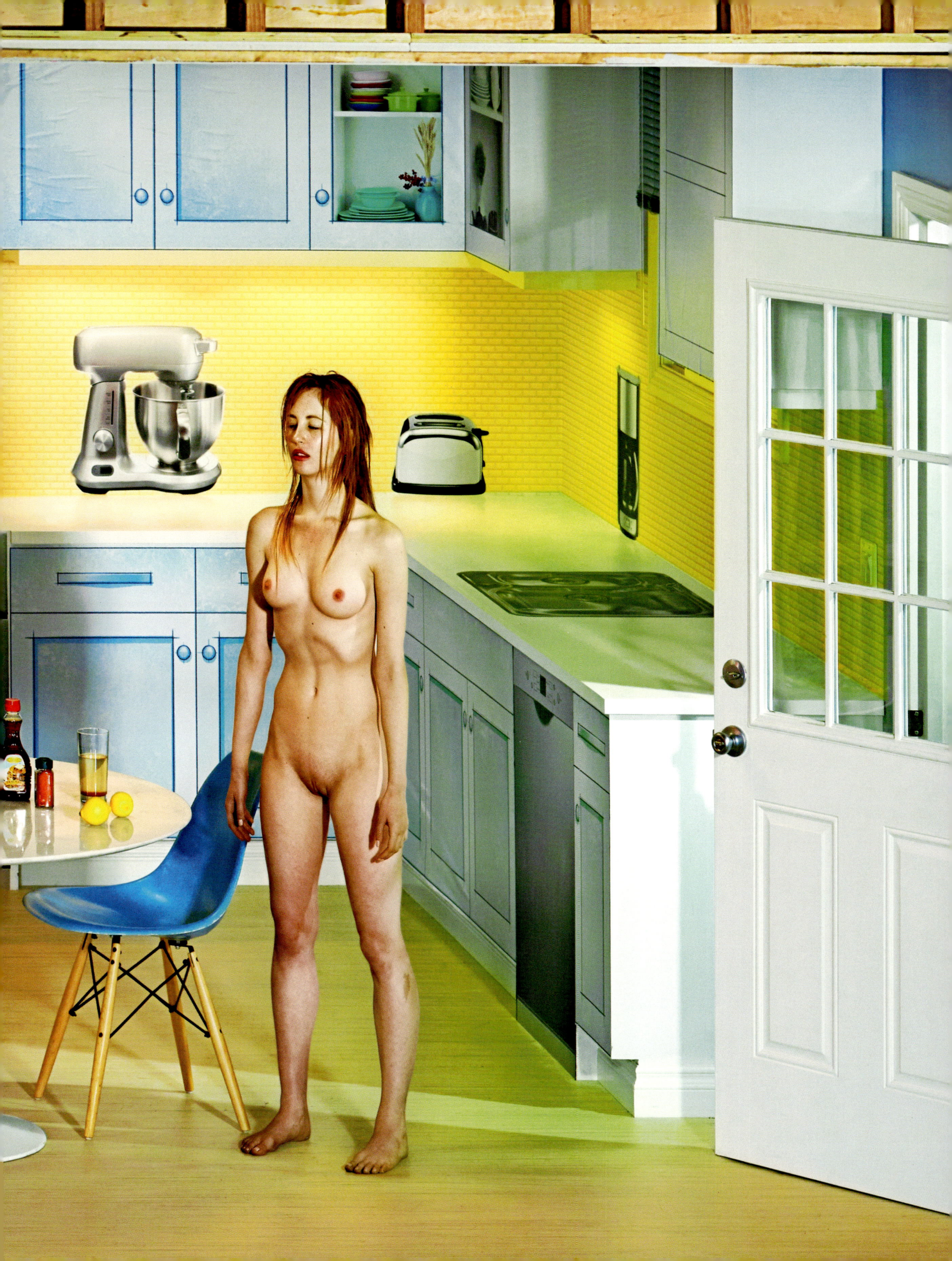

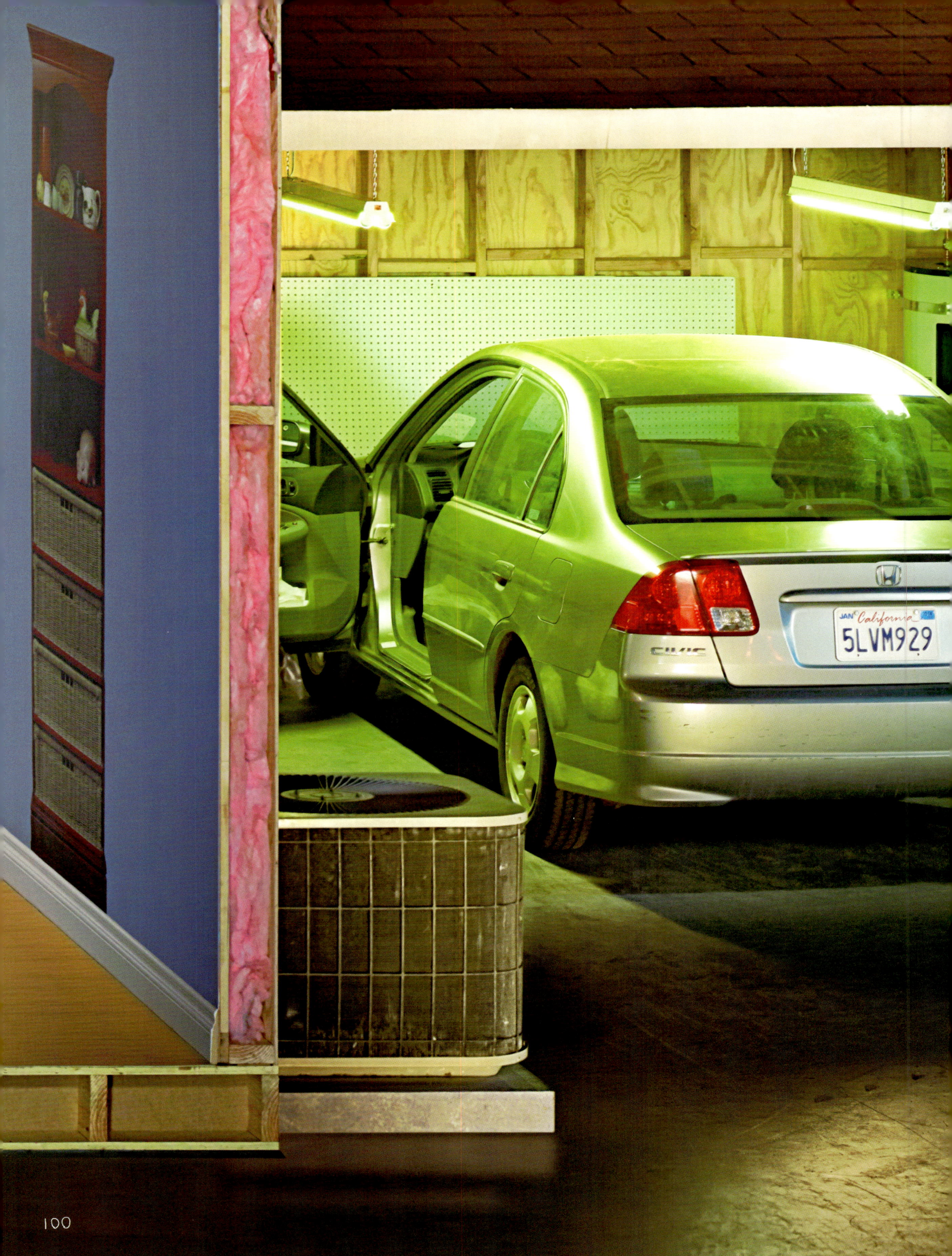
California
5LVM929

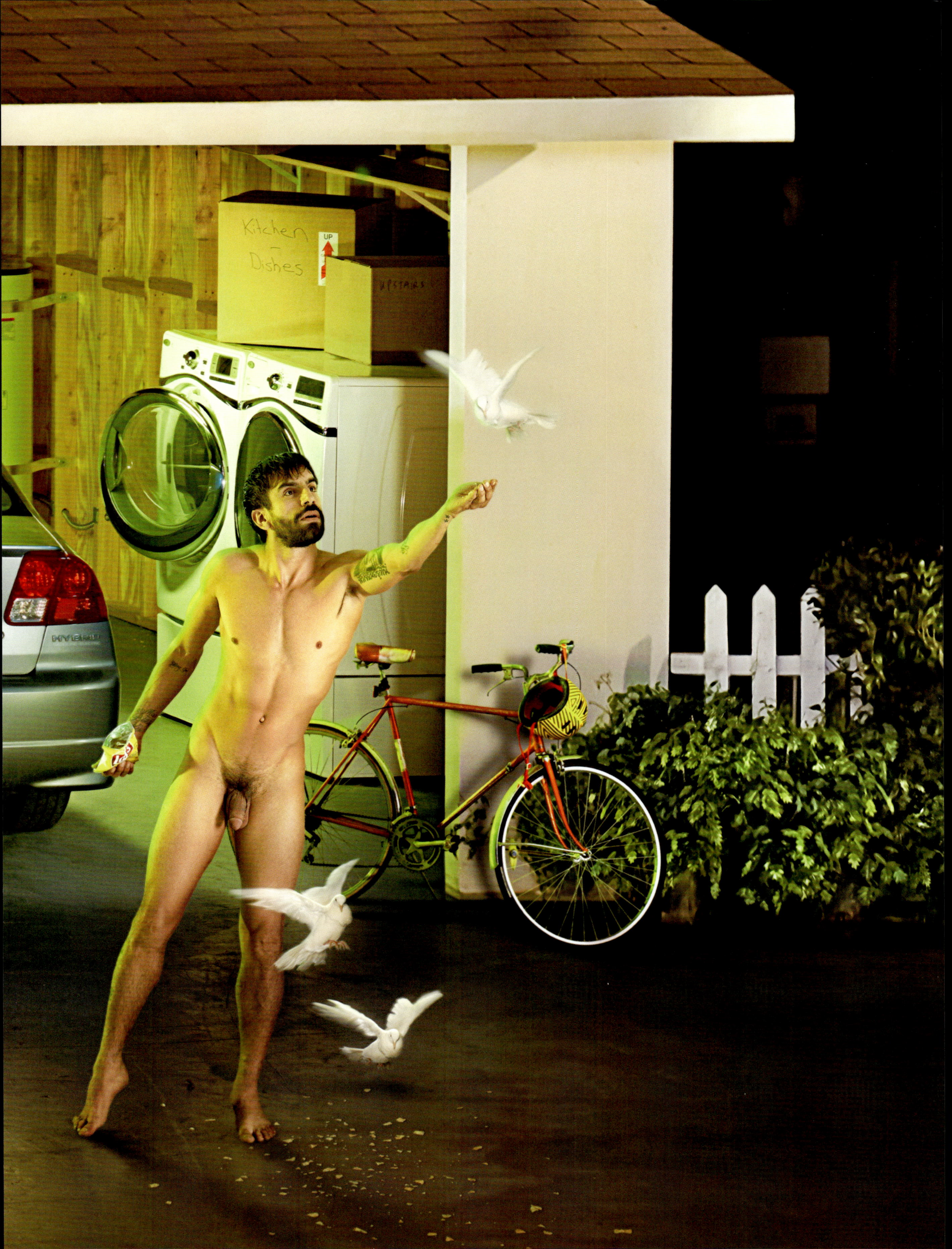
Kitchen
–
Dishes
UP
HYBRID

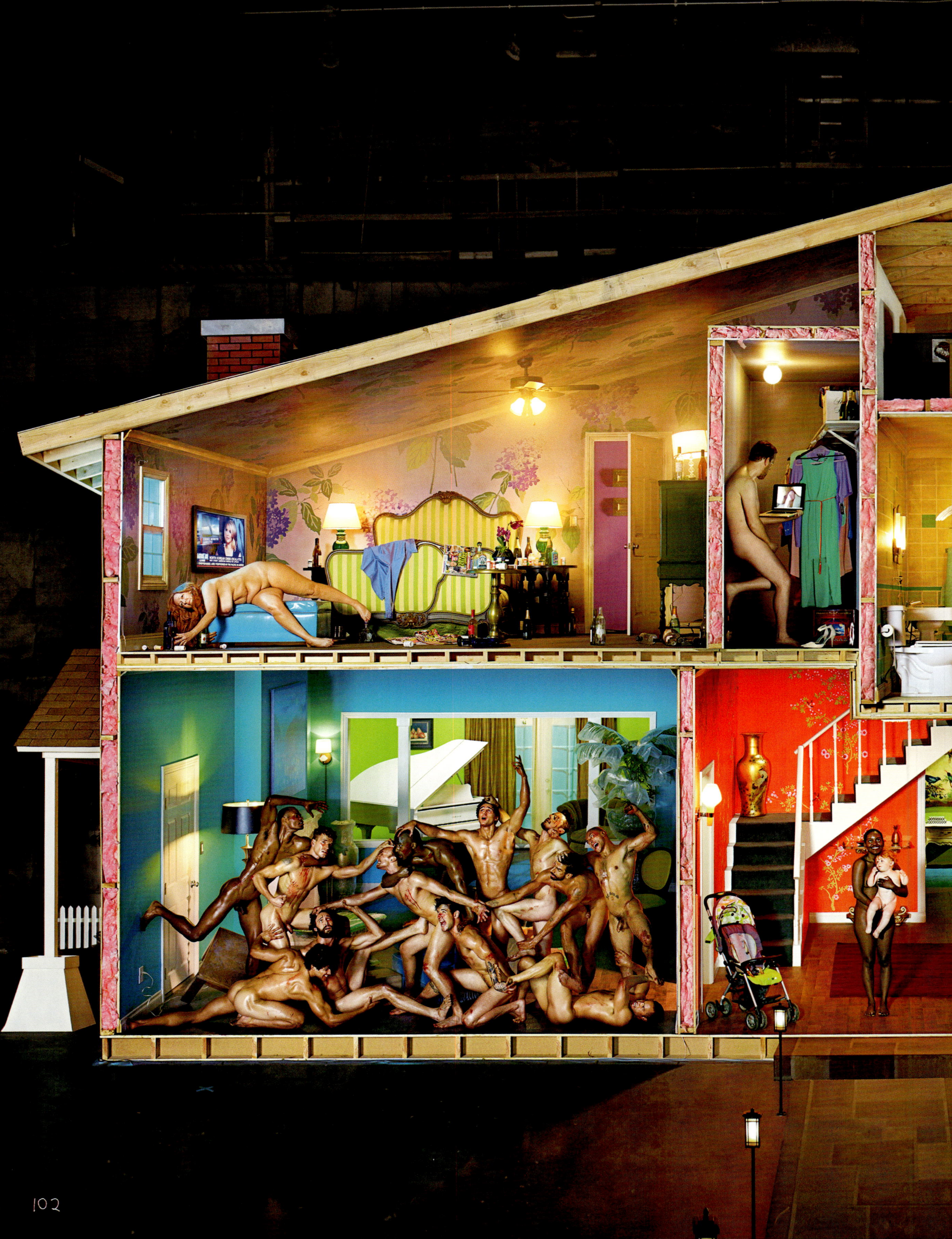

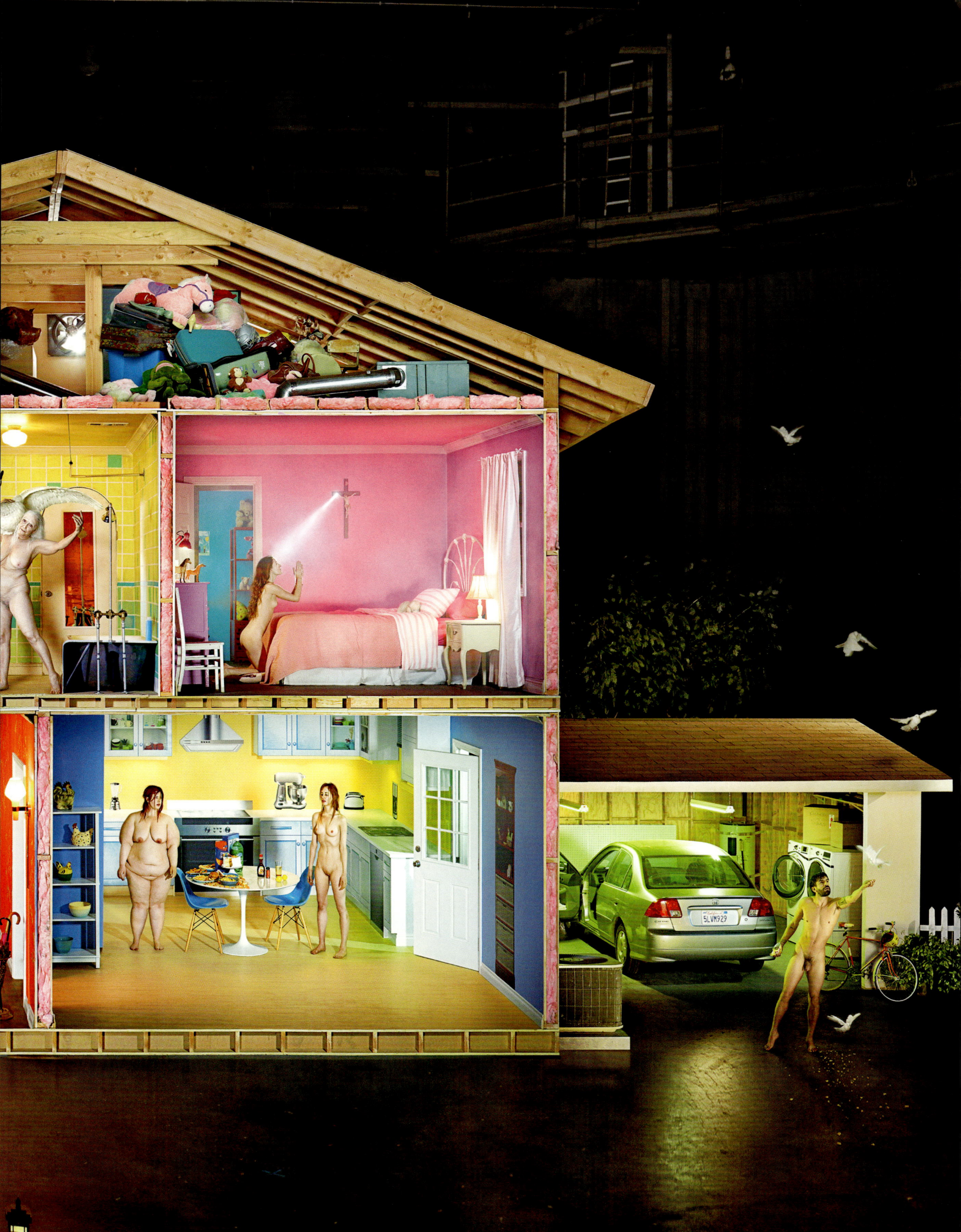
5LVM929

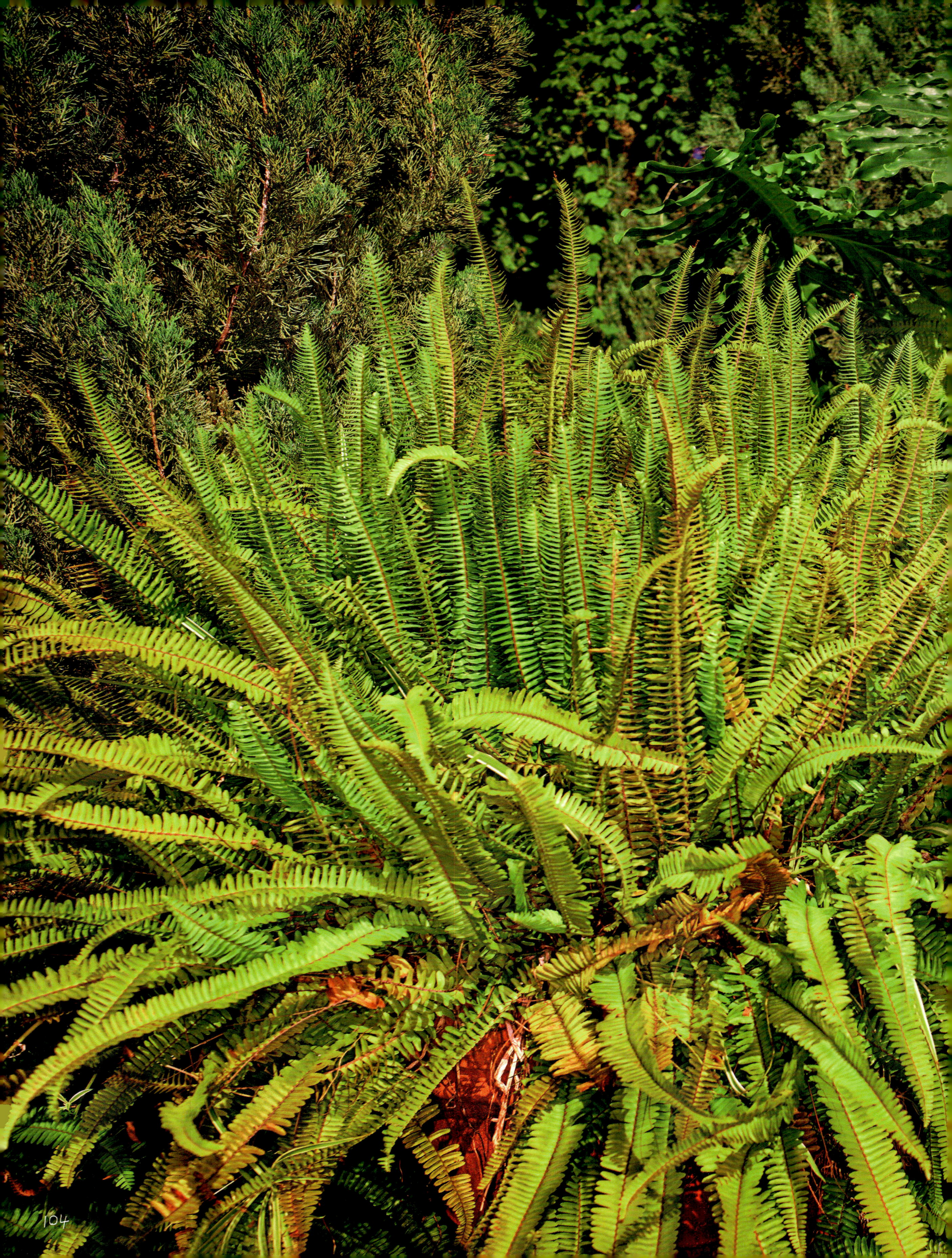

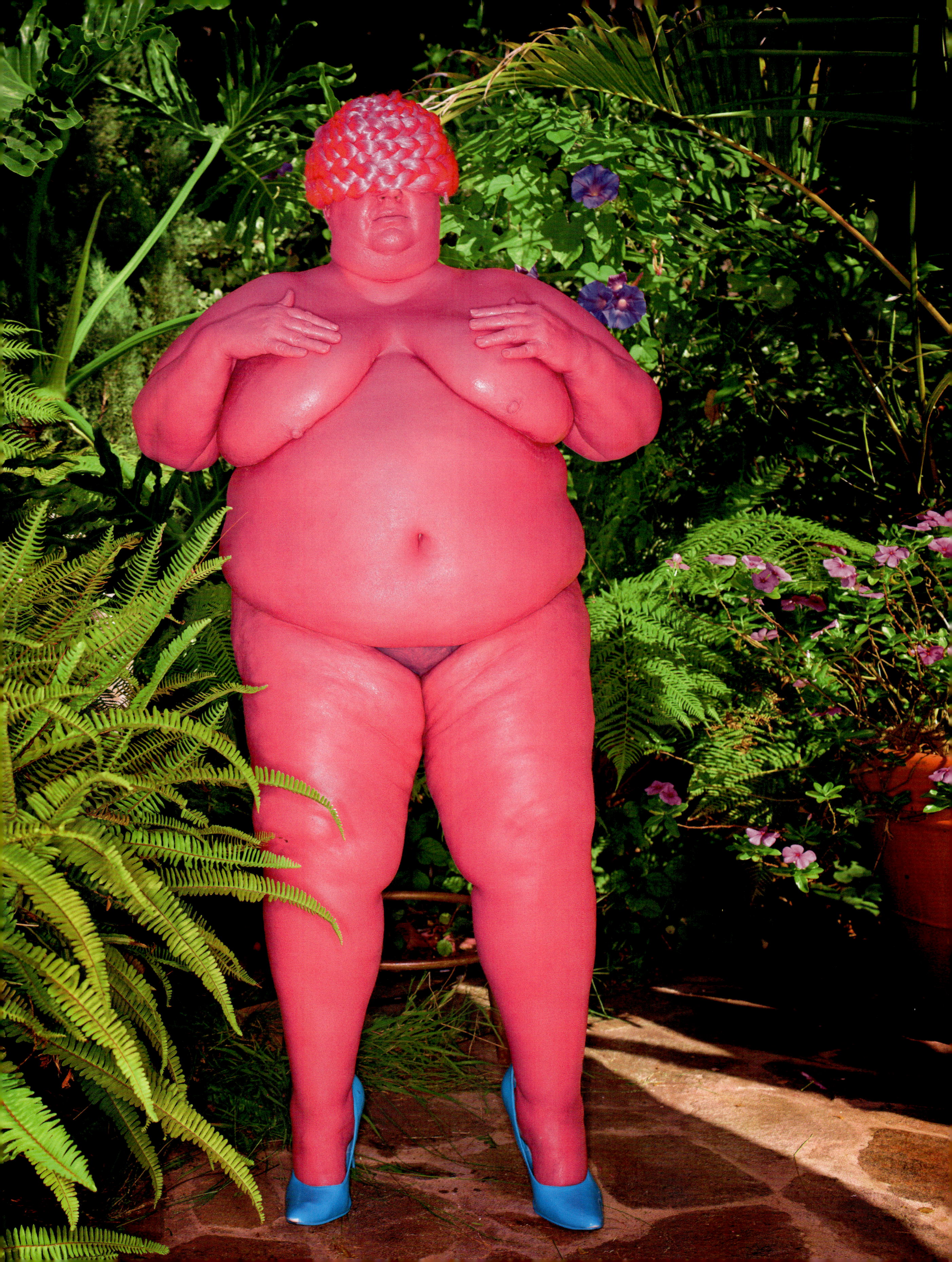

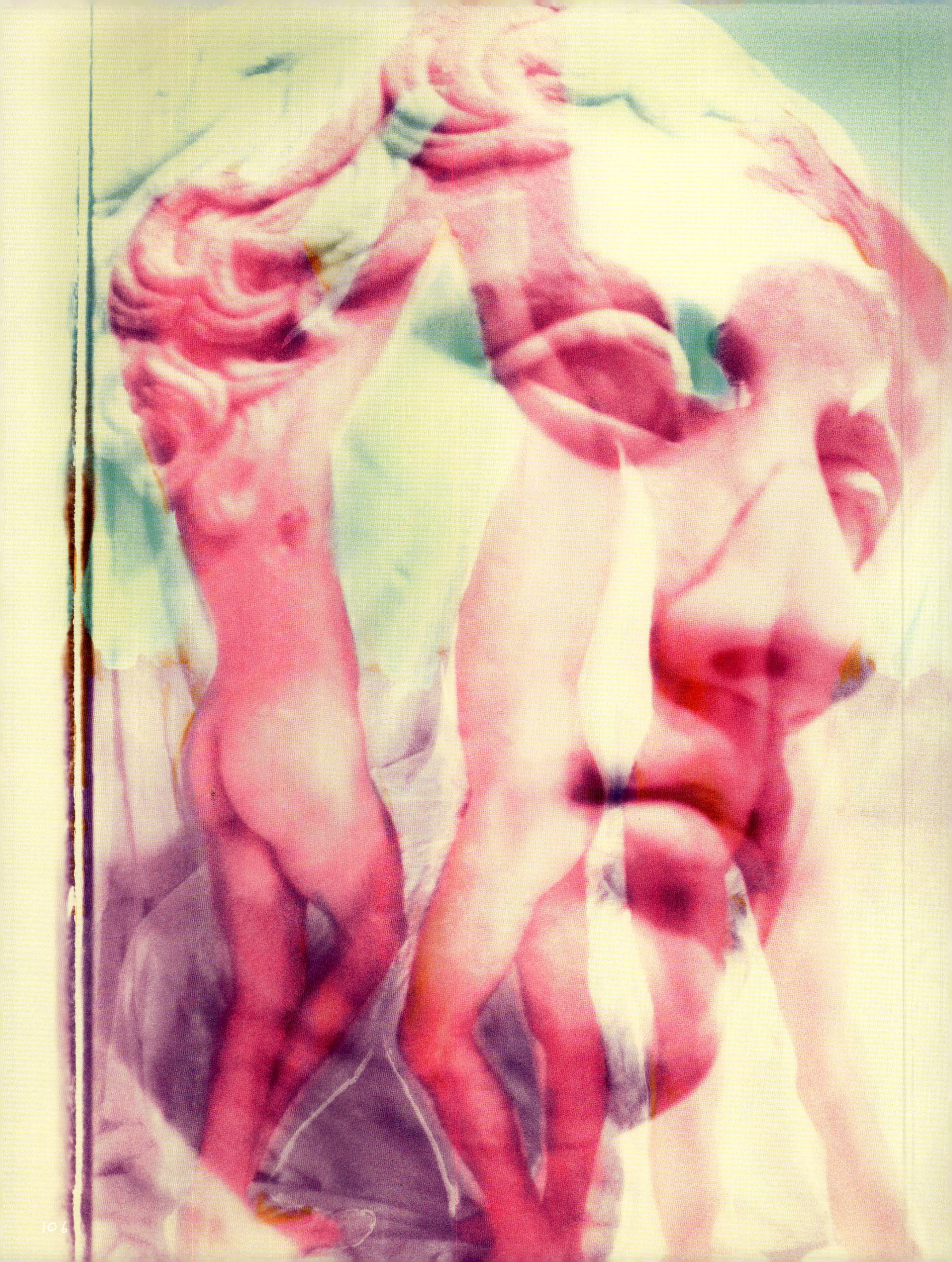

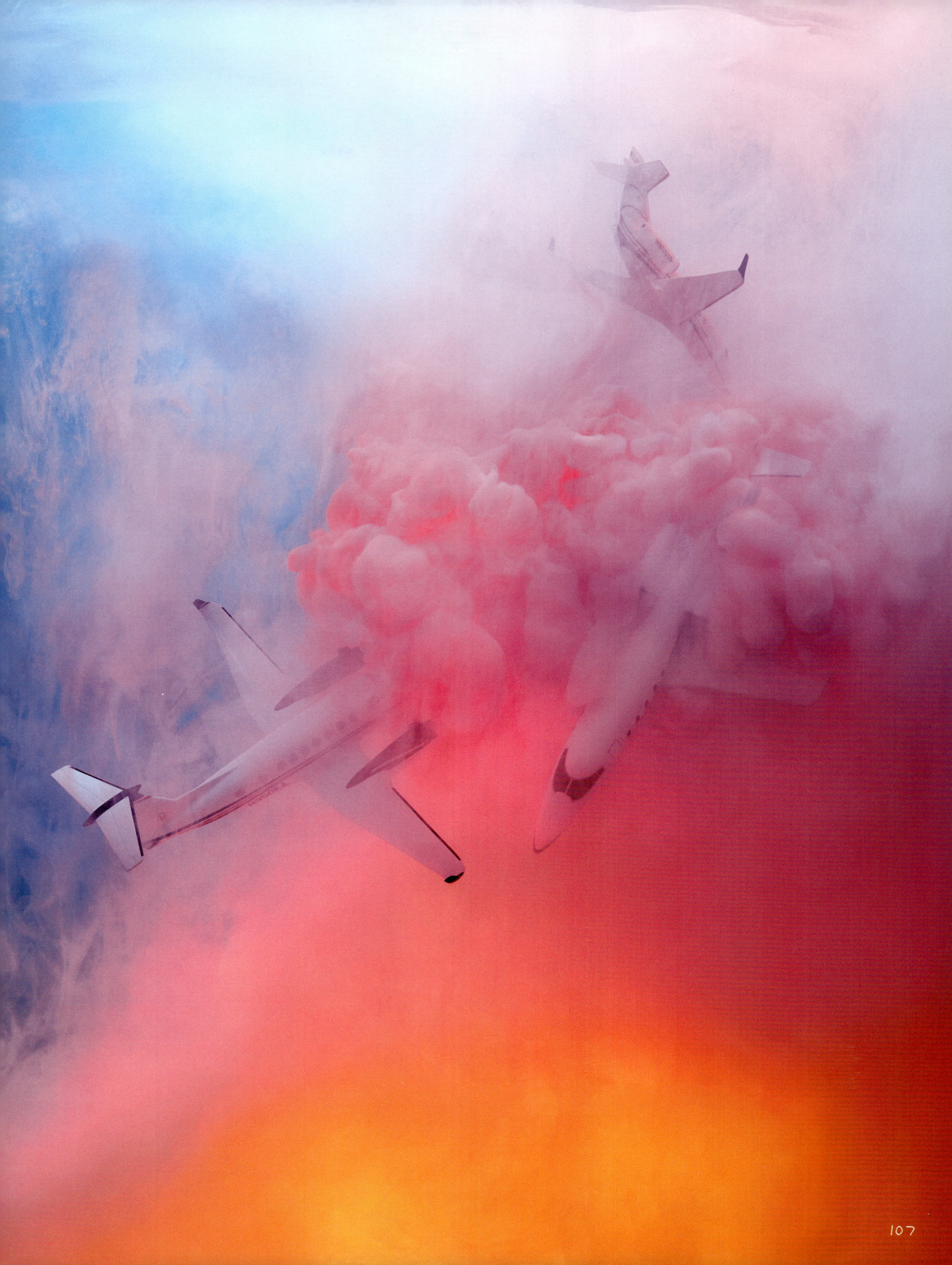

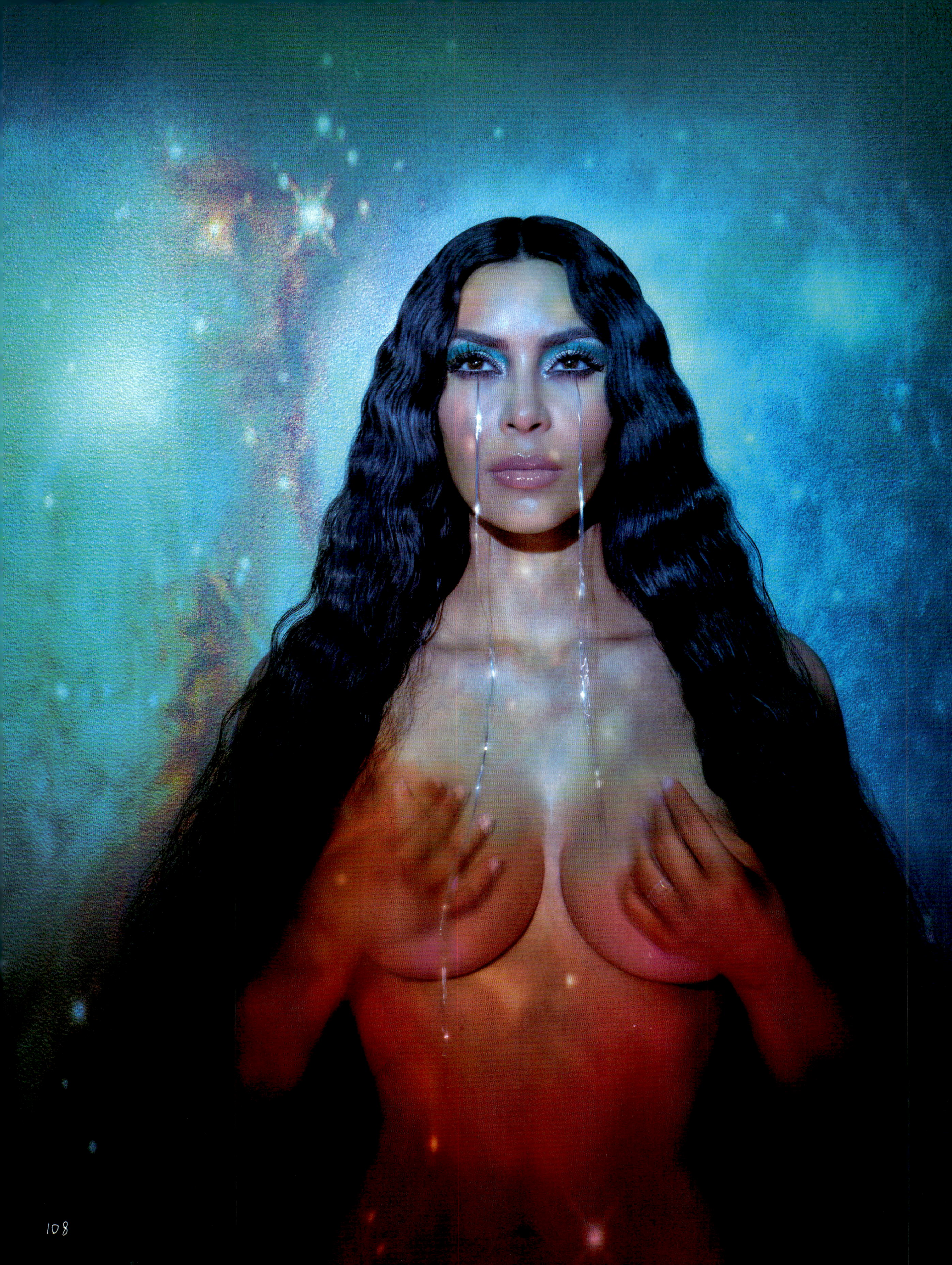

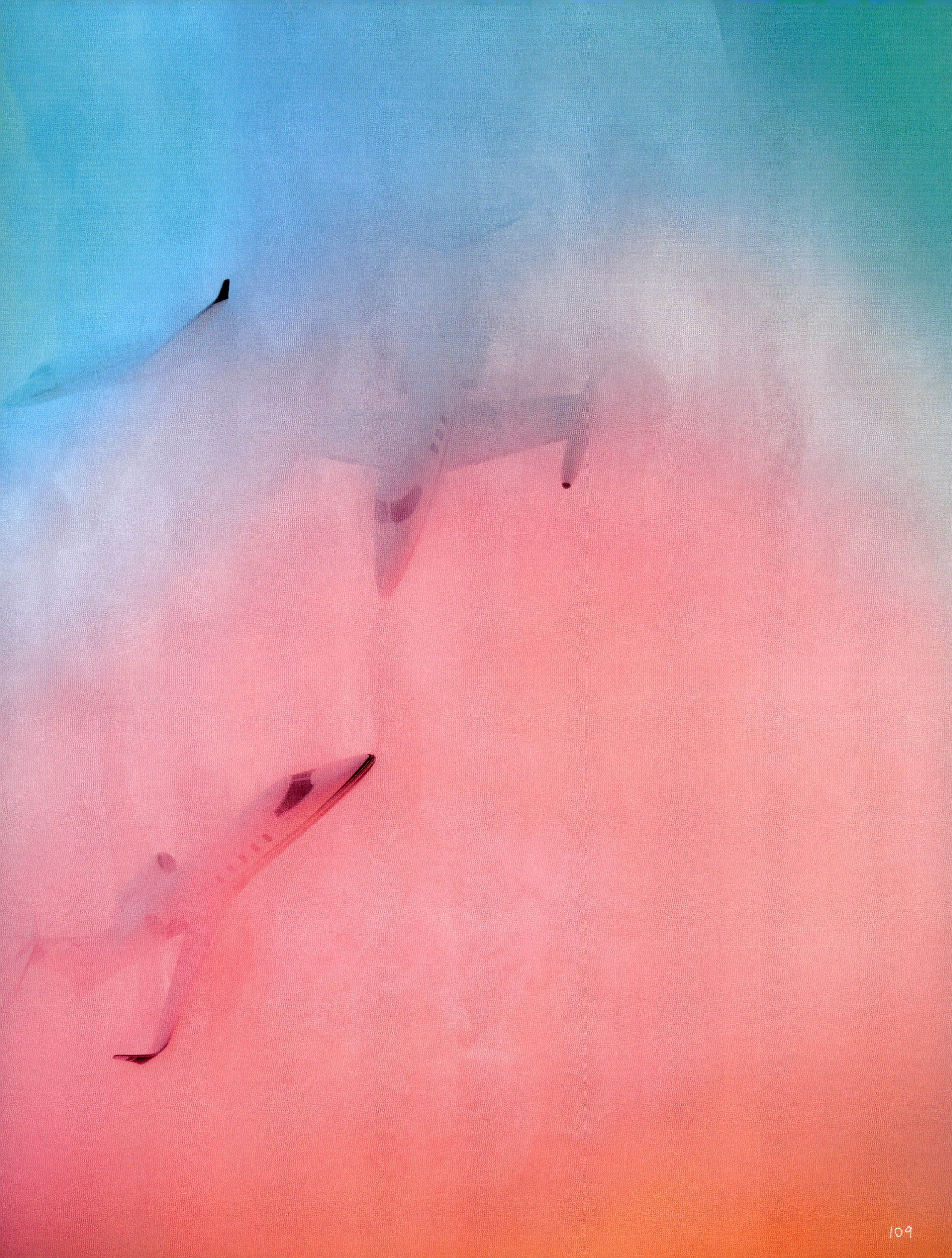

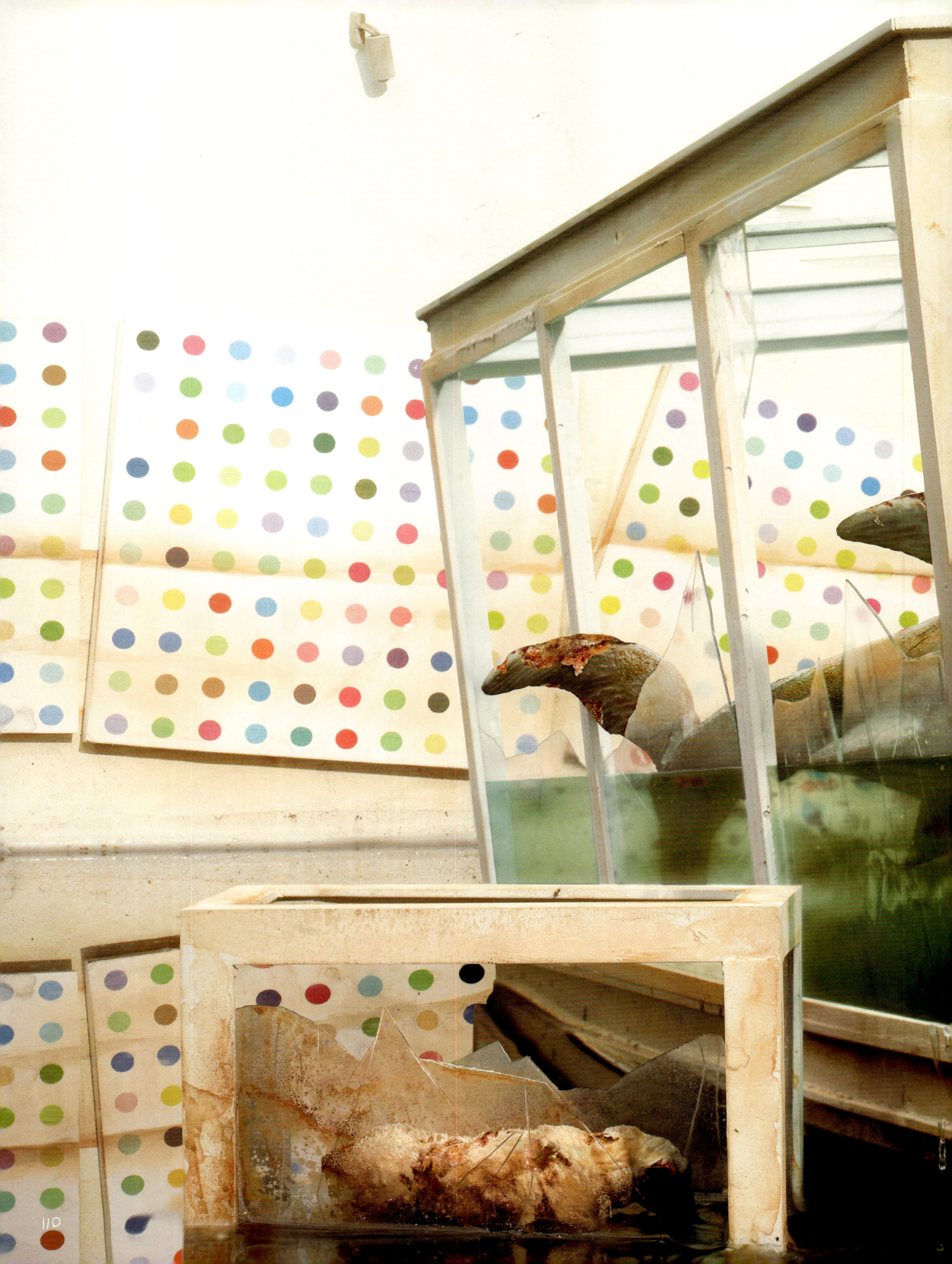

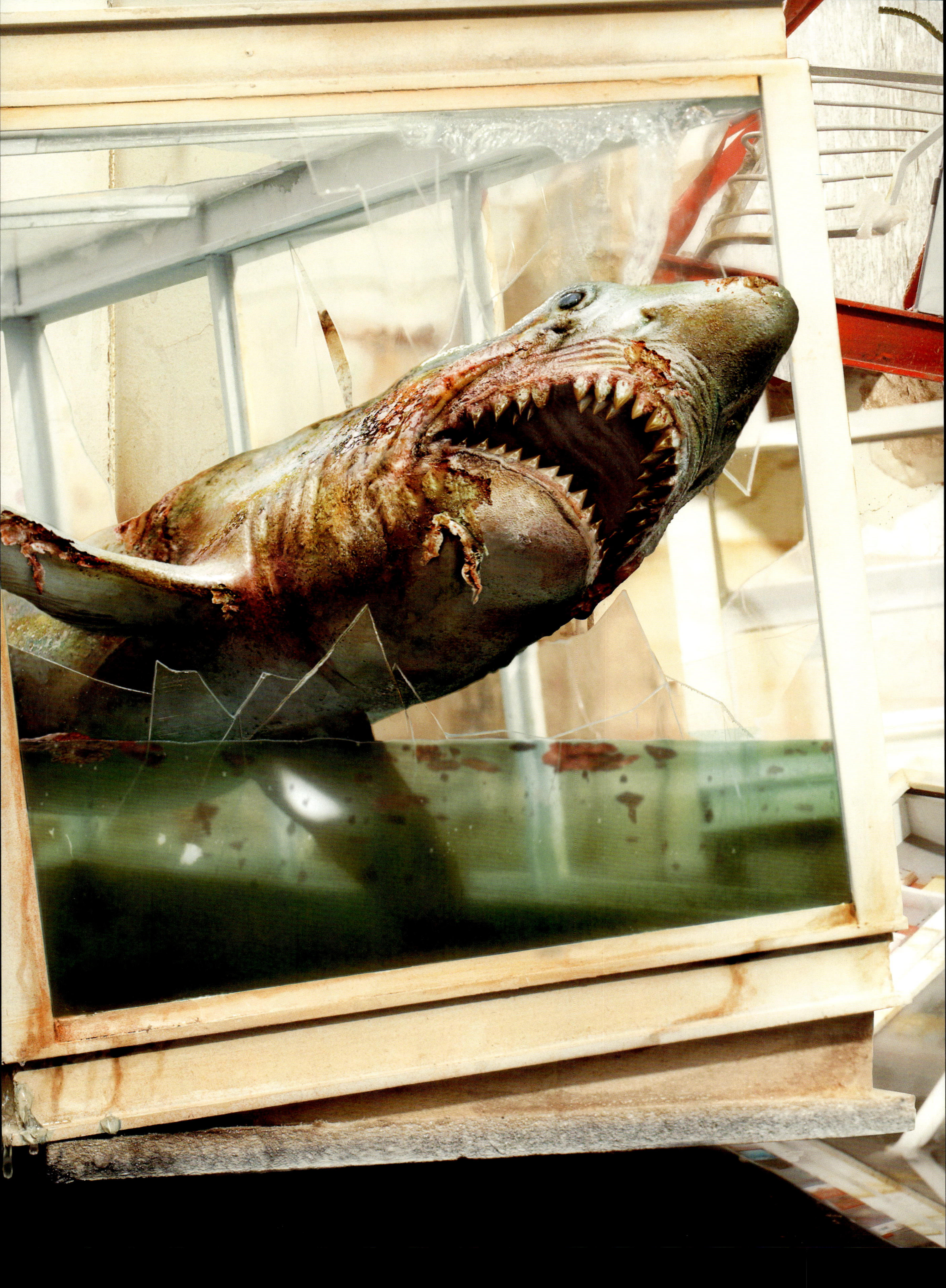

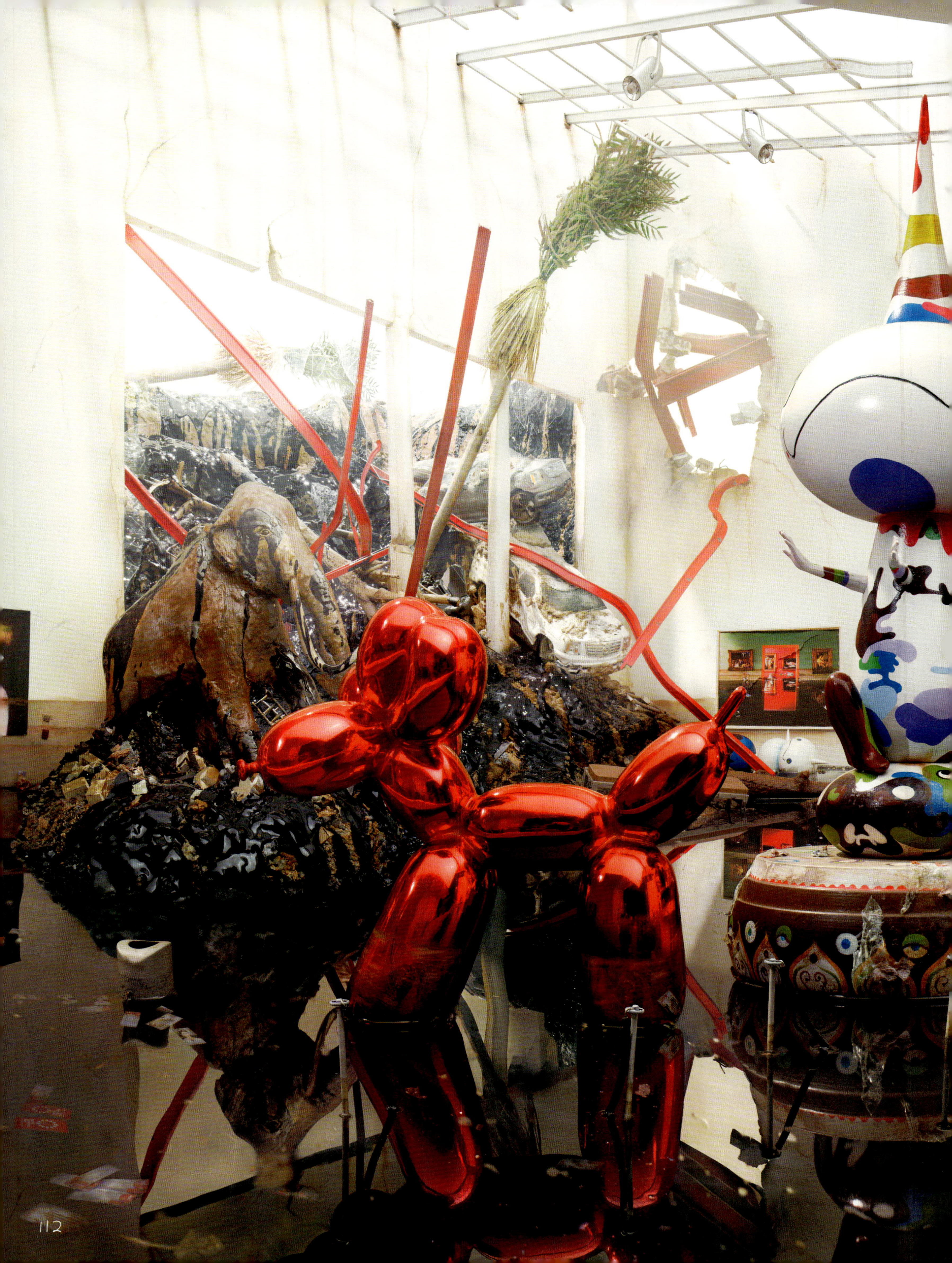

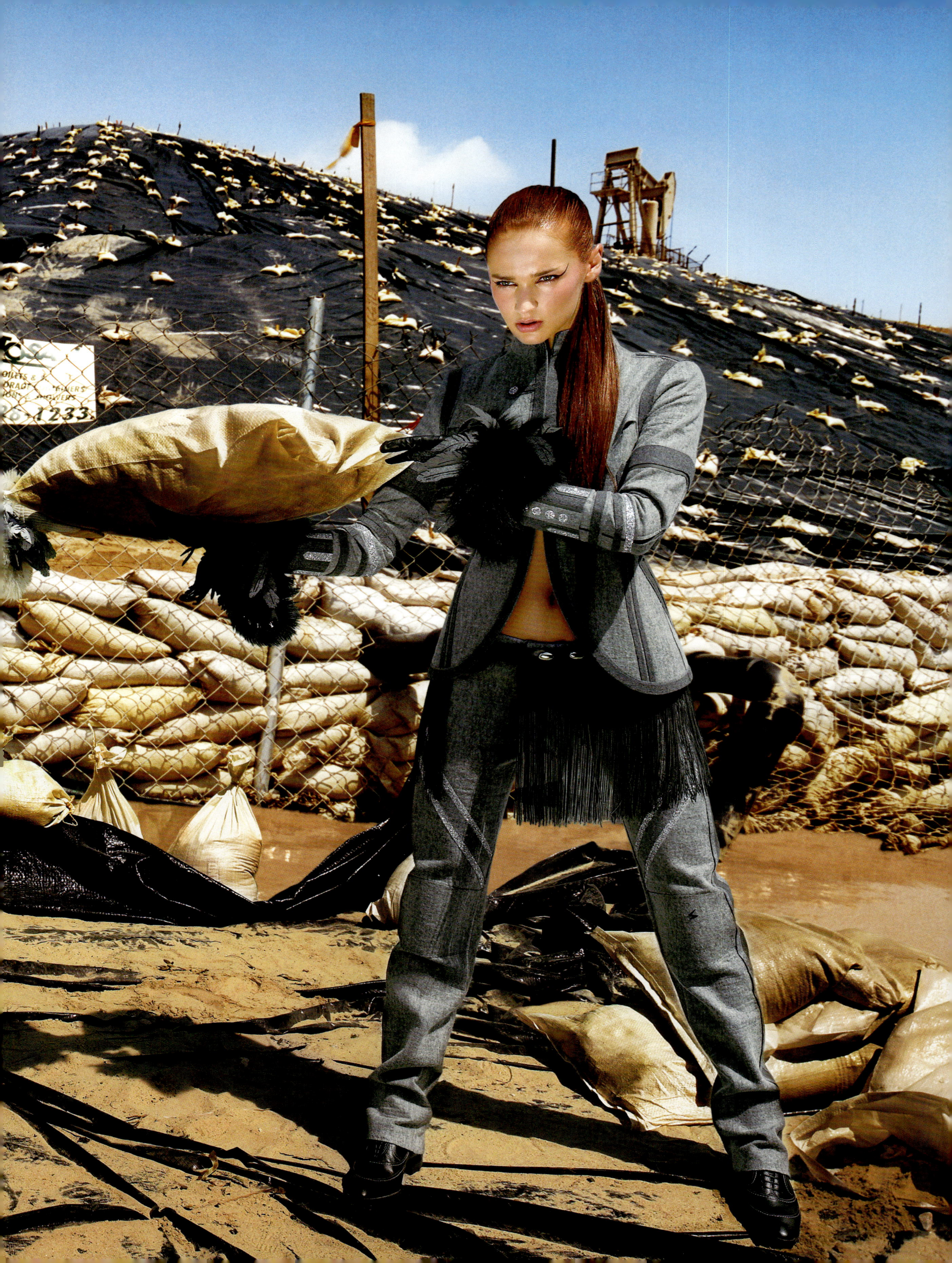
1233

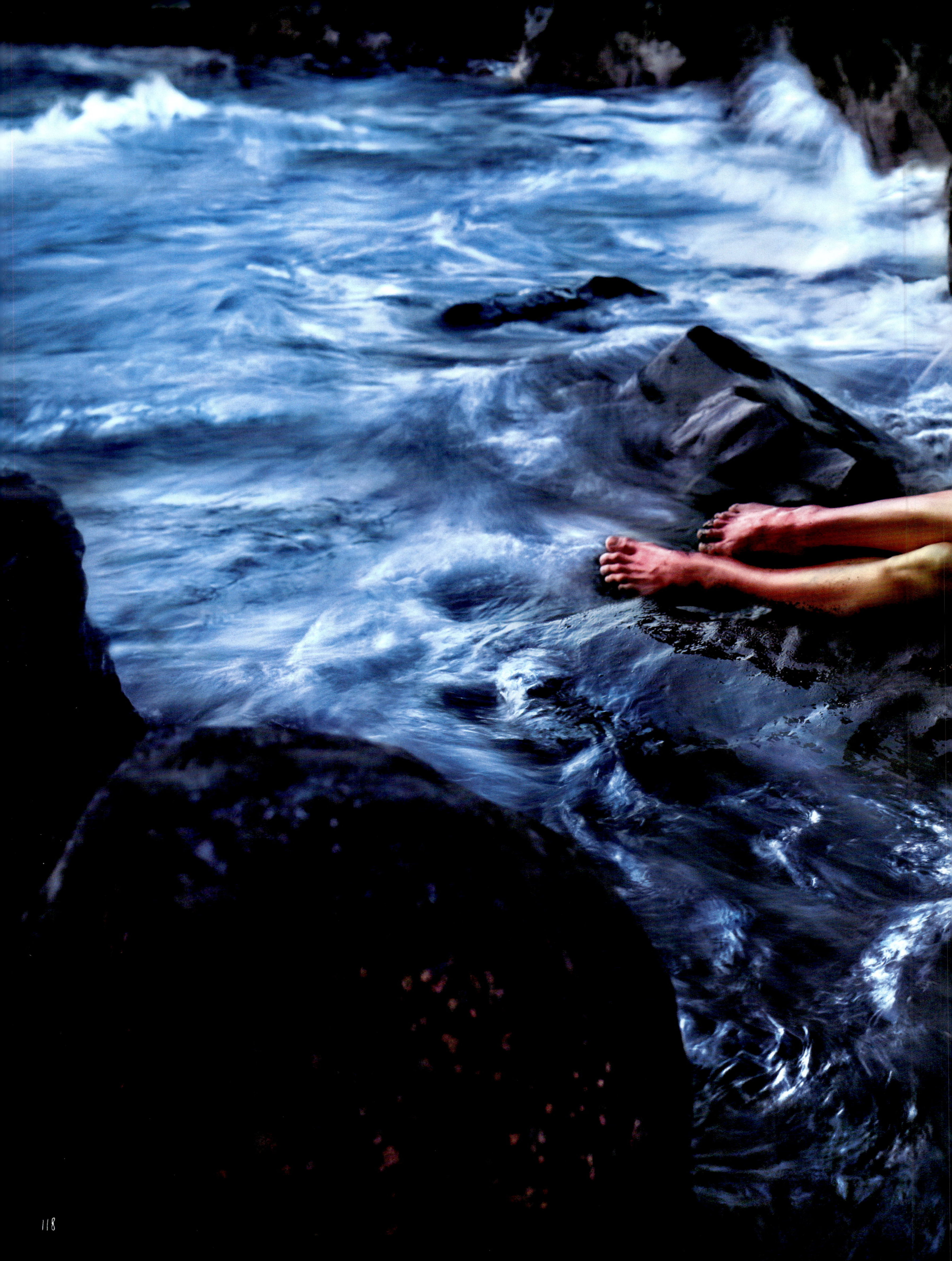

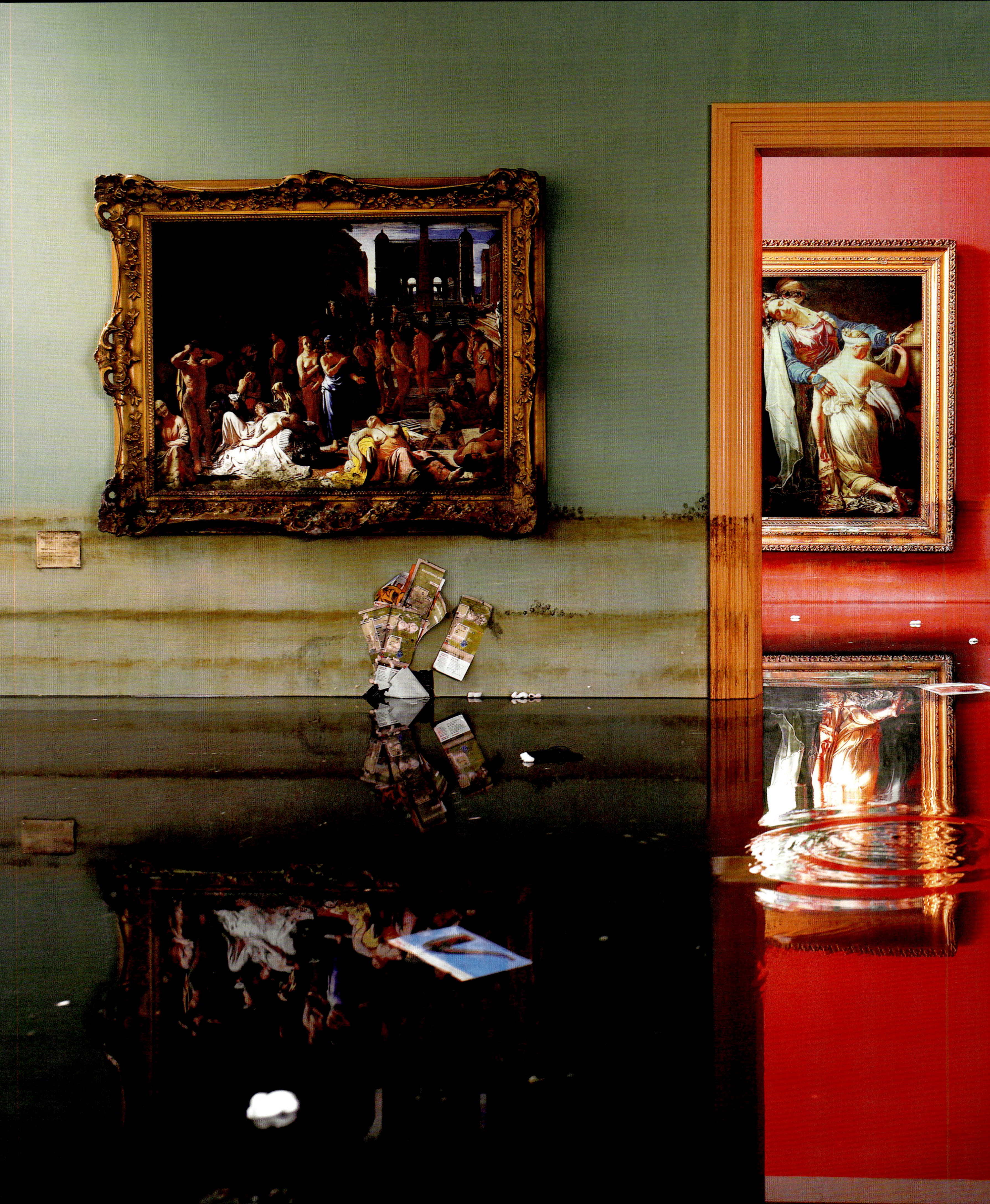

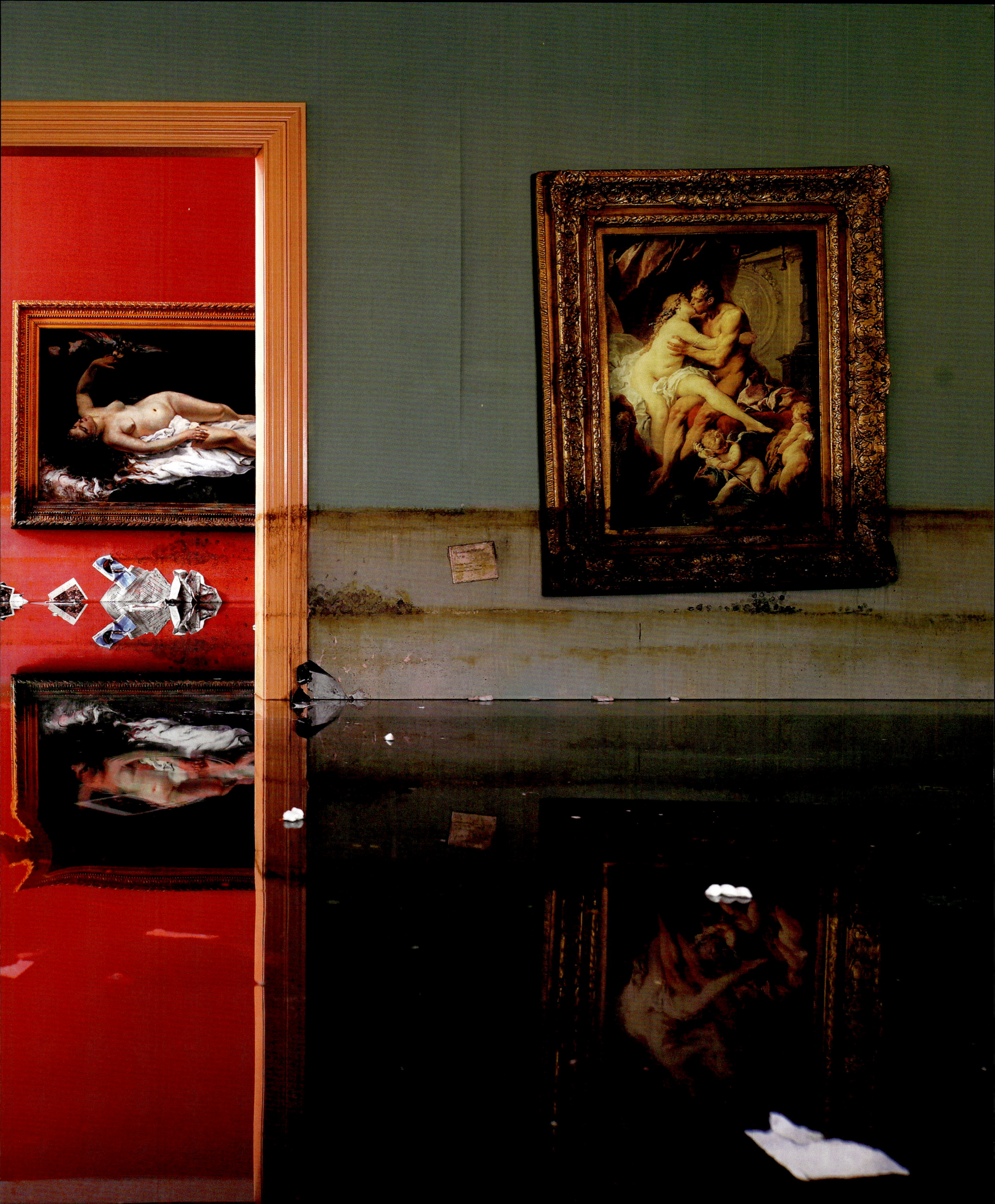

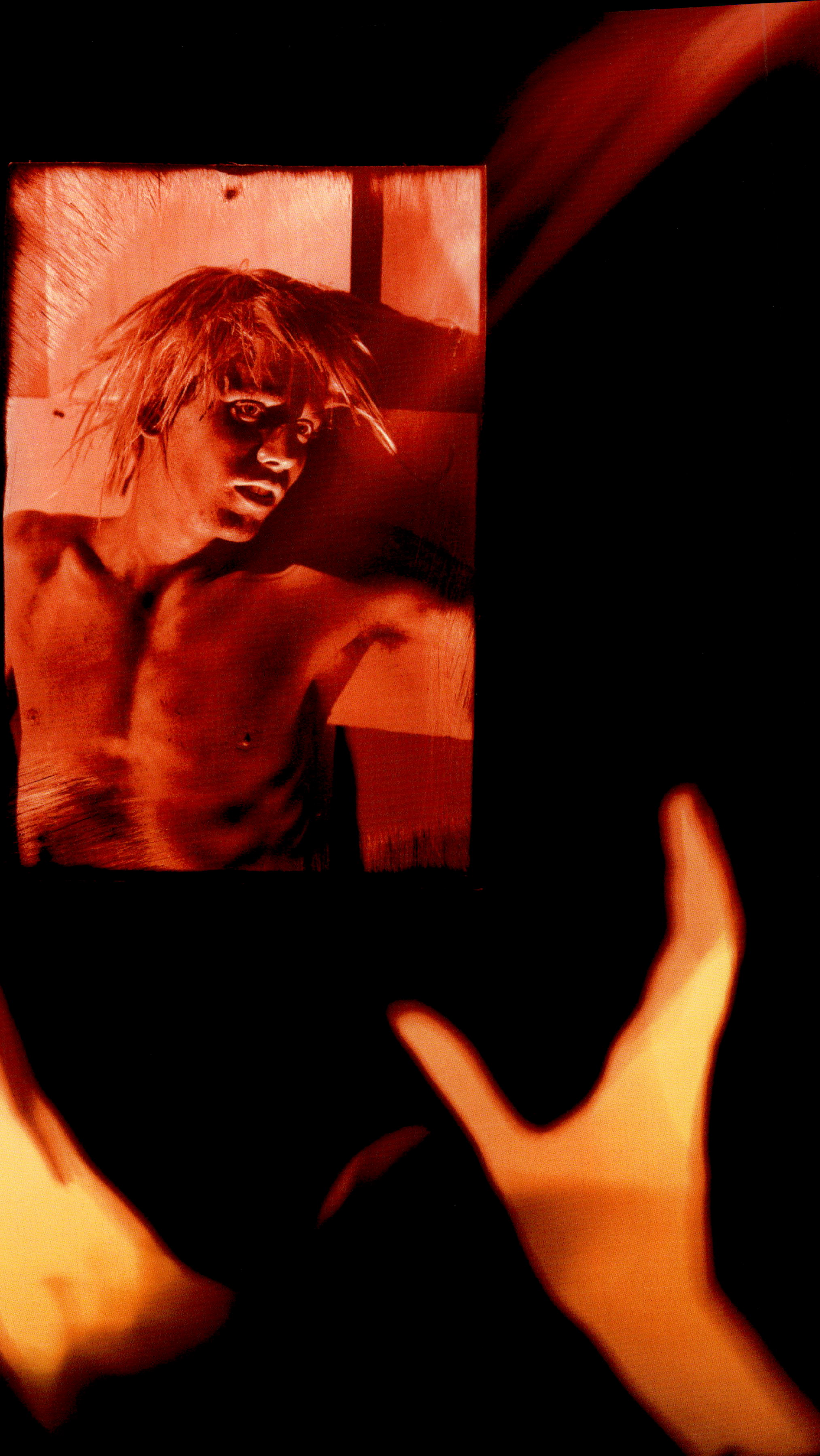

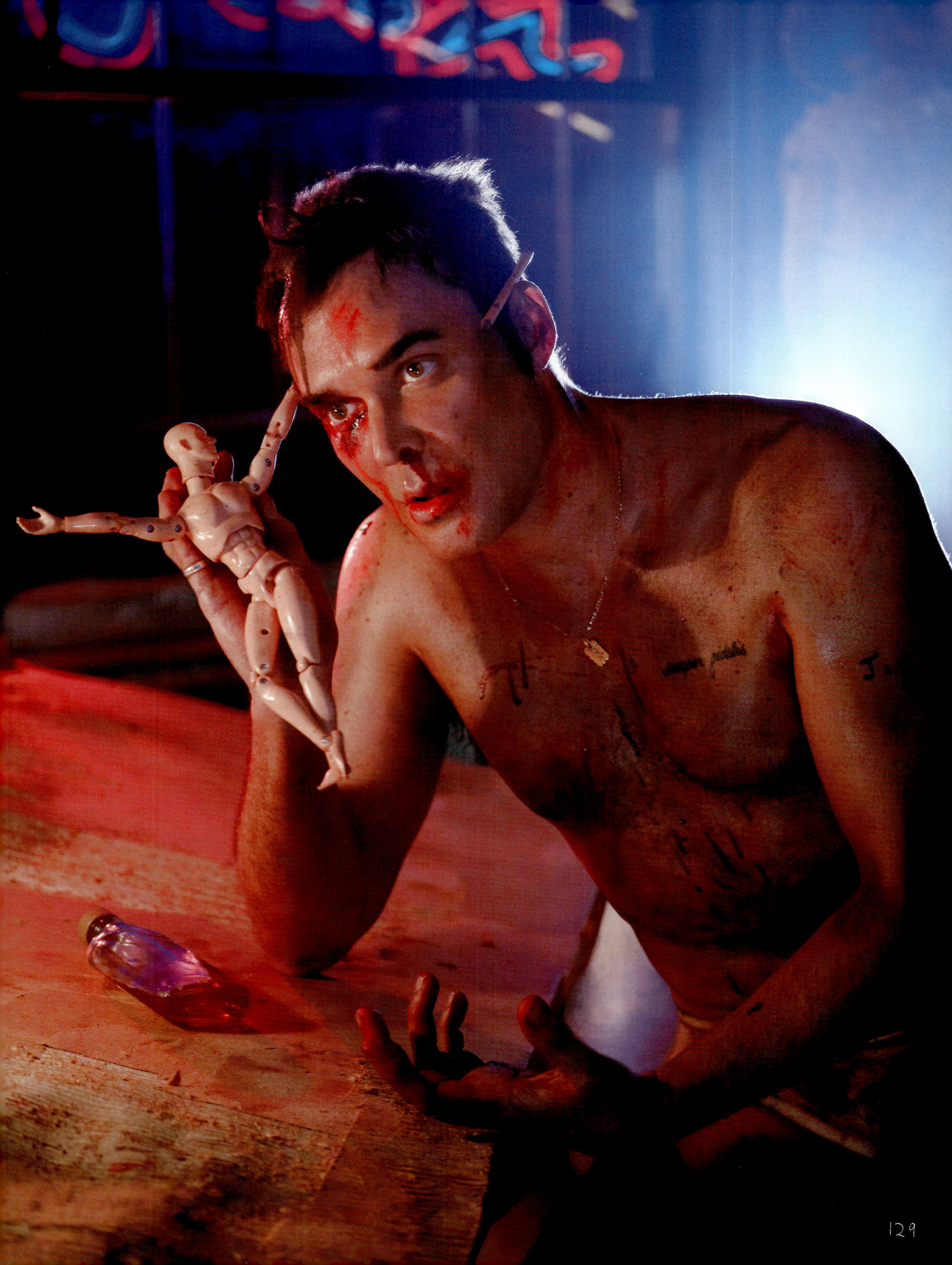

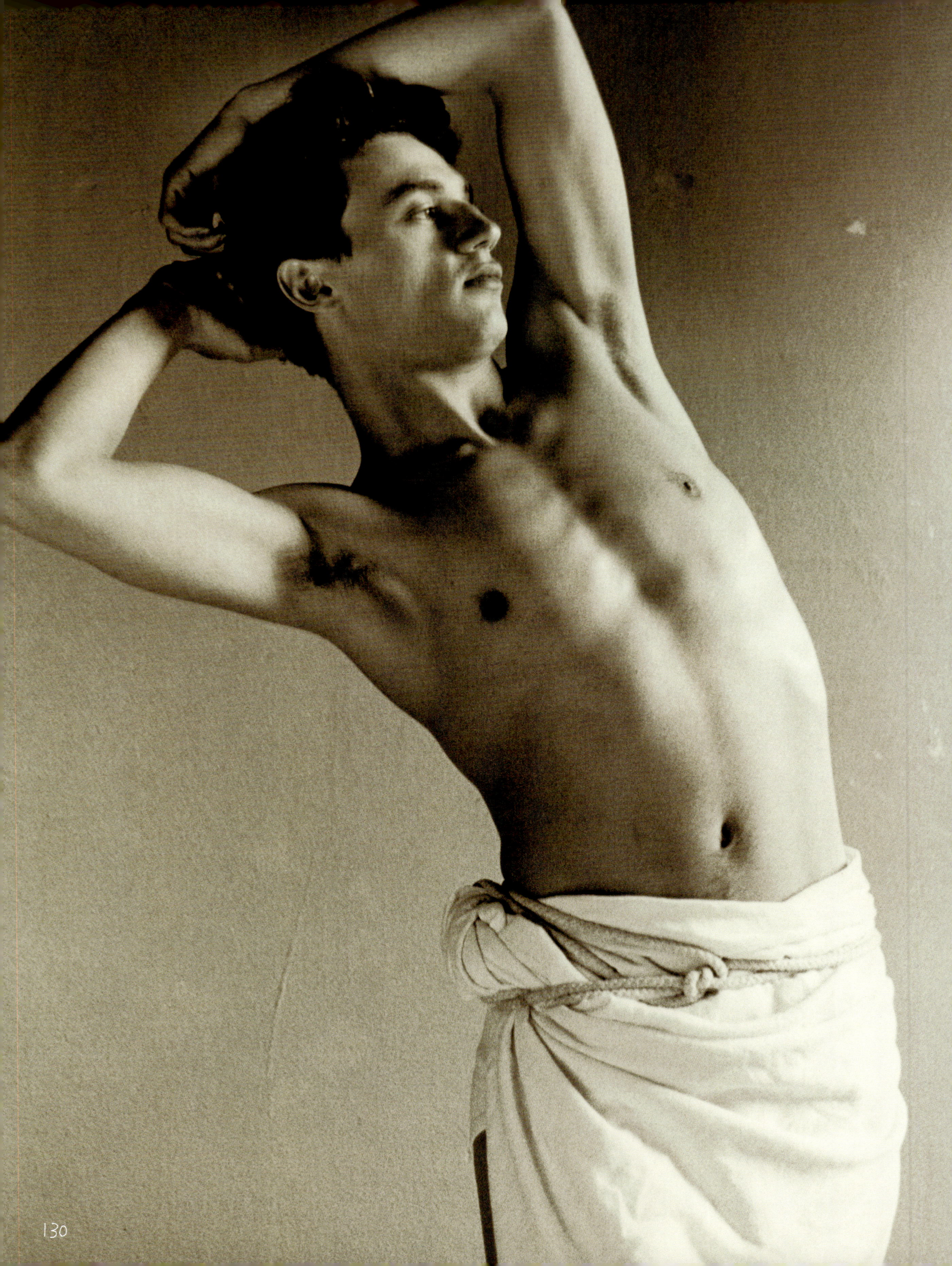

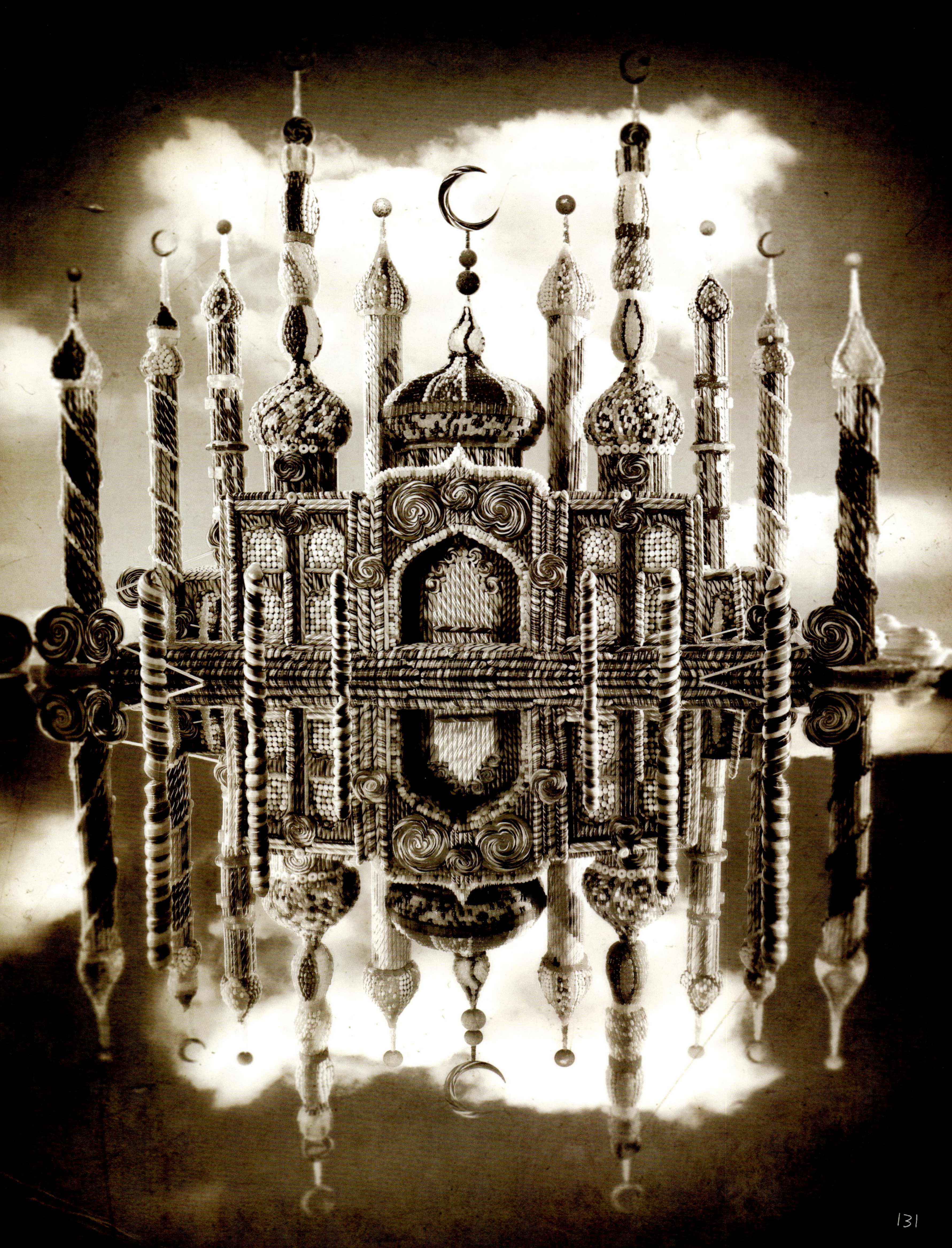

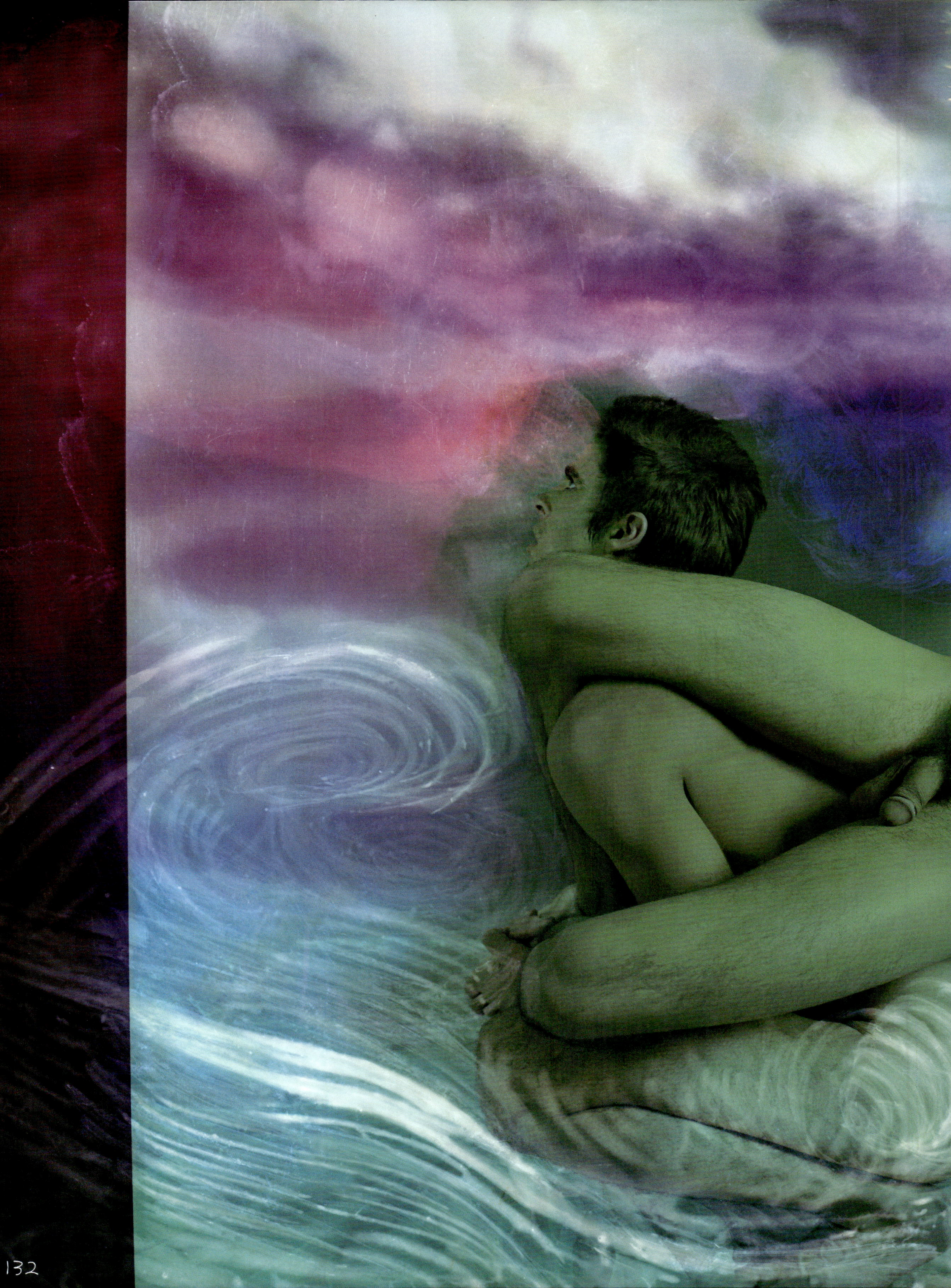

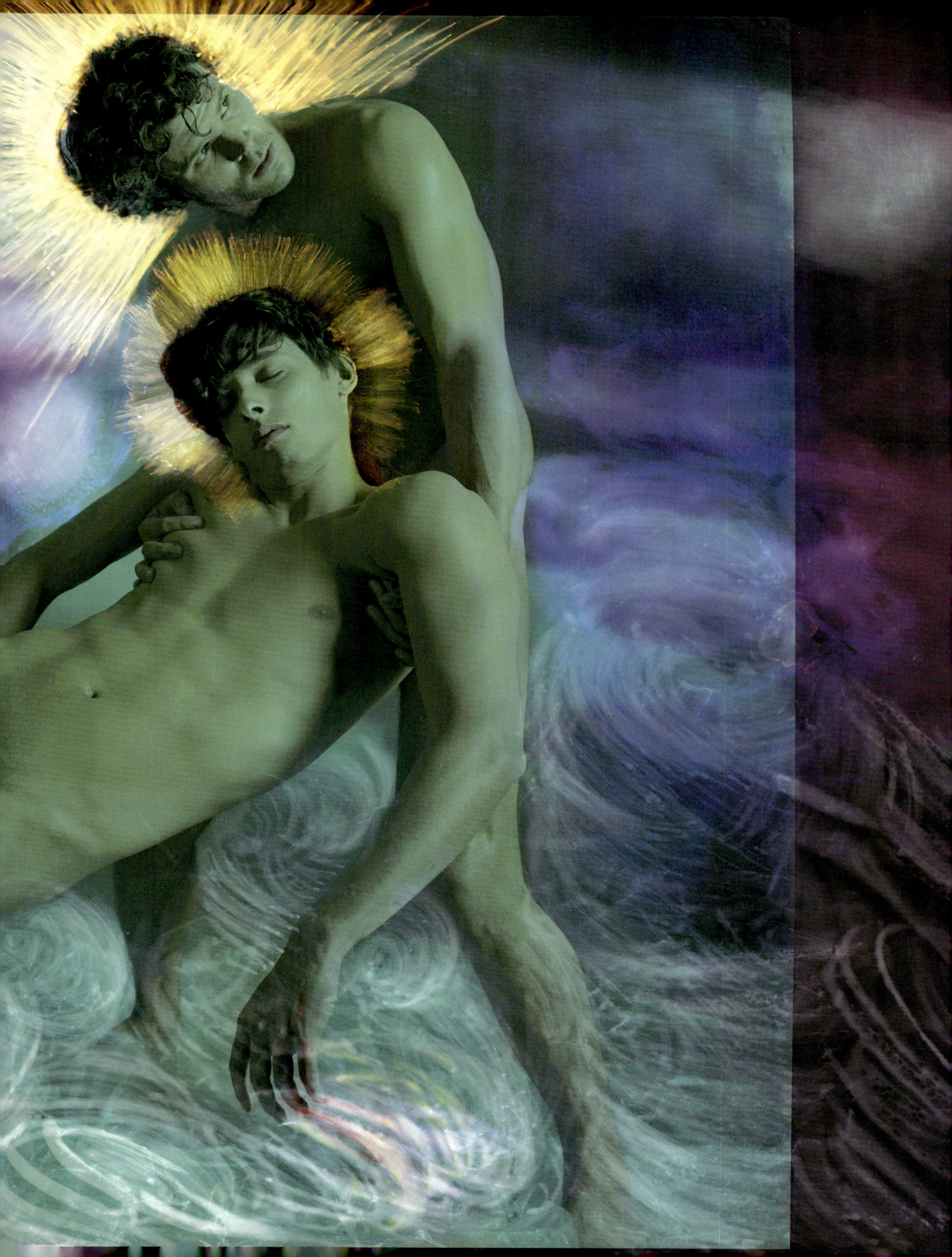

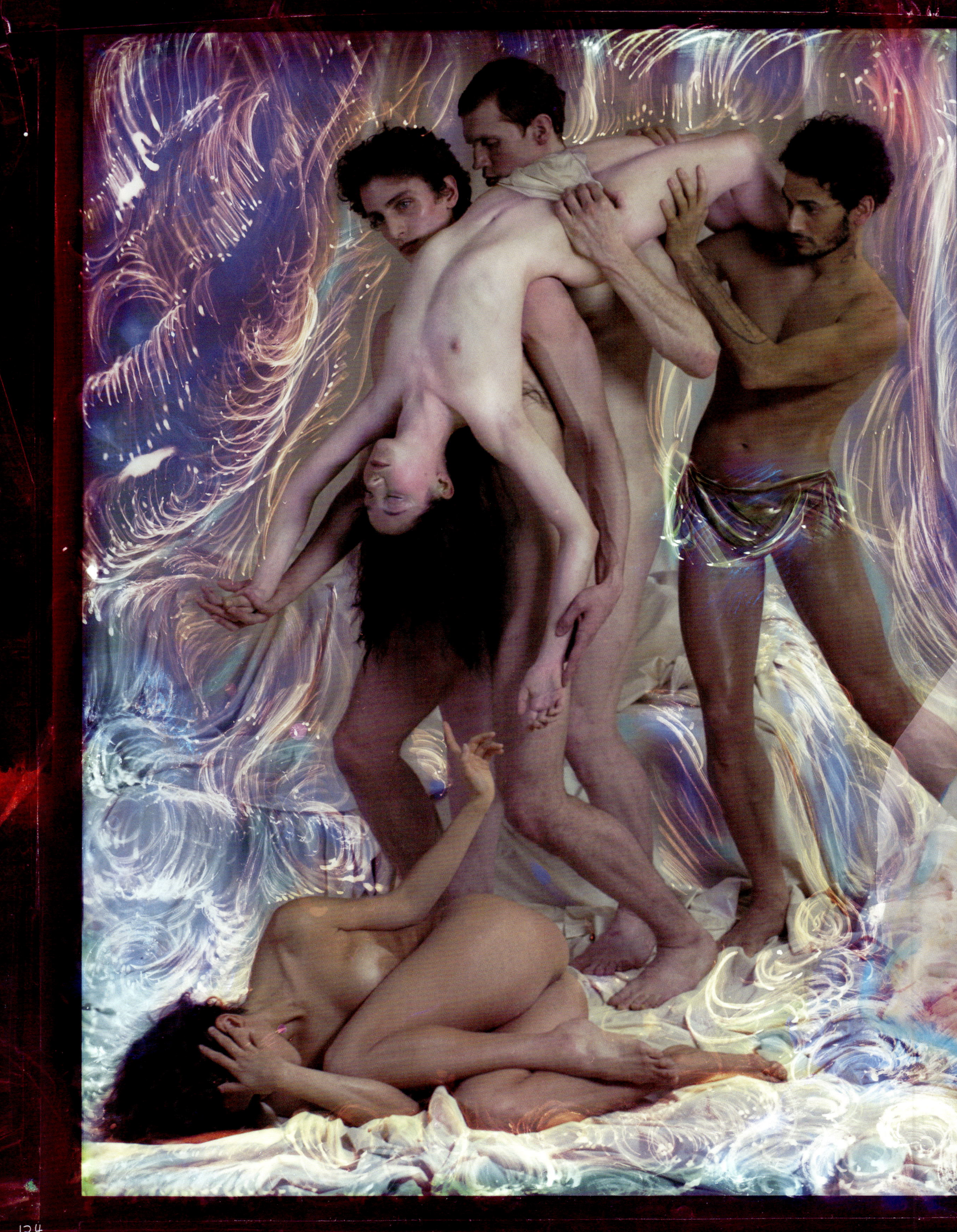

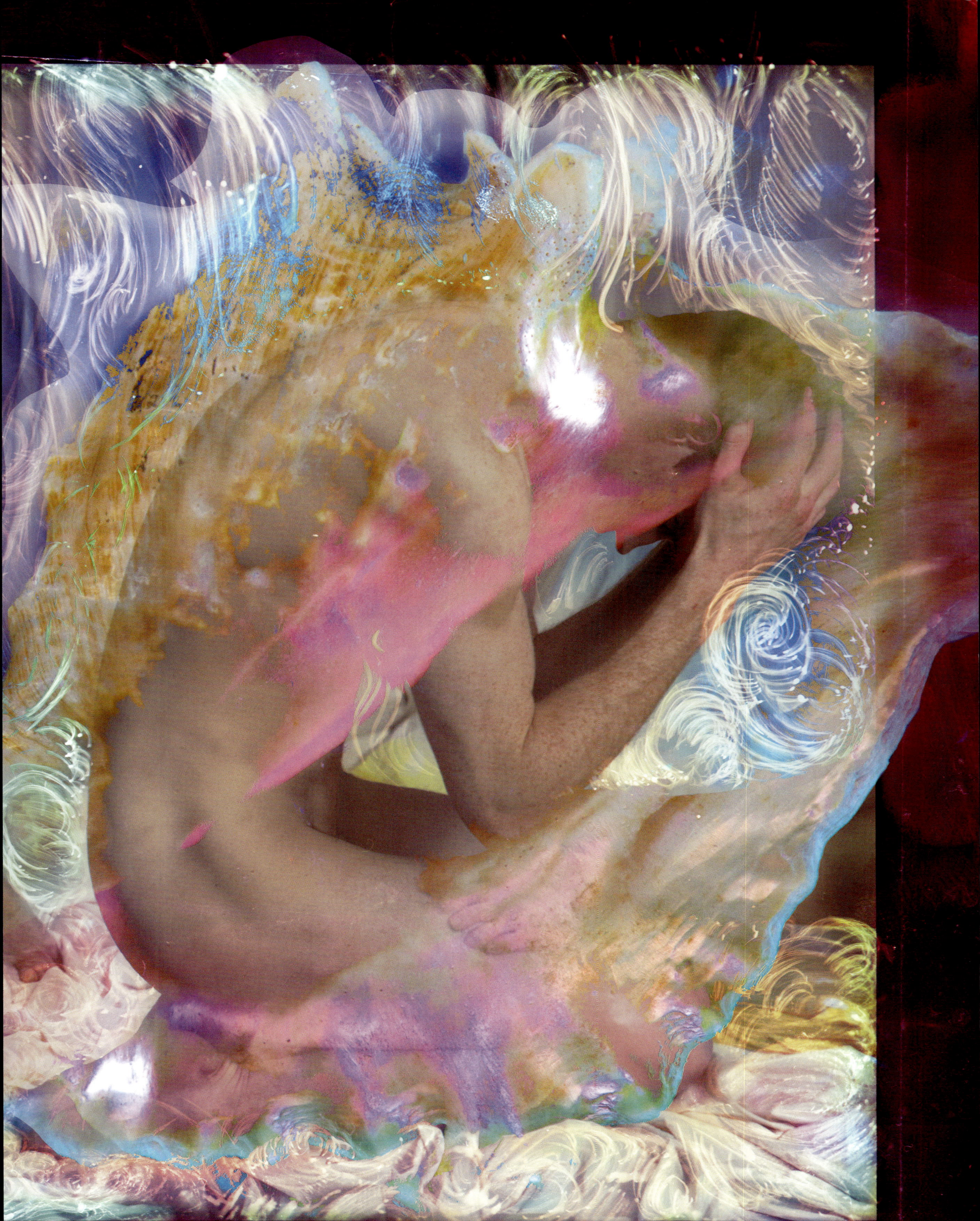

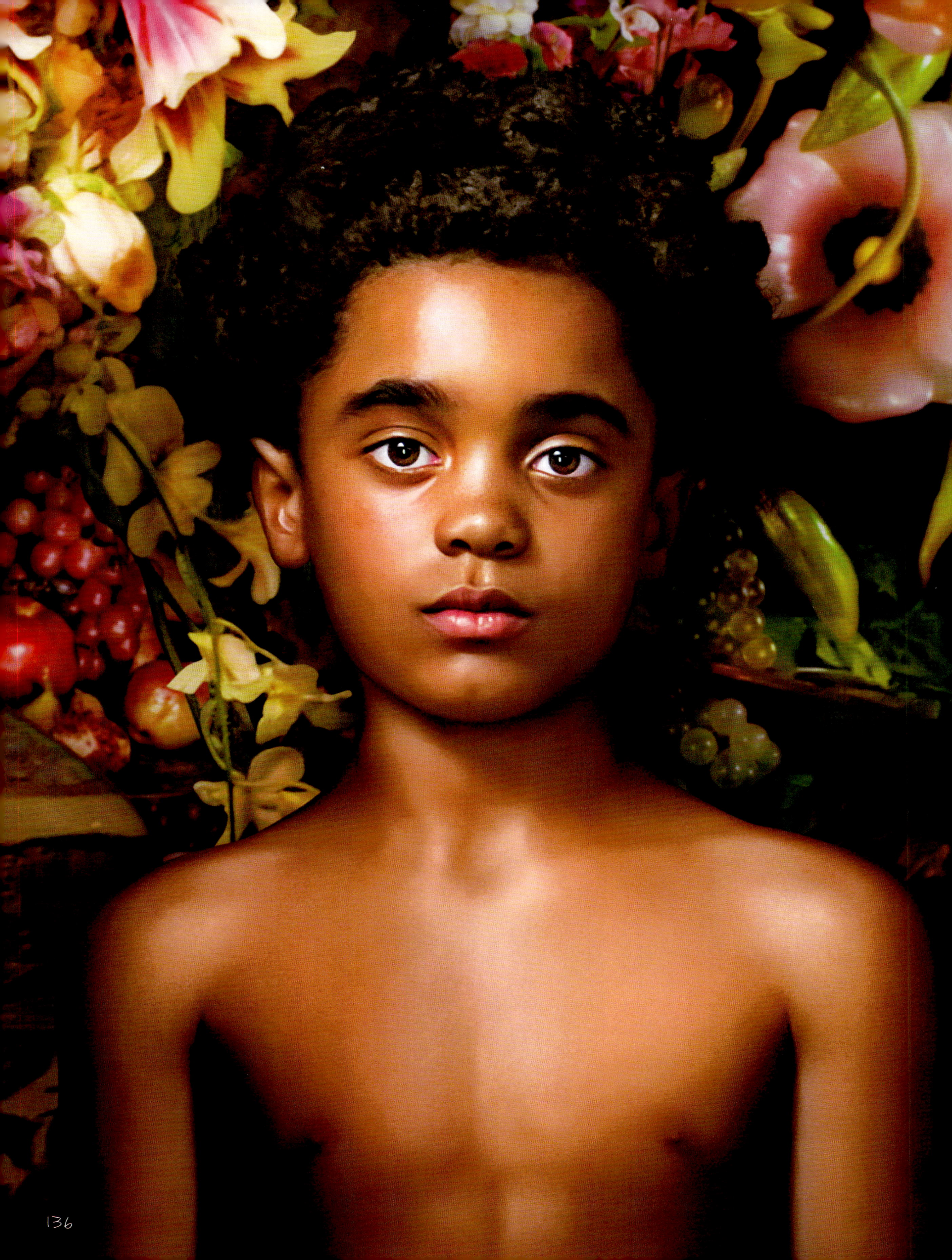

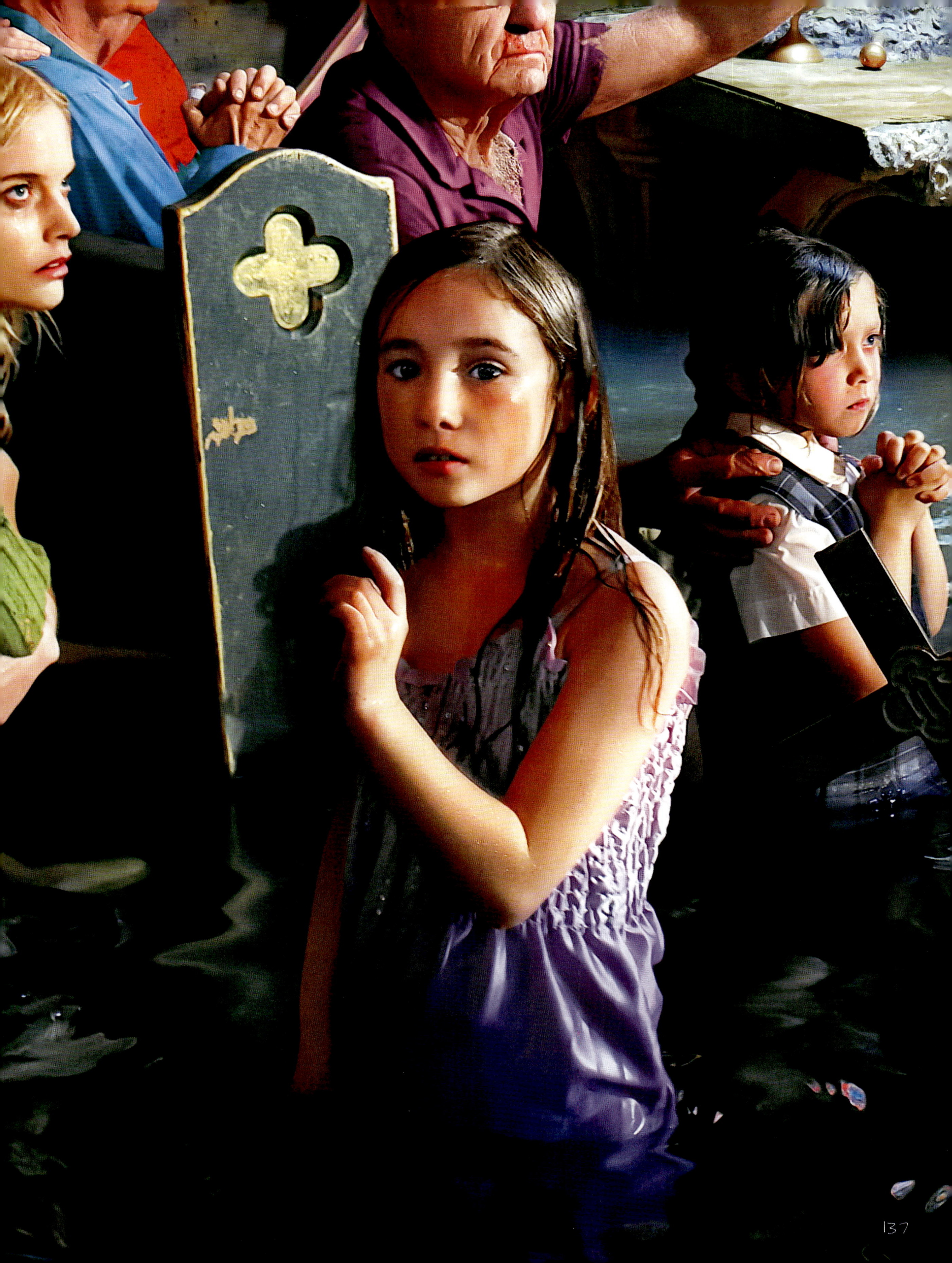

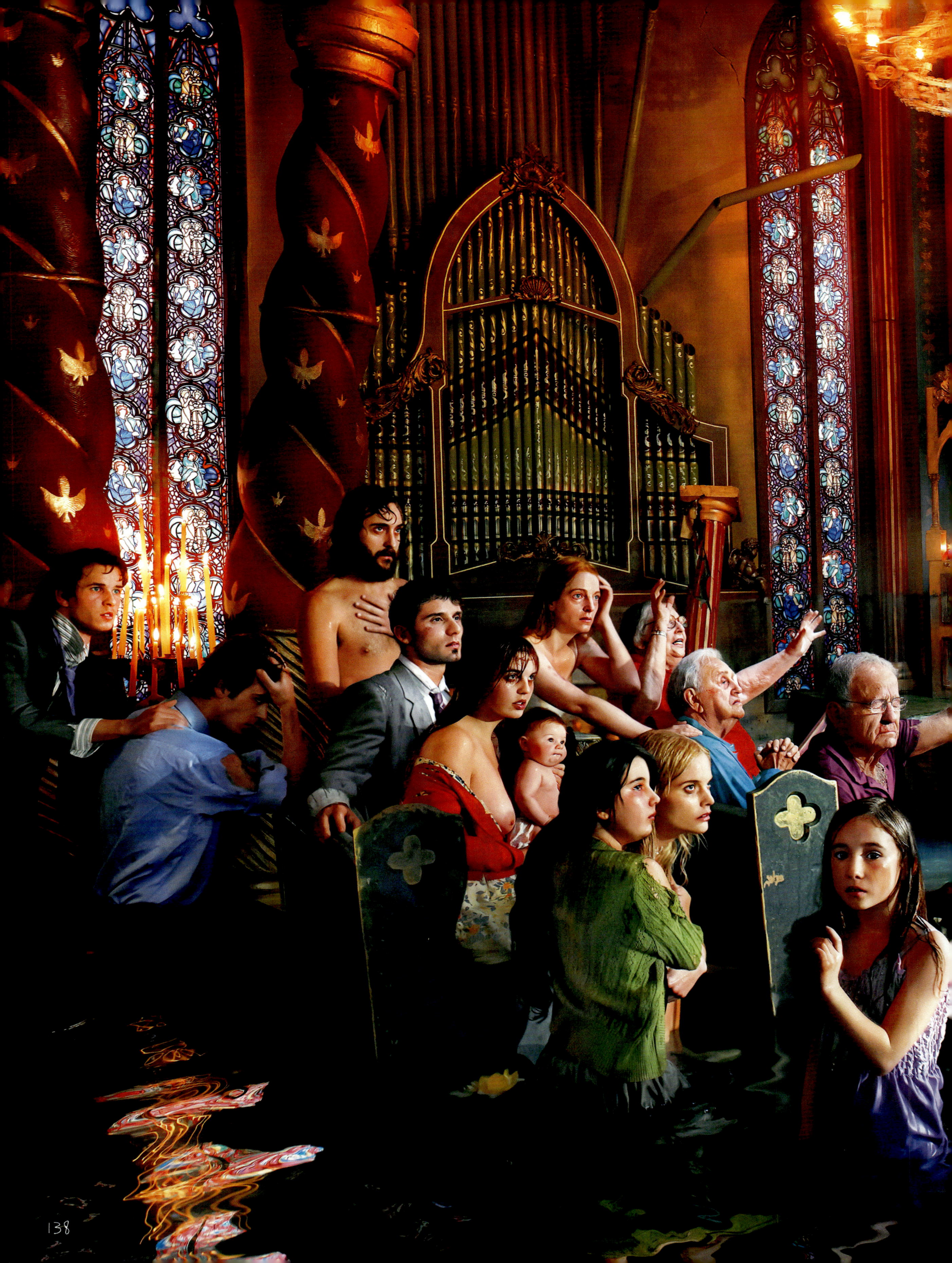

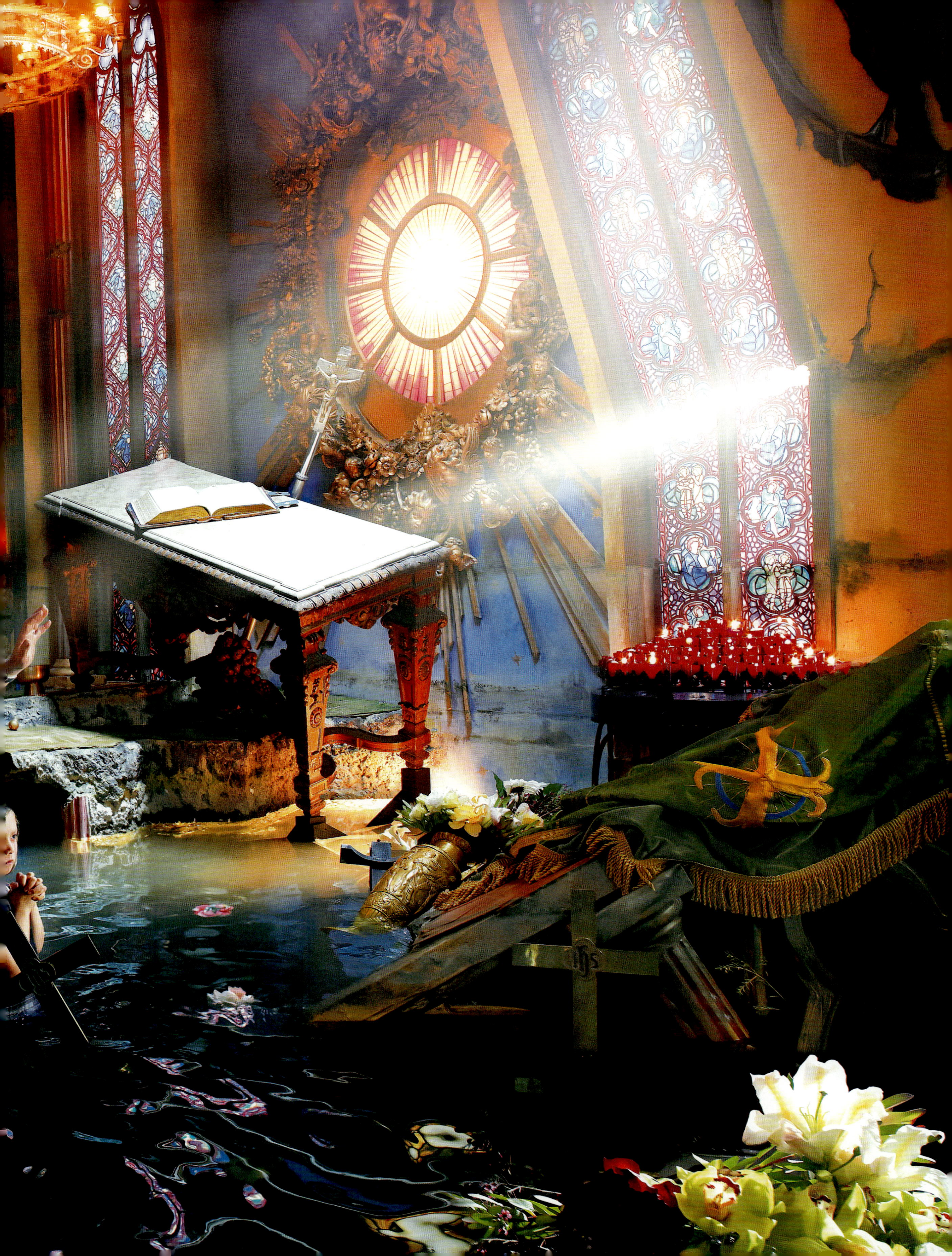

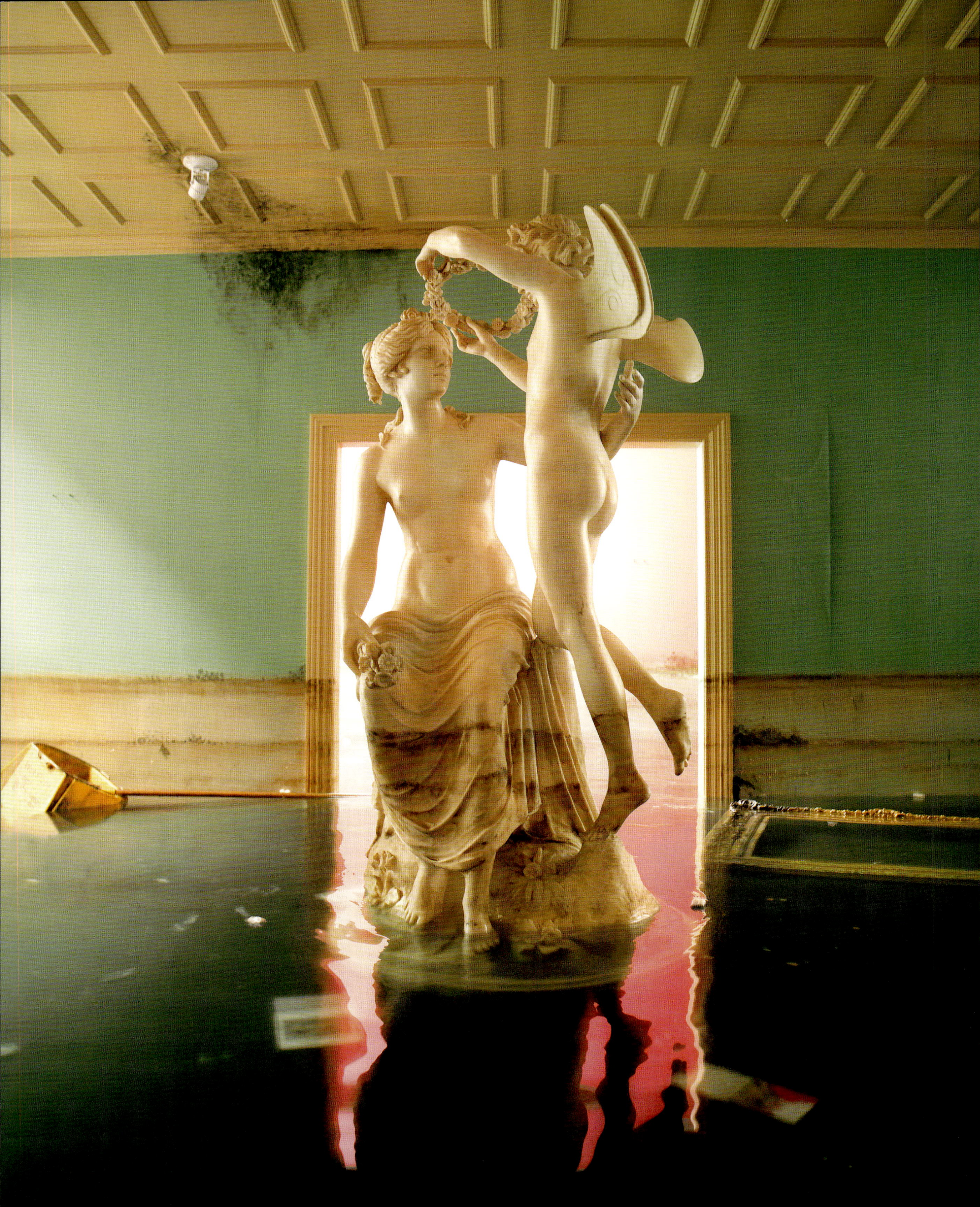

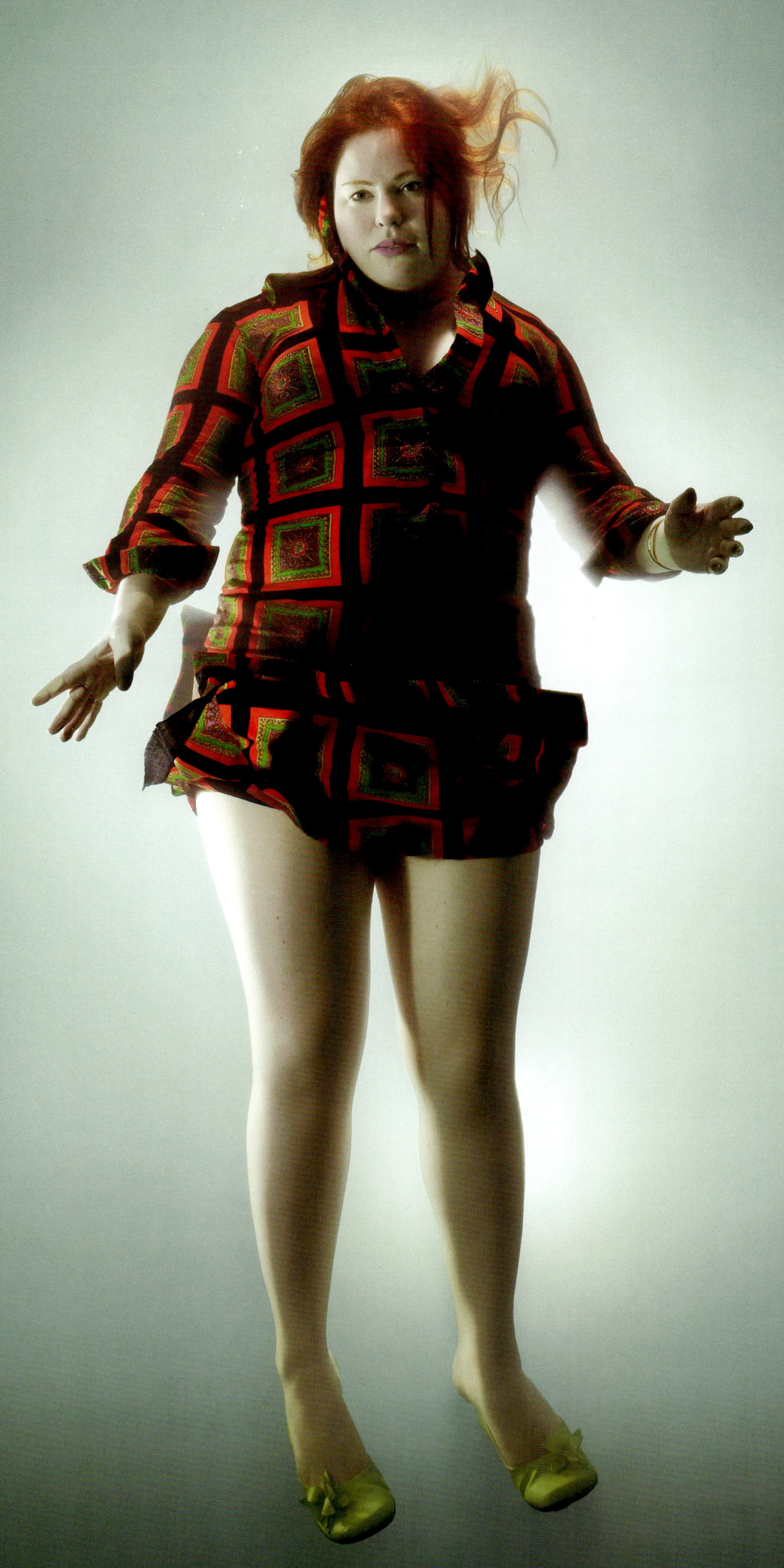

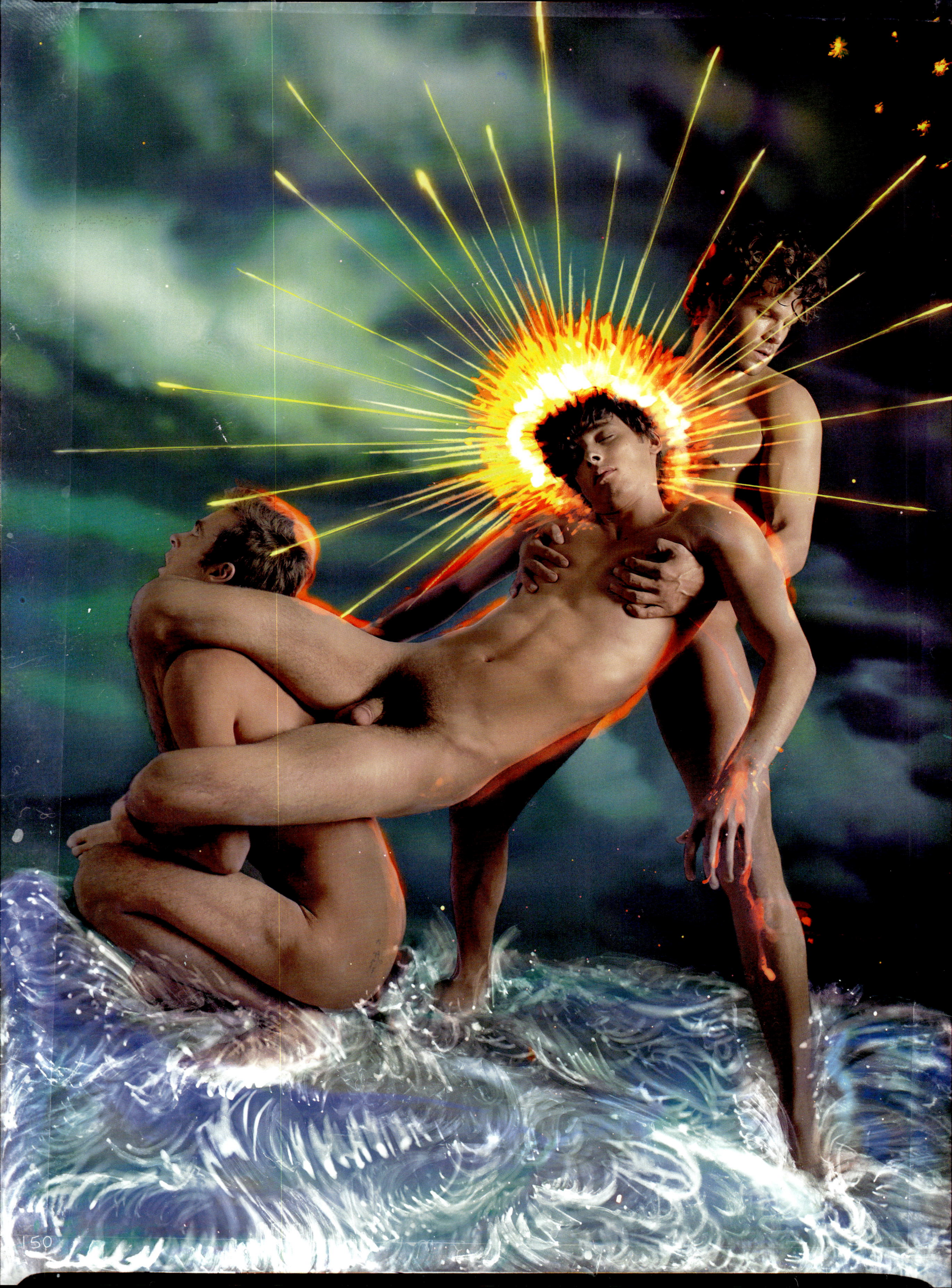

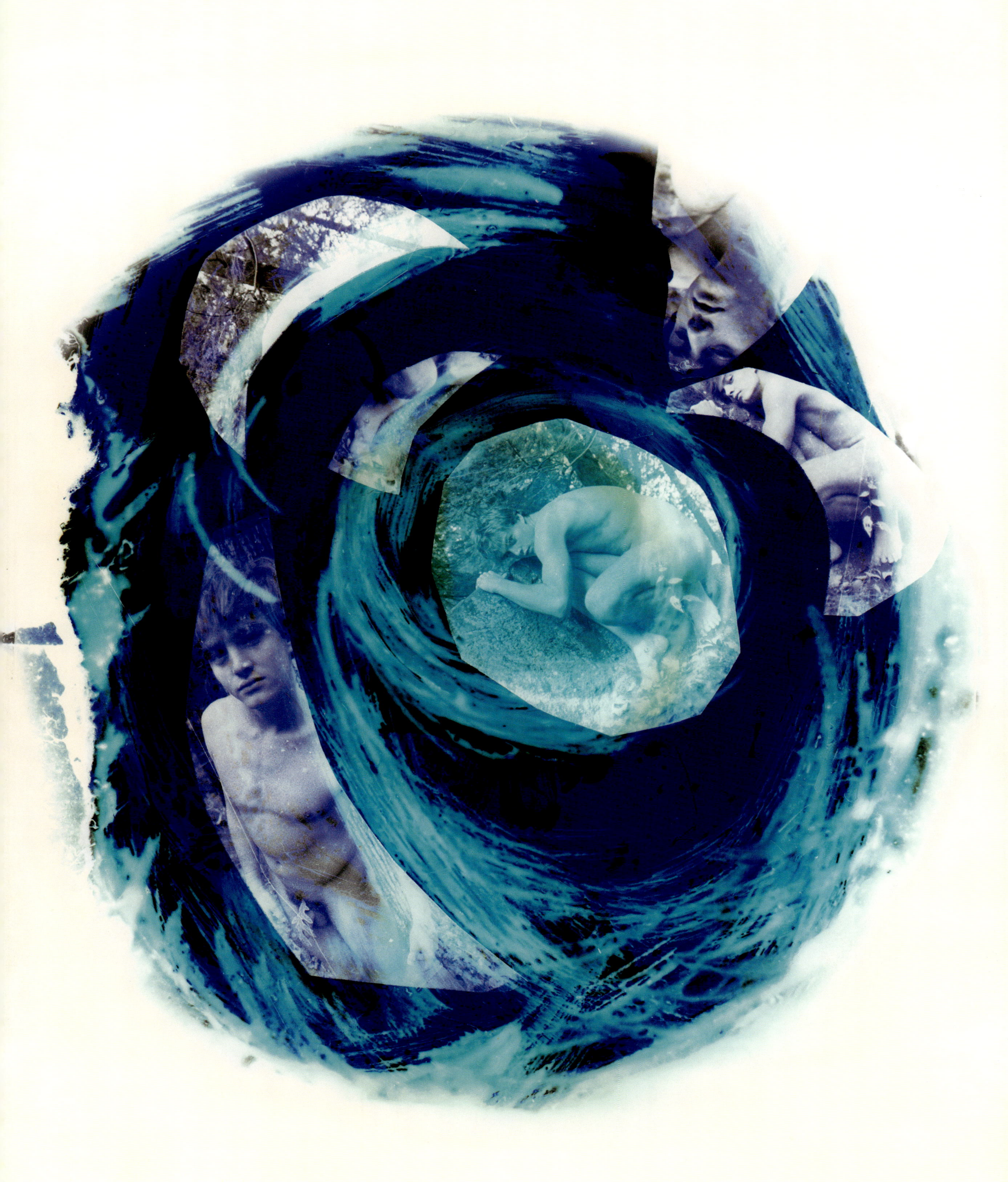

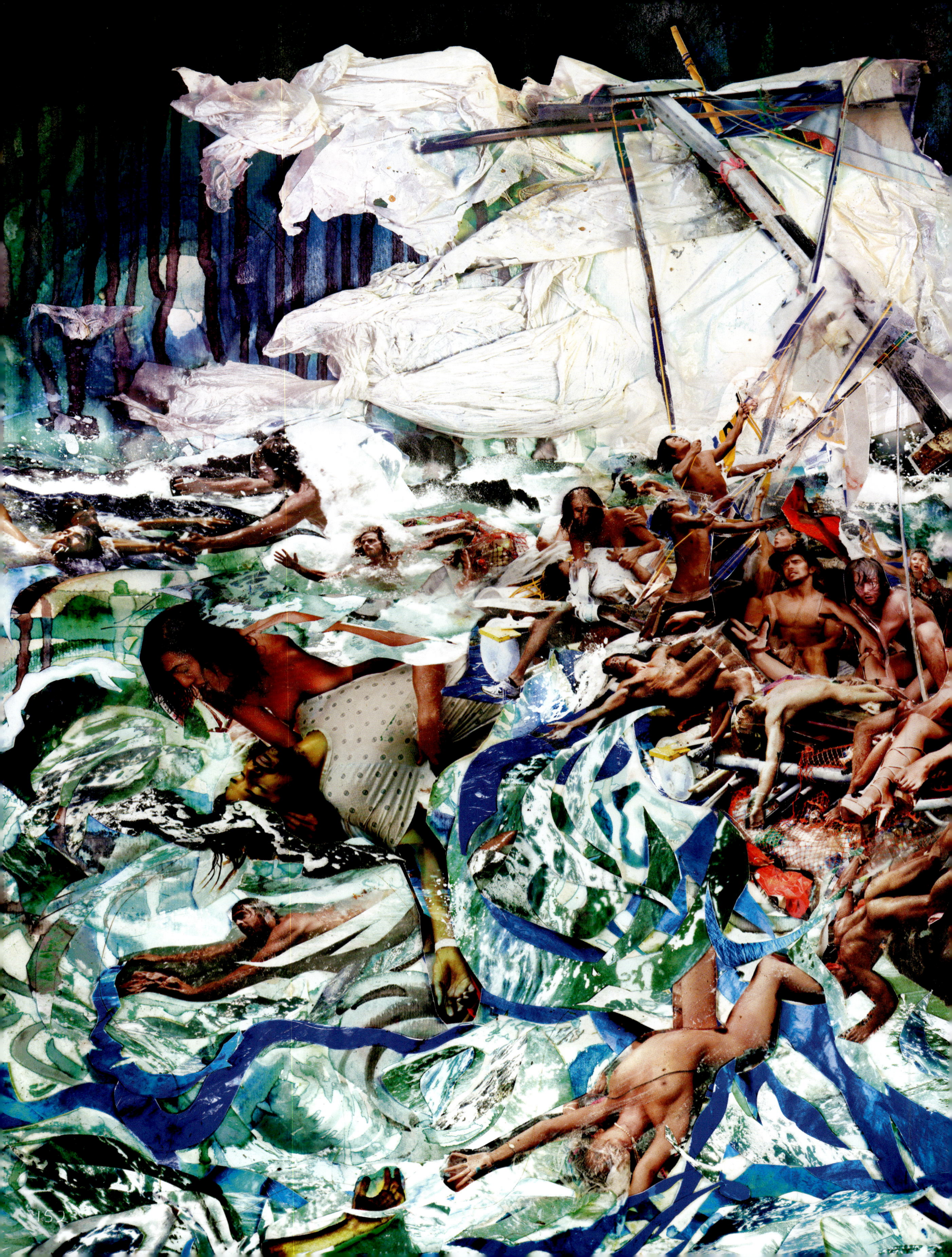

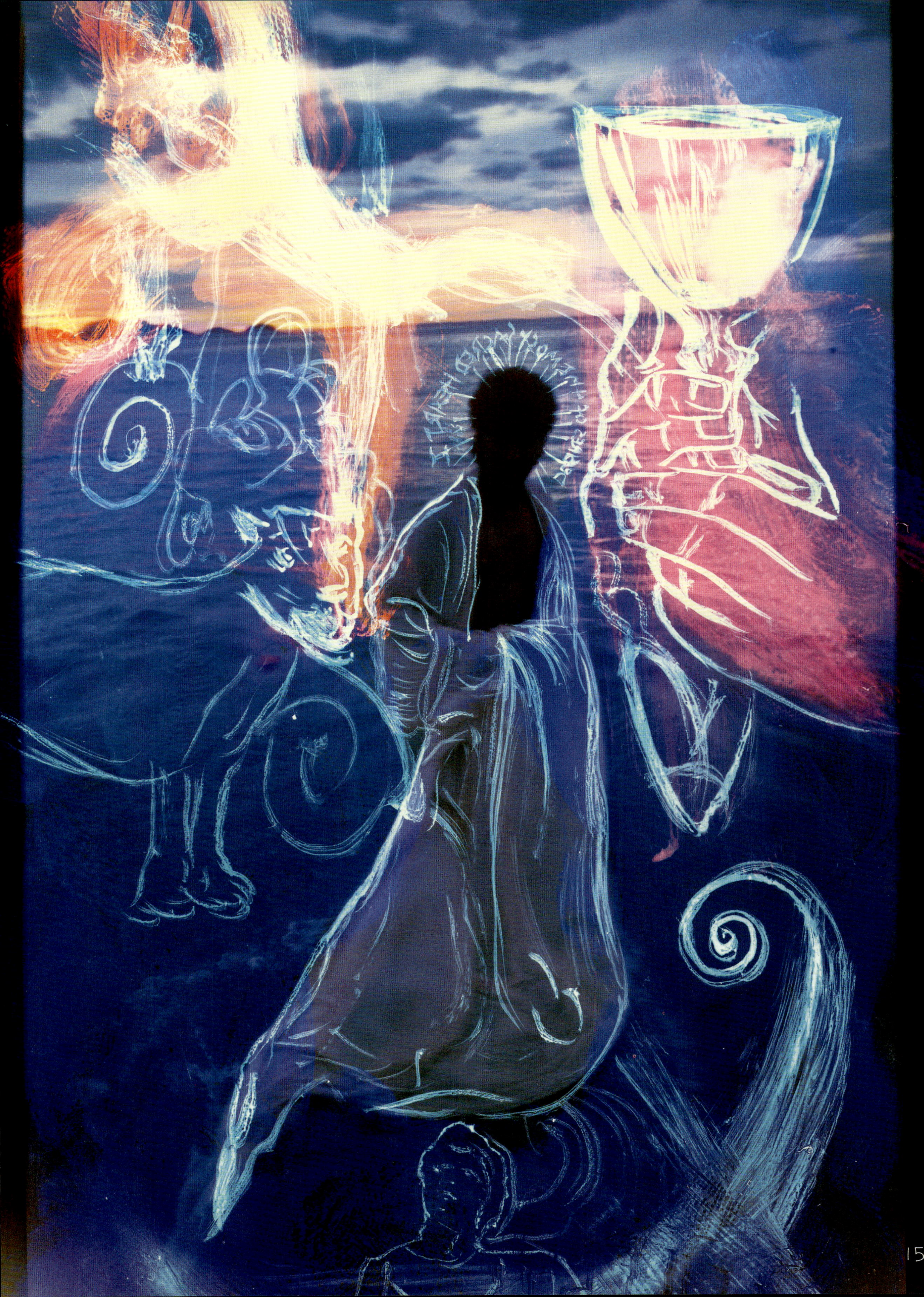
15

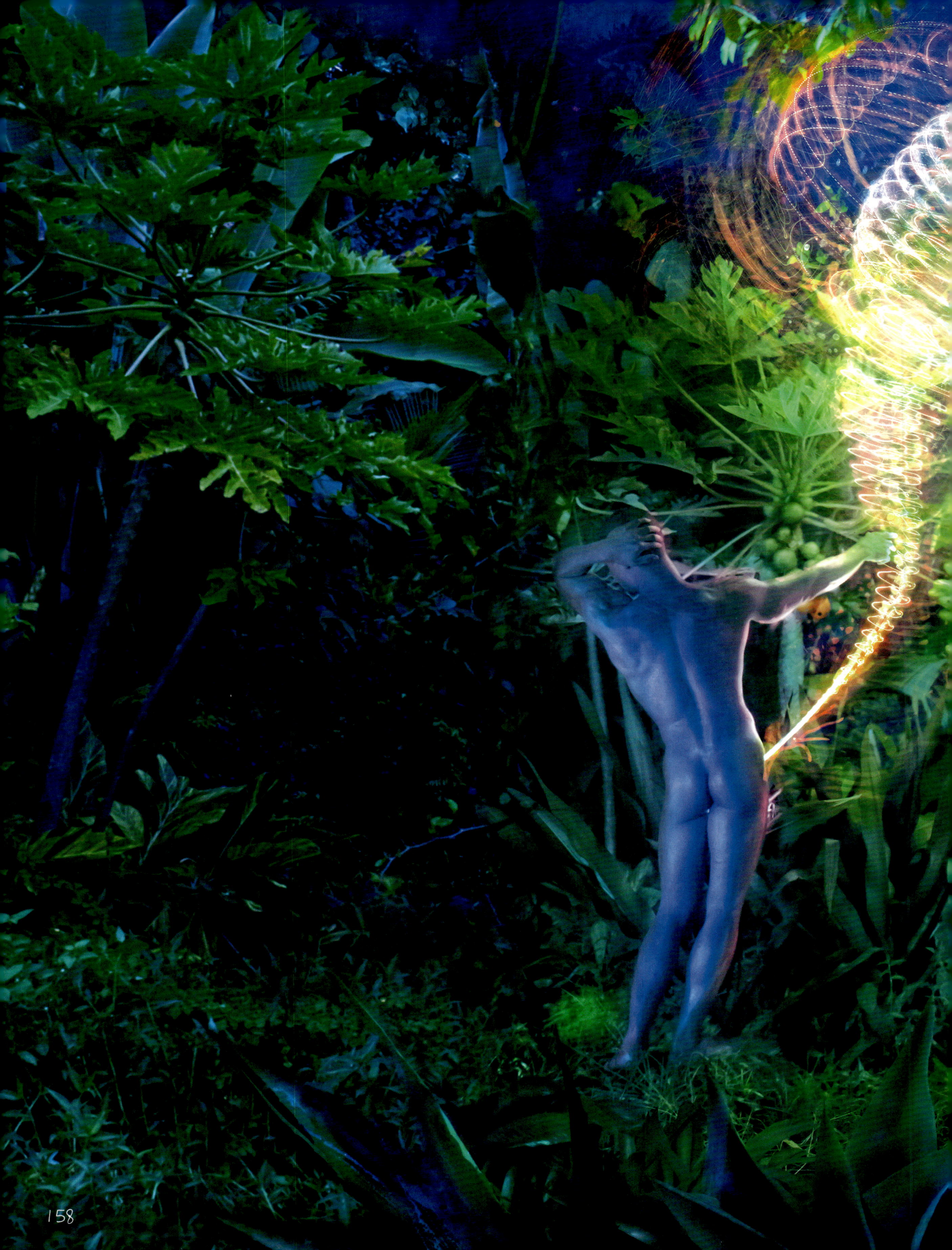

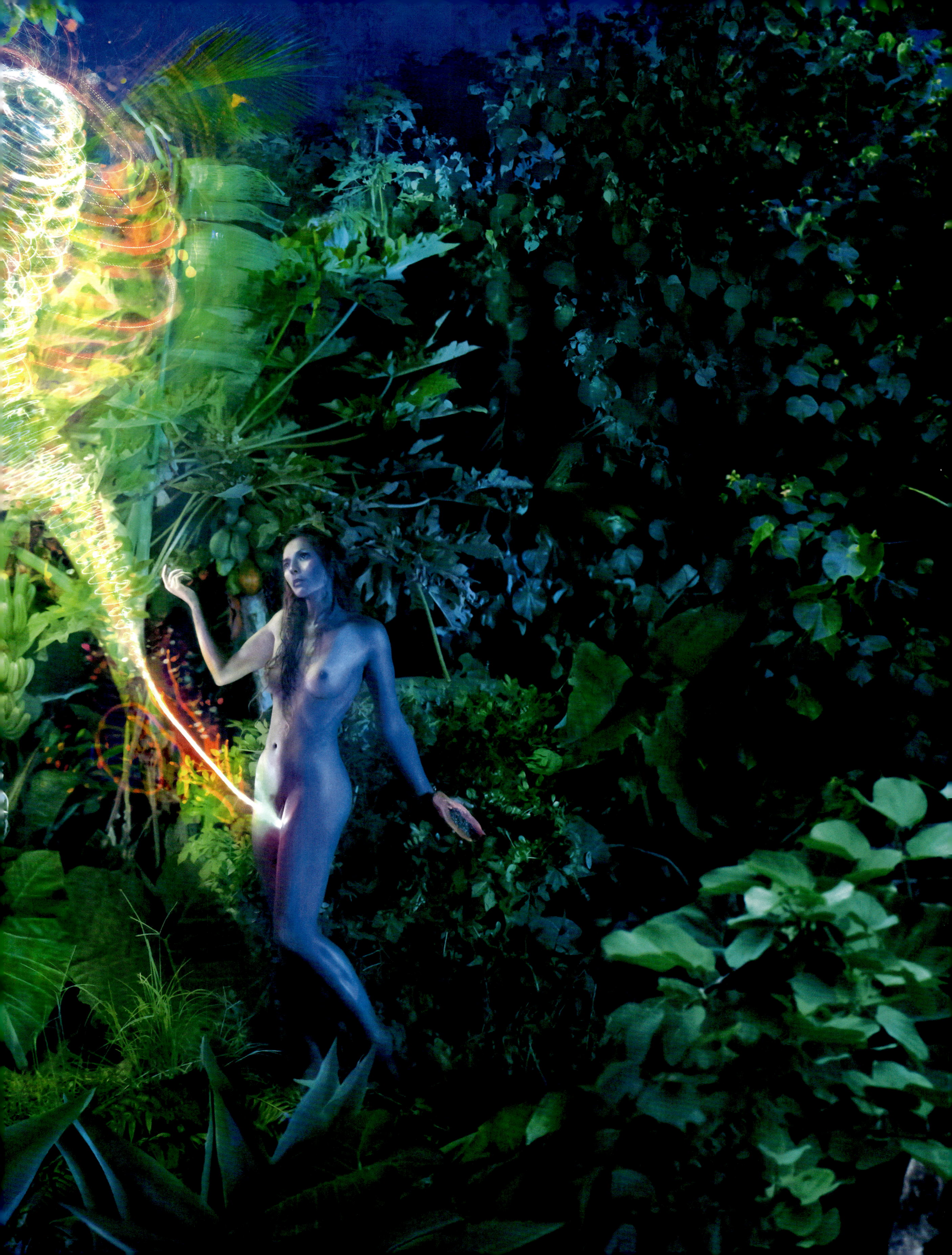

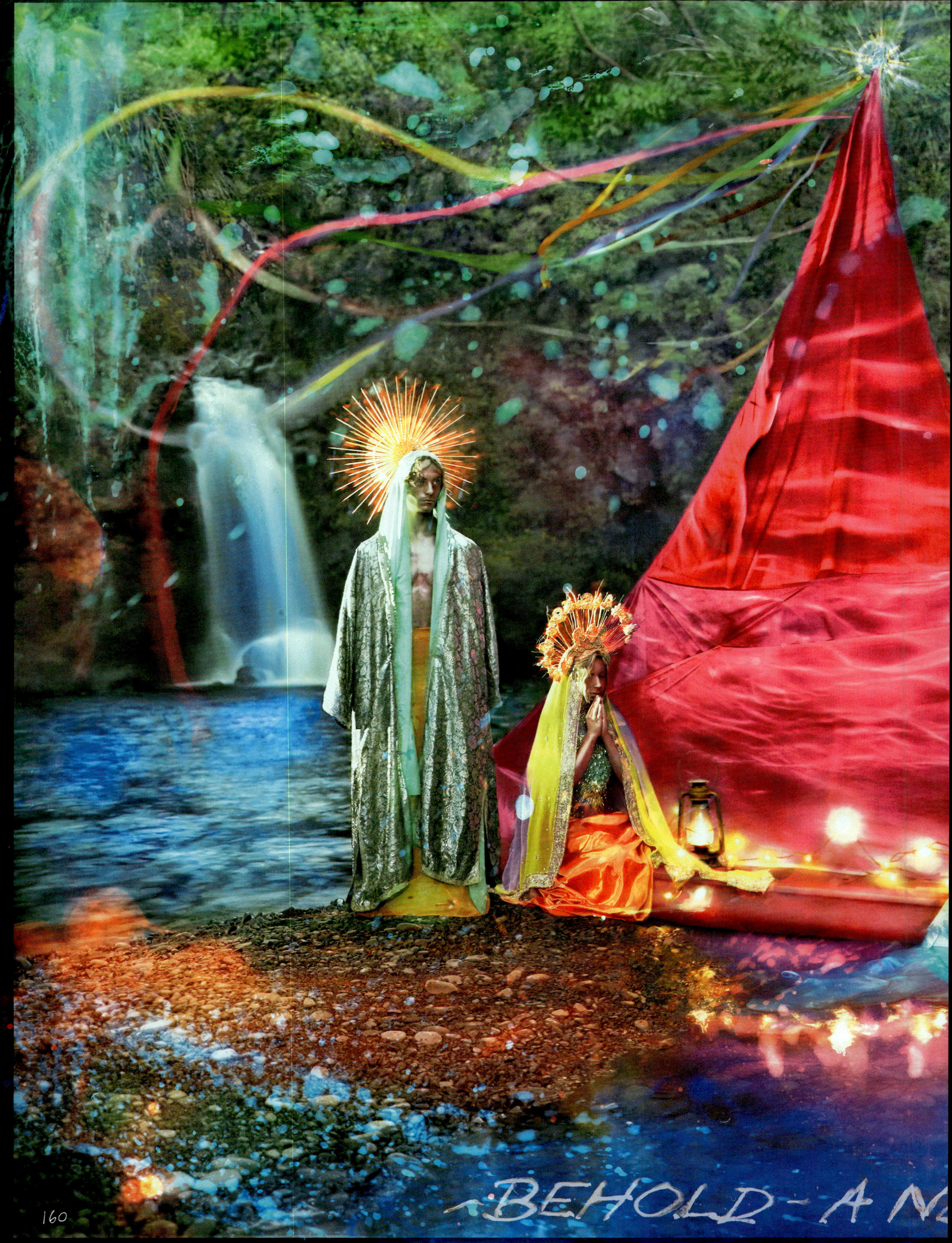
BEHOLD - A

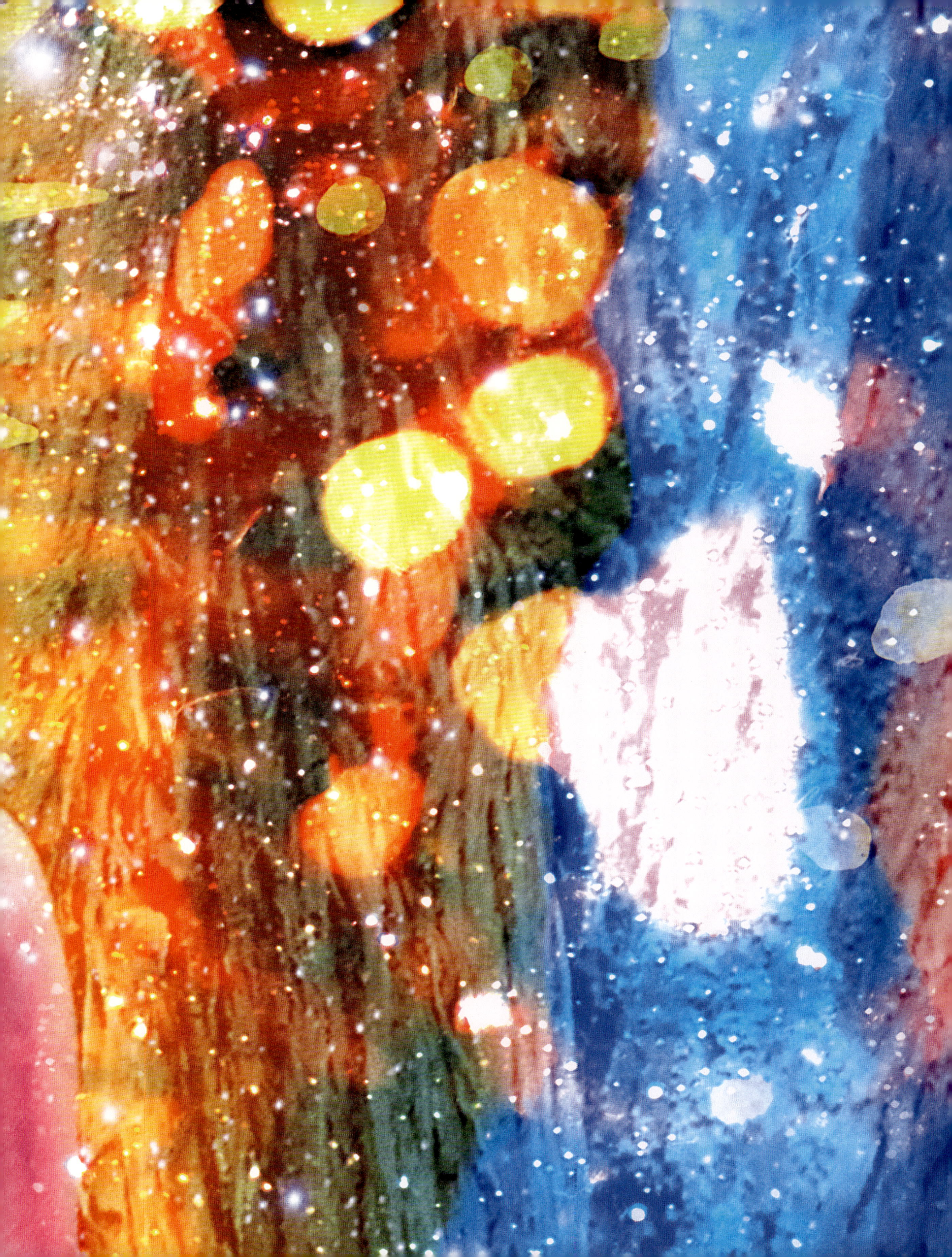

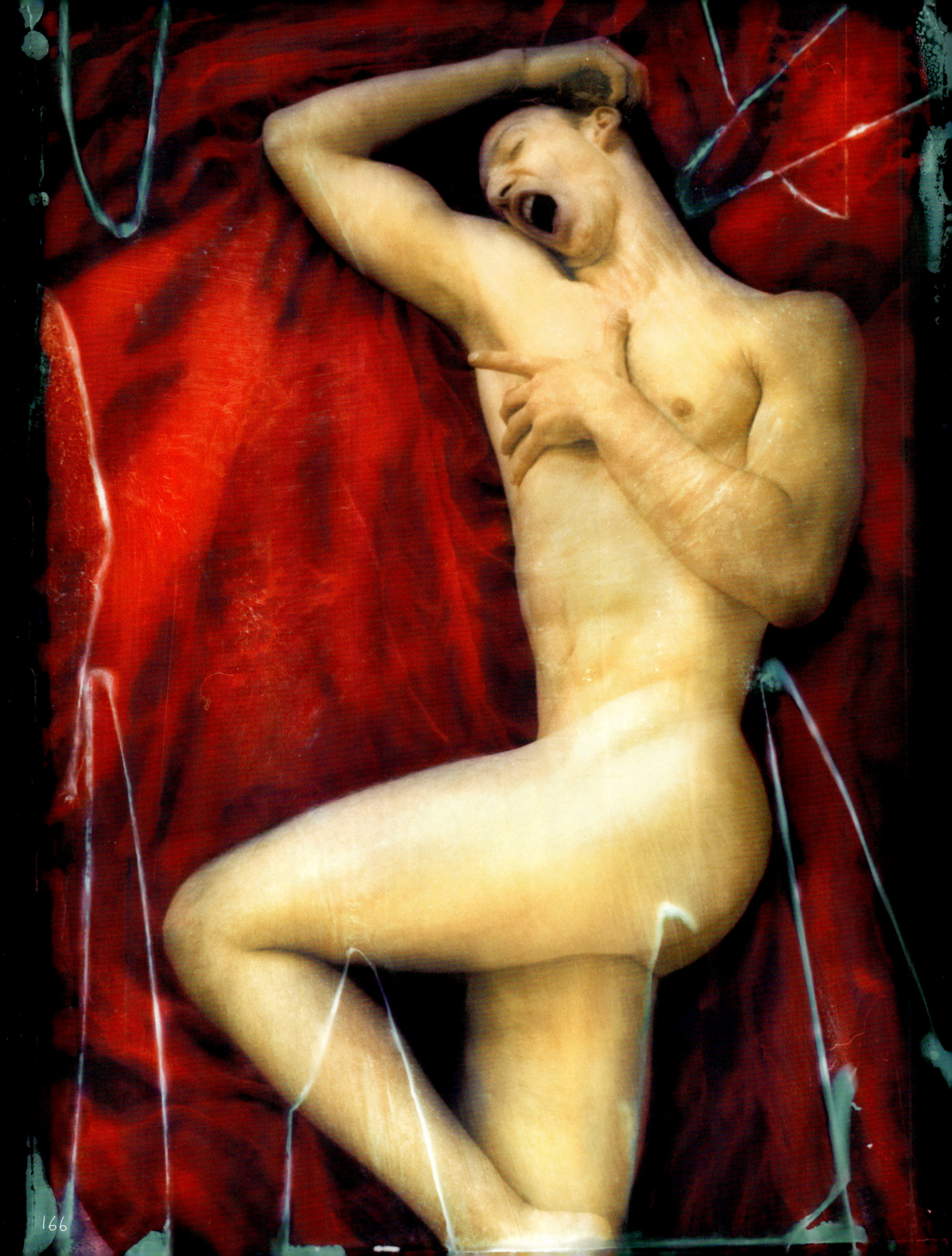

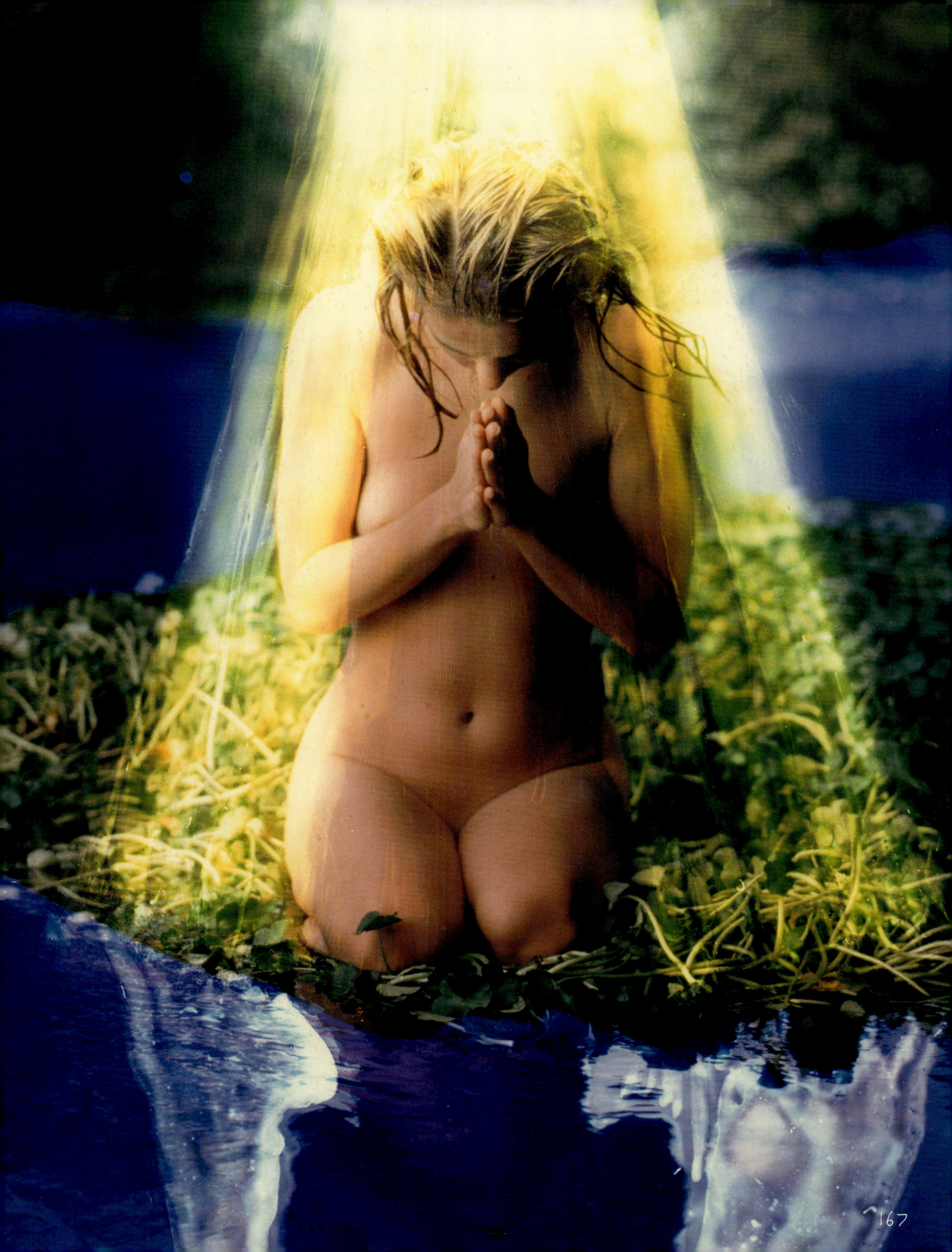

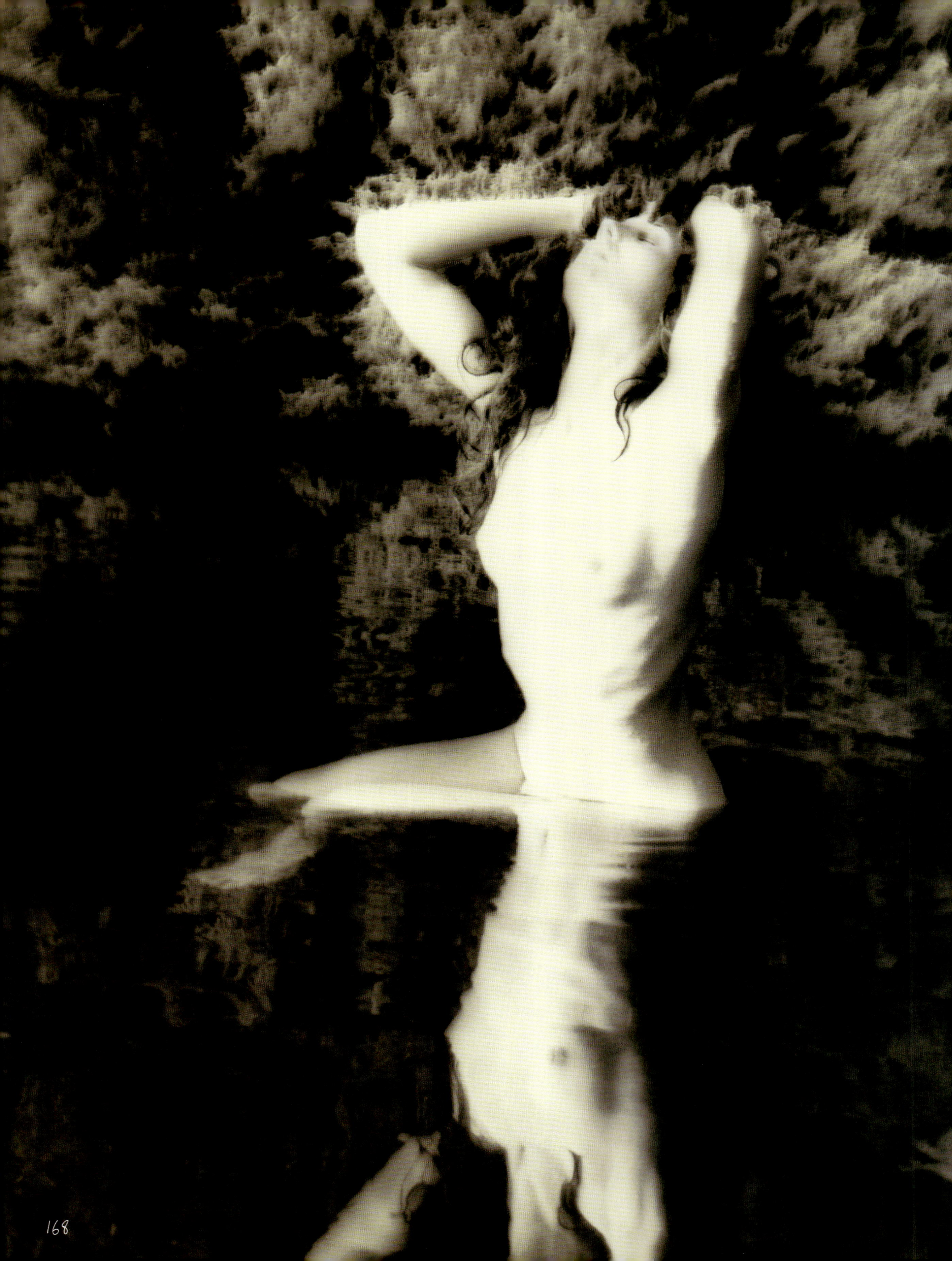

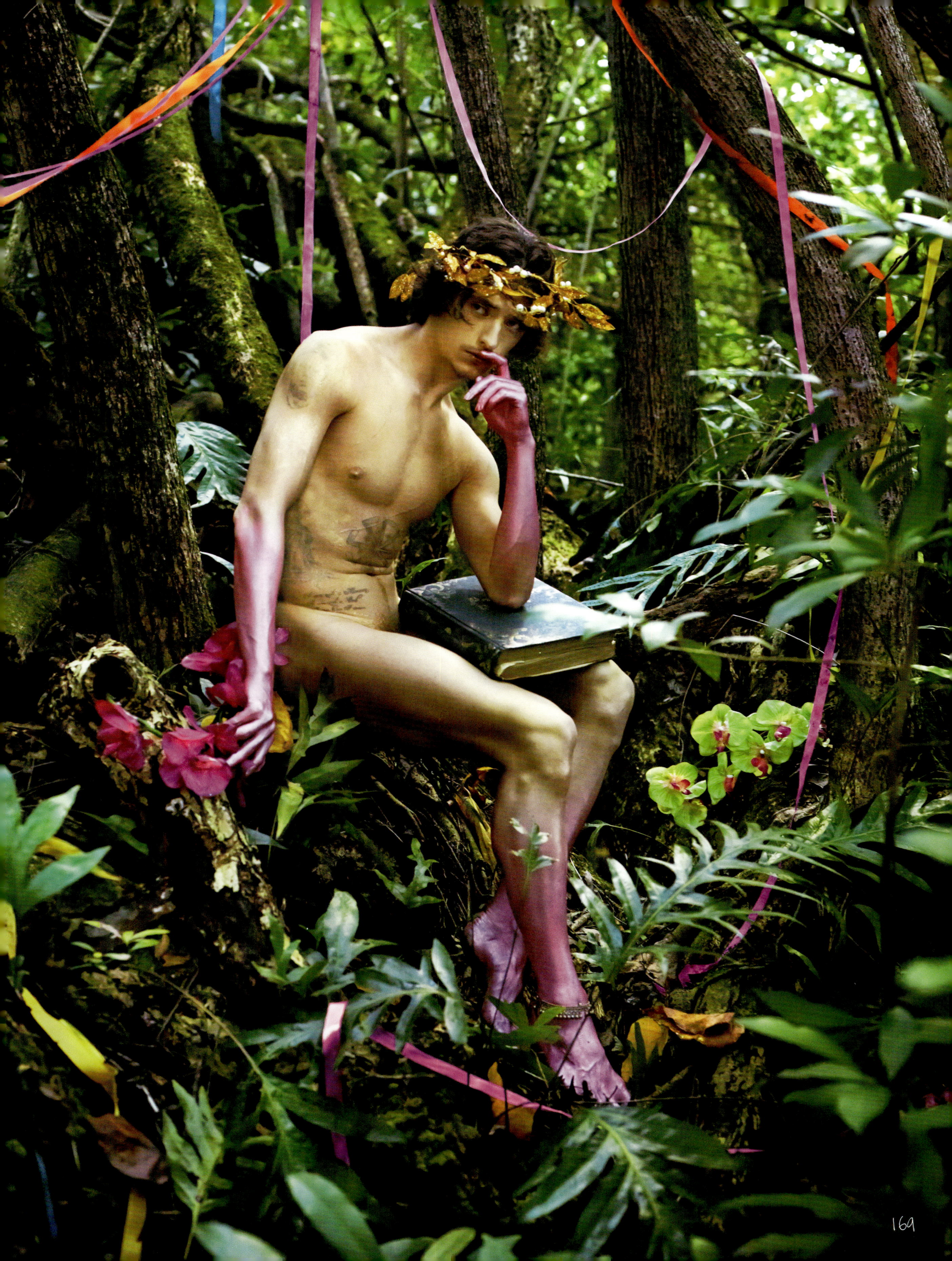

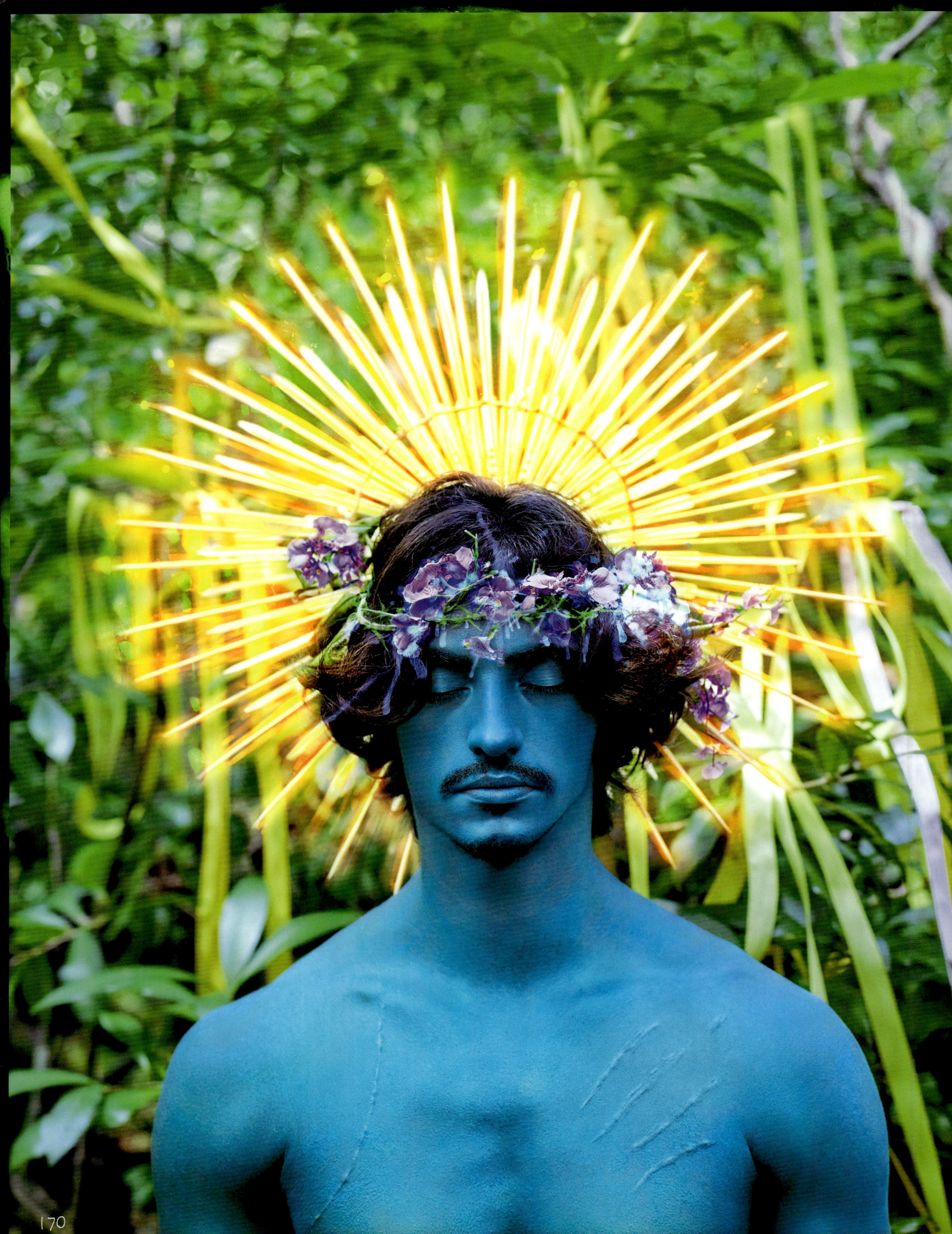

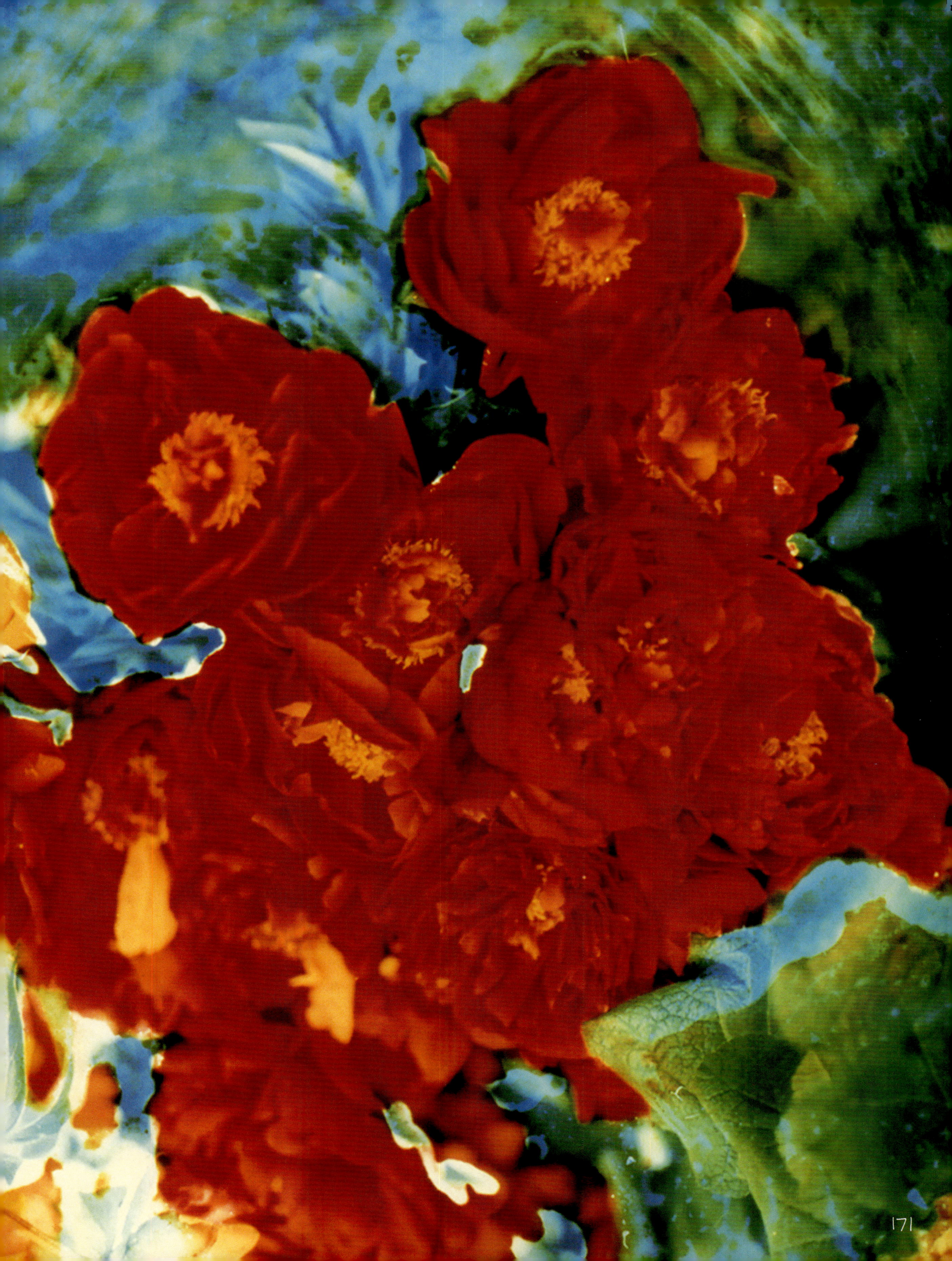

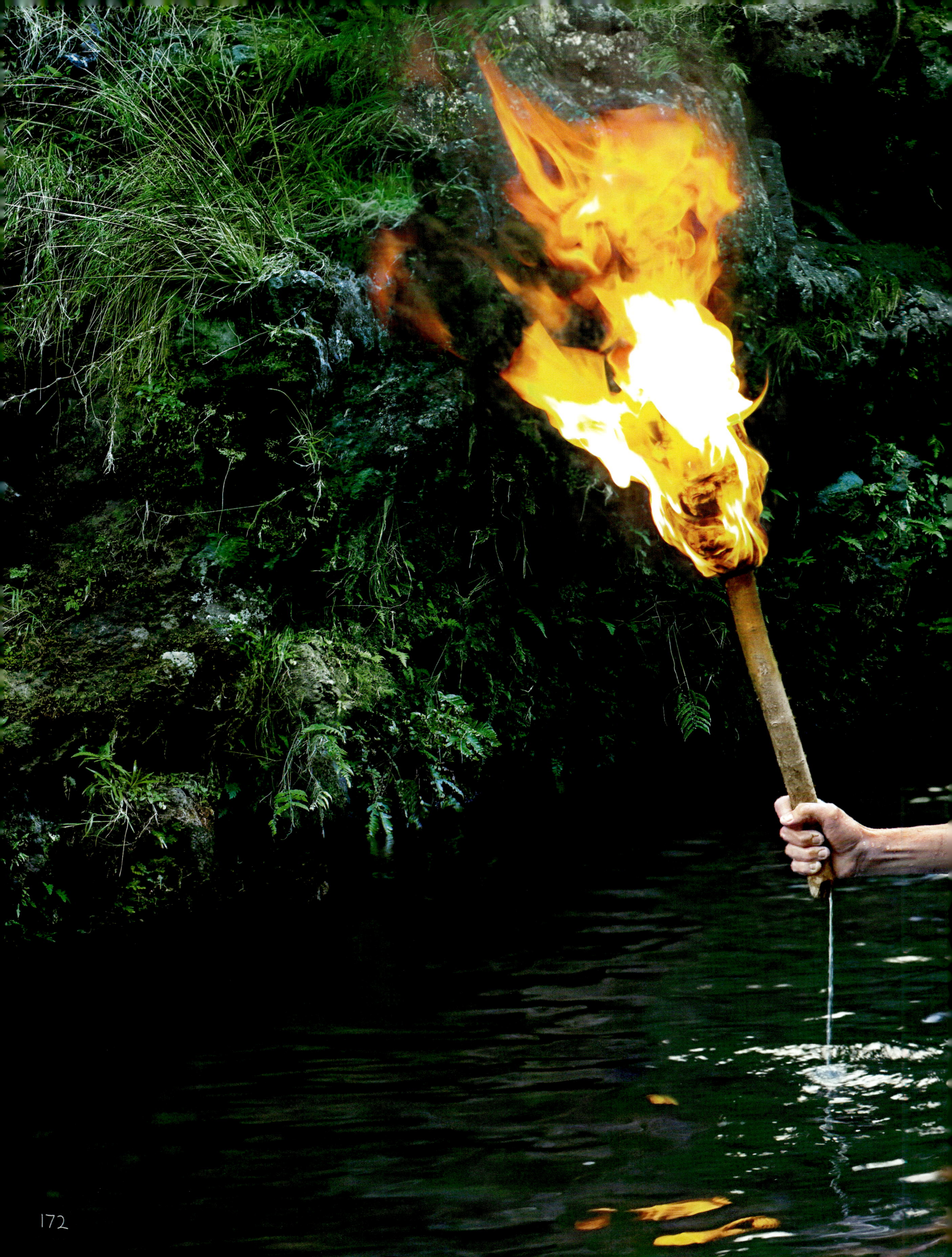

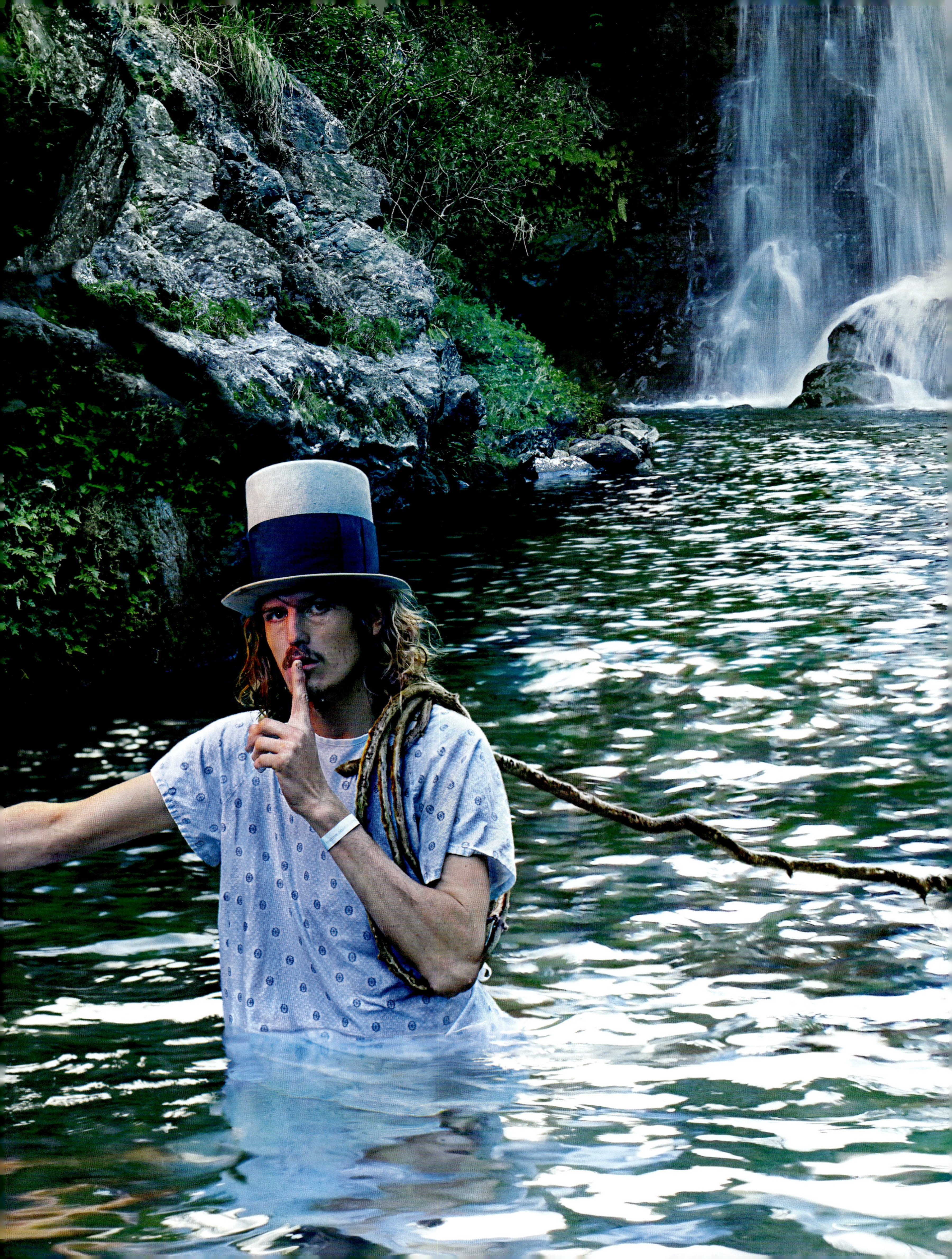

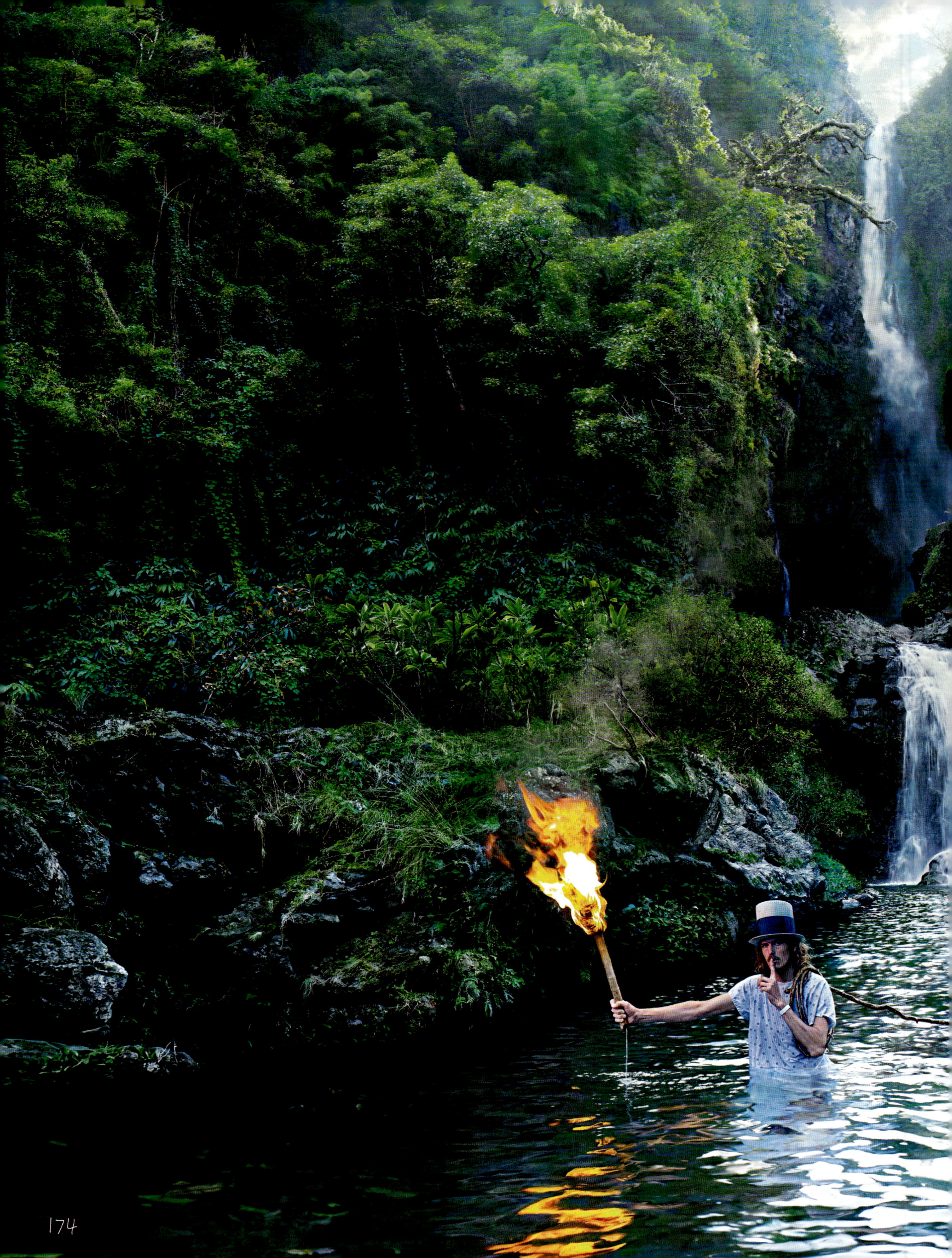

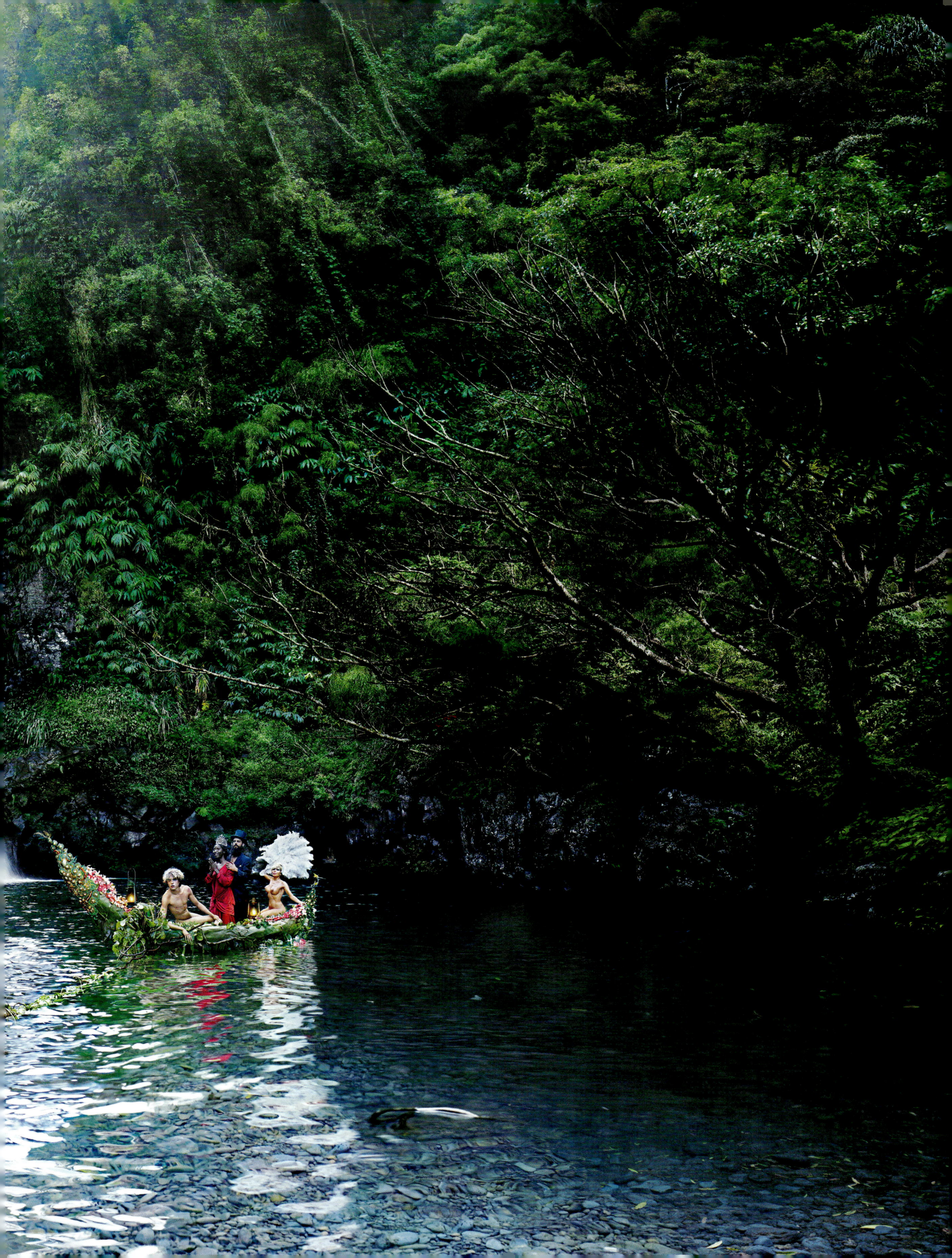

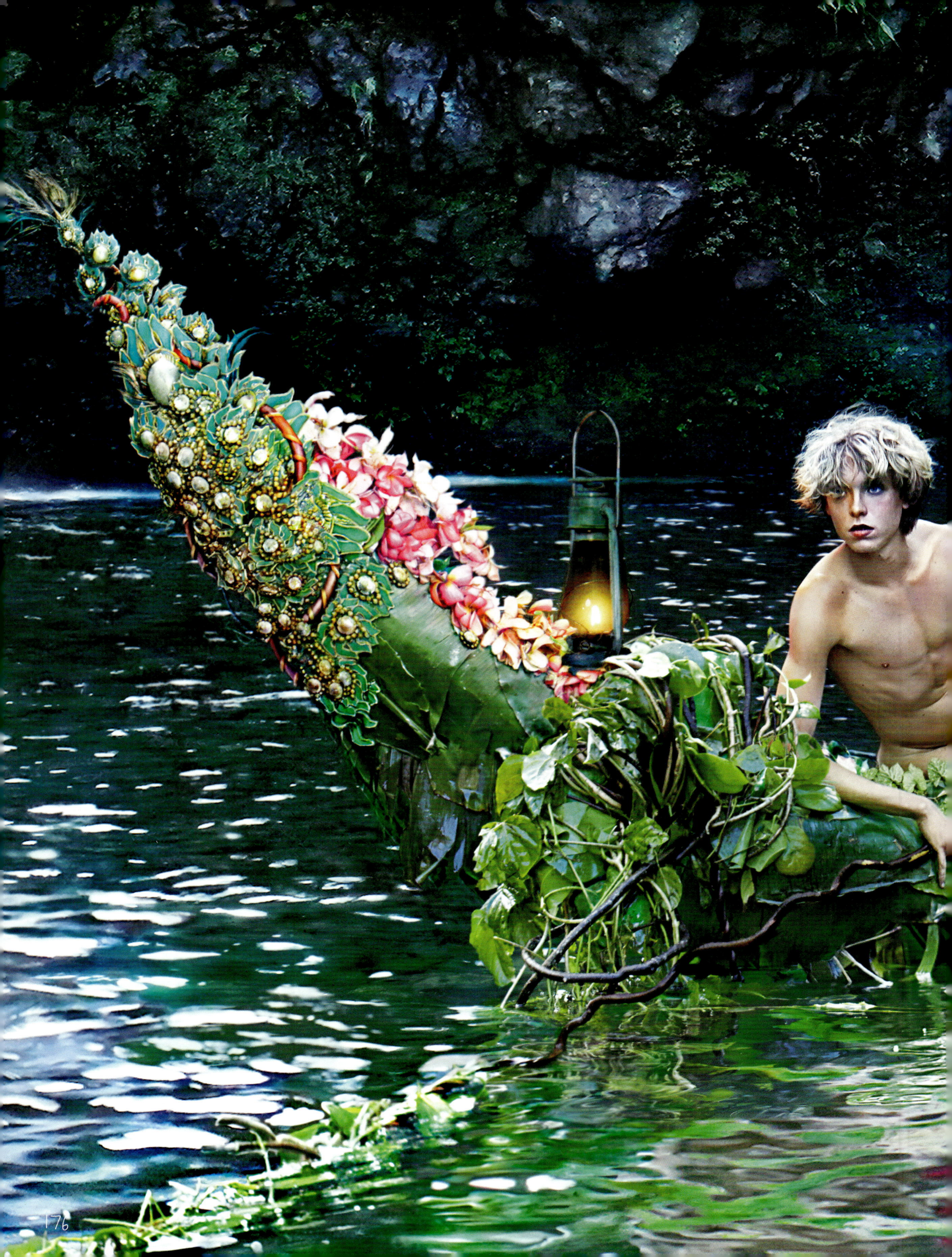

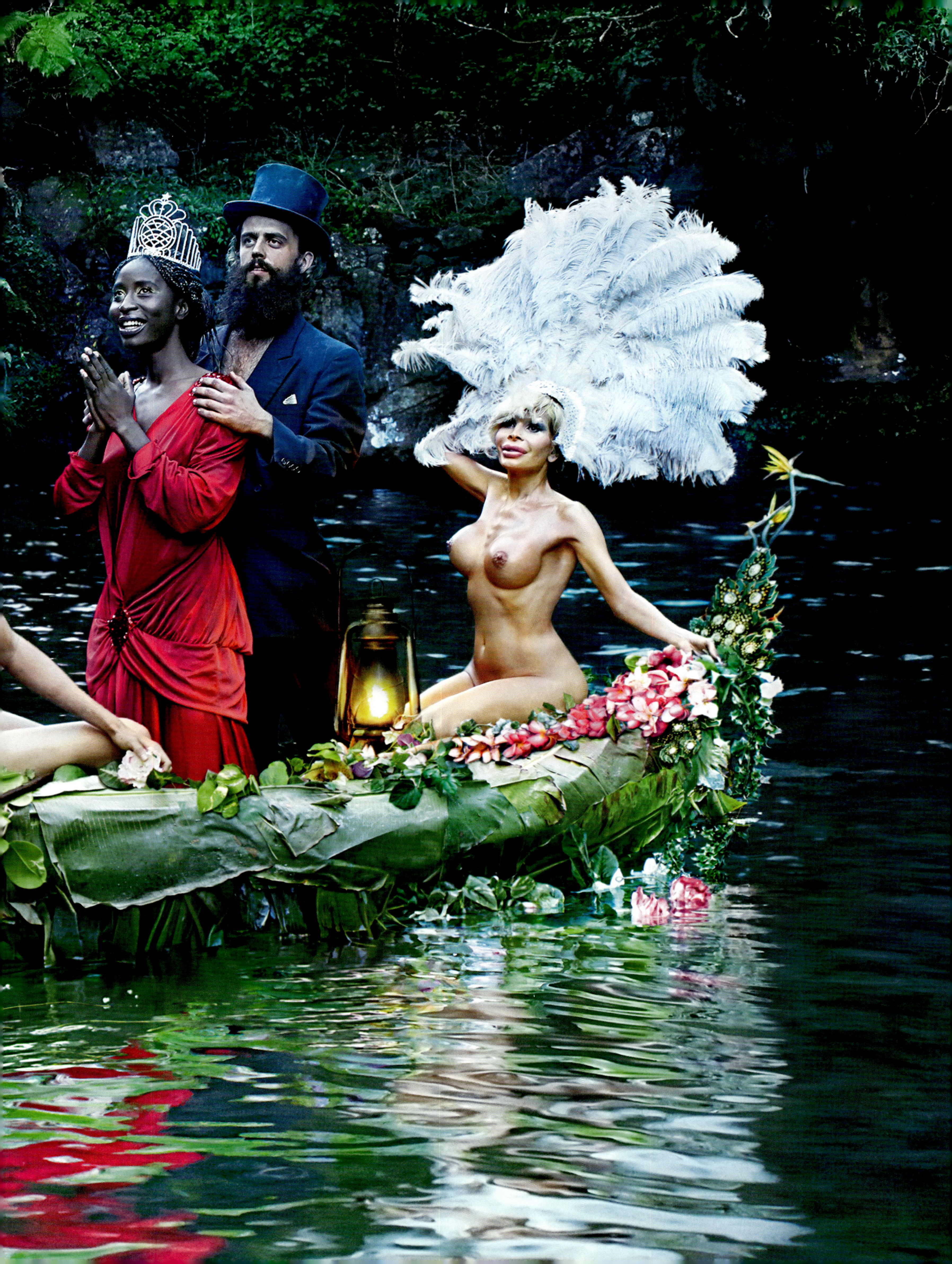

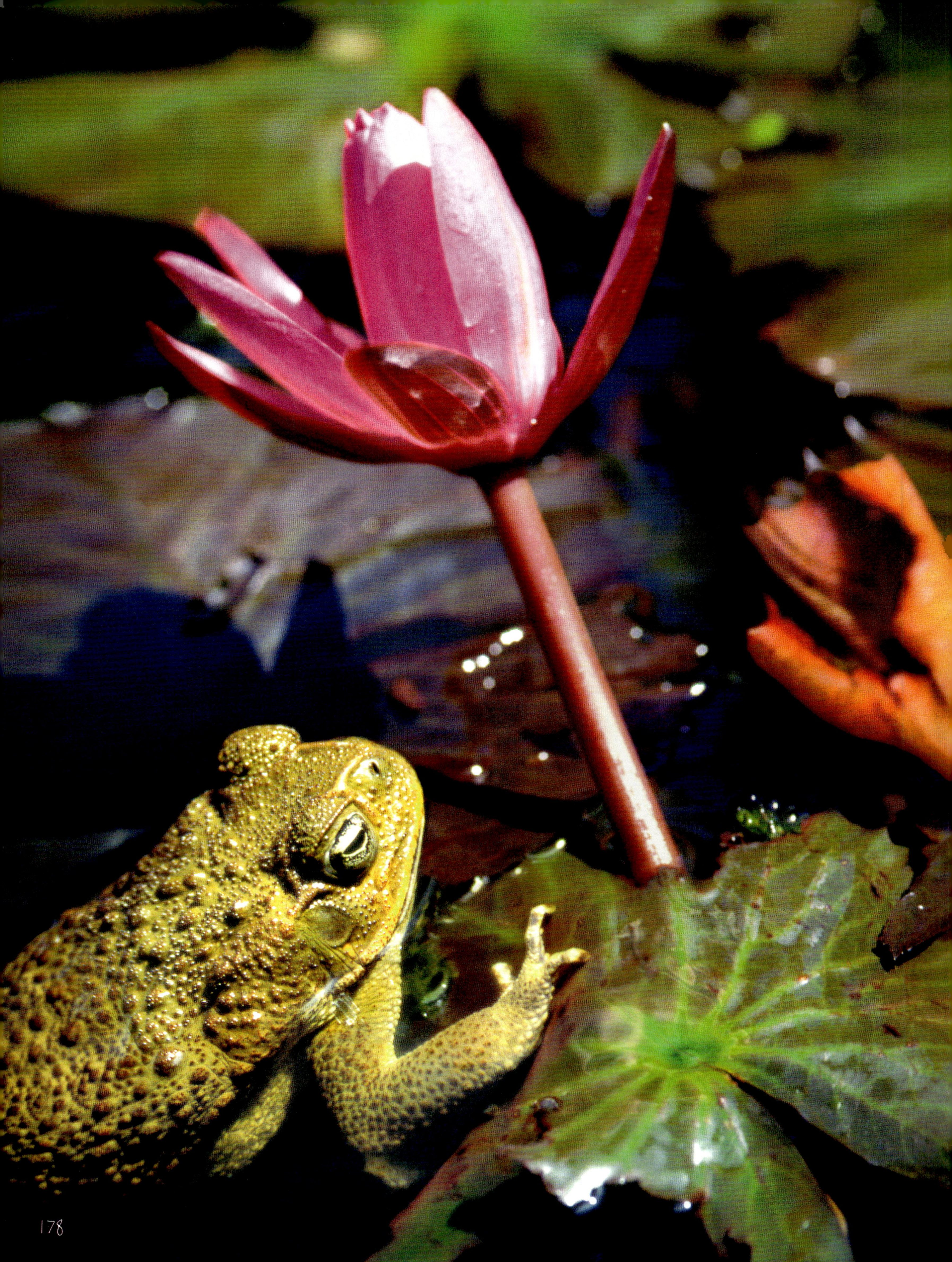

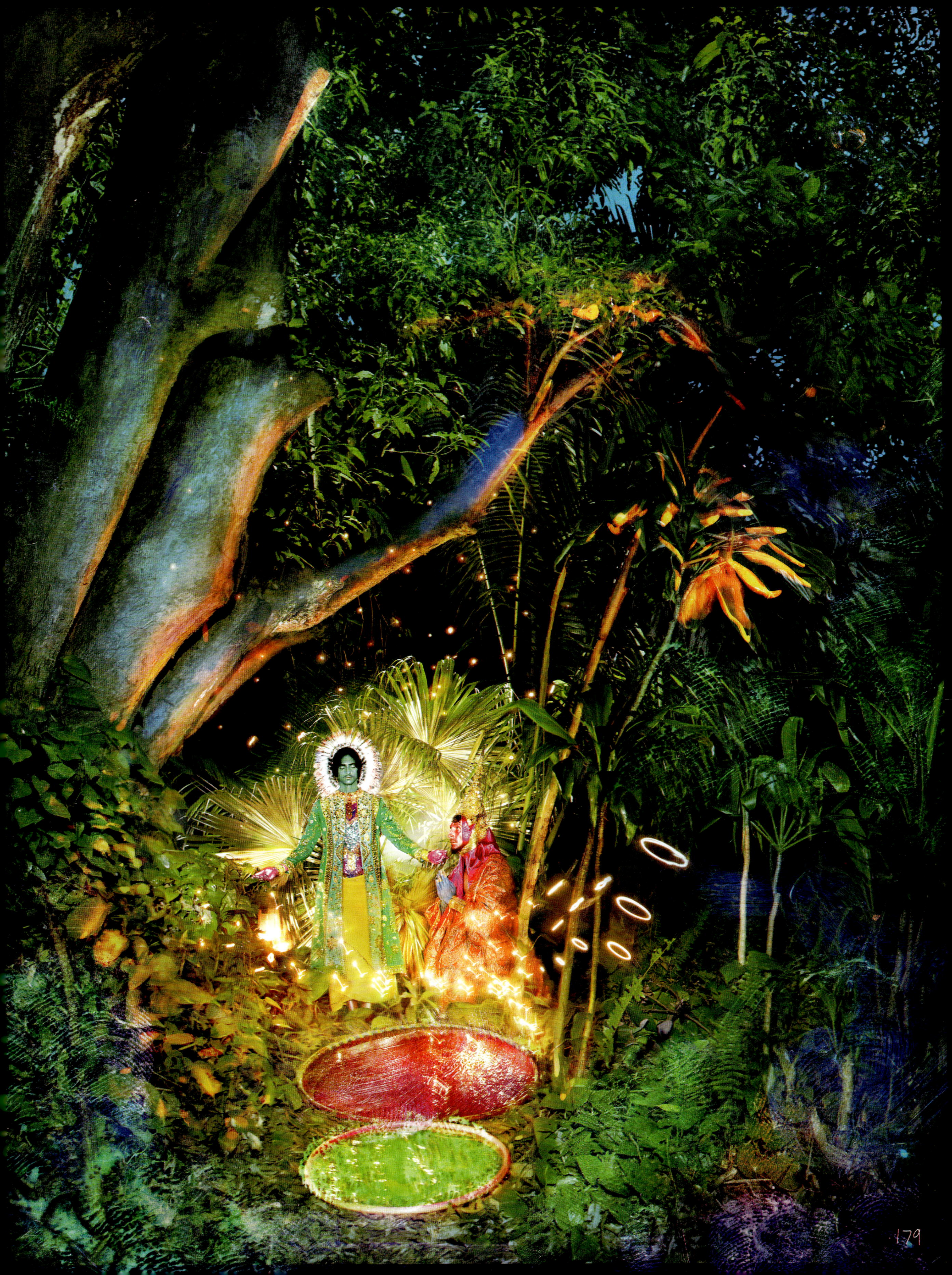

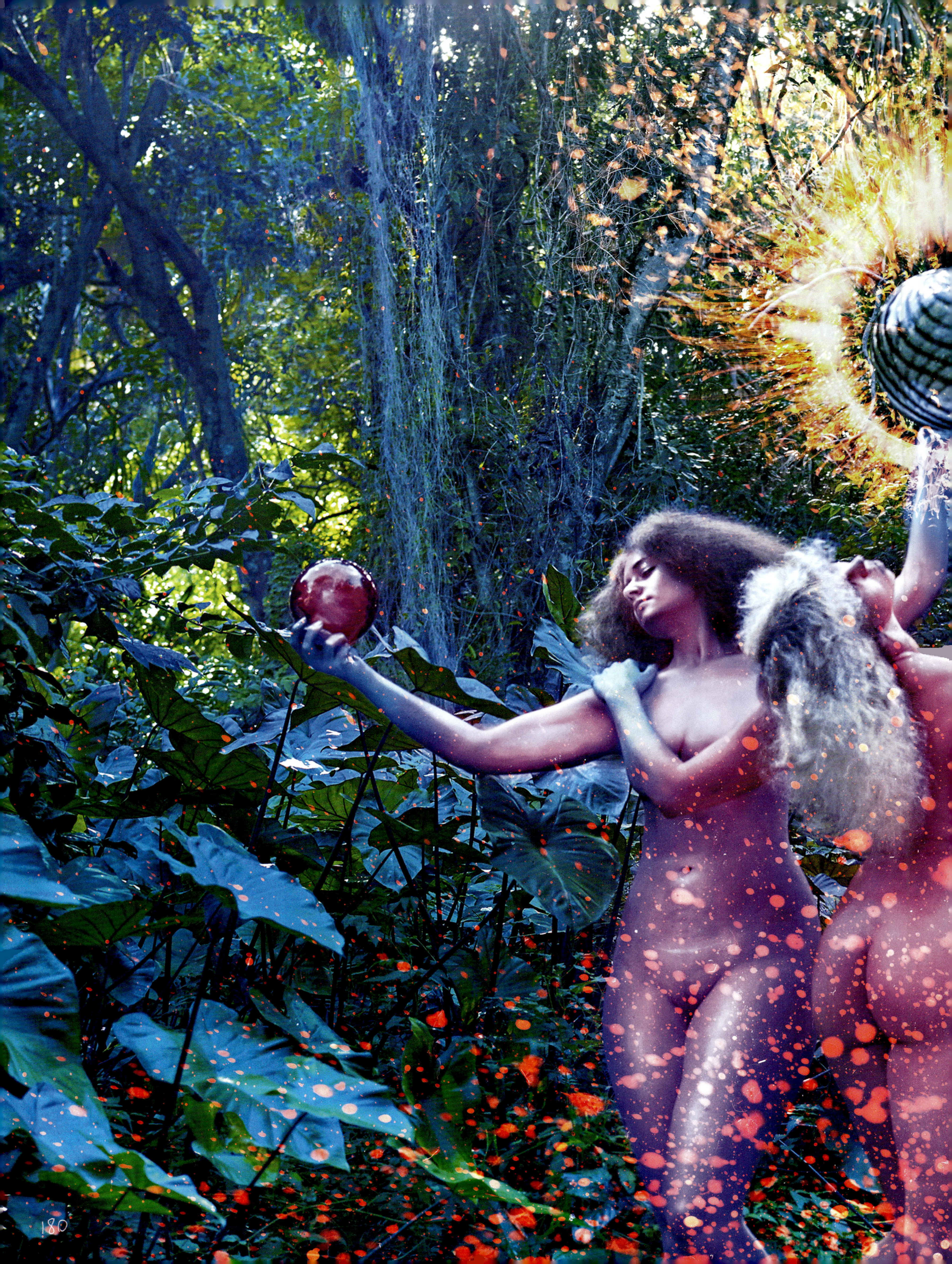

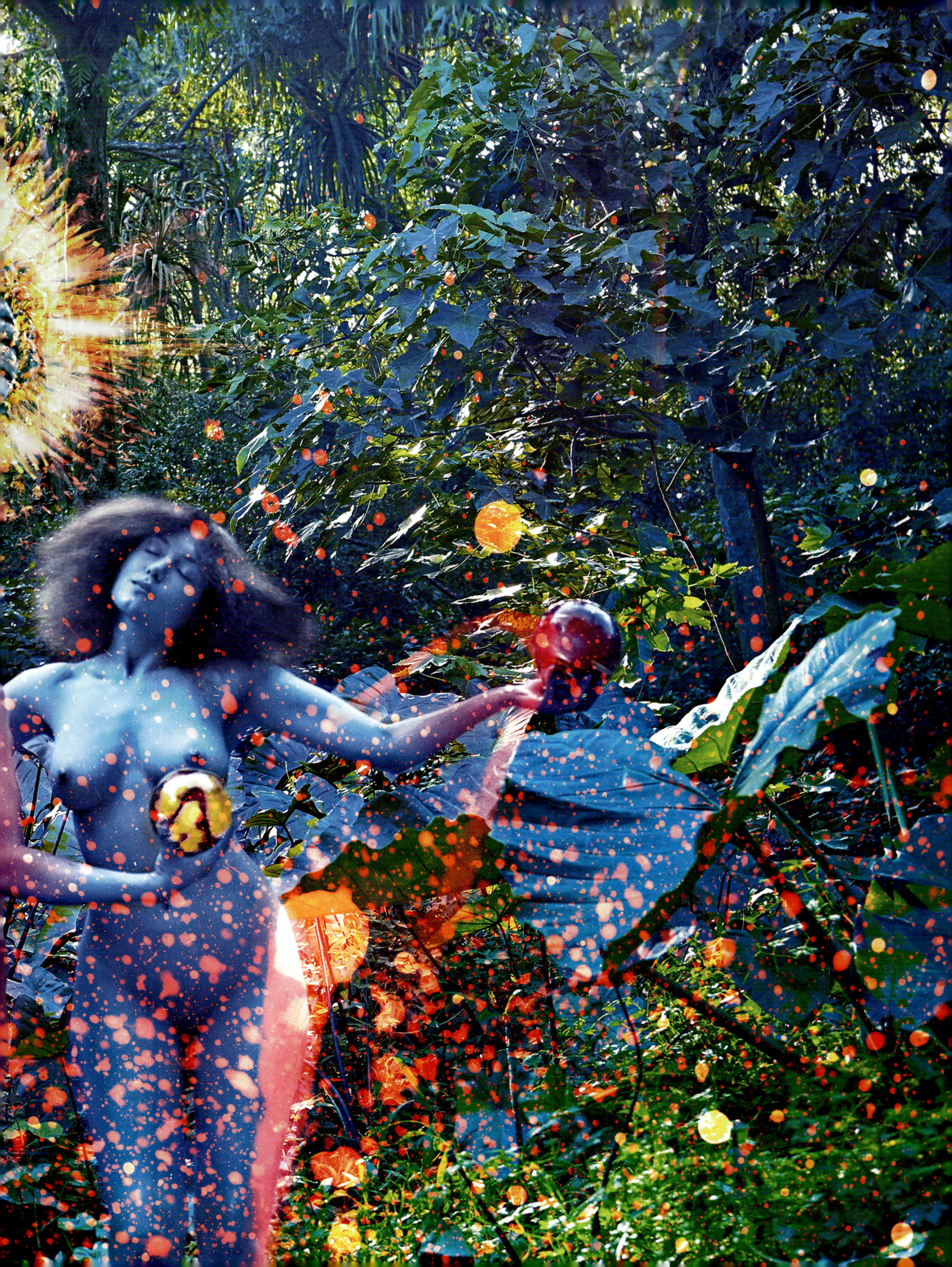

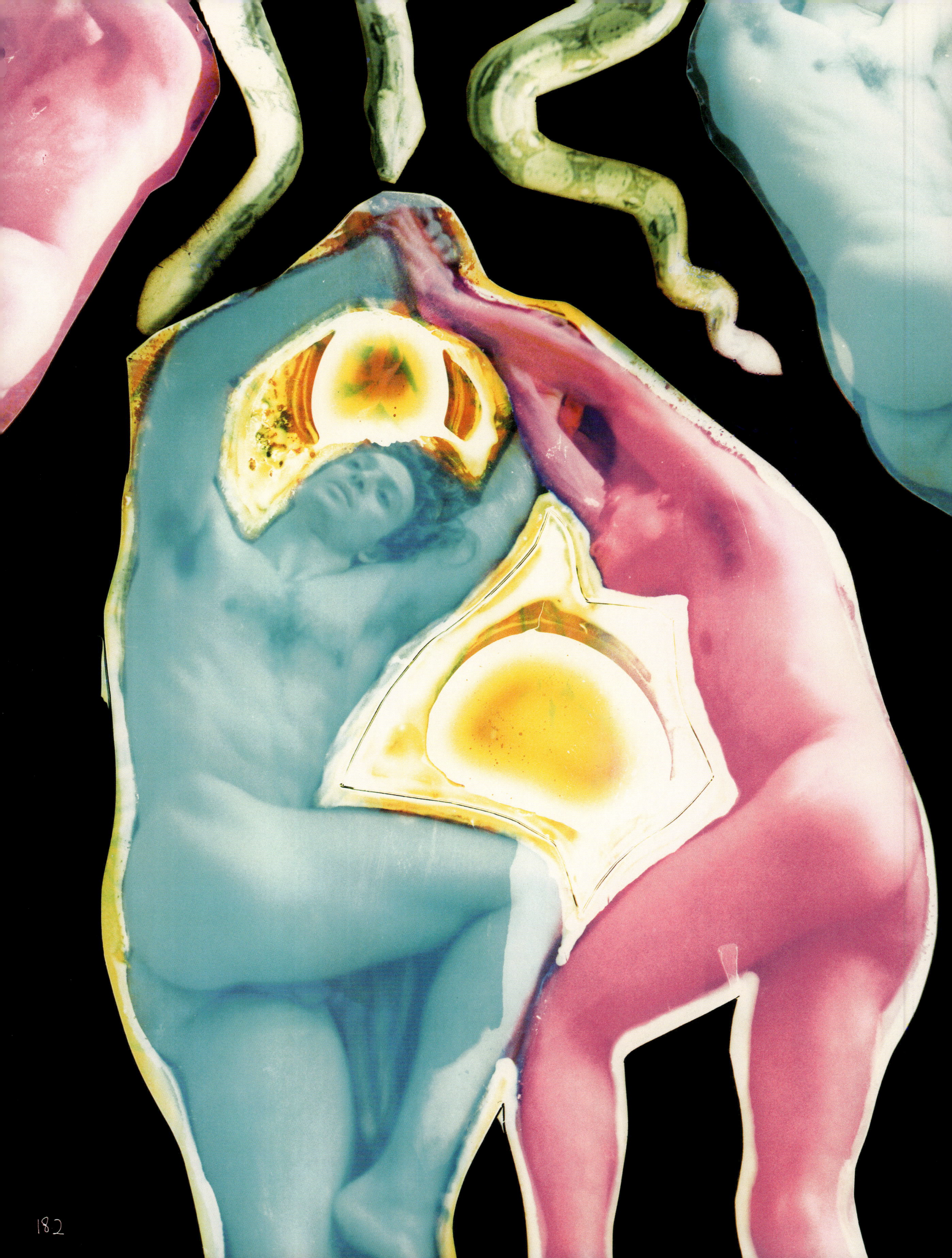

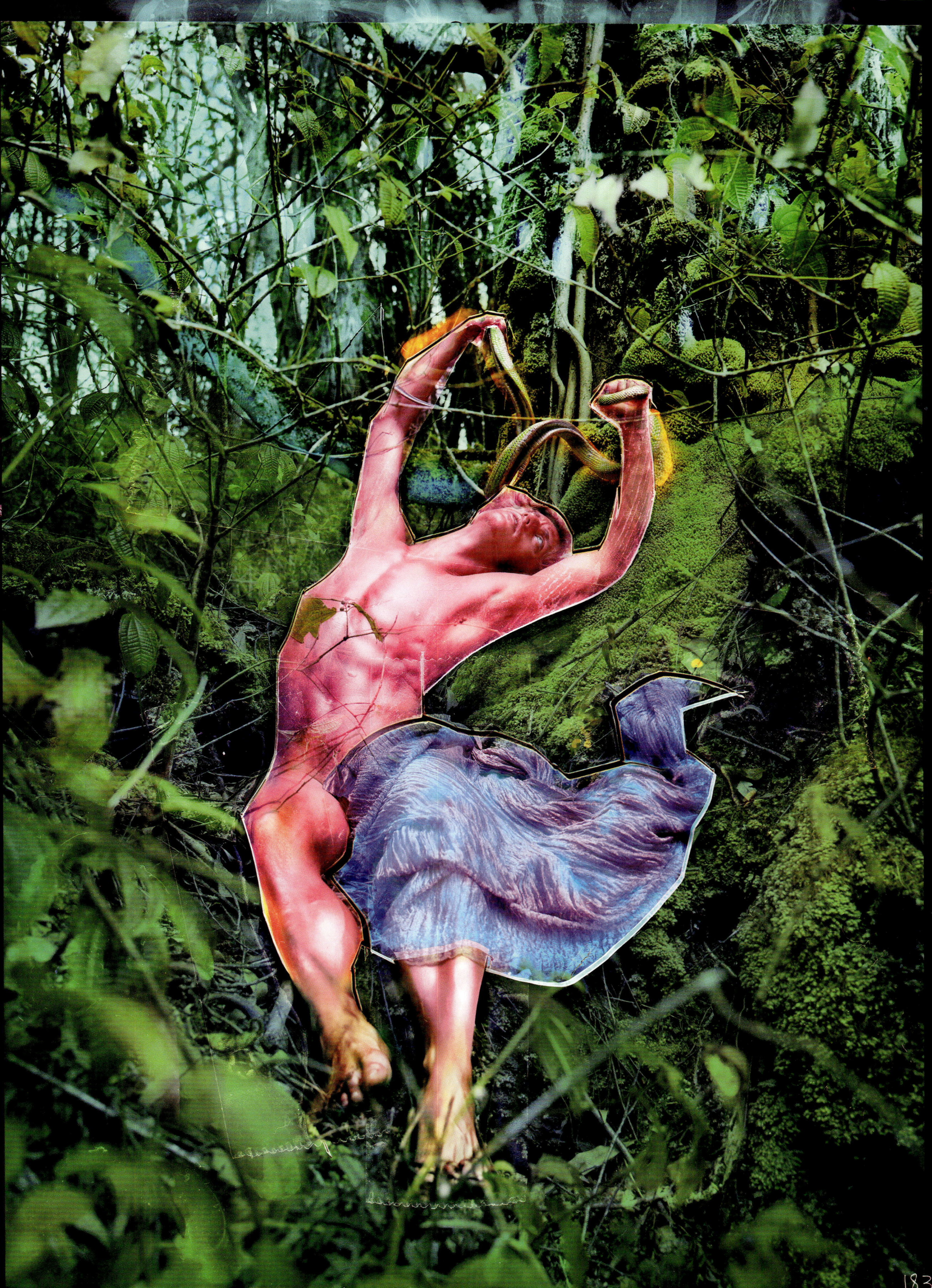

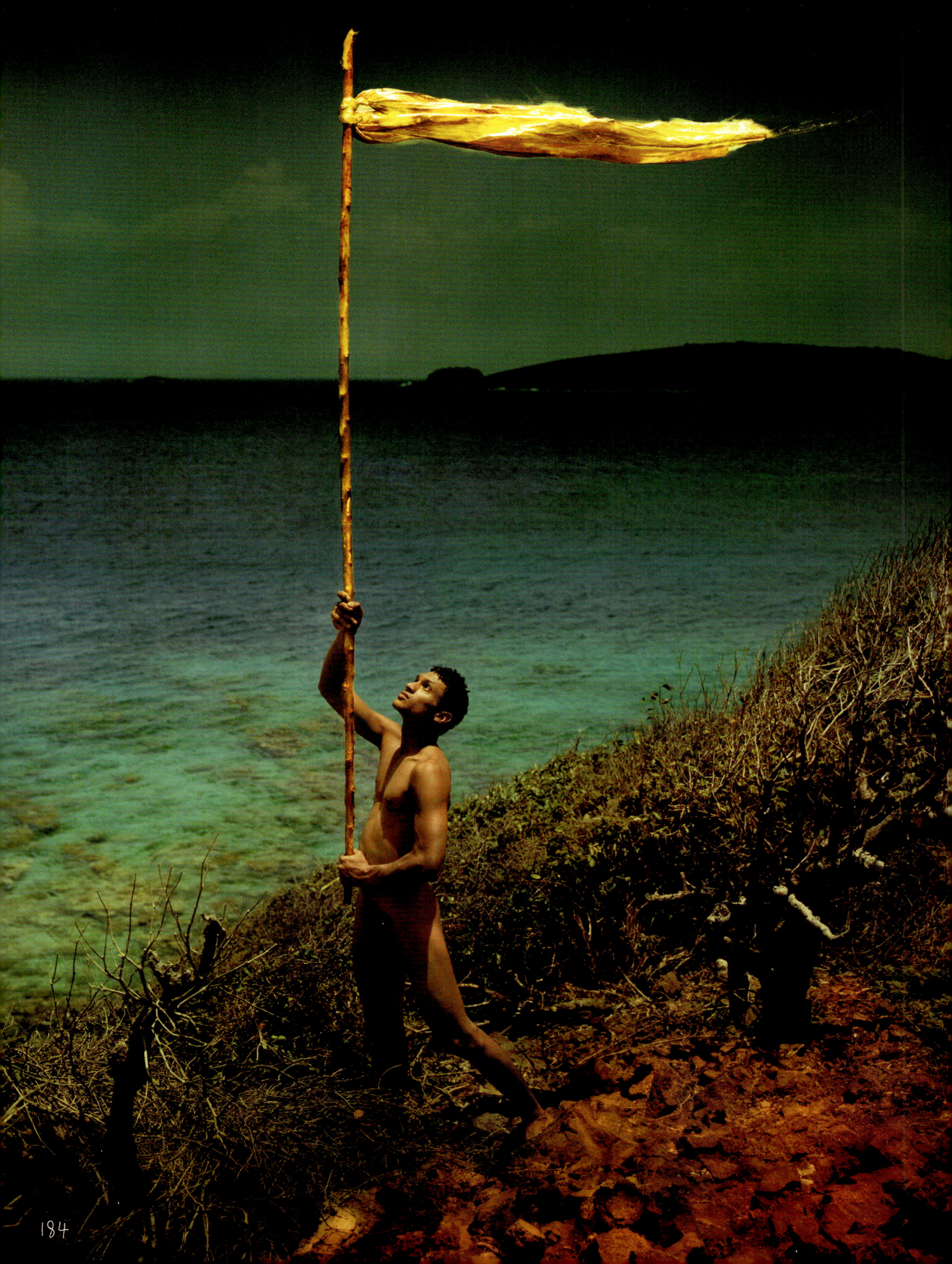

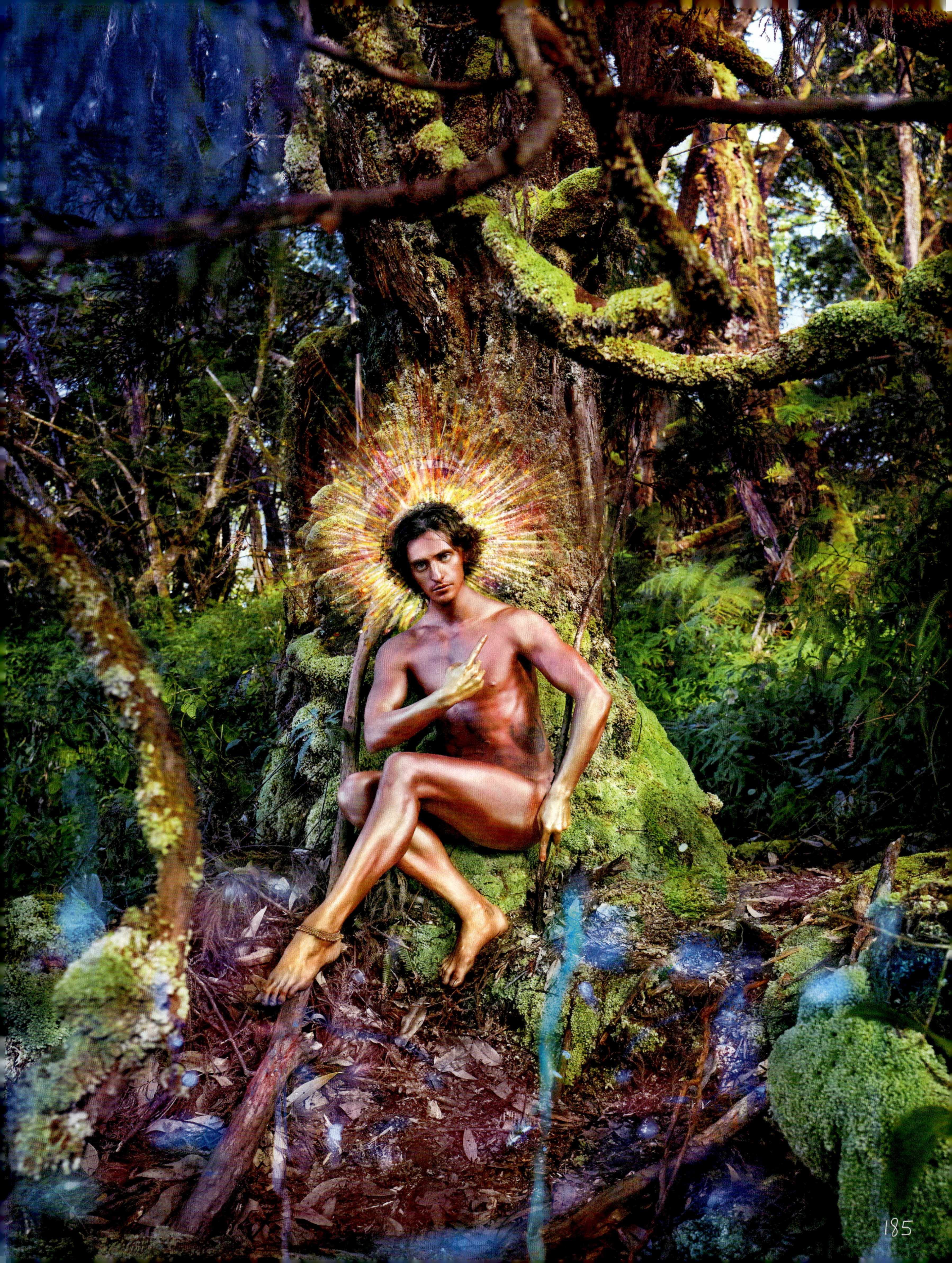

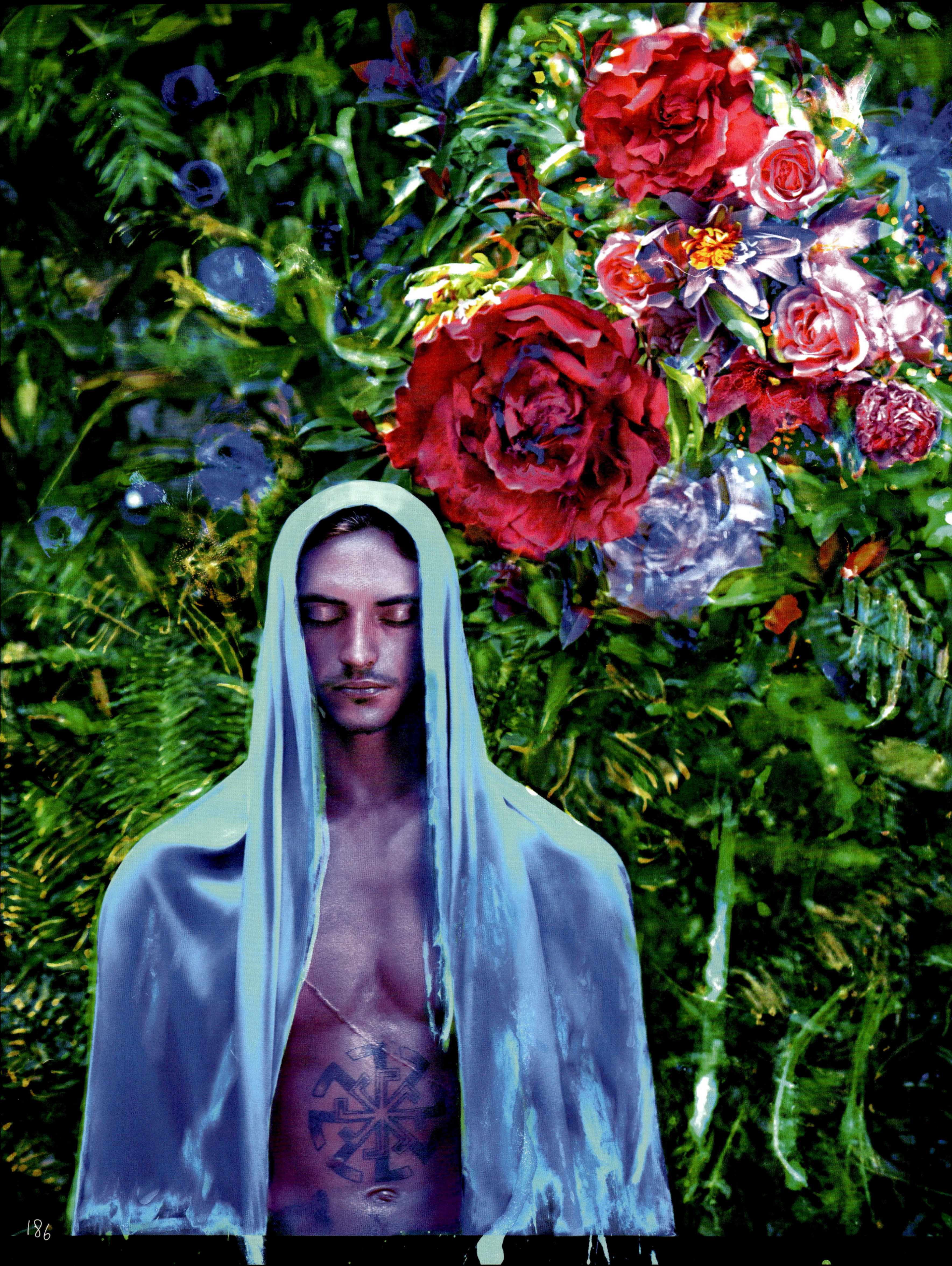

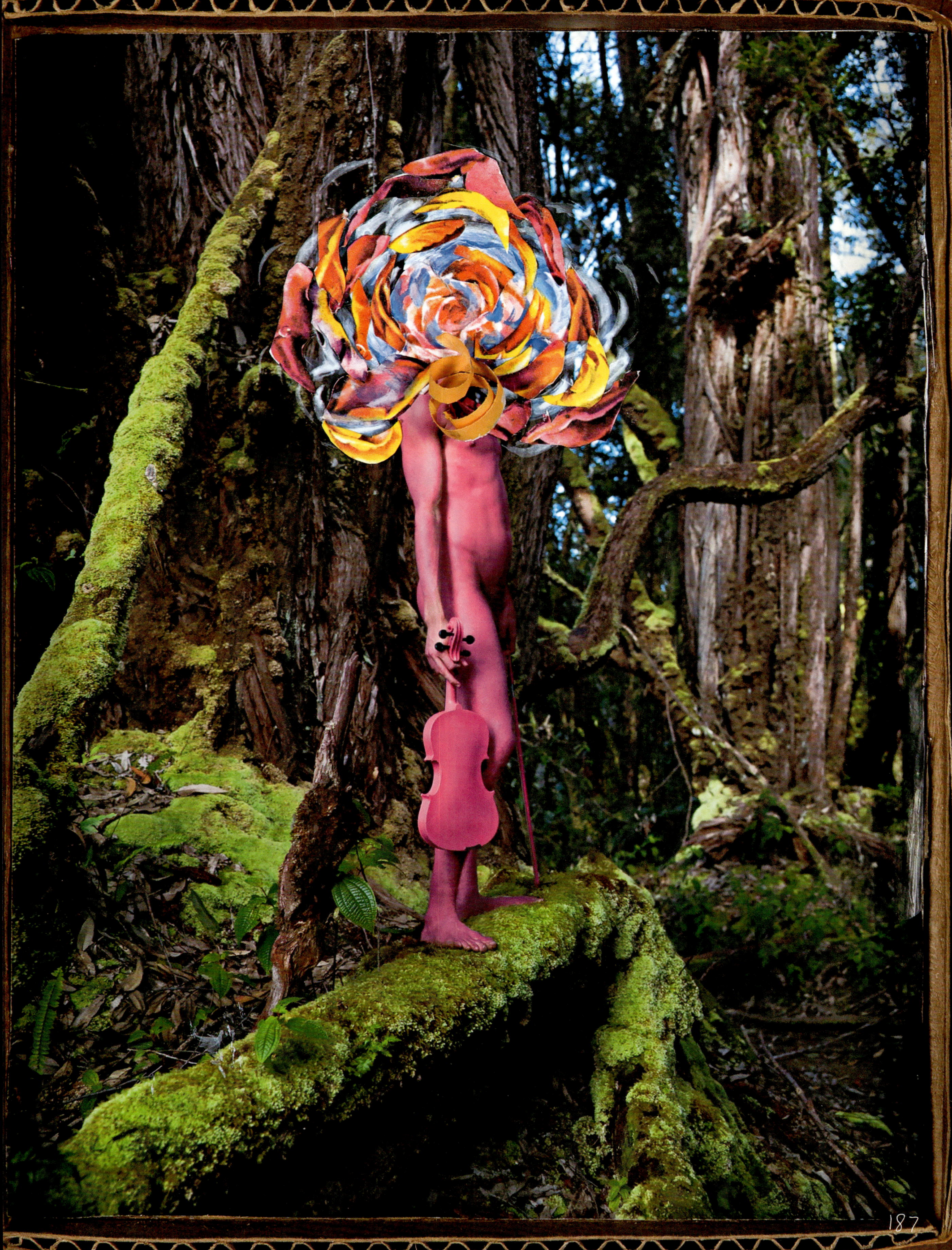

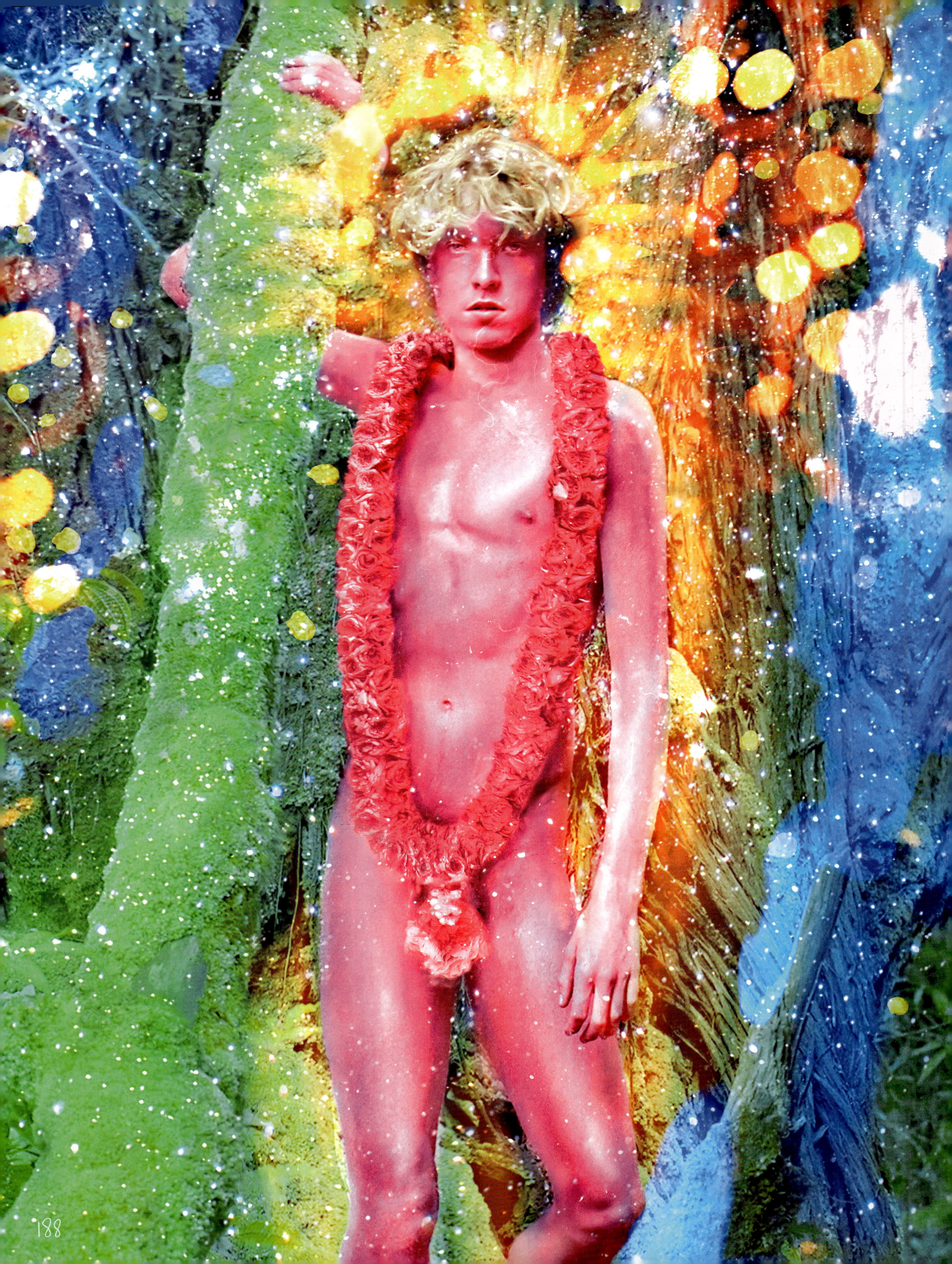

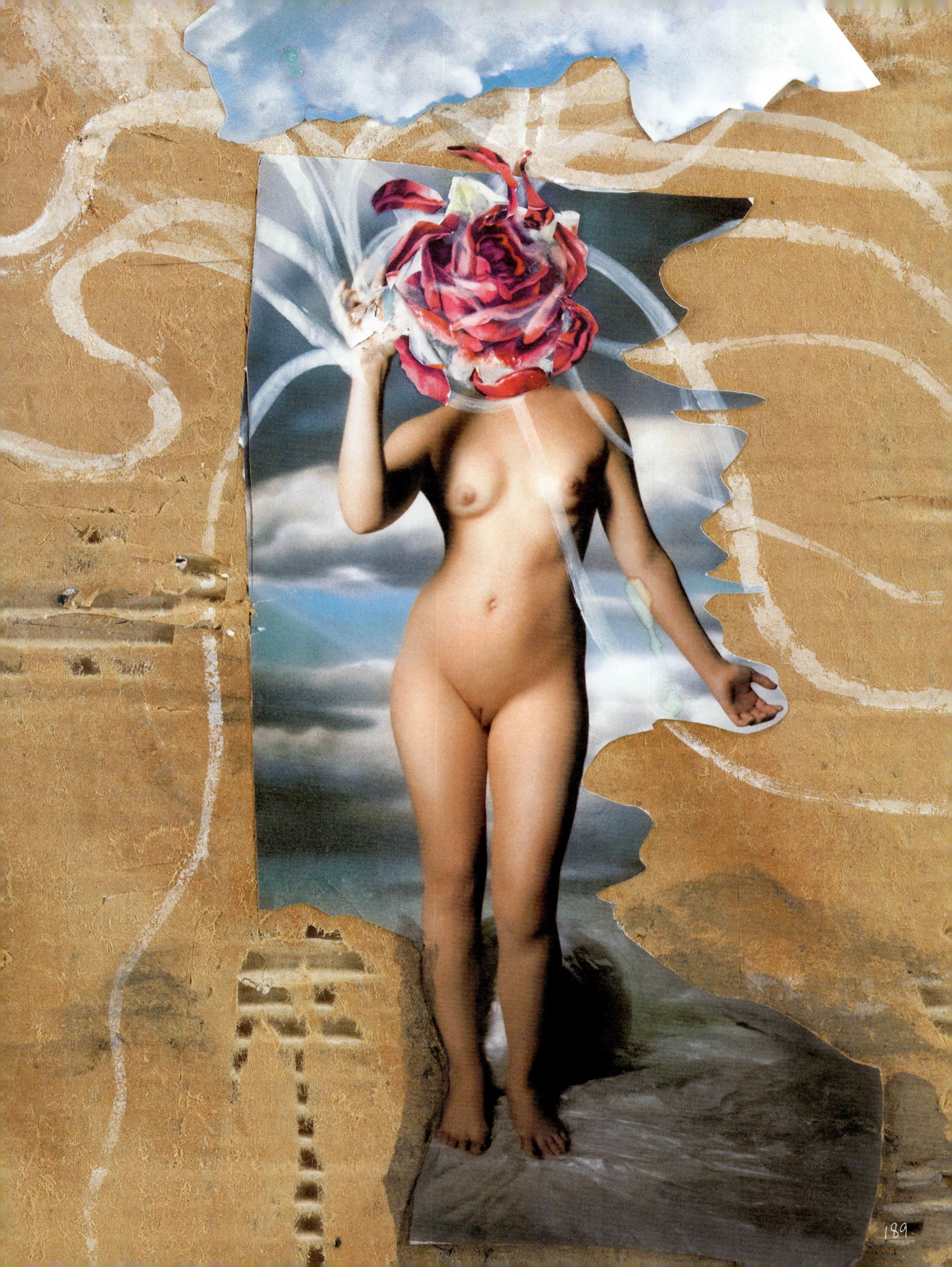

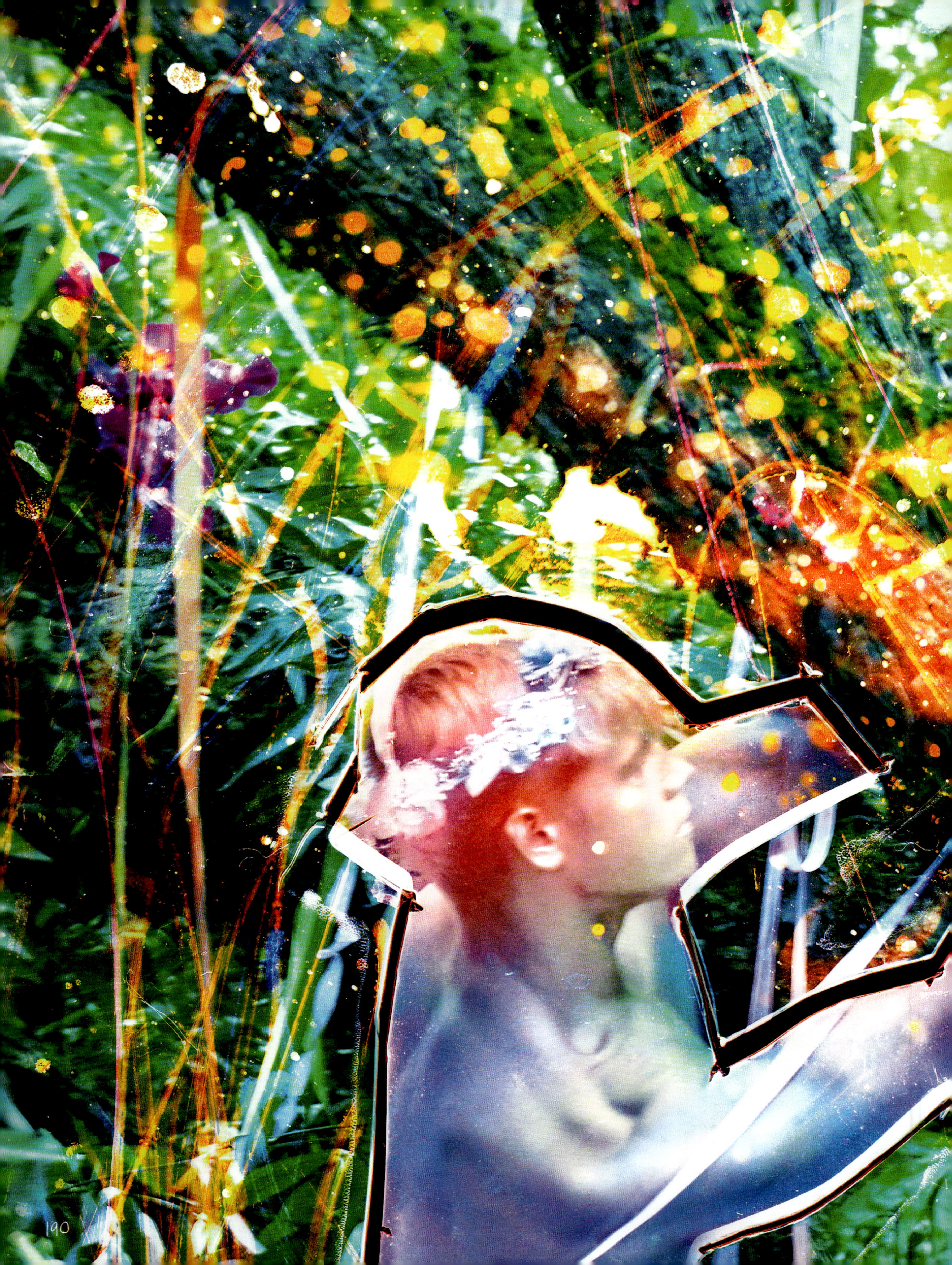

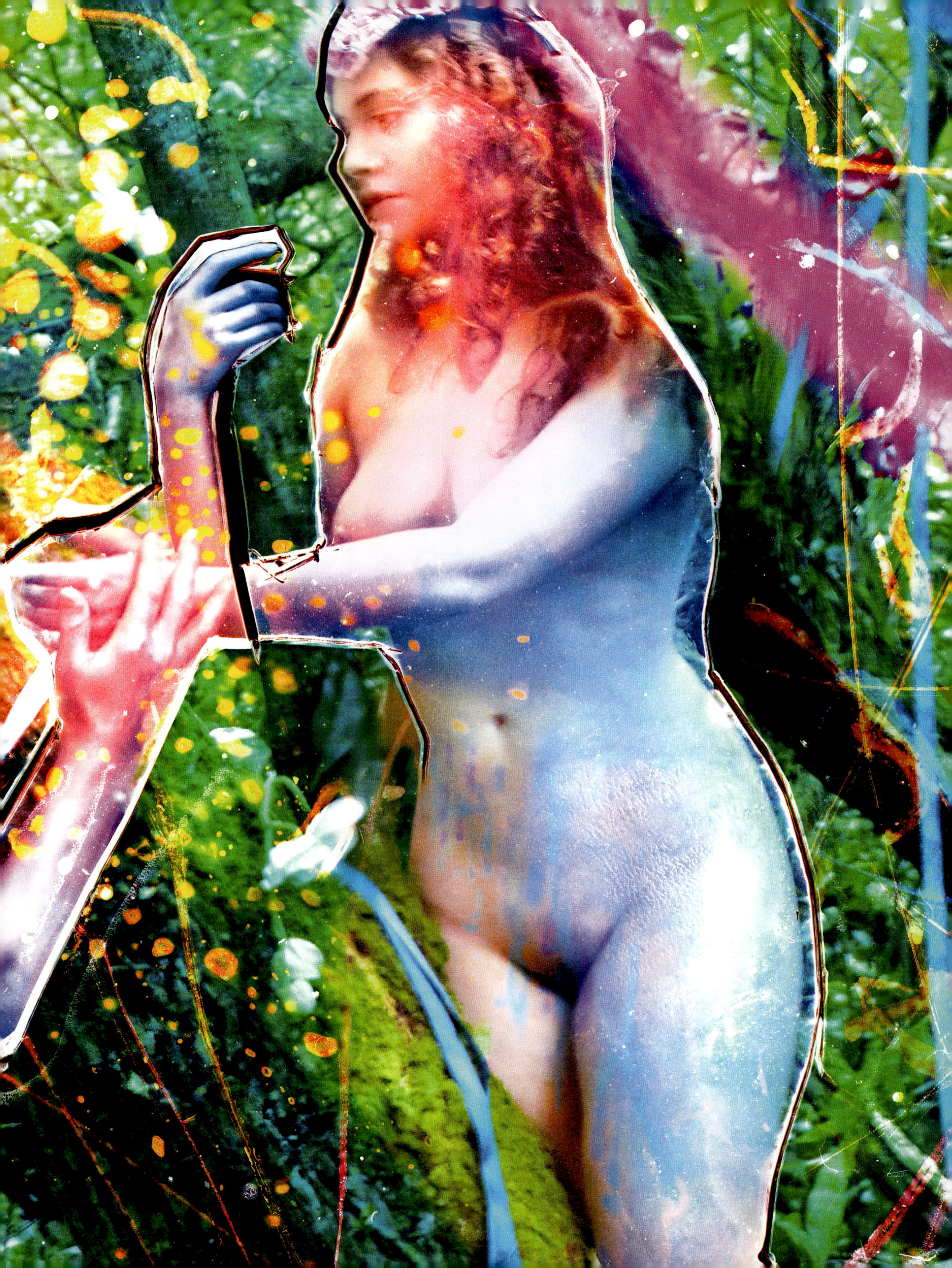

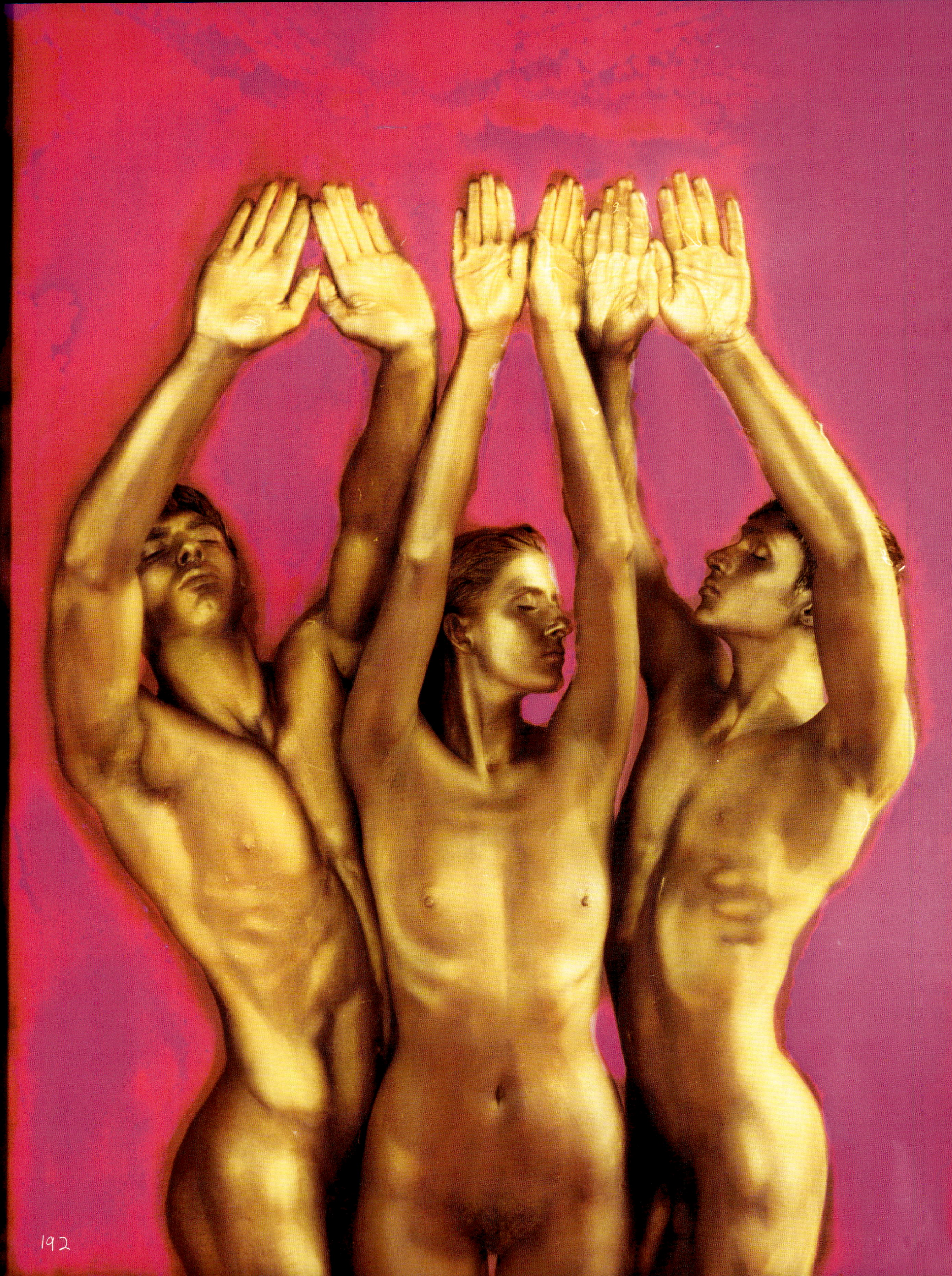

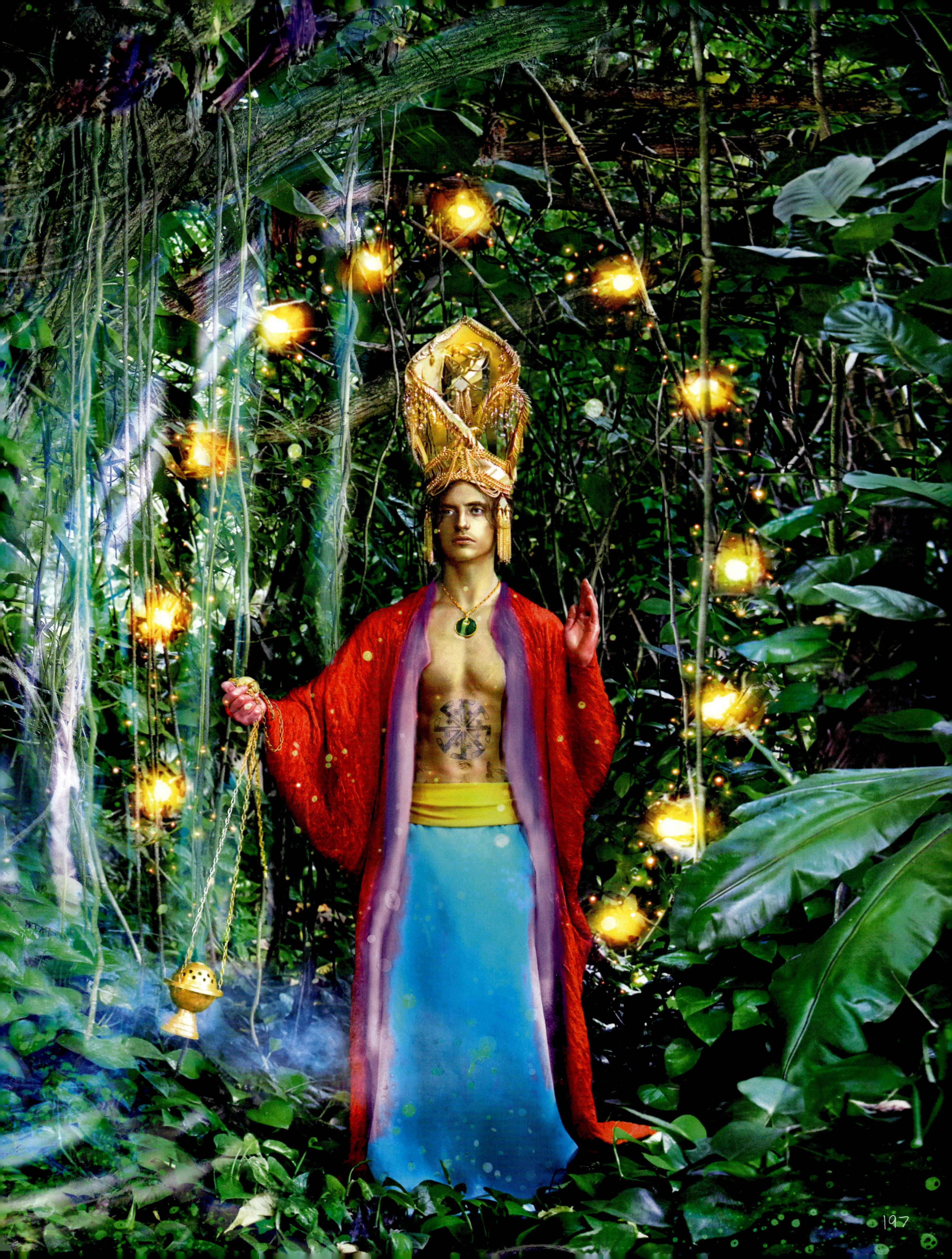

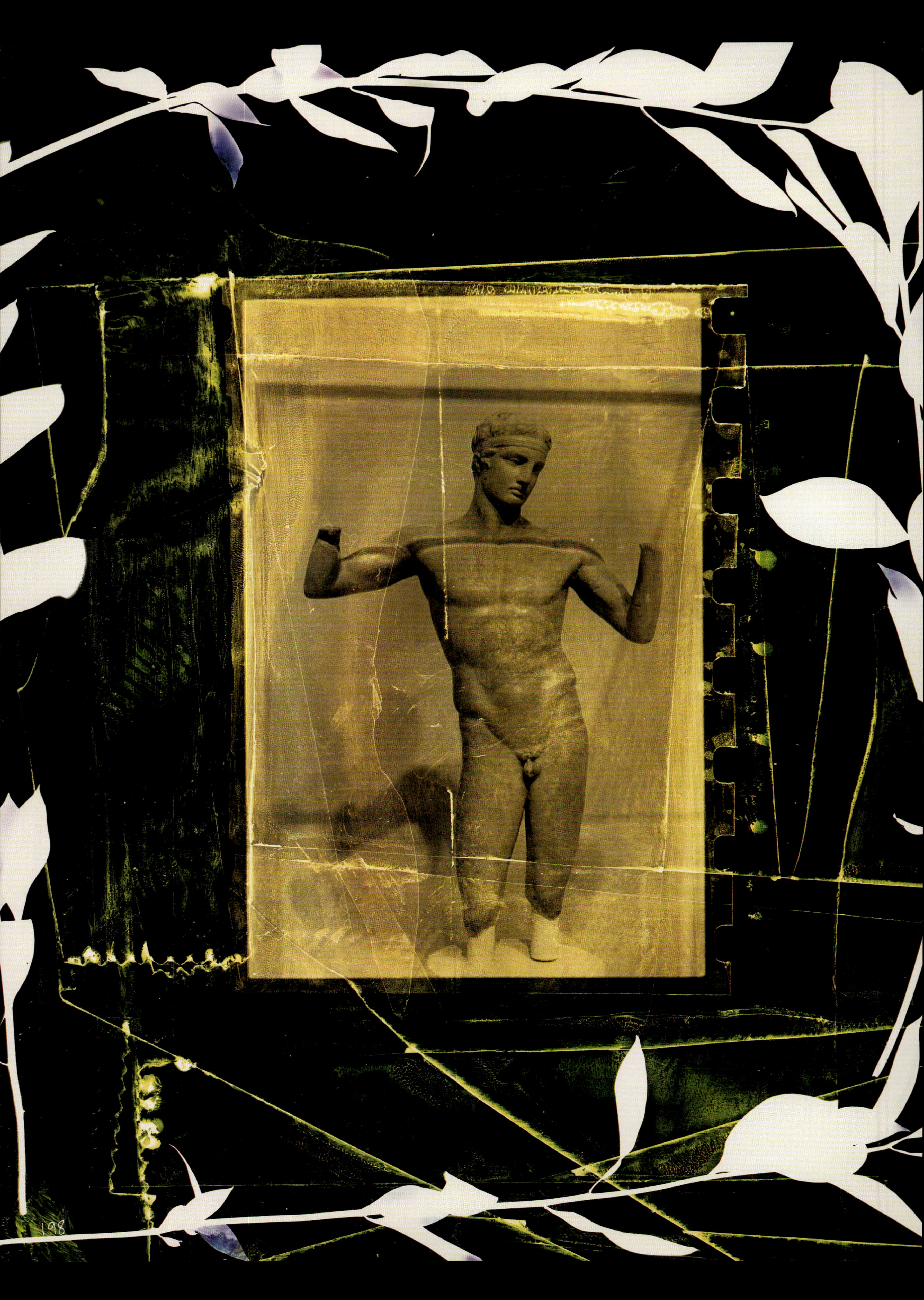
198

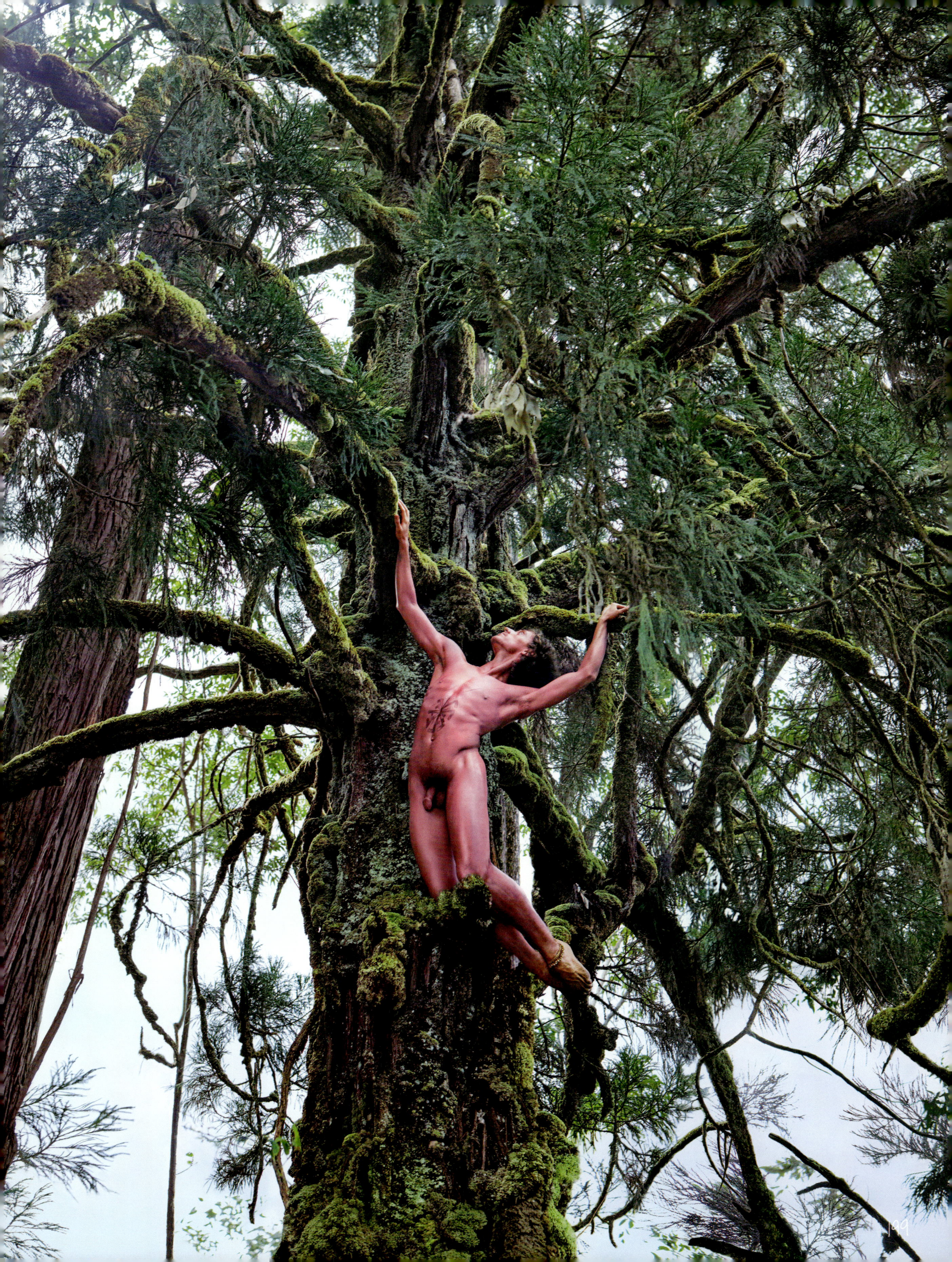

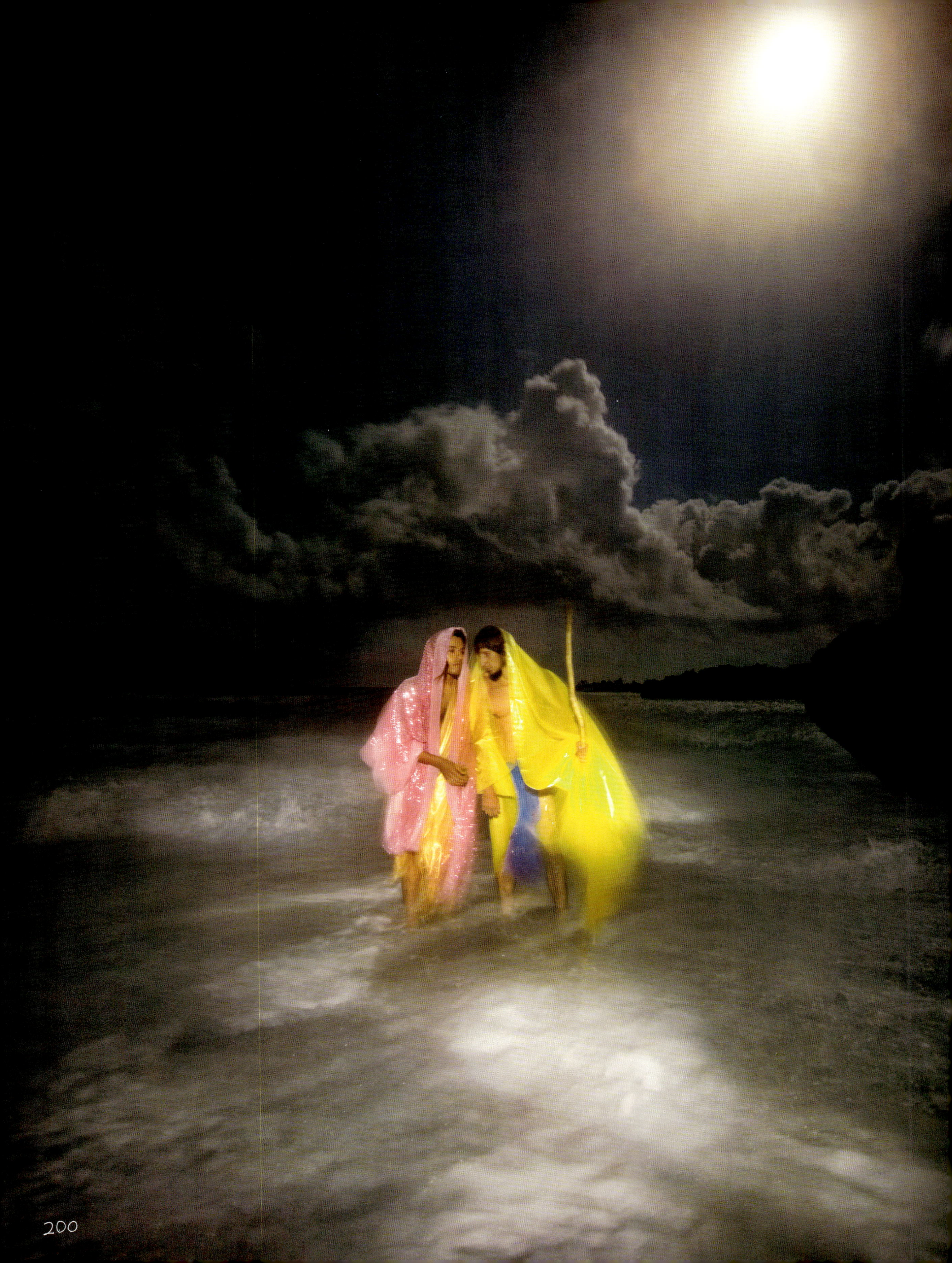

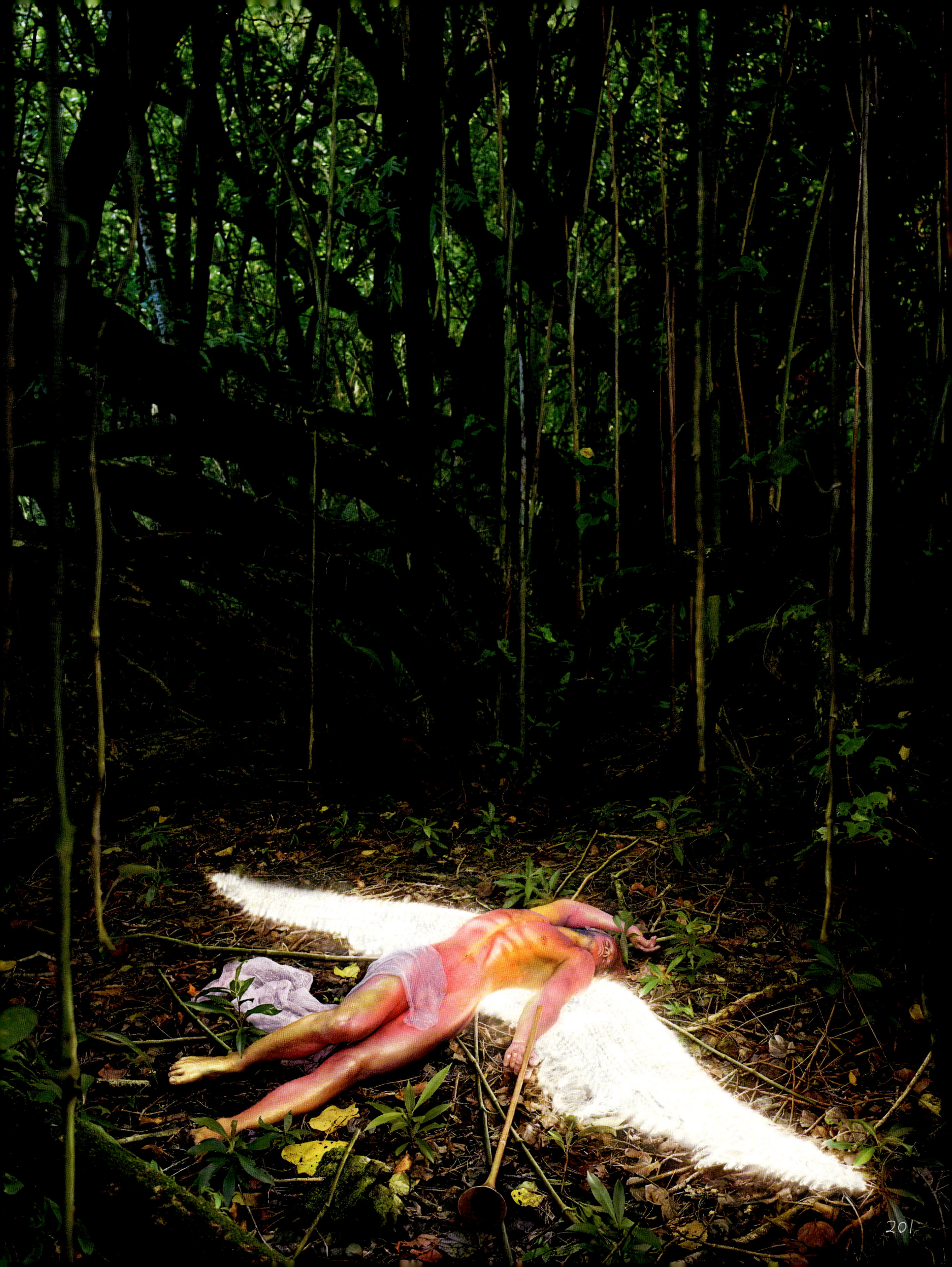

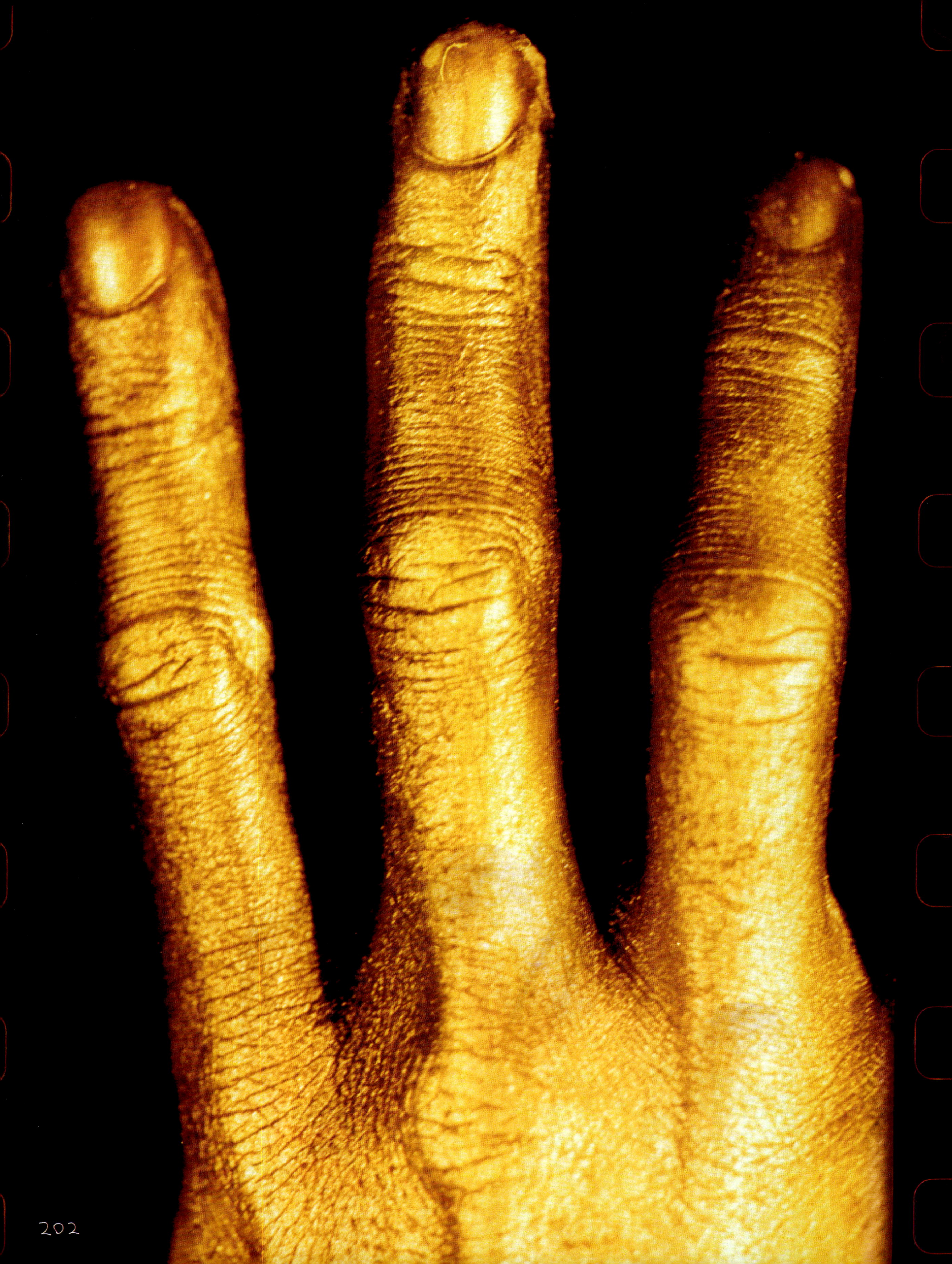

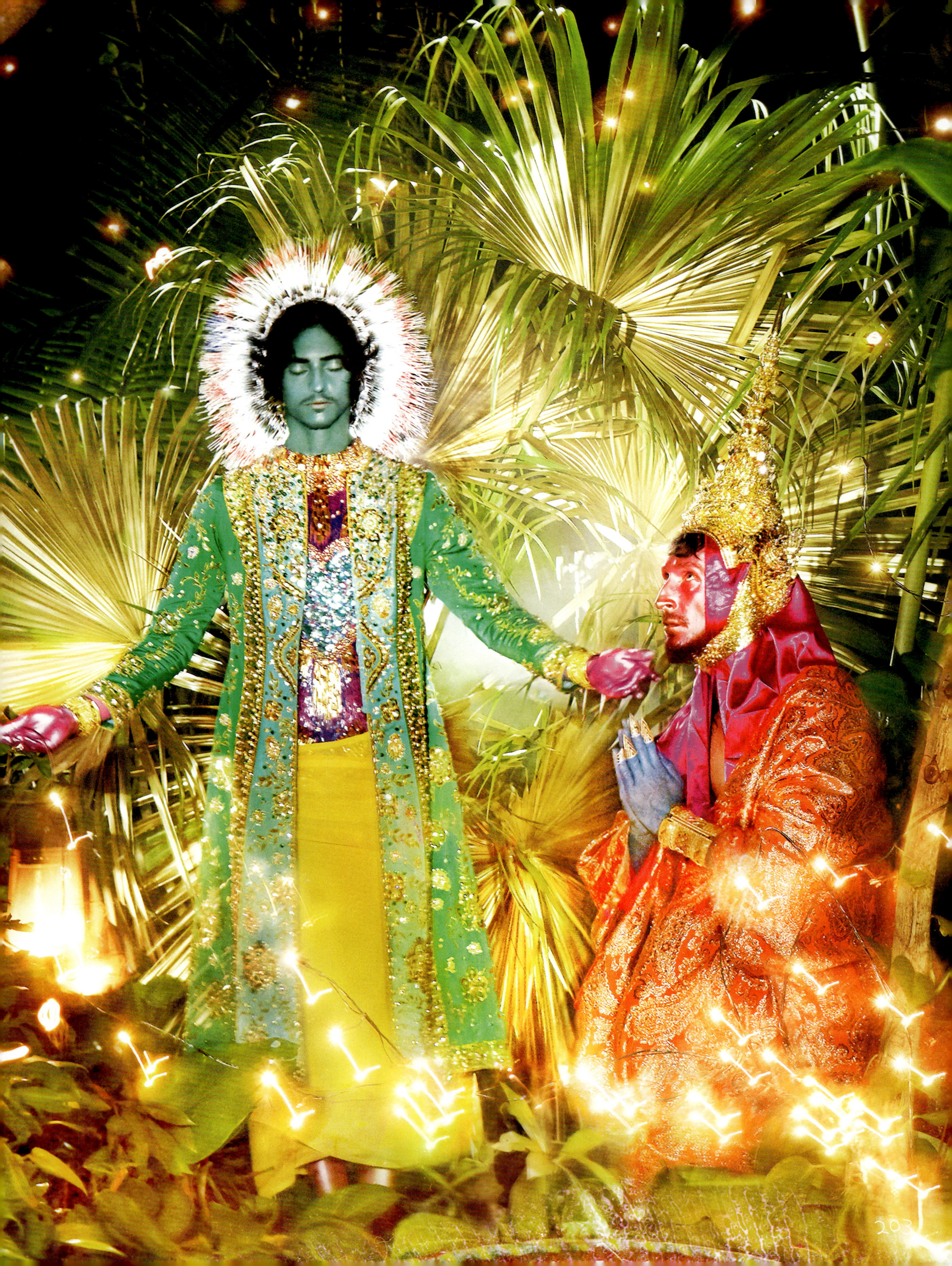

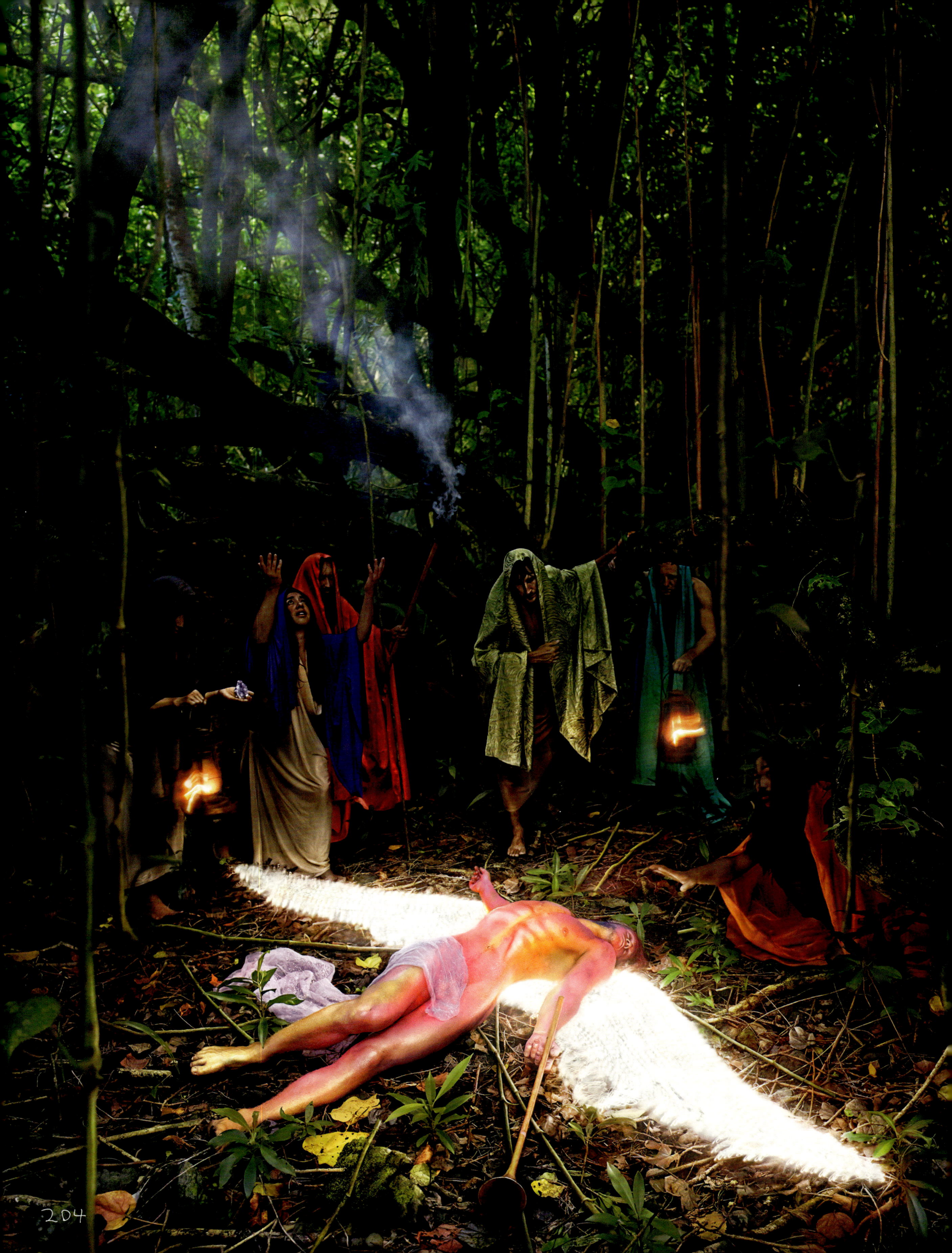

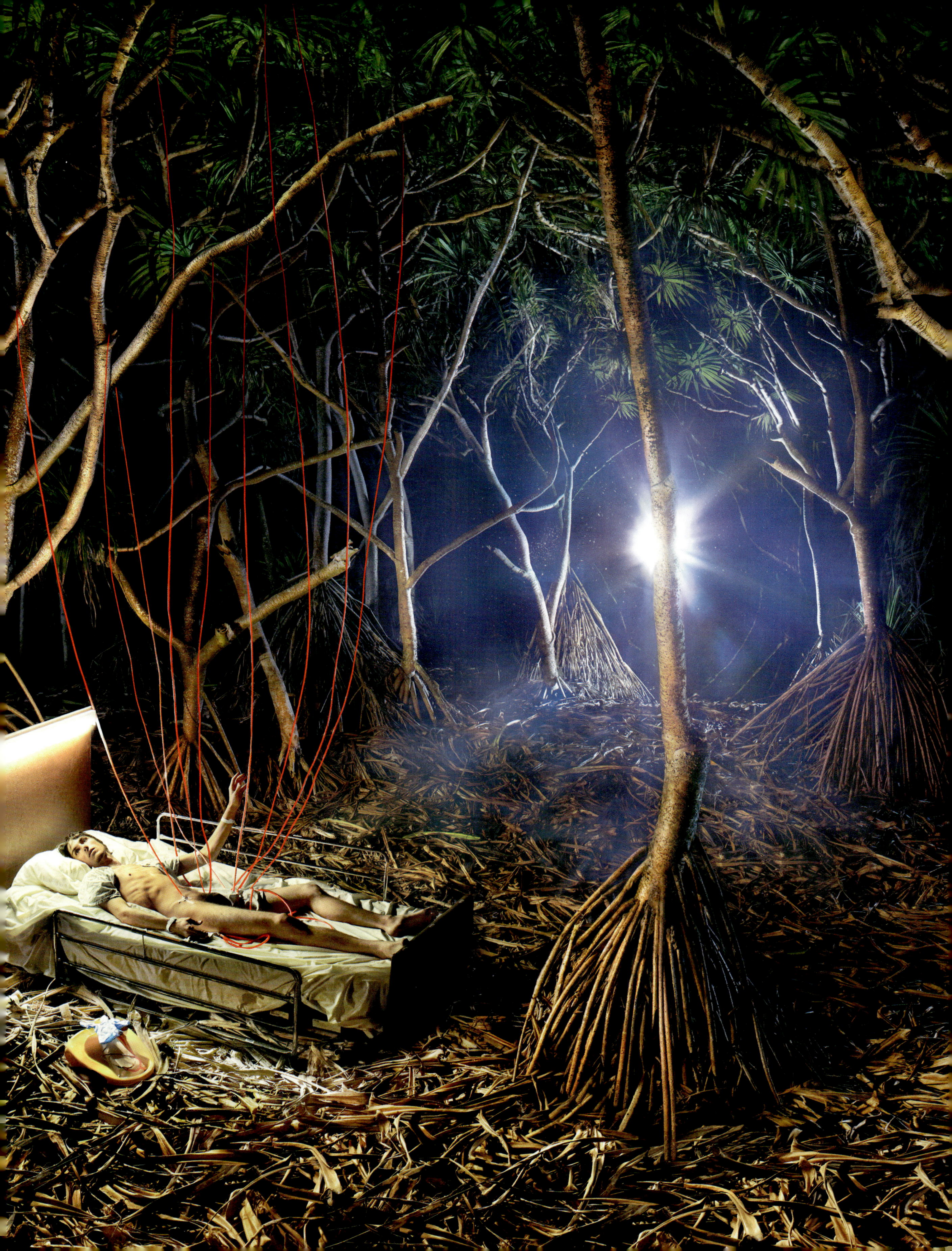

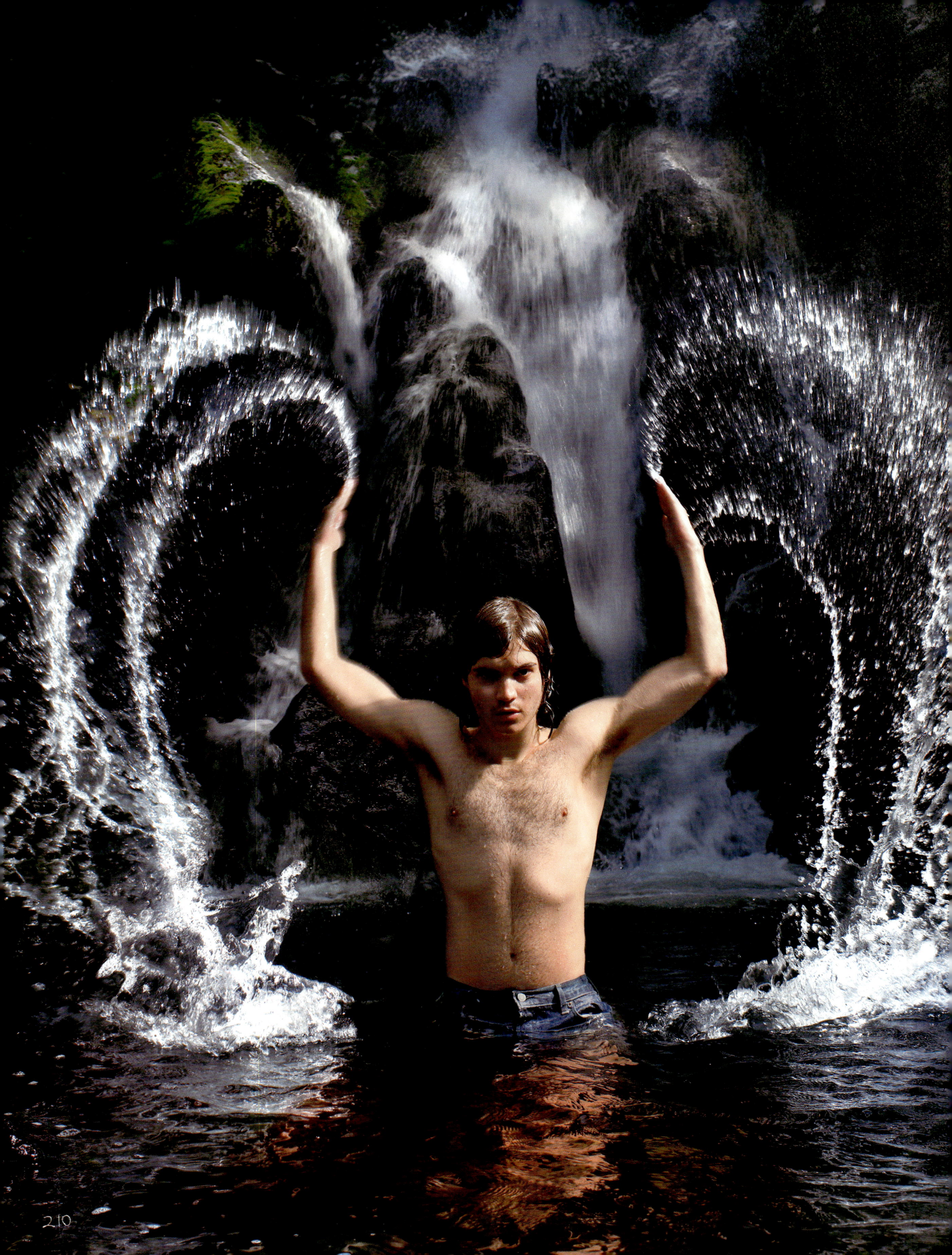

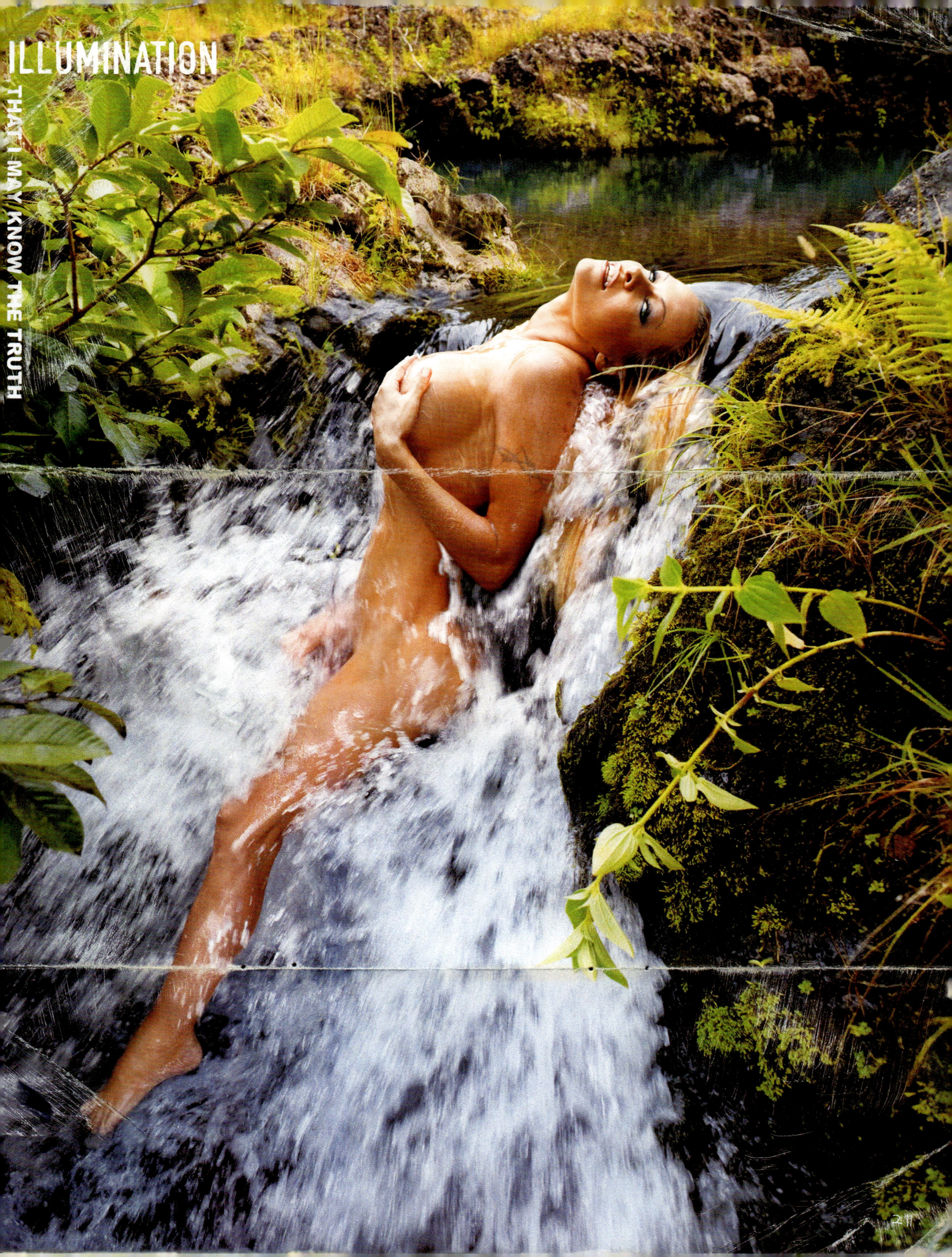
ILLUMINATION
THAT I MAY KNOW THE TRUTH

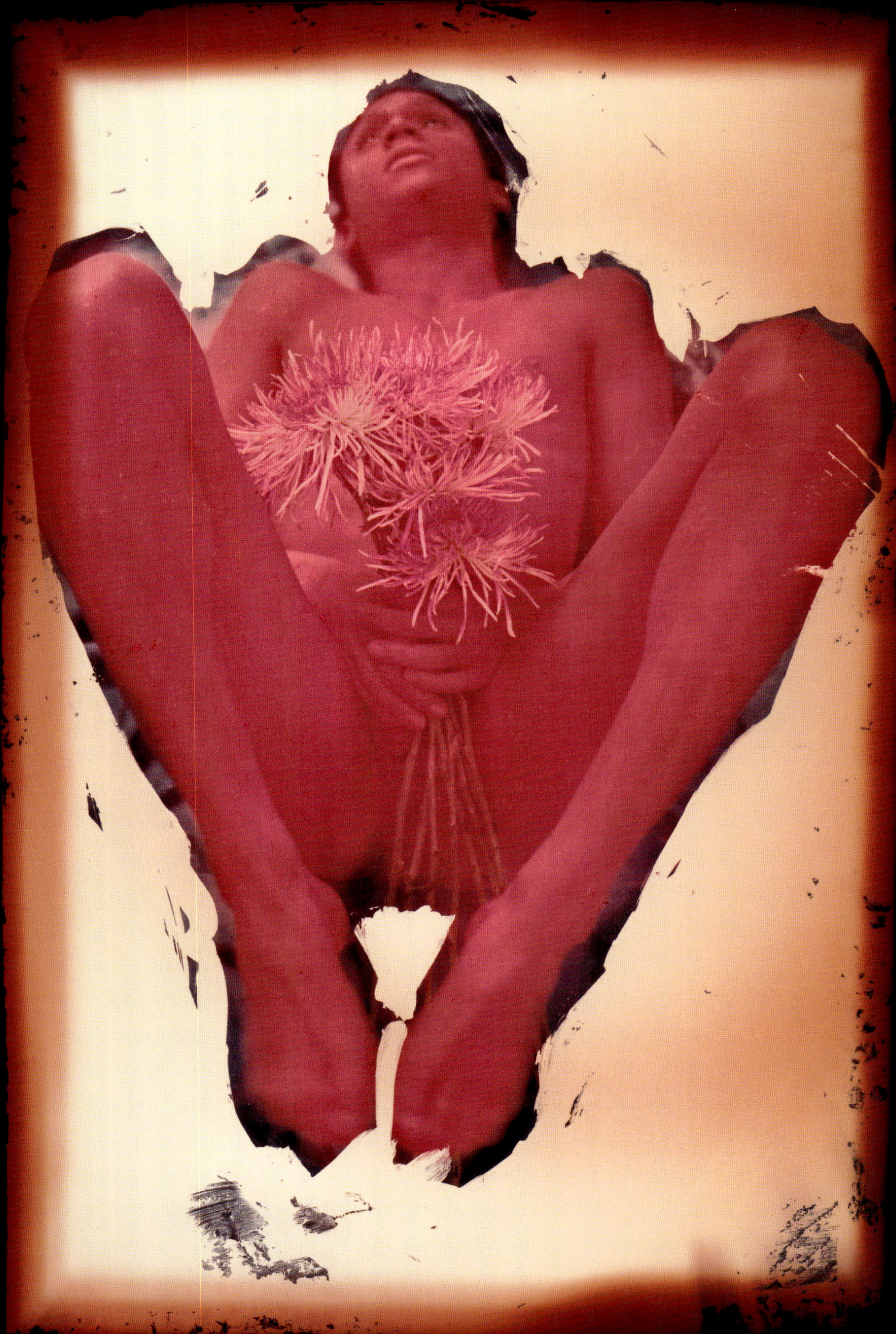

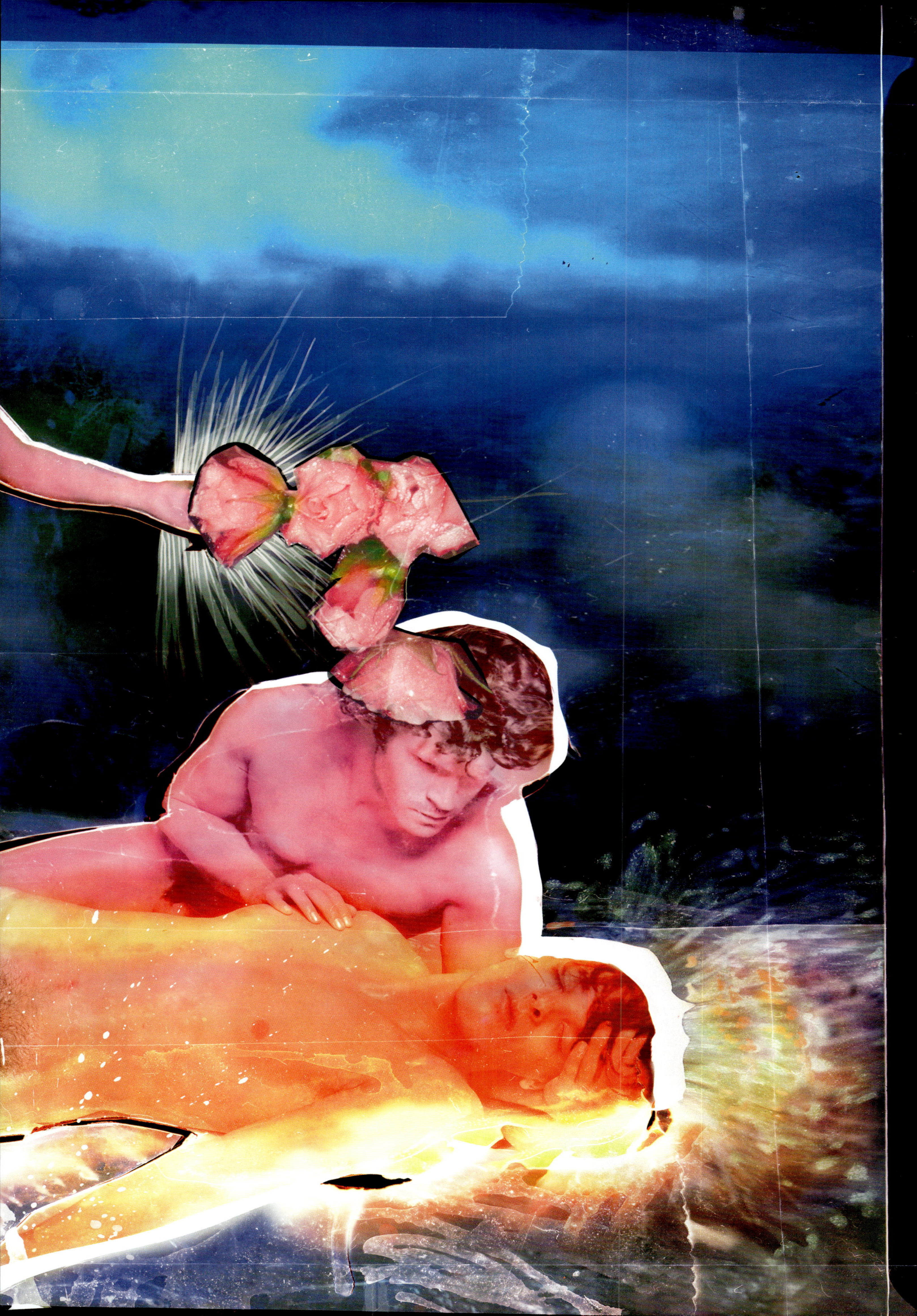

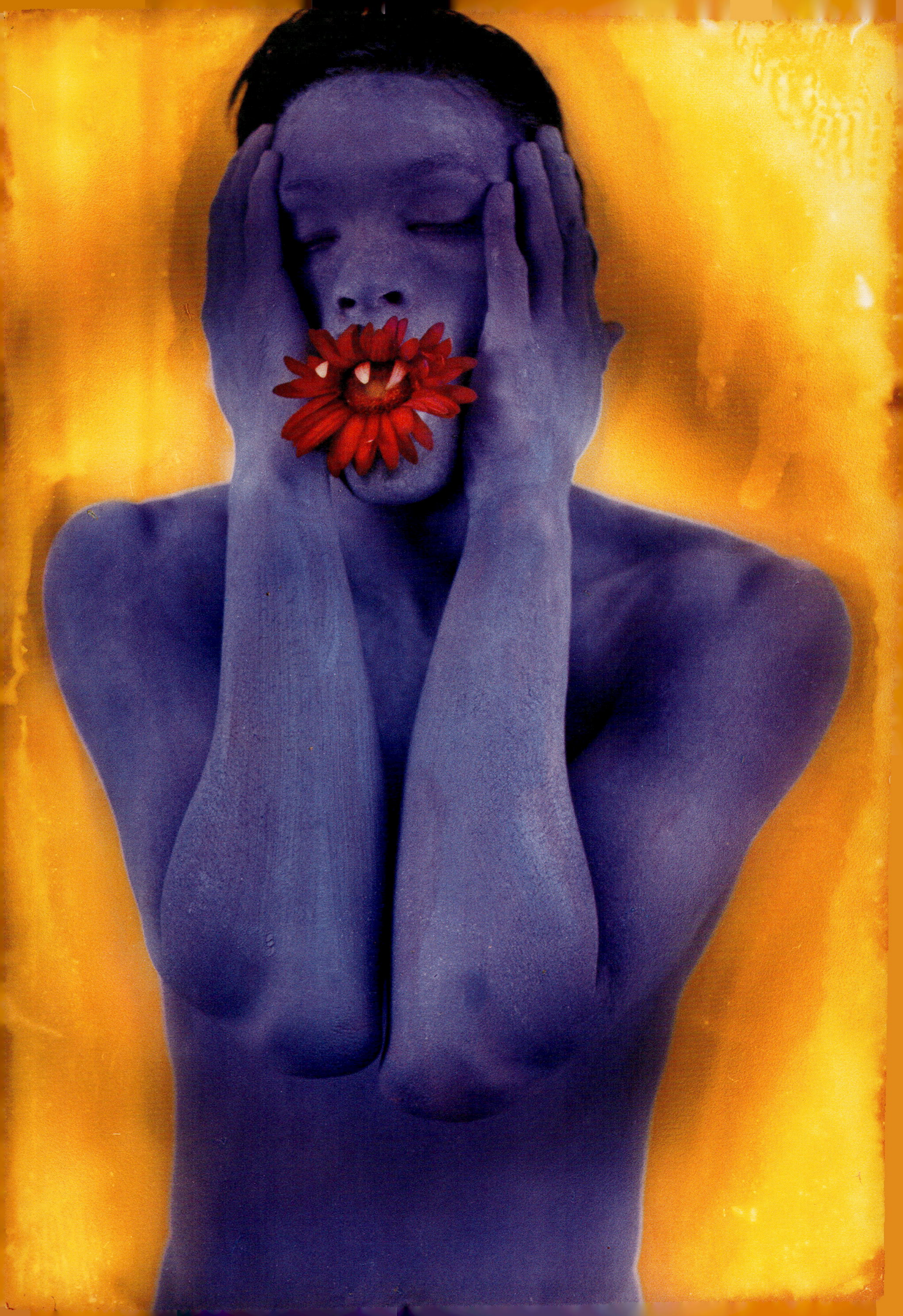

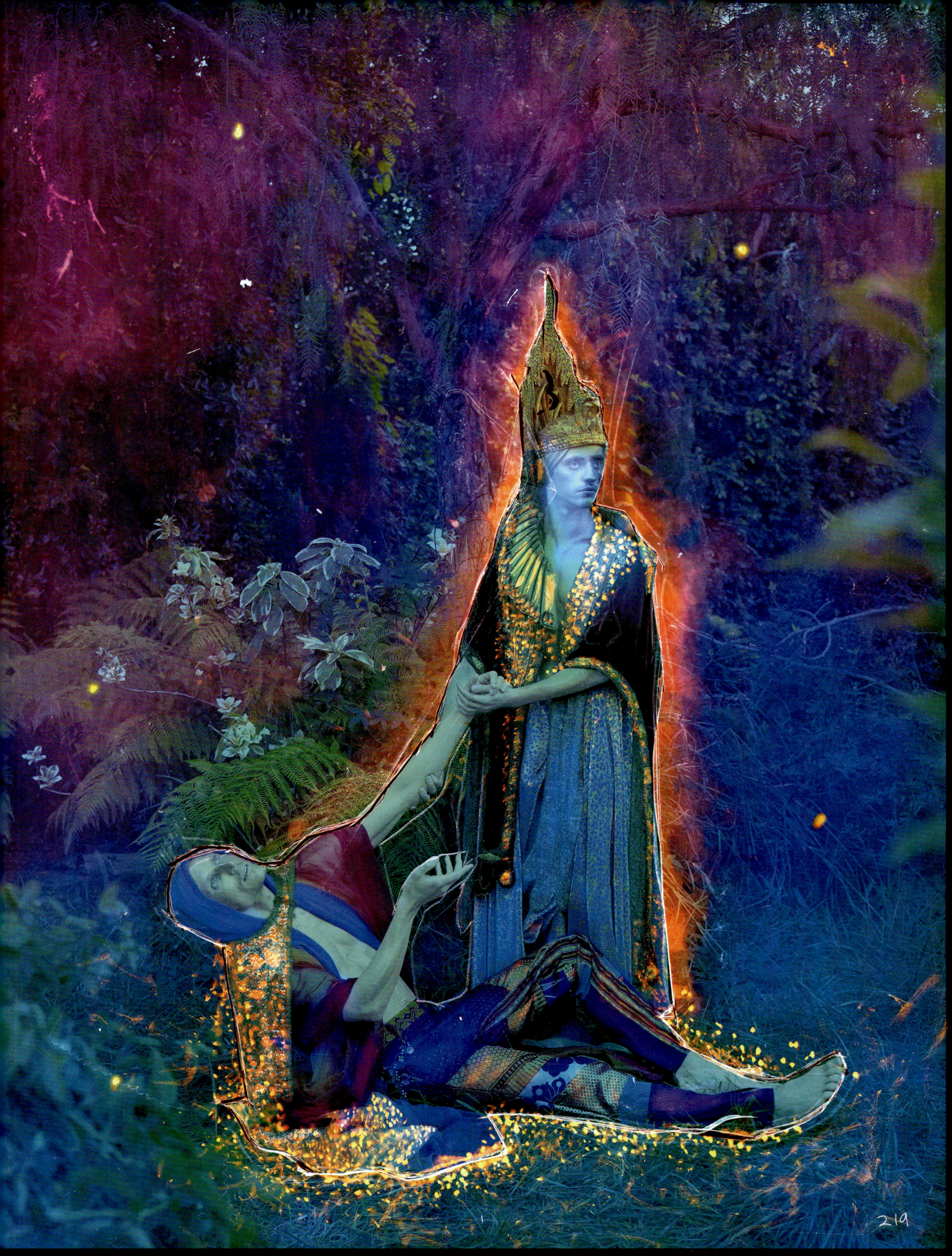

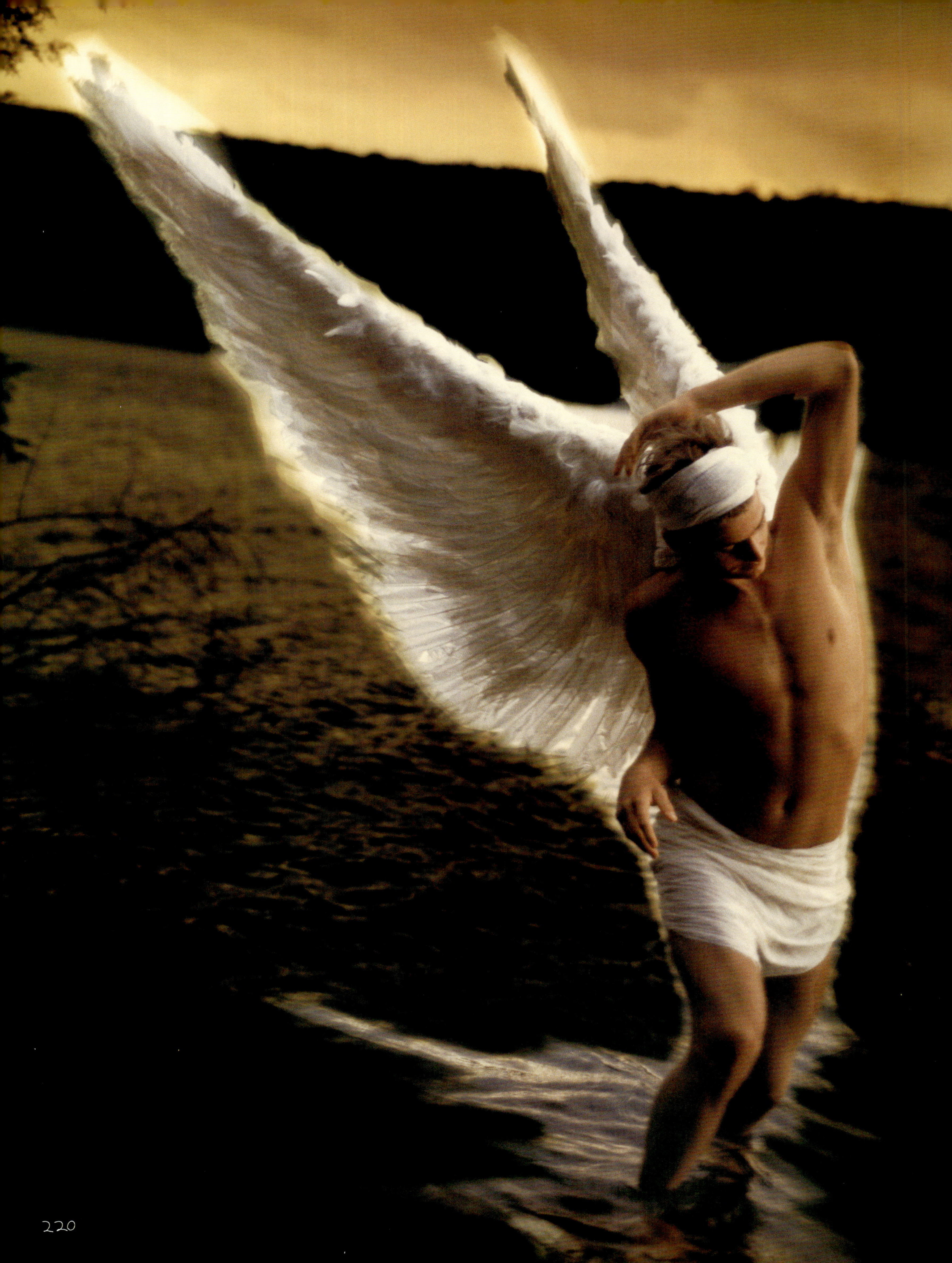

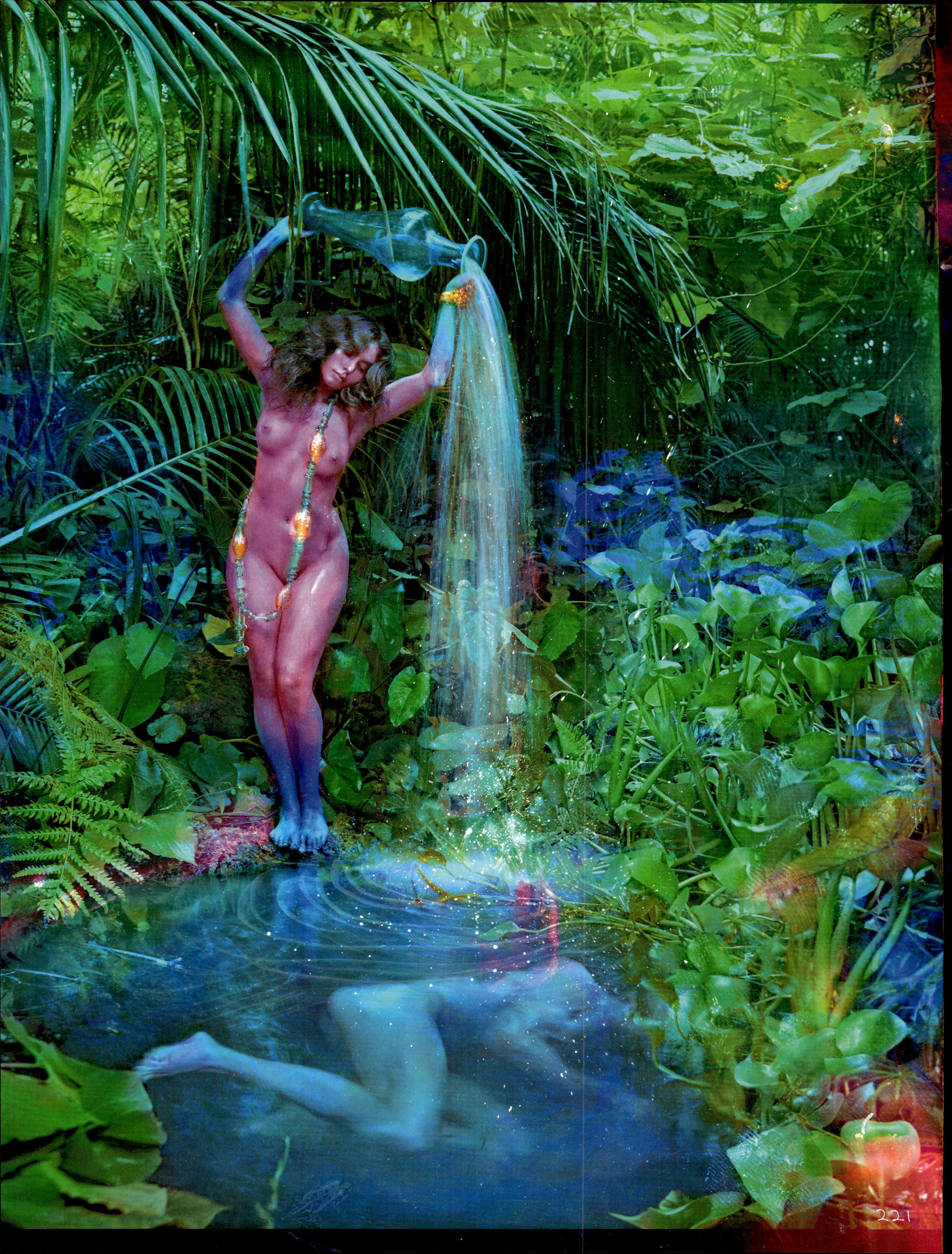

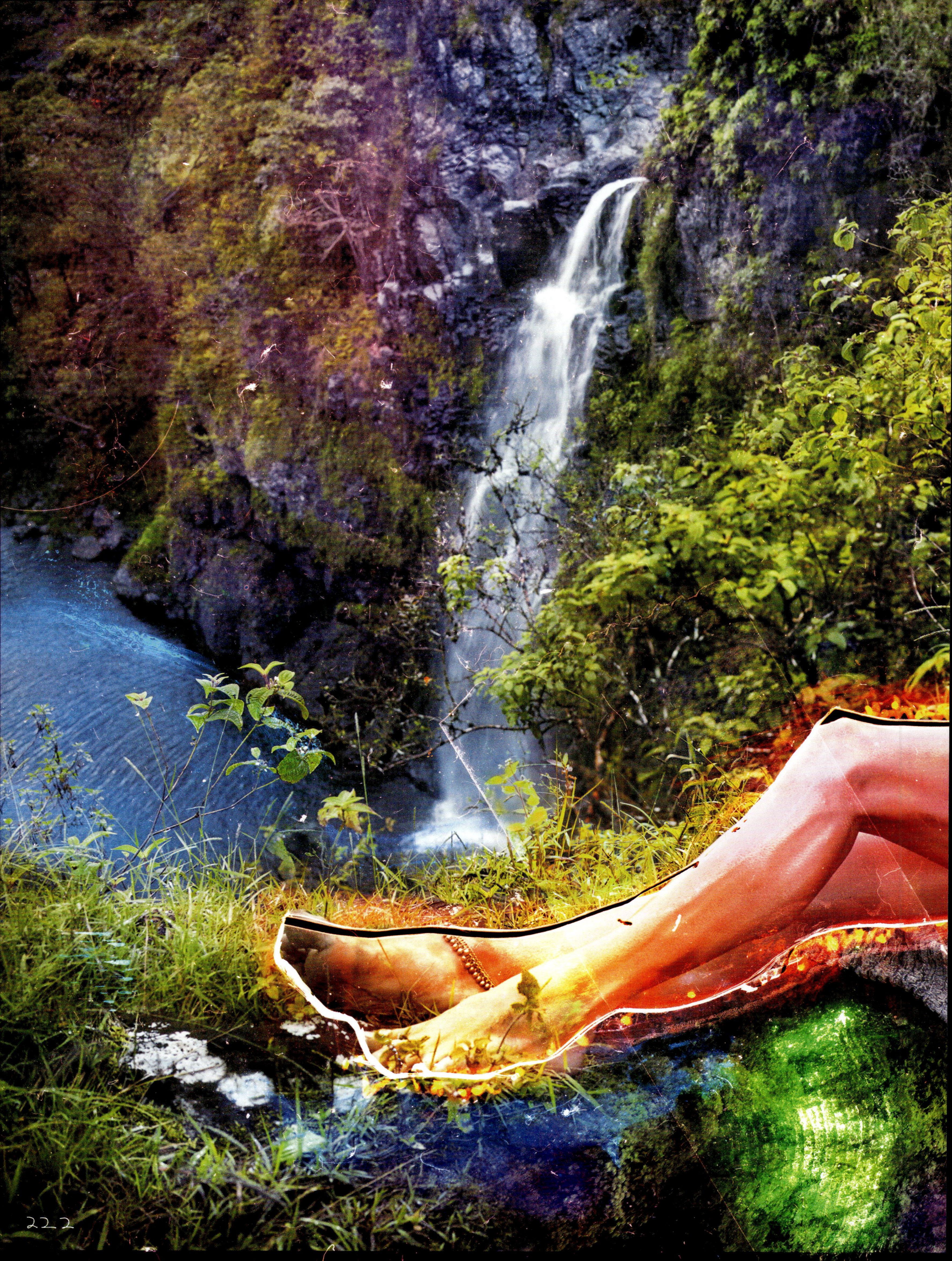

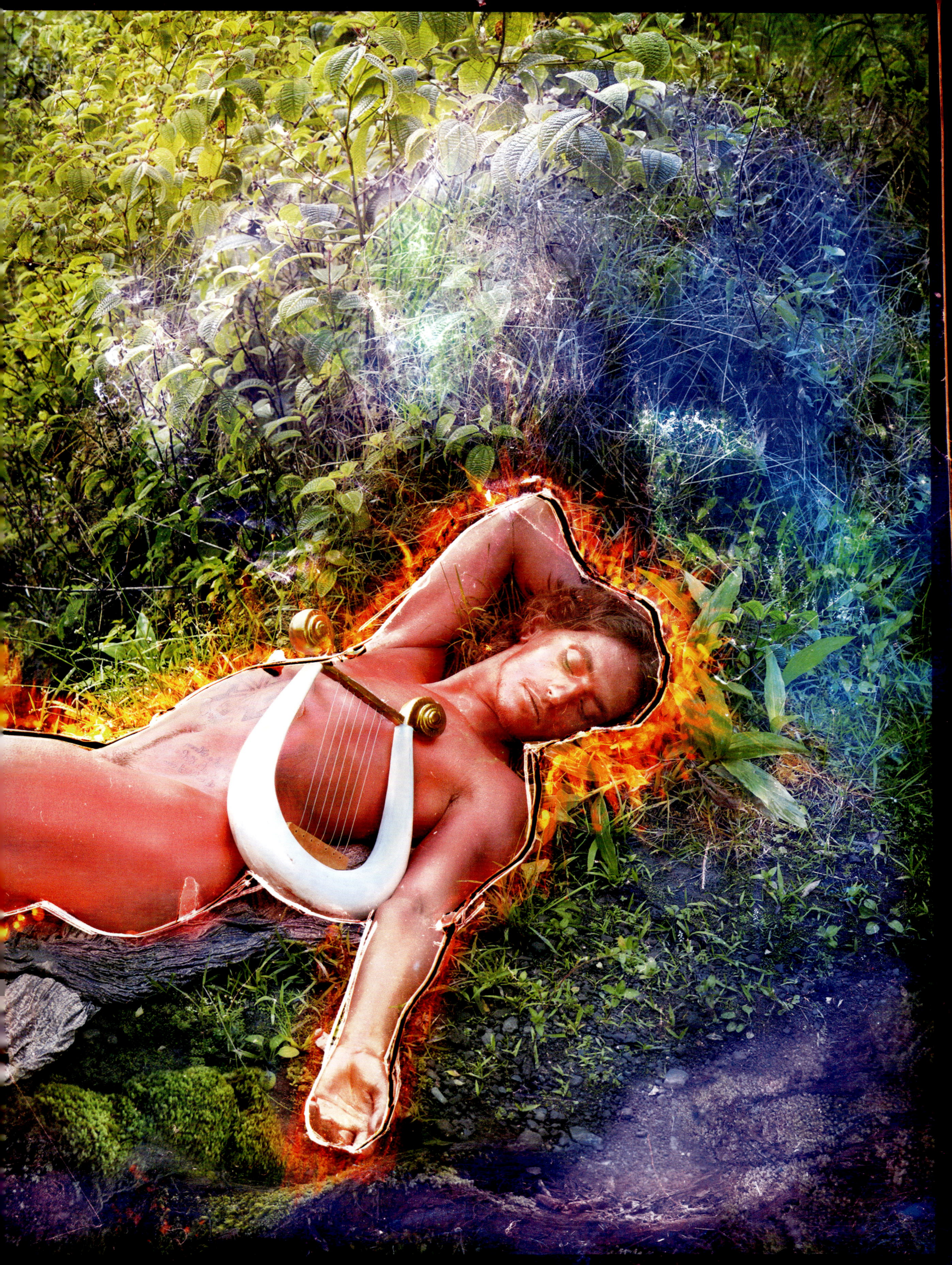

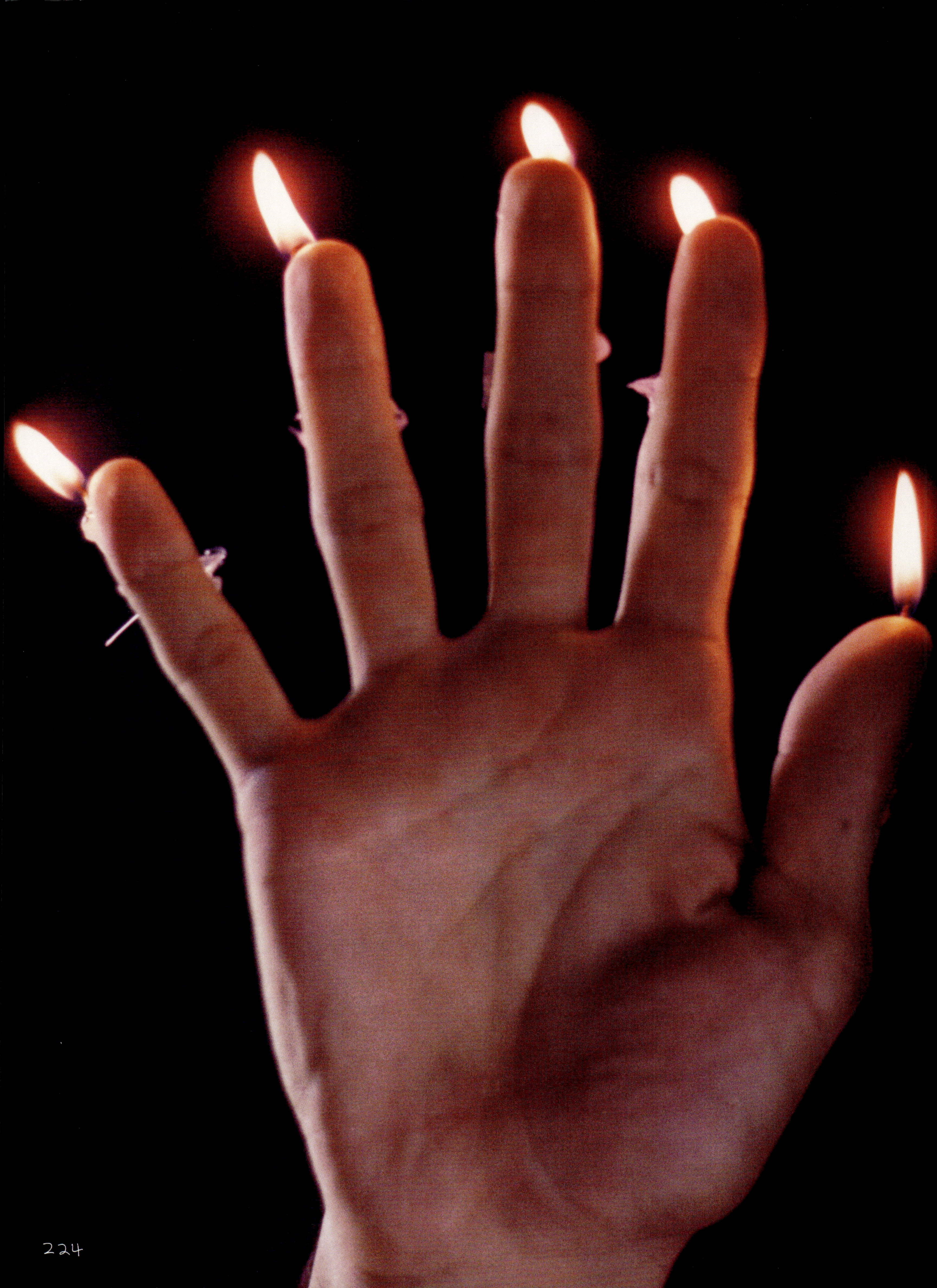

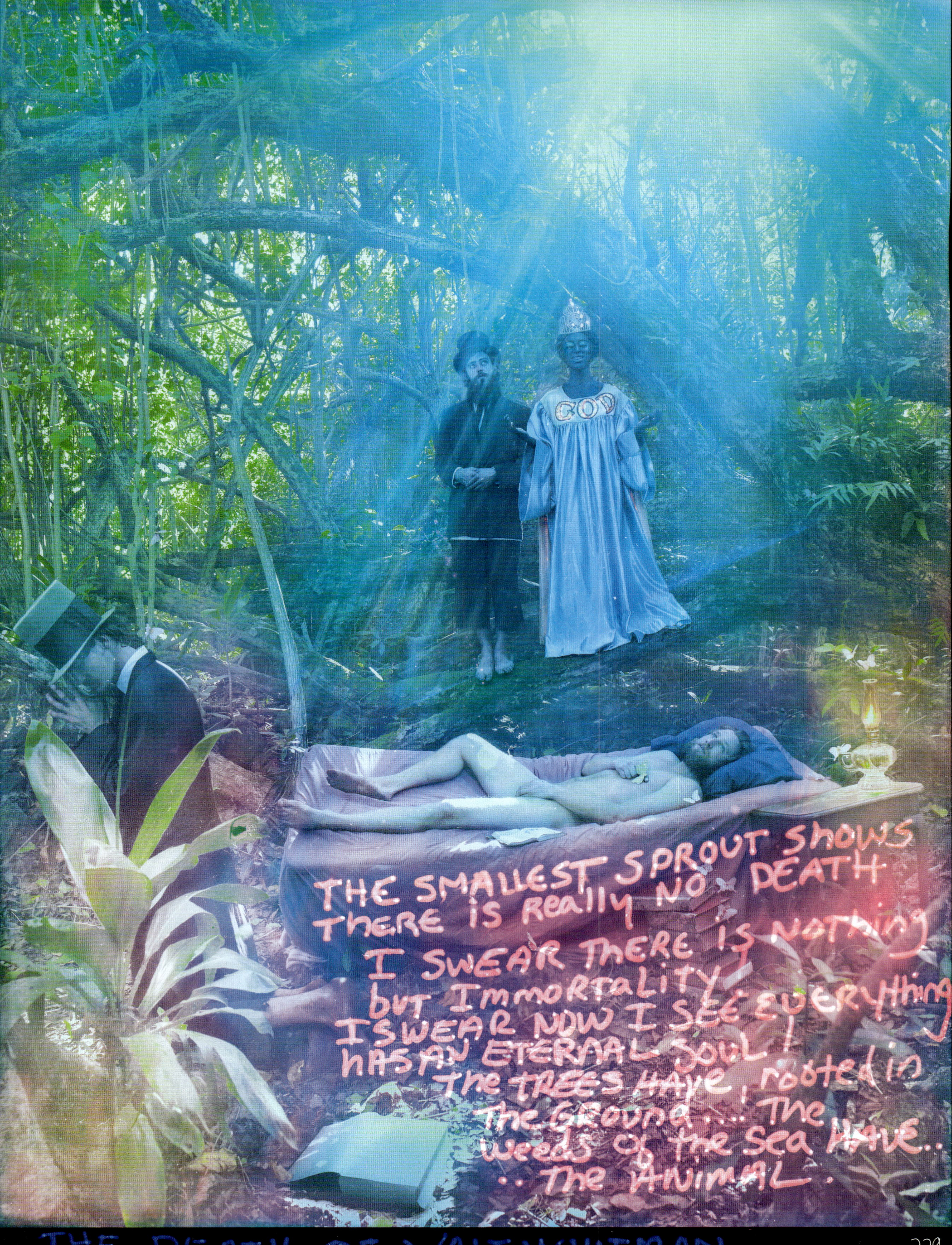

THE DEATH OF WALT WHITMAN

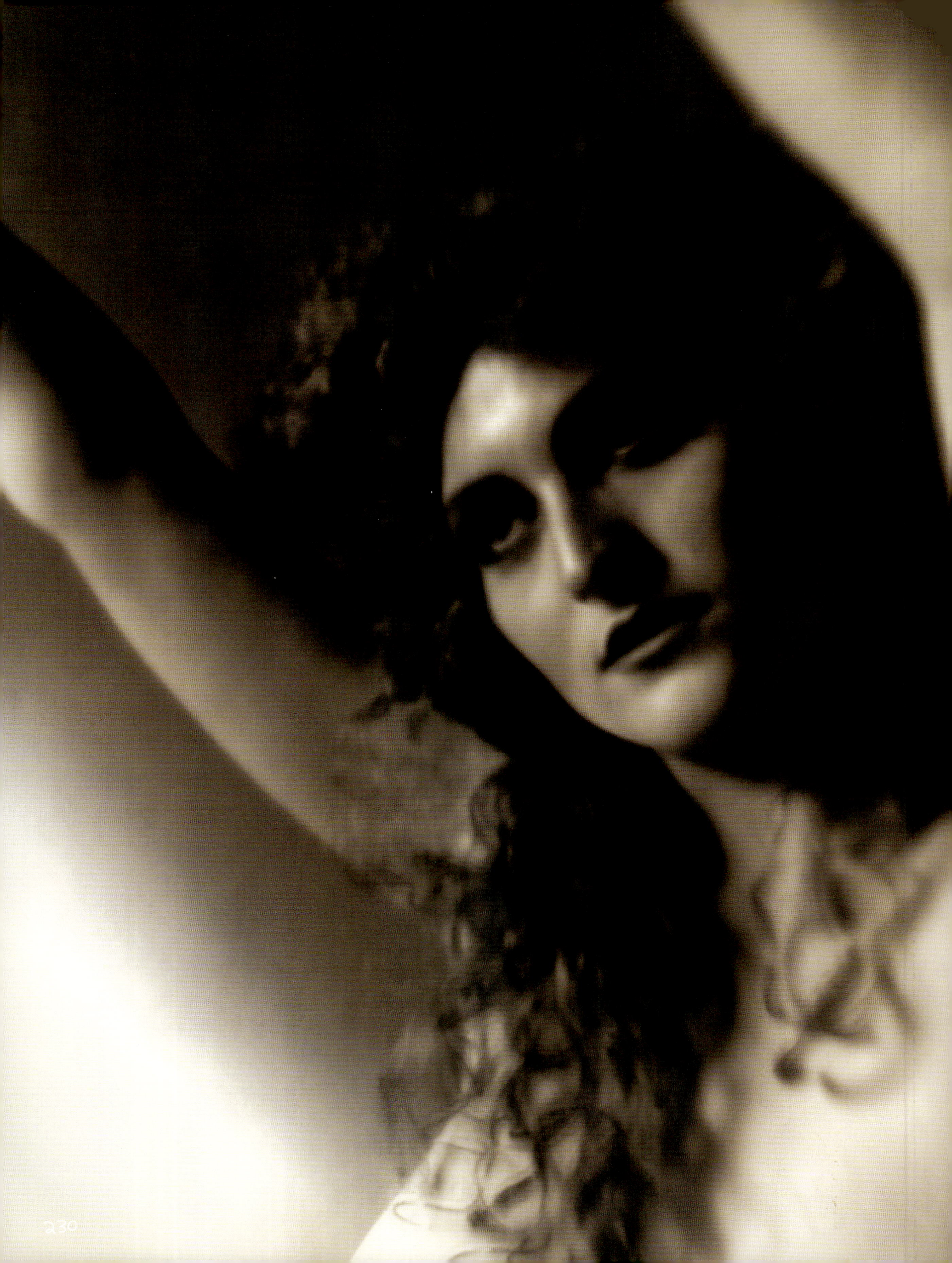

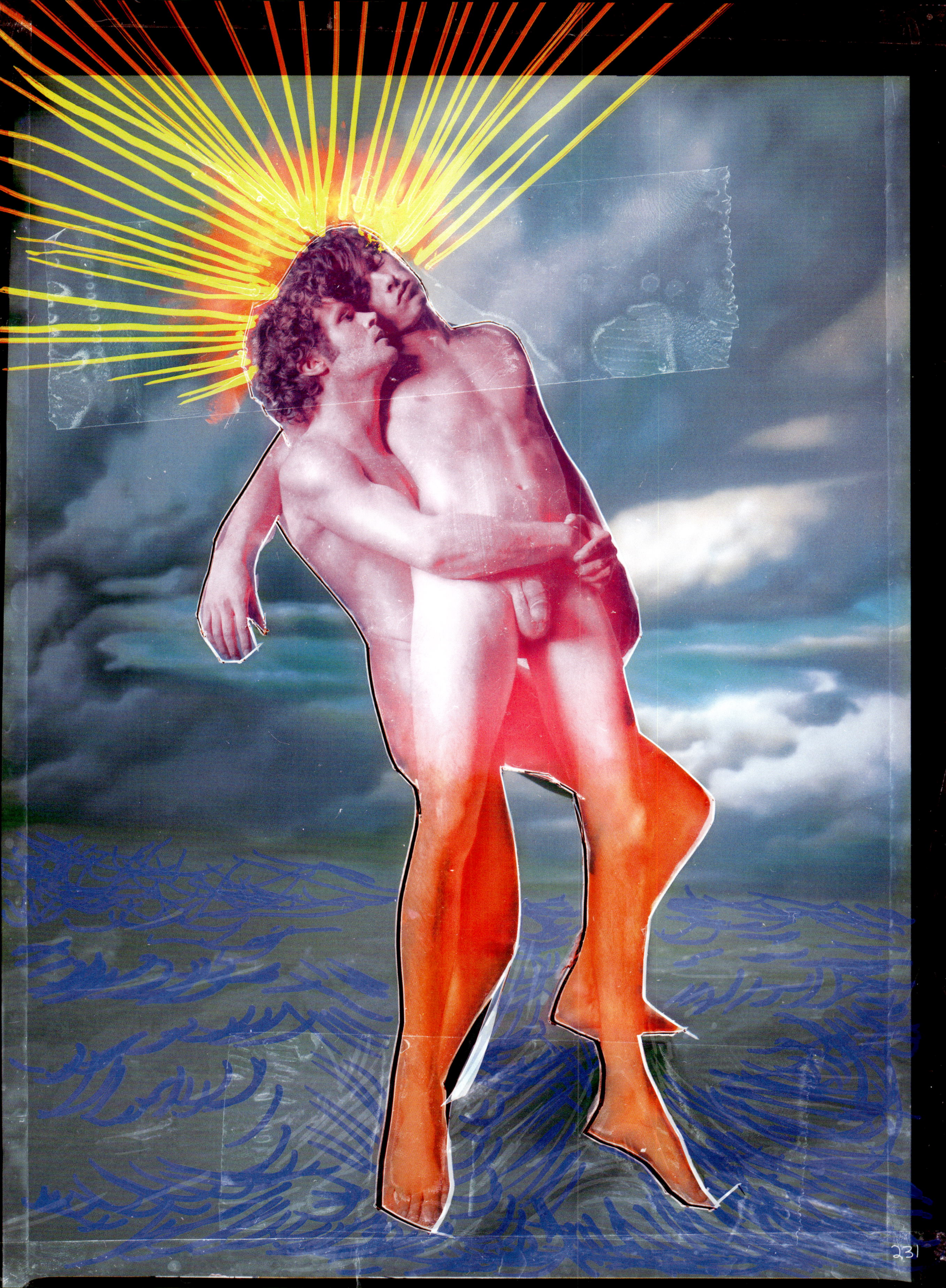
231

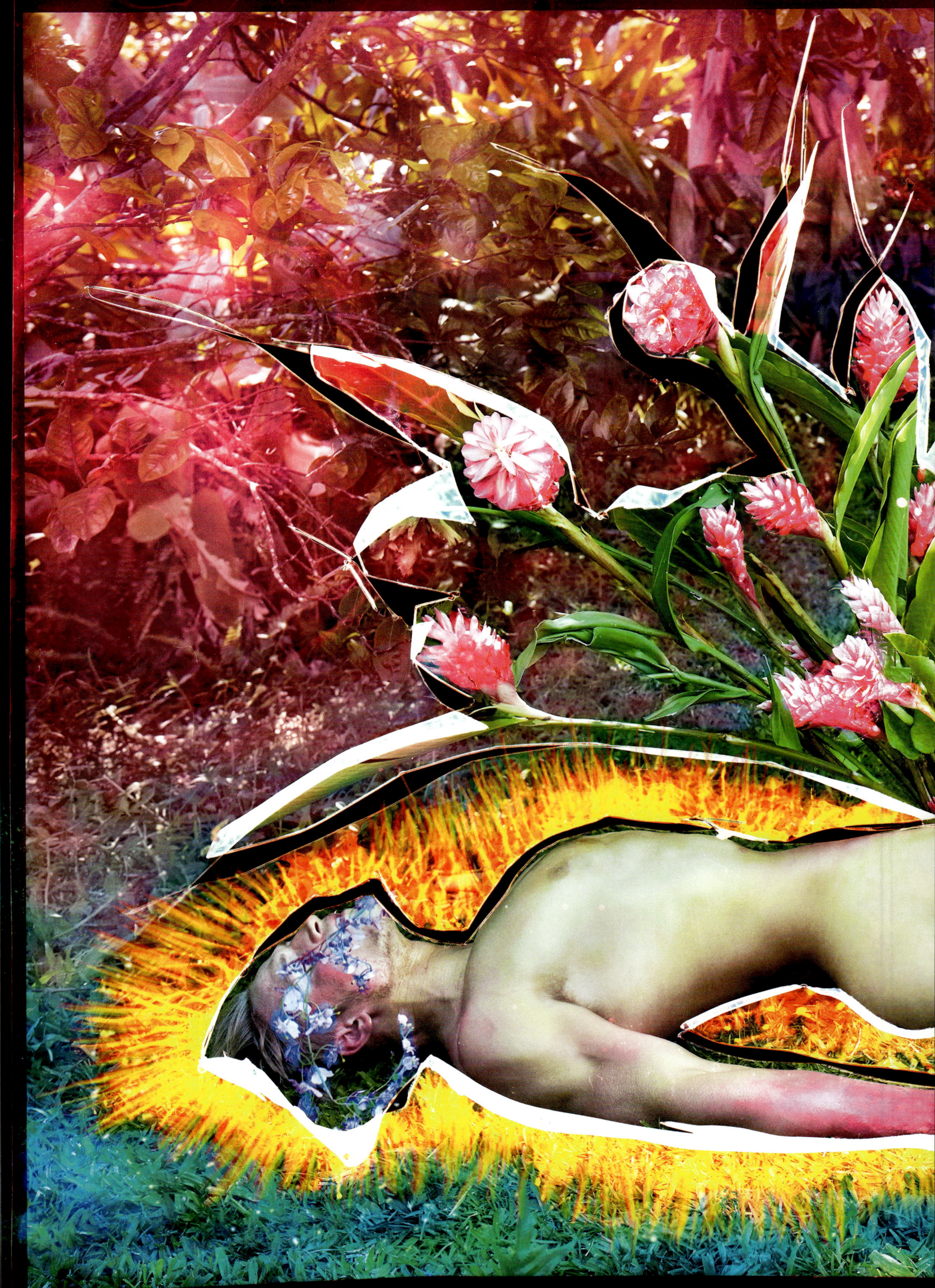

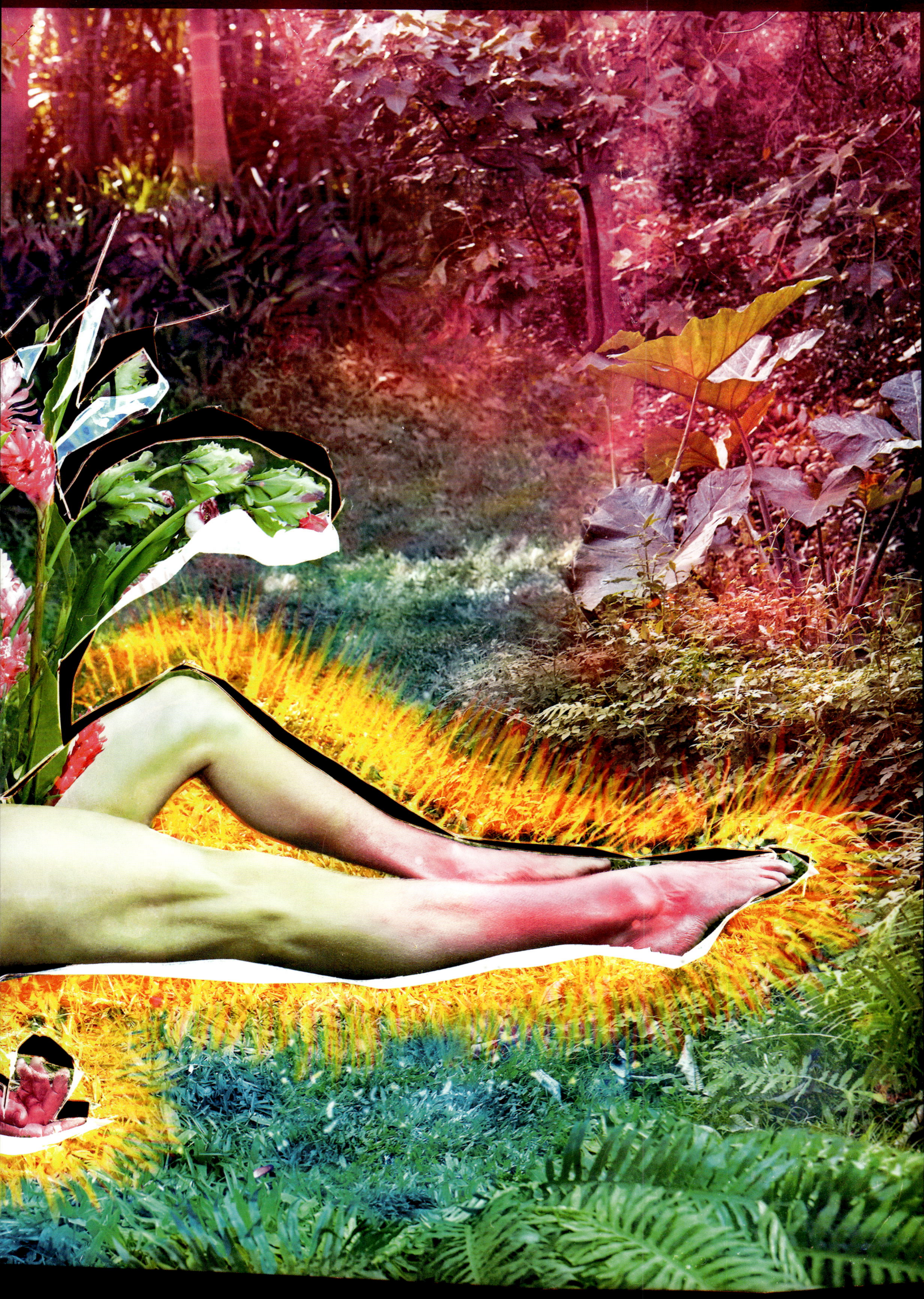

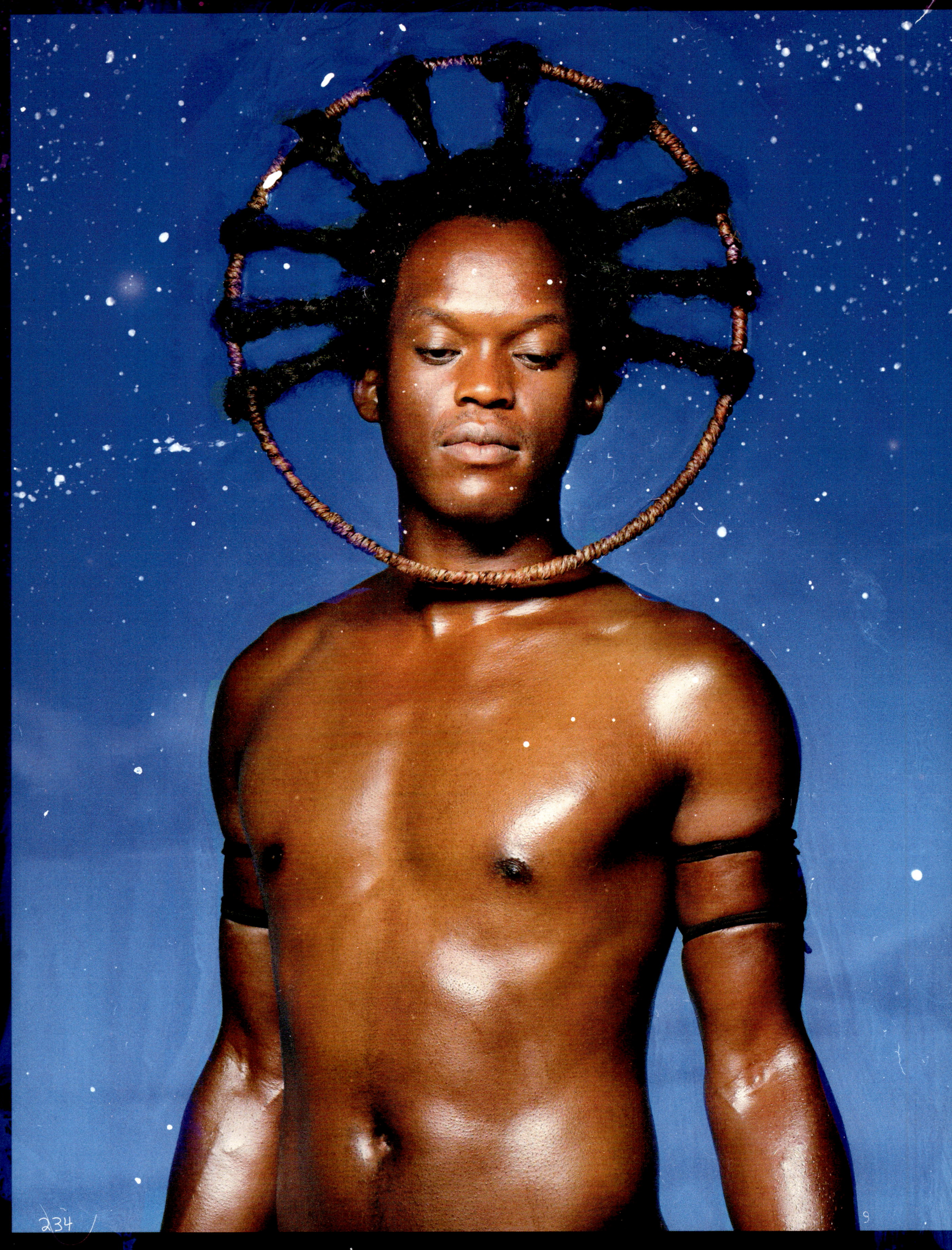

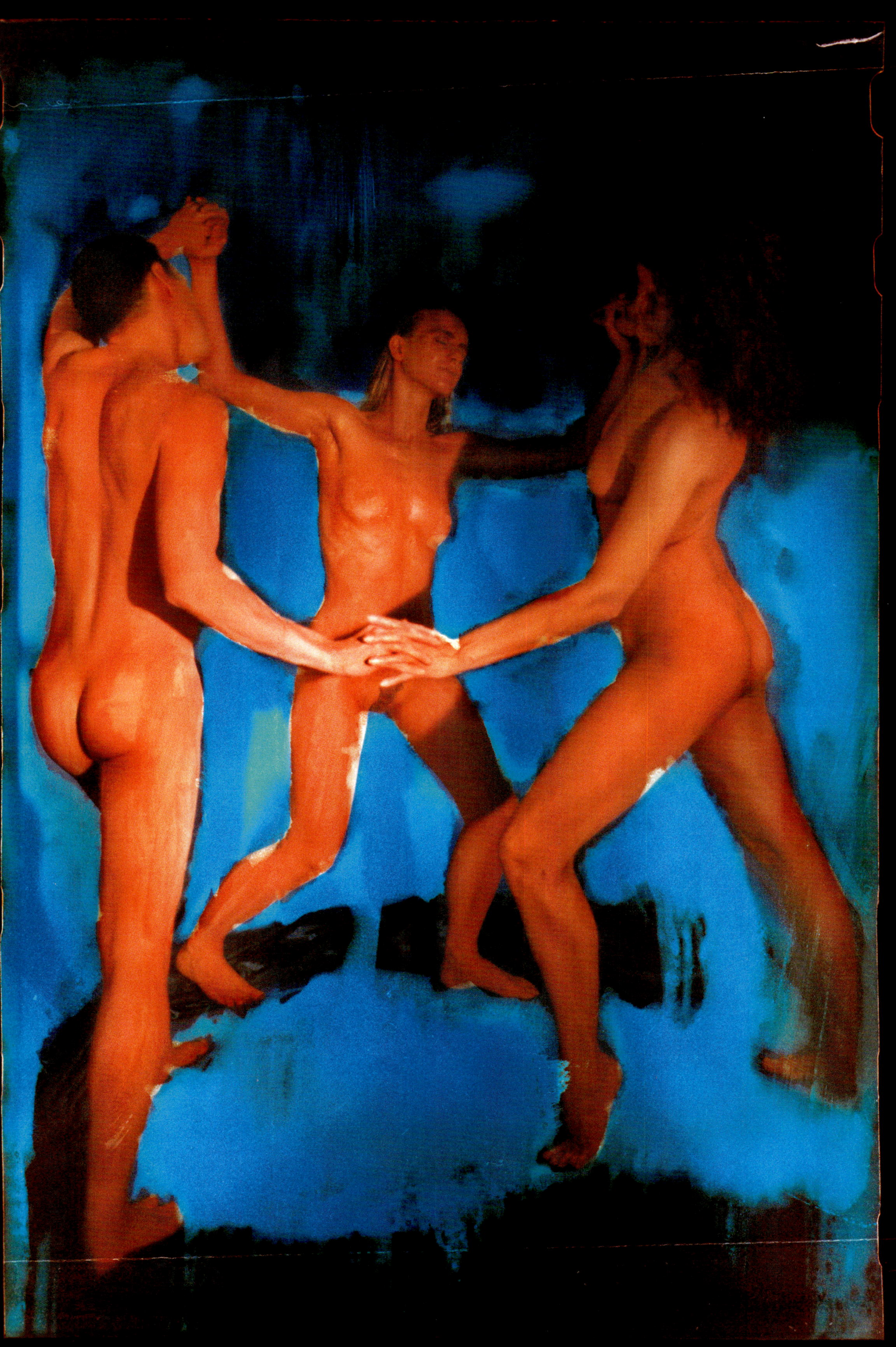

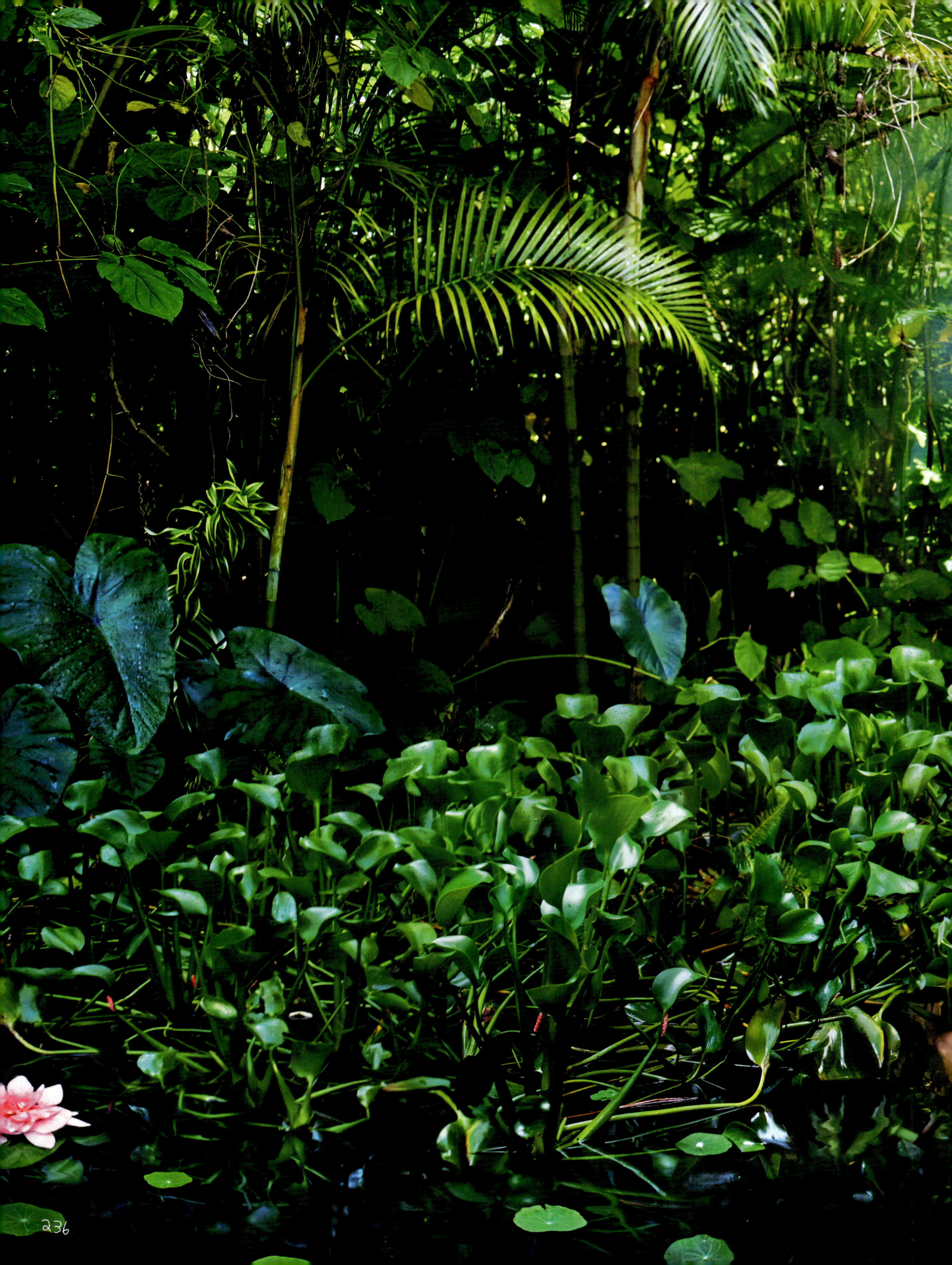

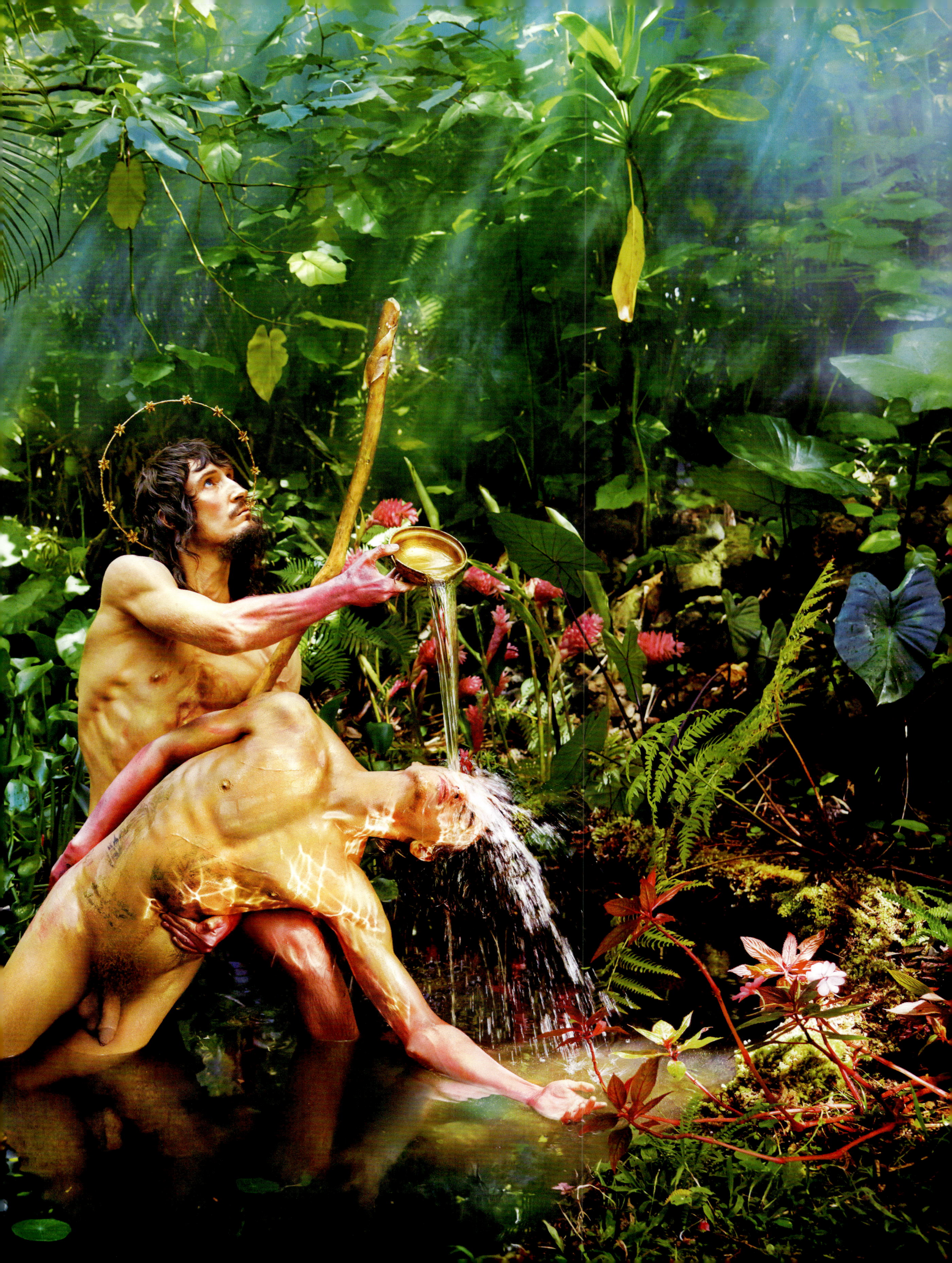

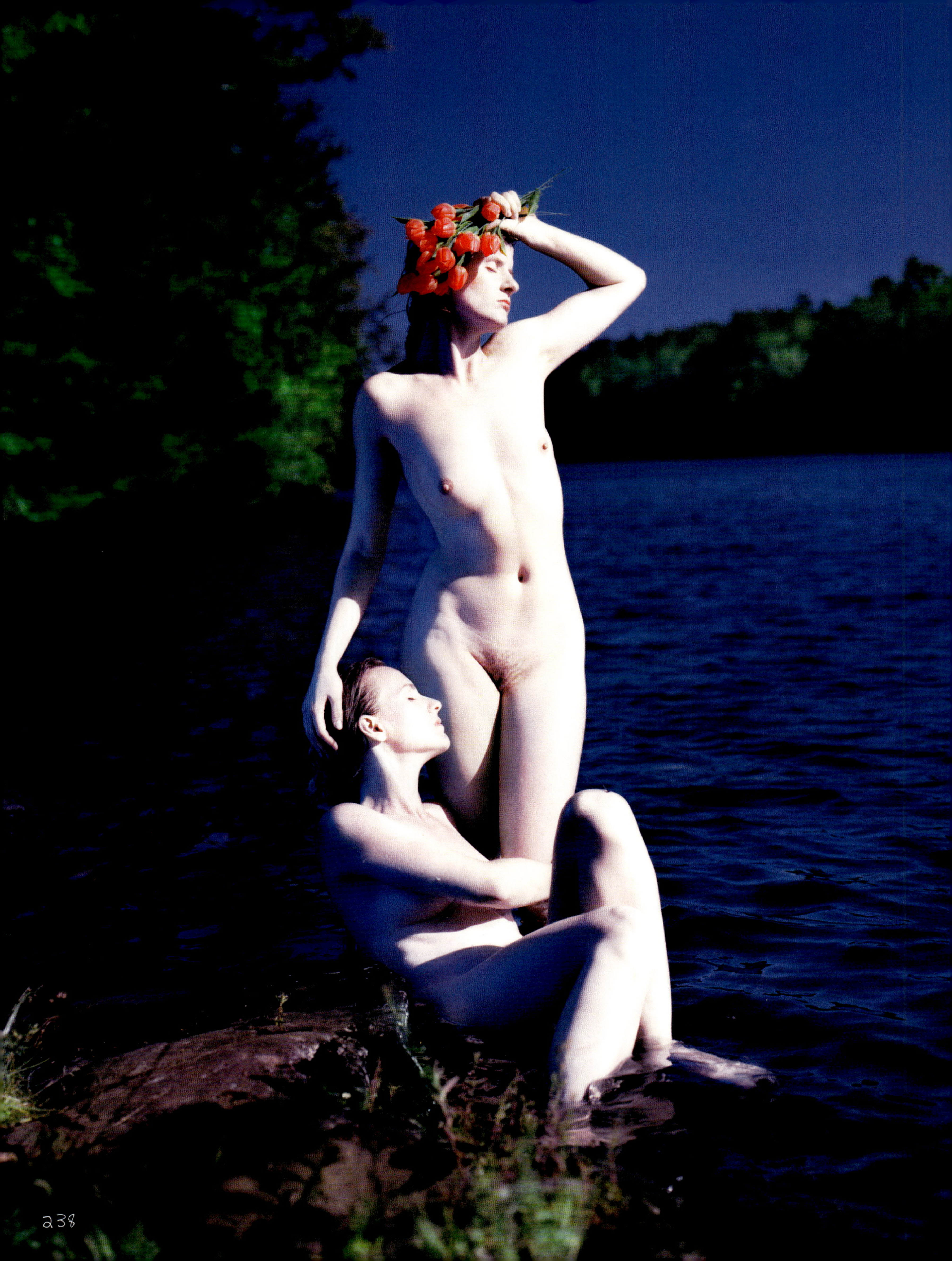

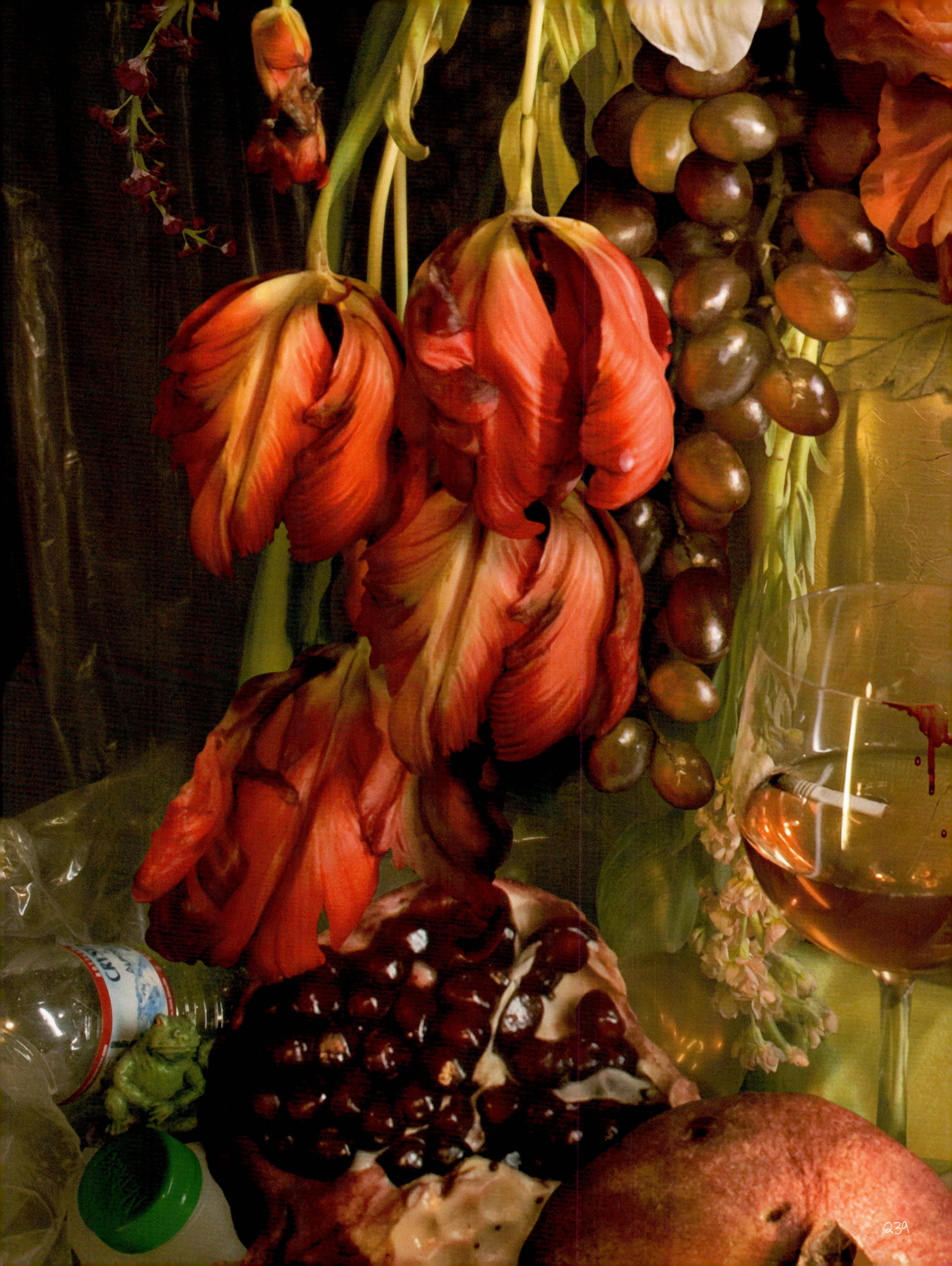

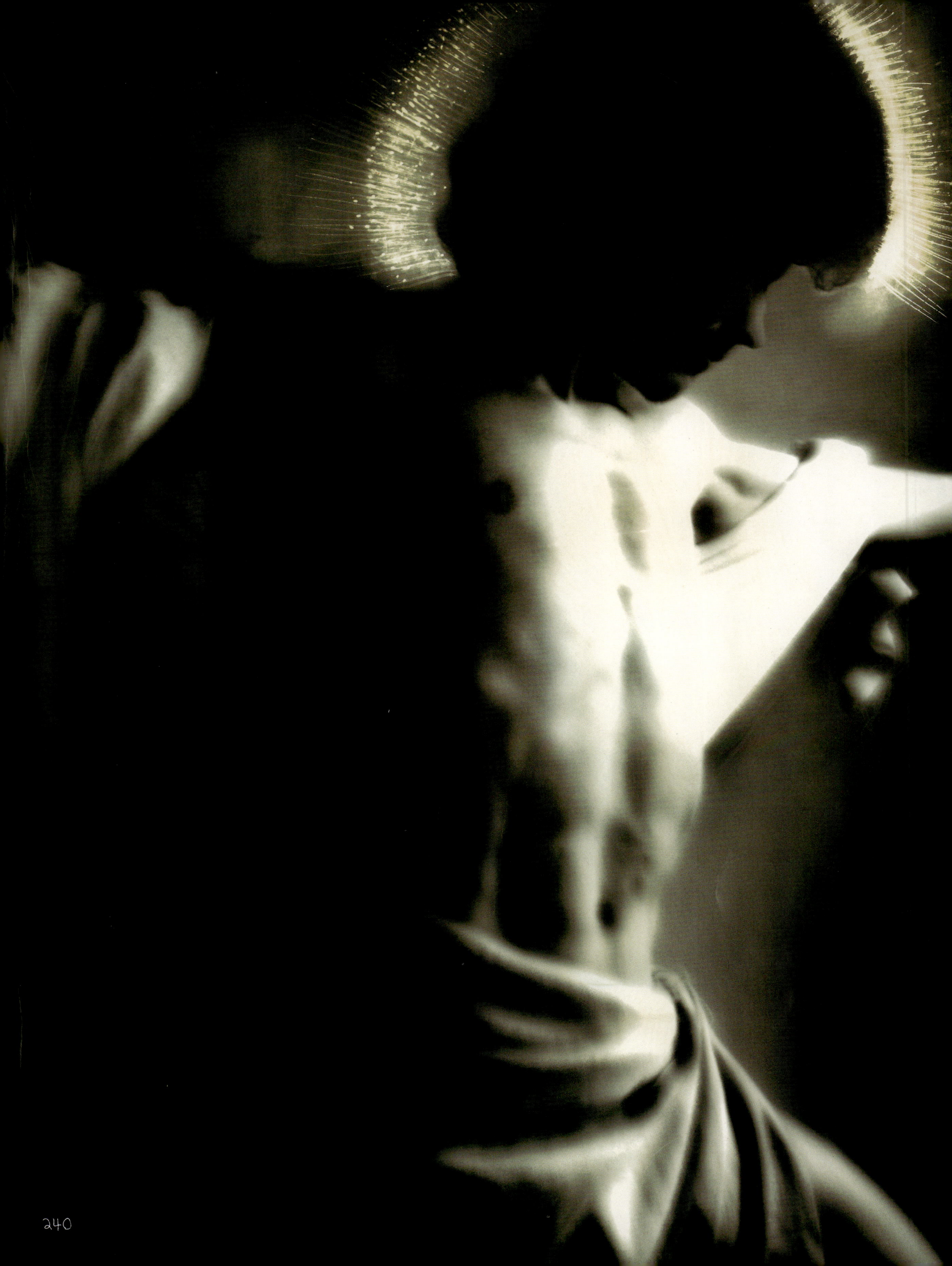

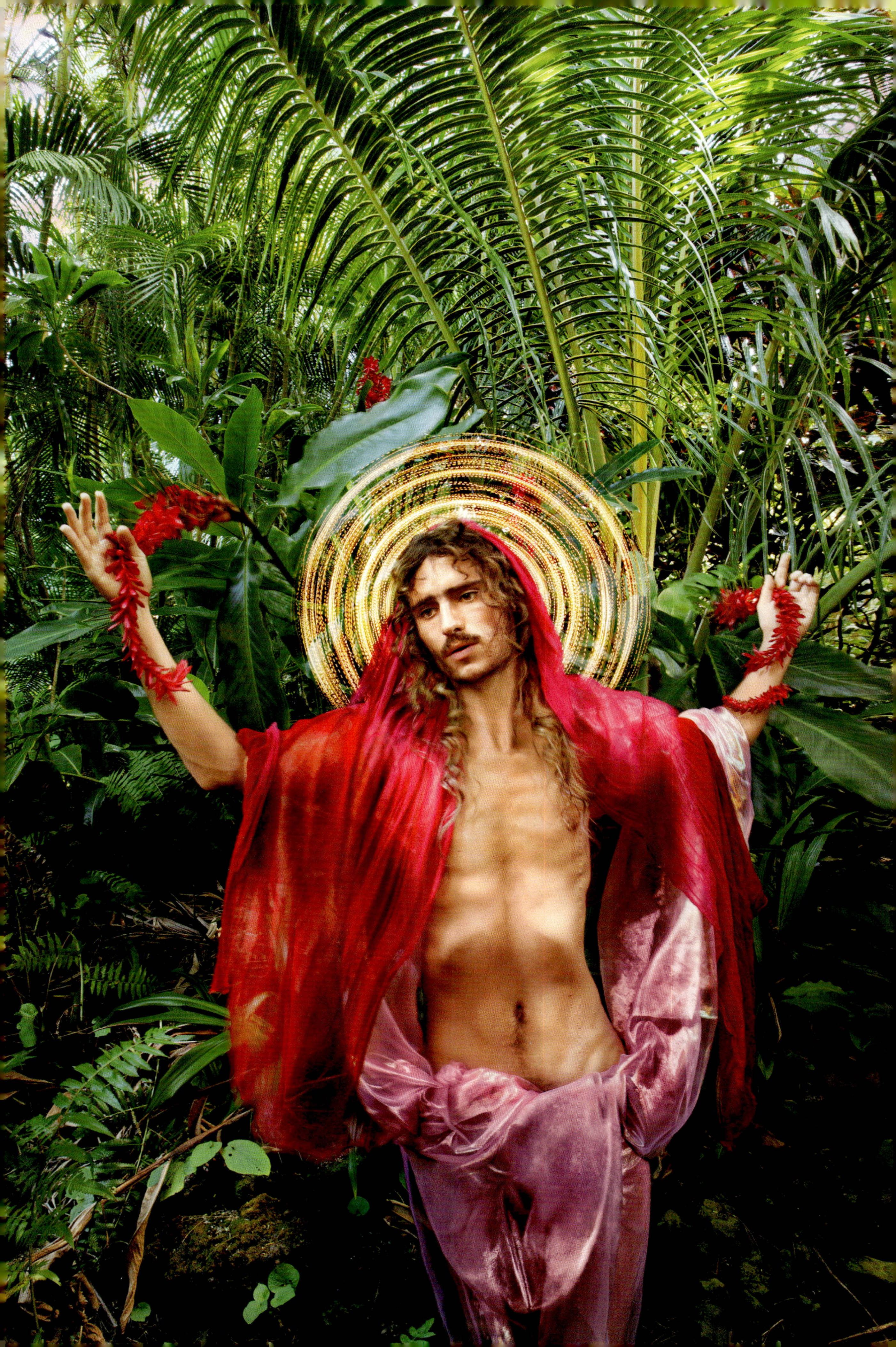

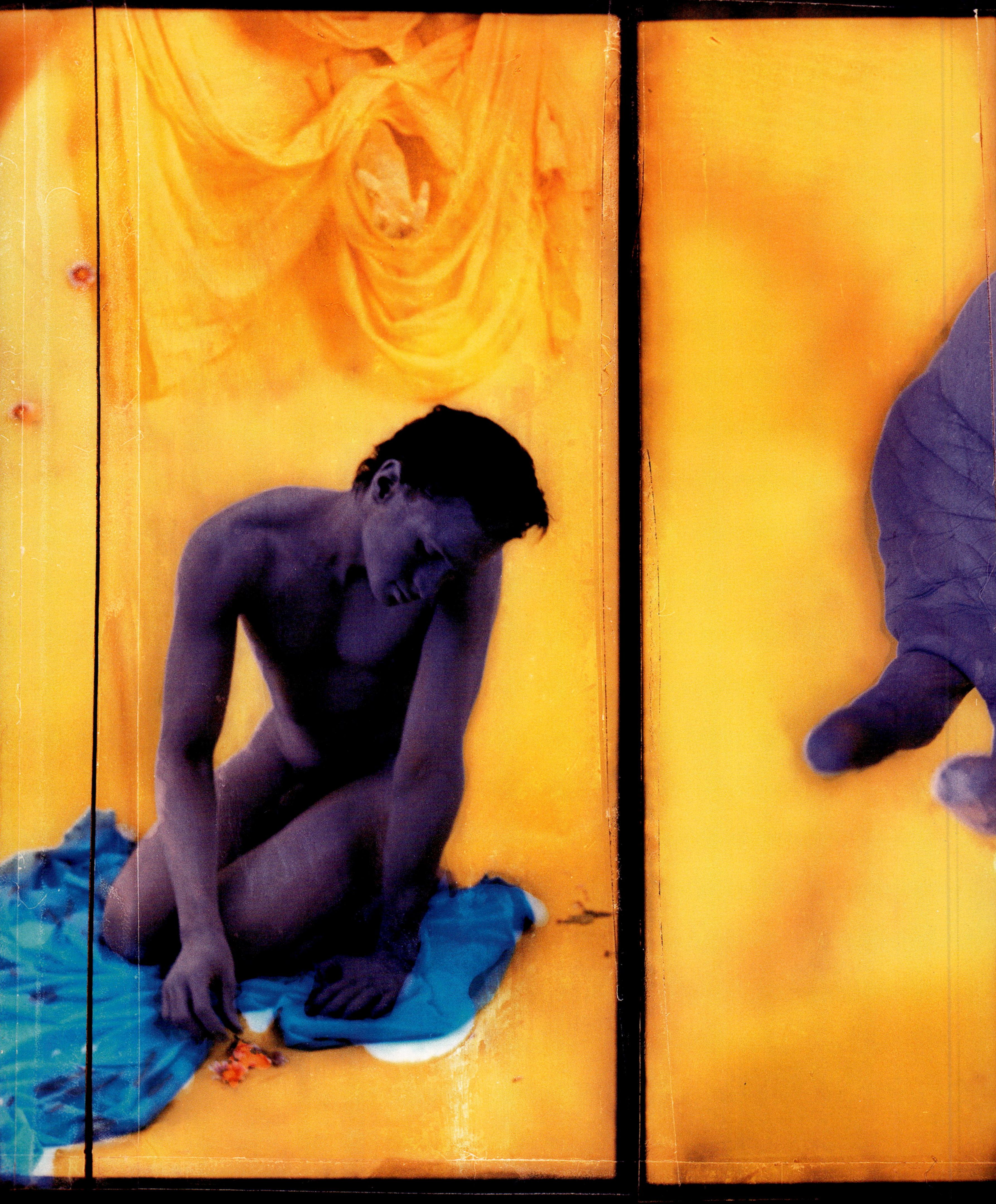

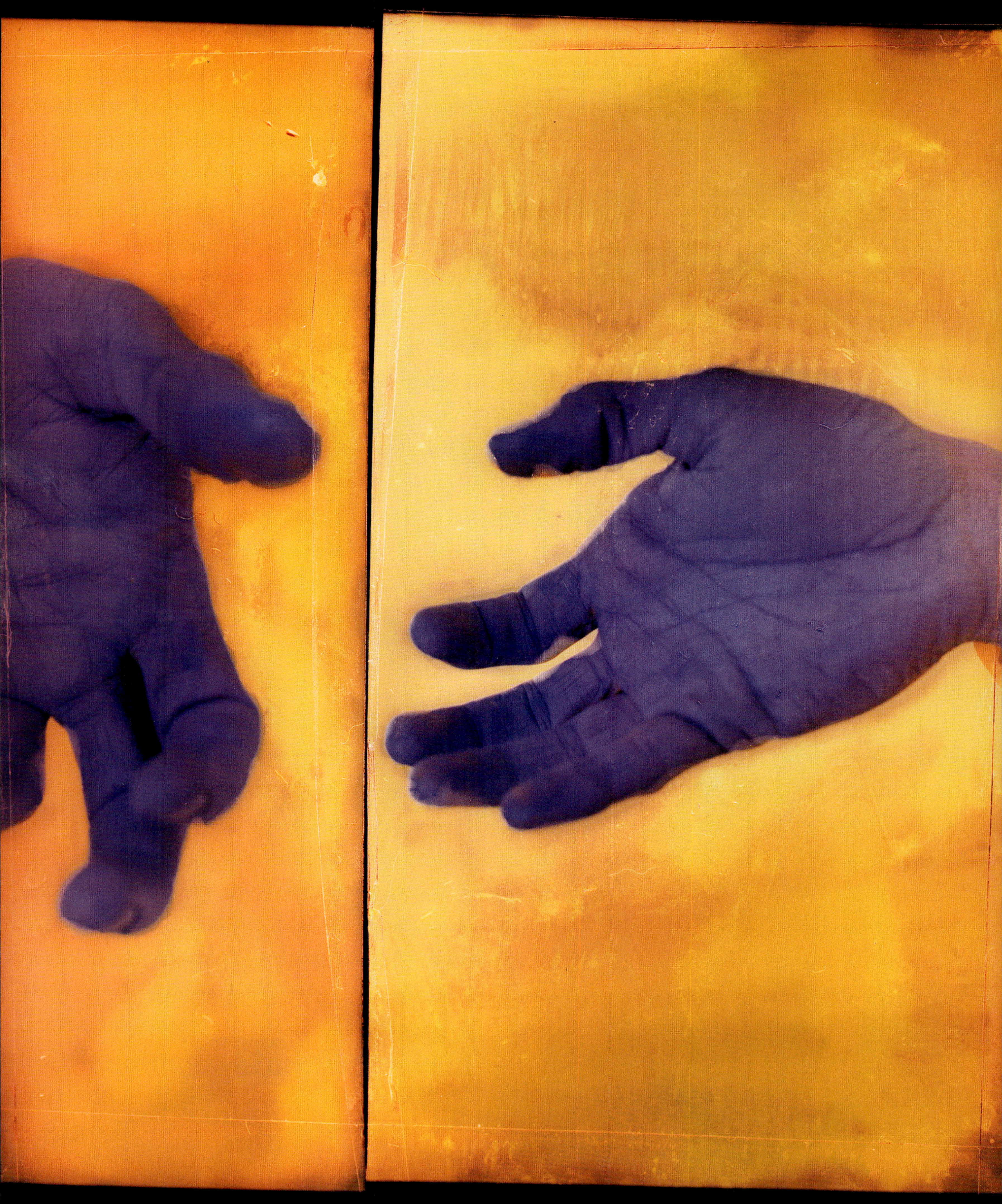

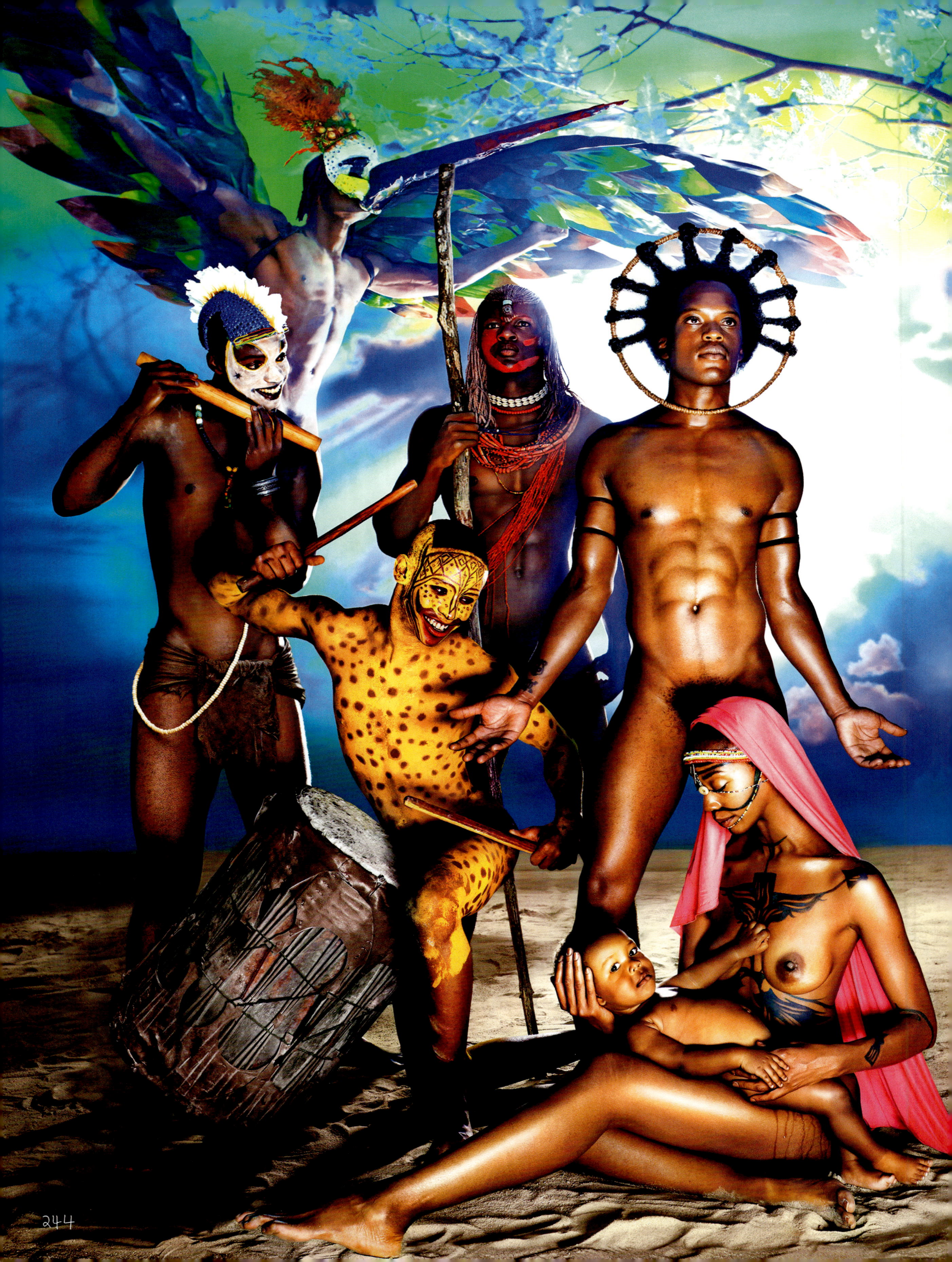

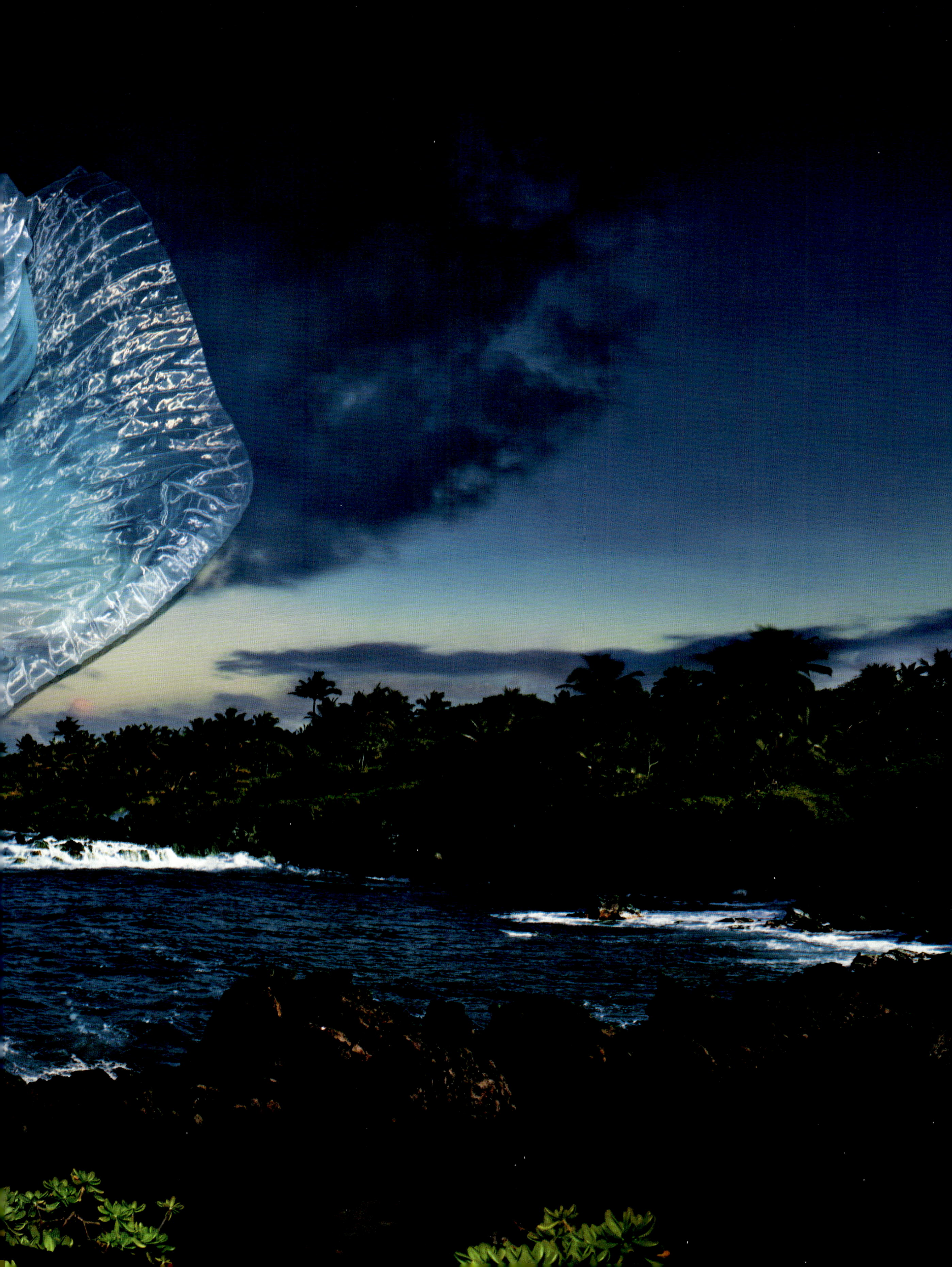

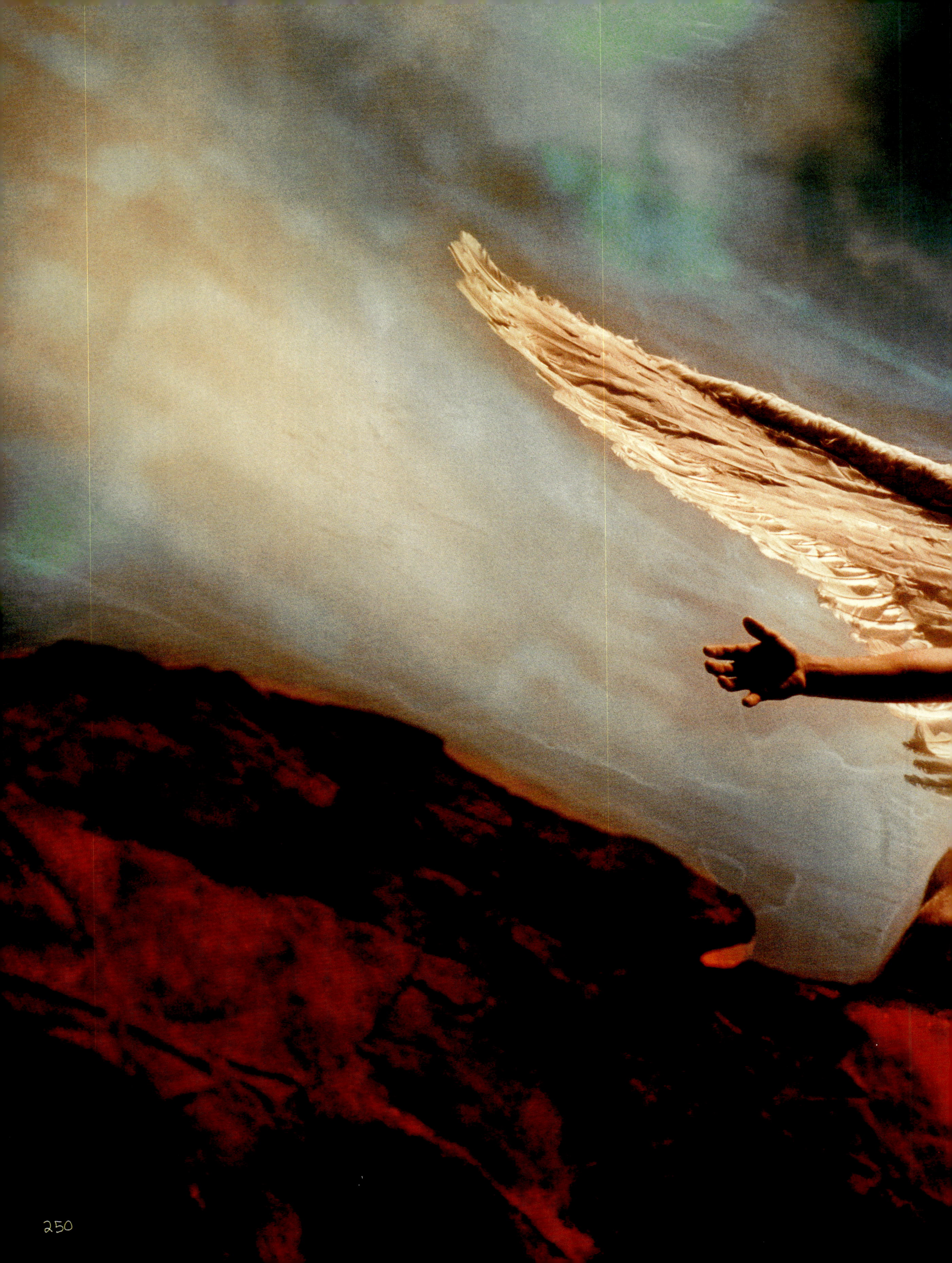

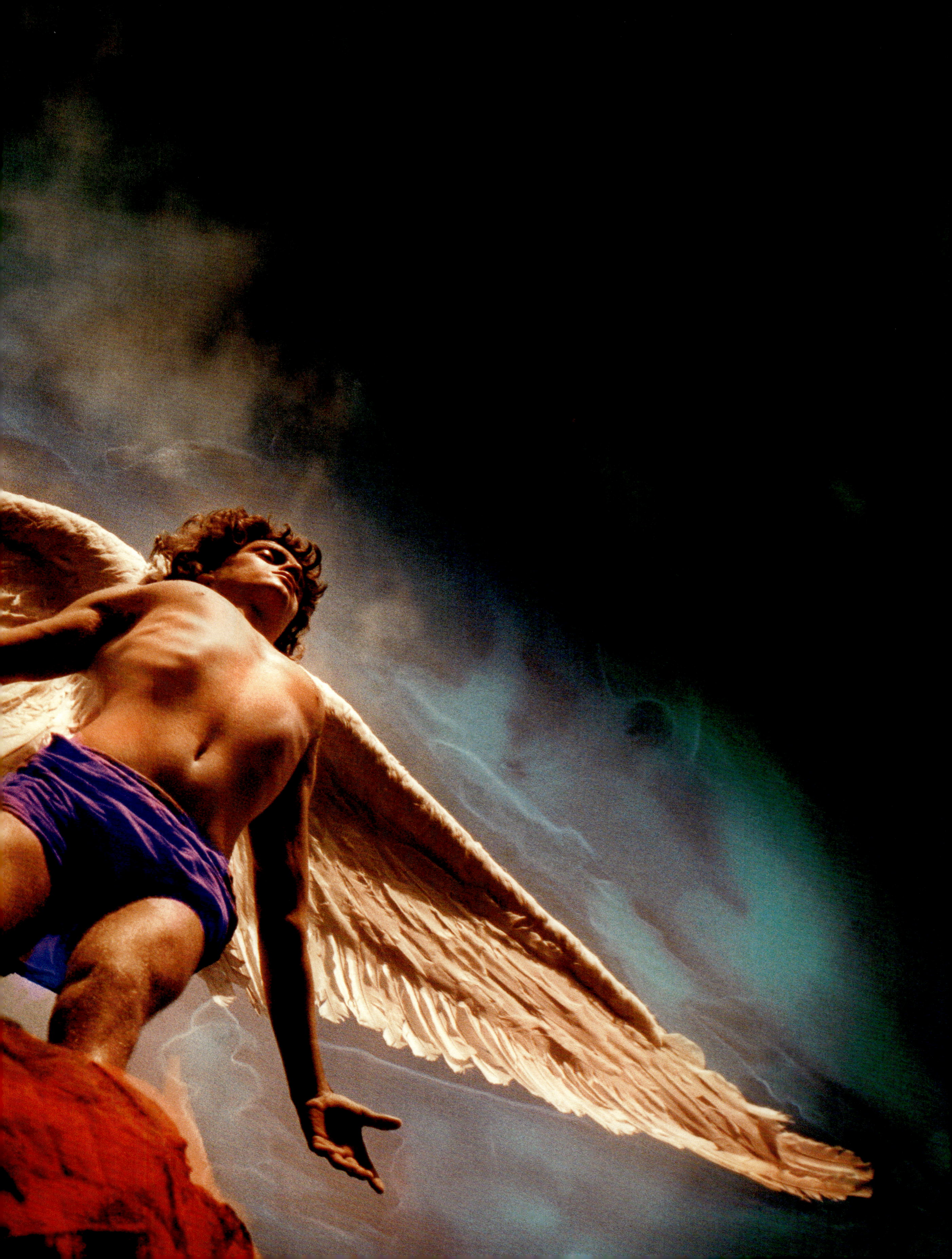

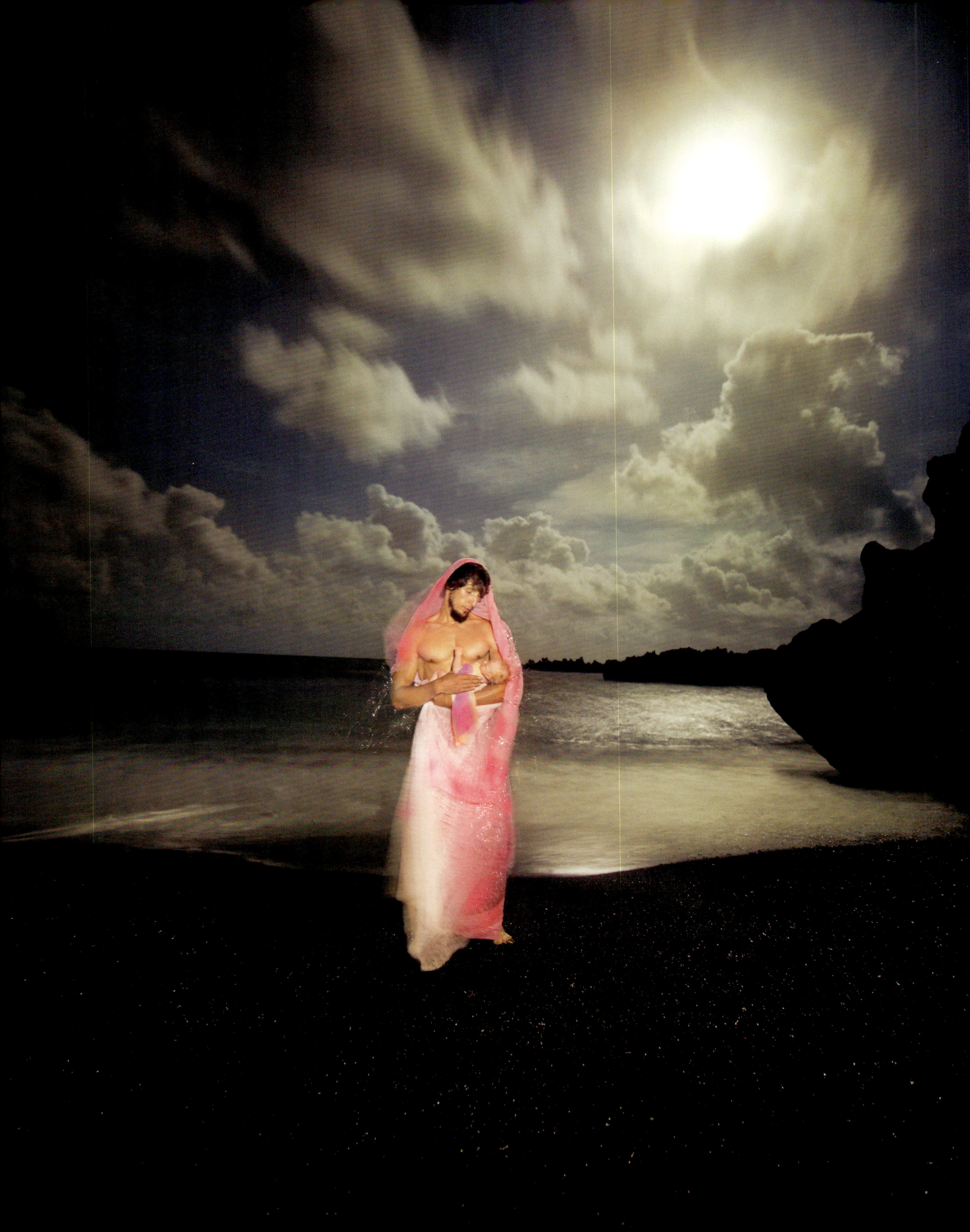

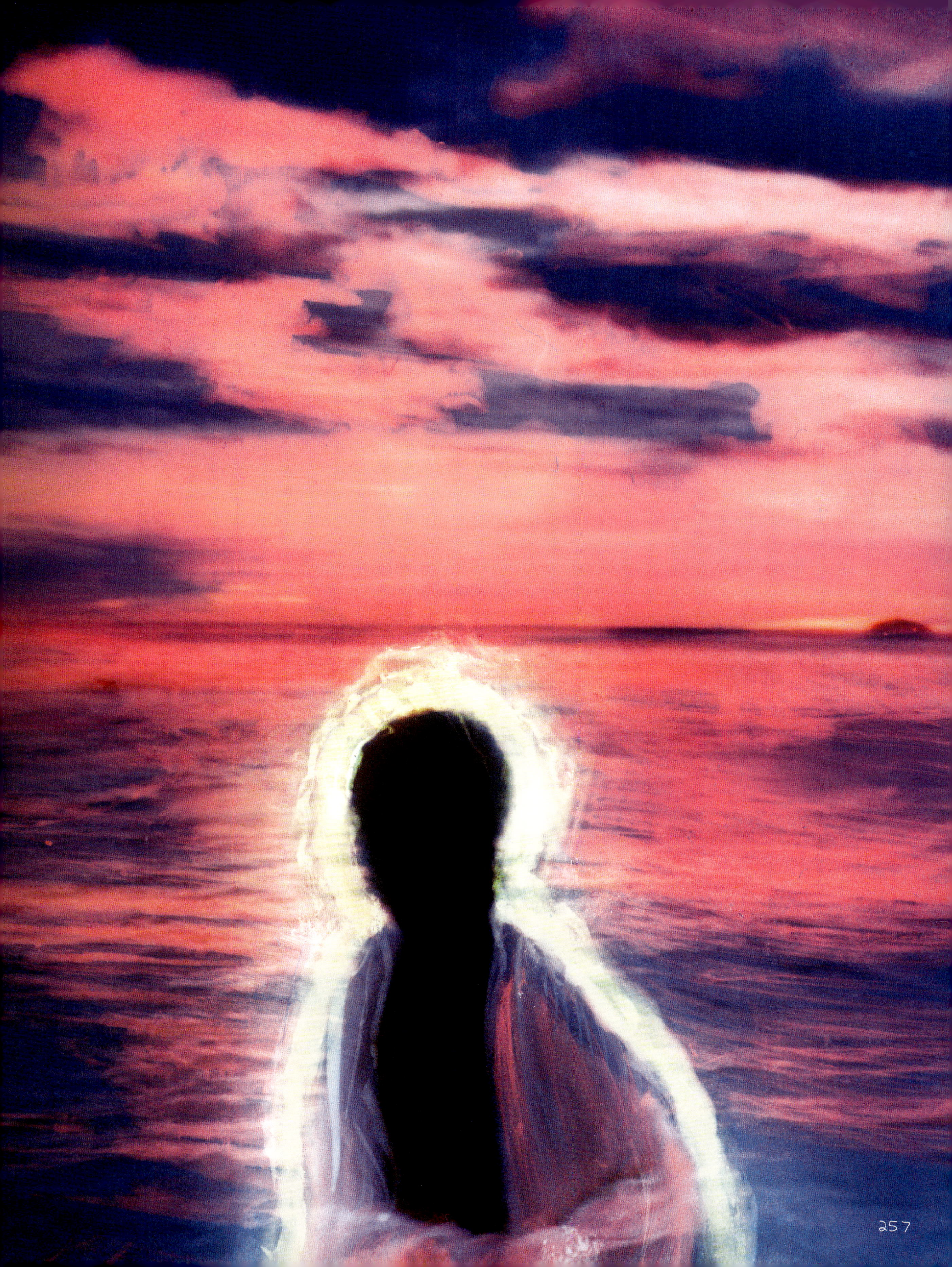

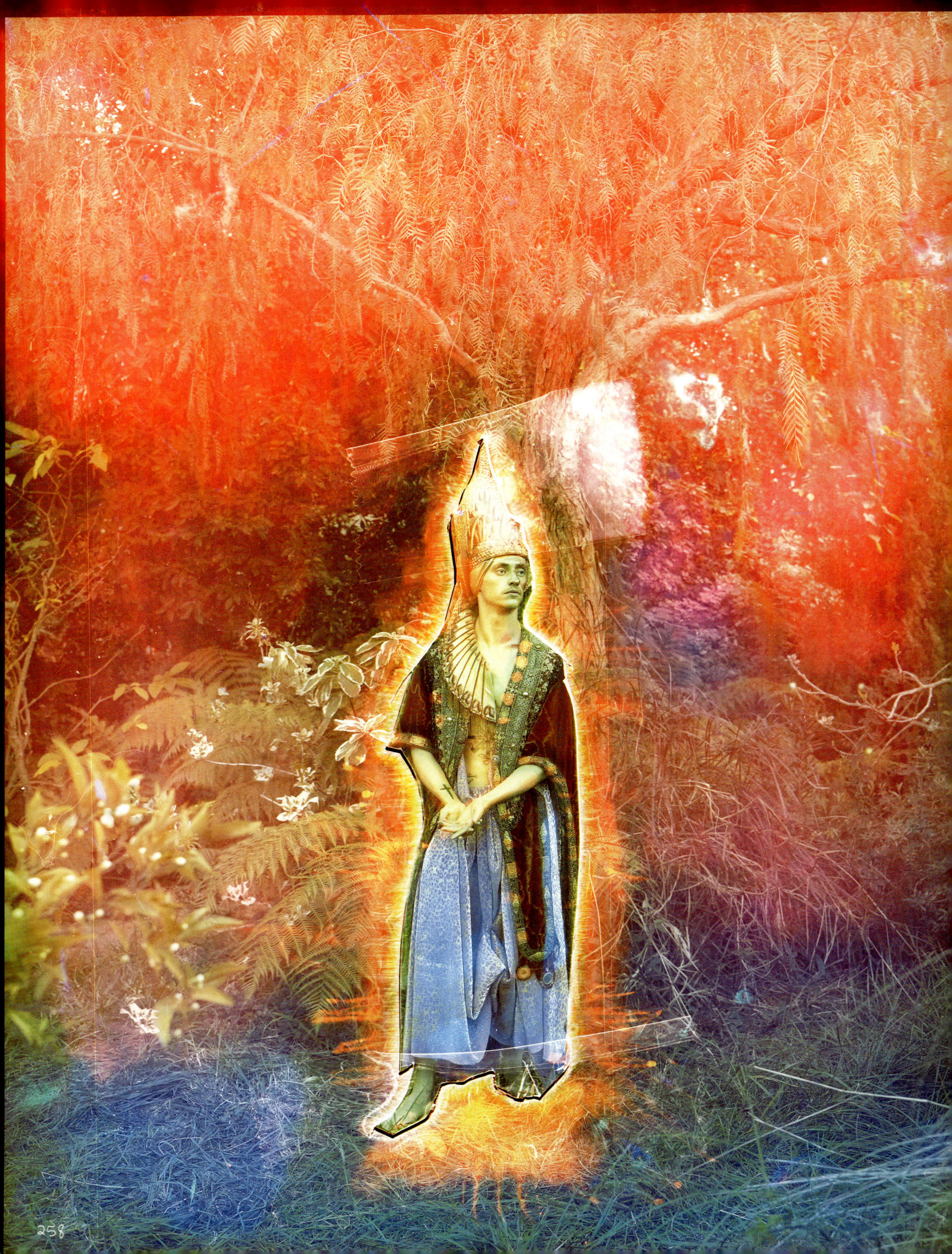
258

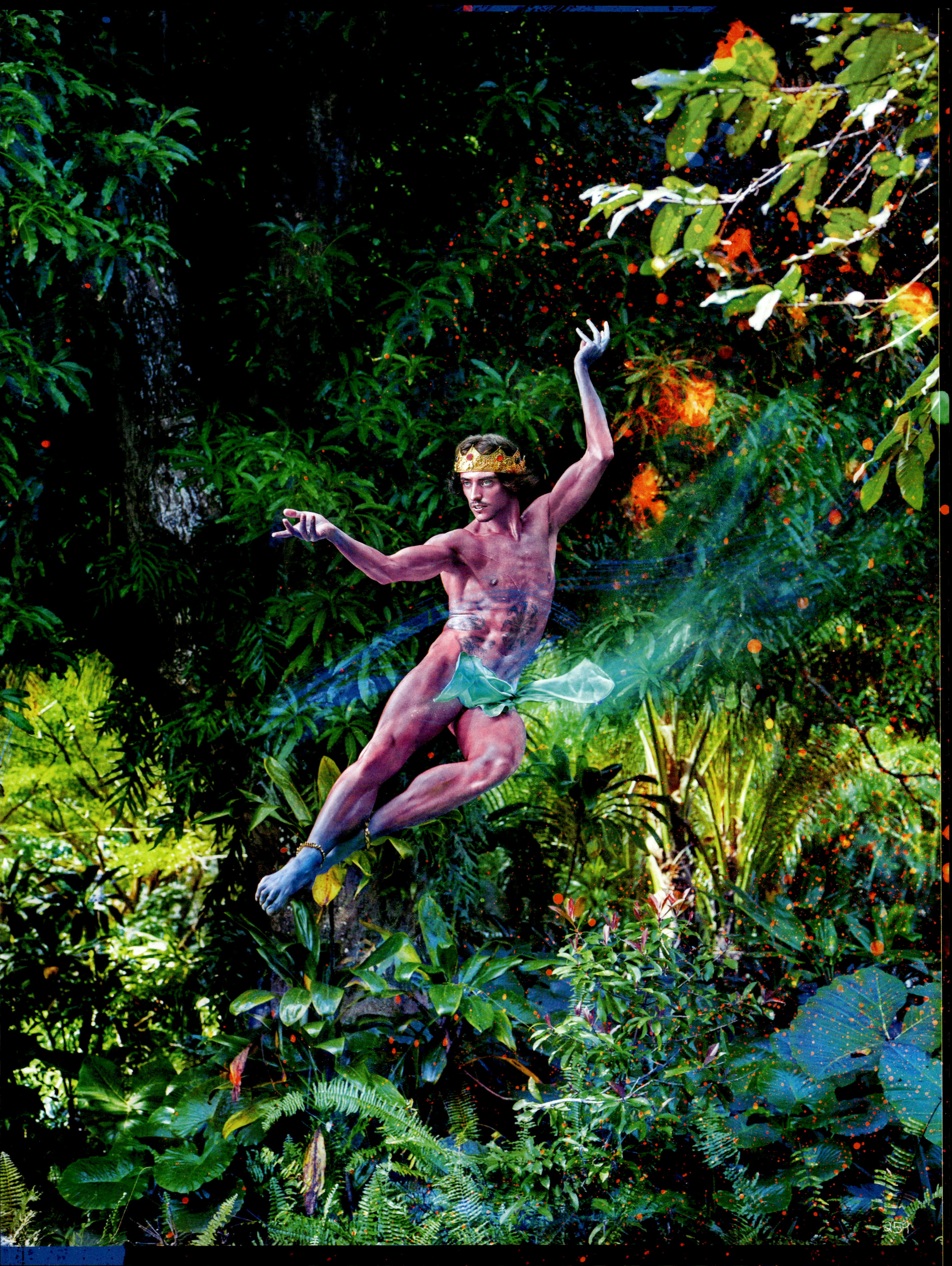

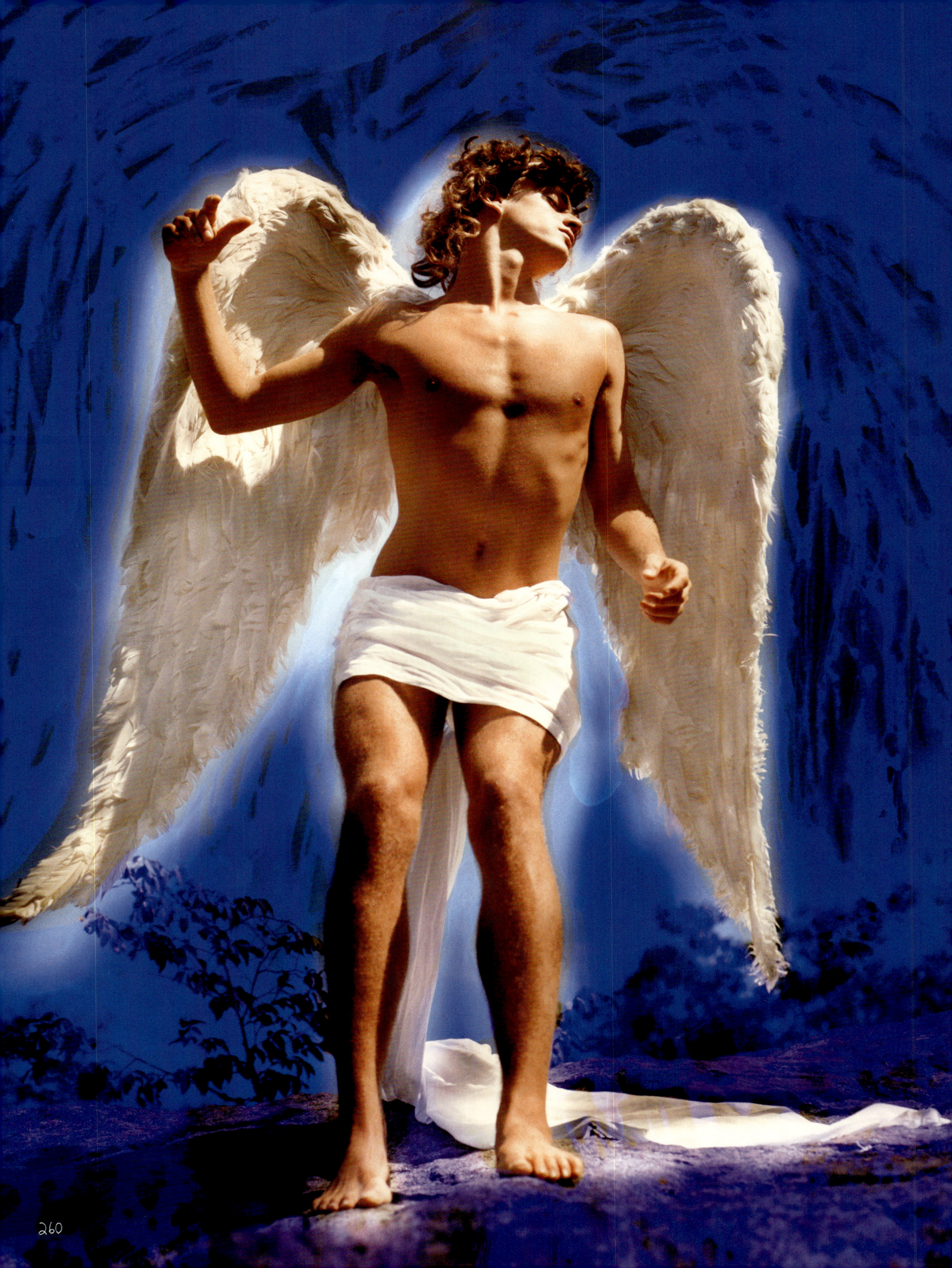

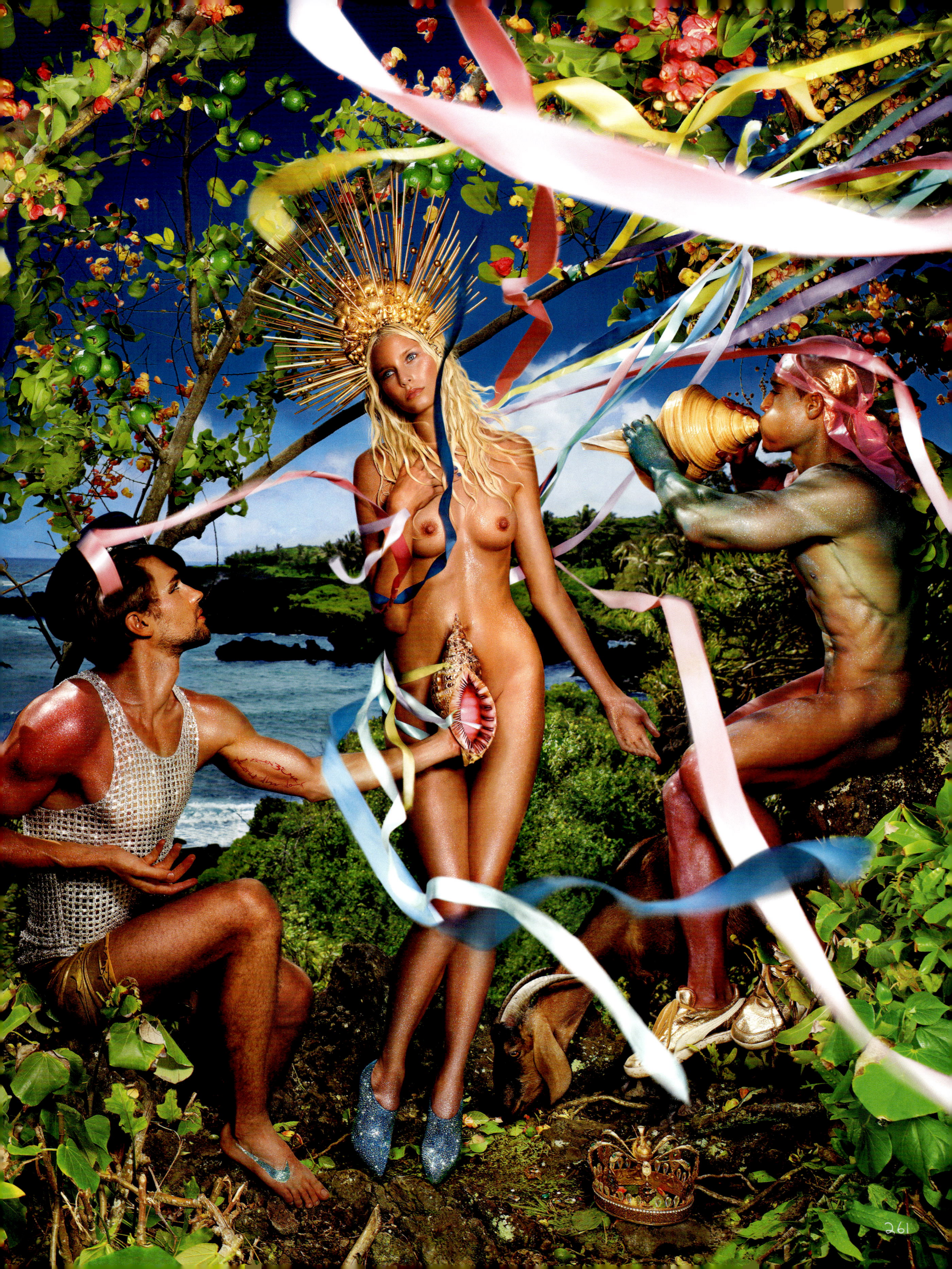

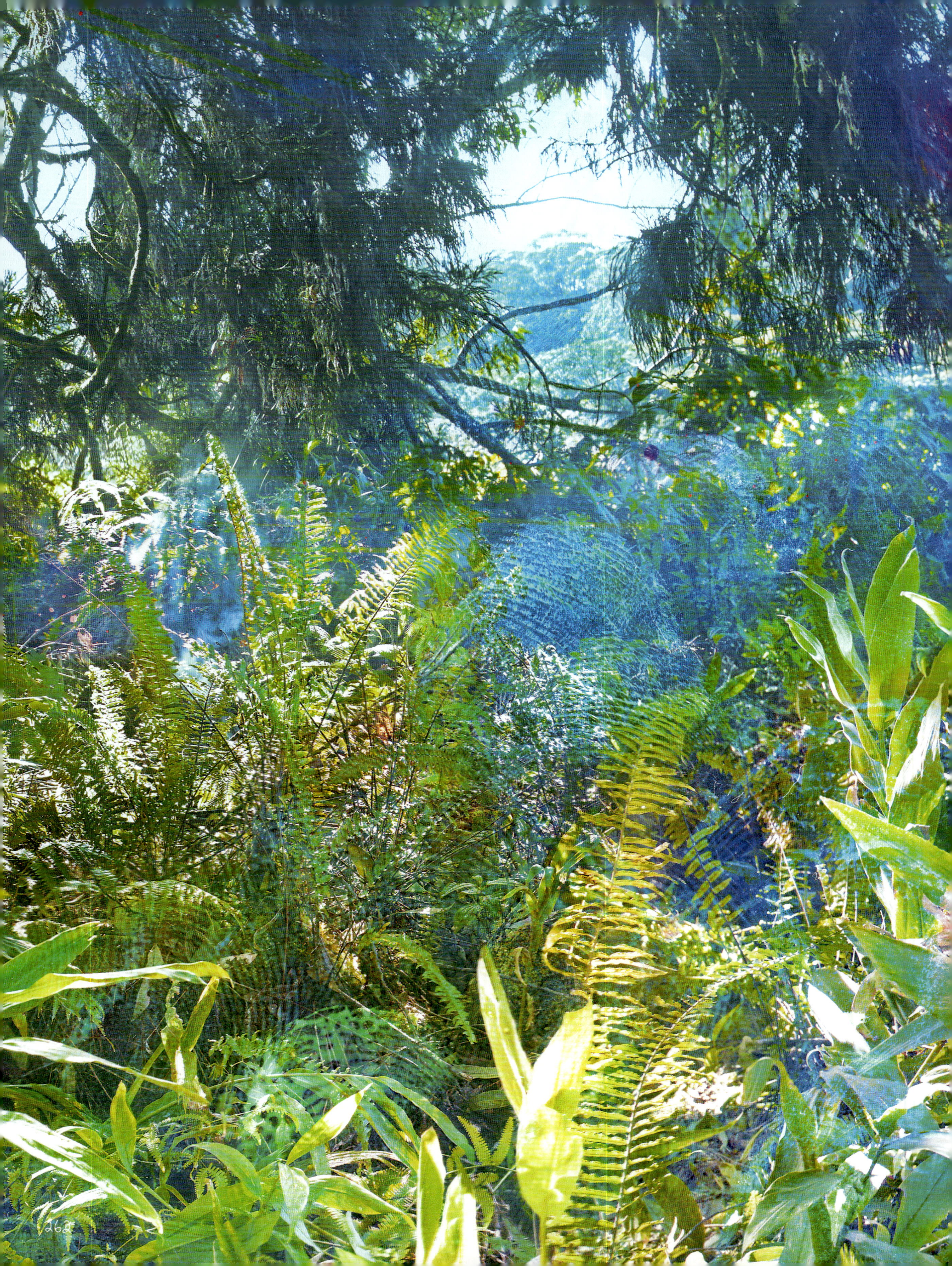

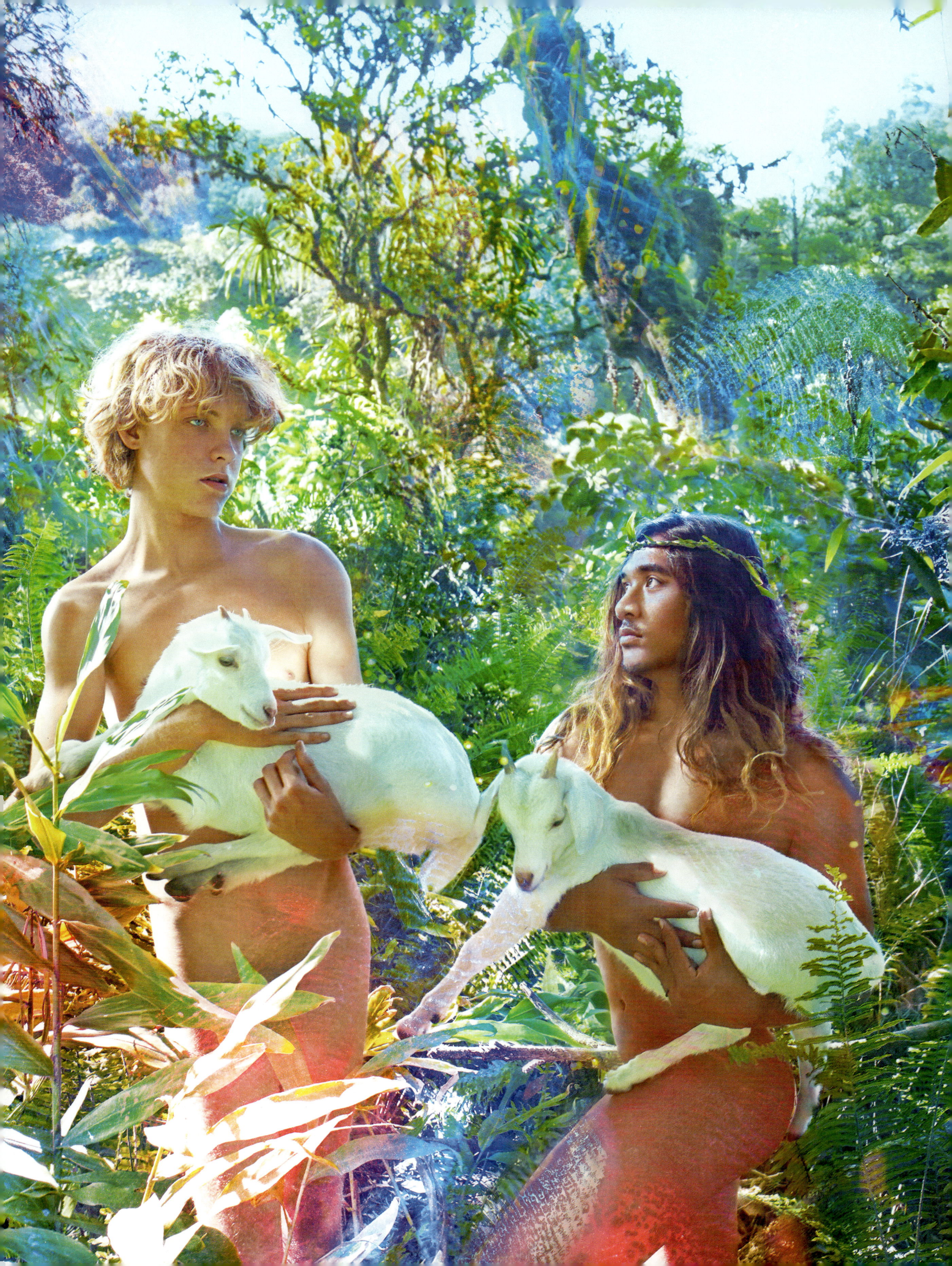

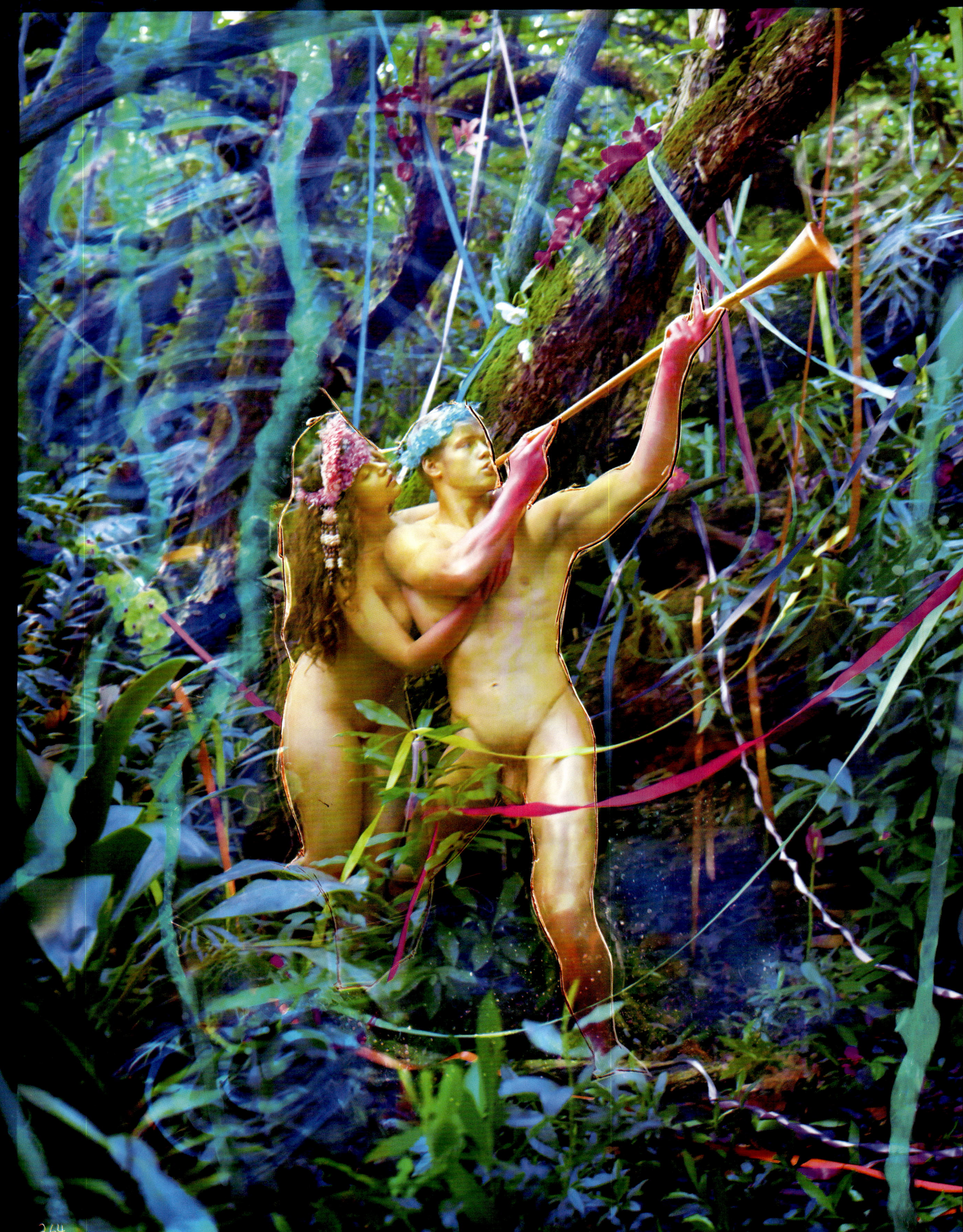

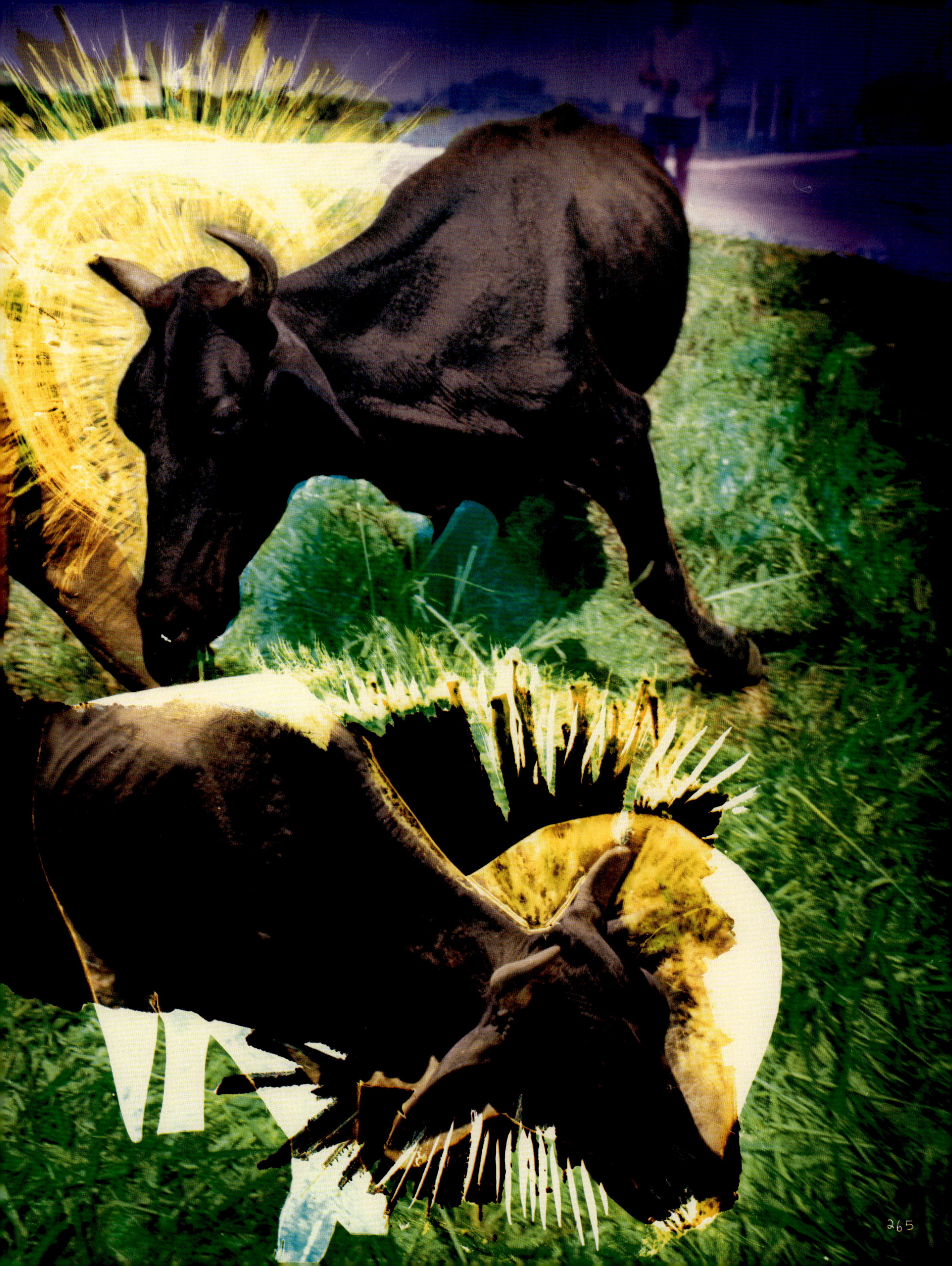

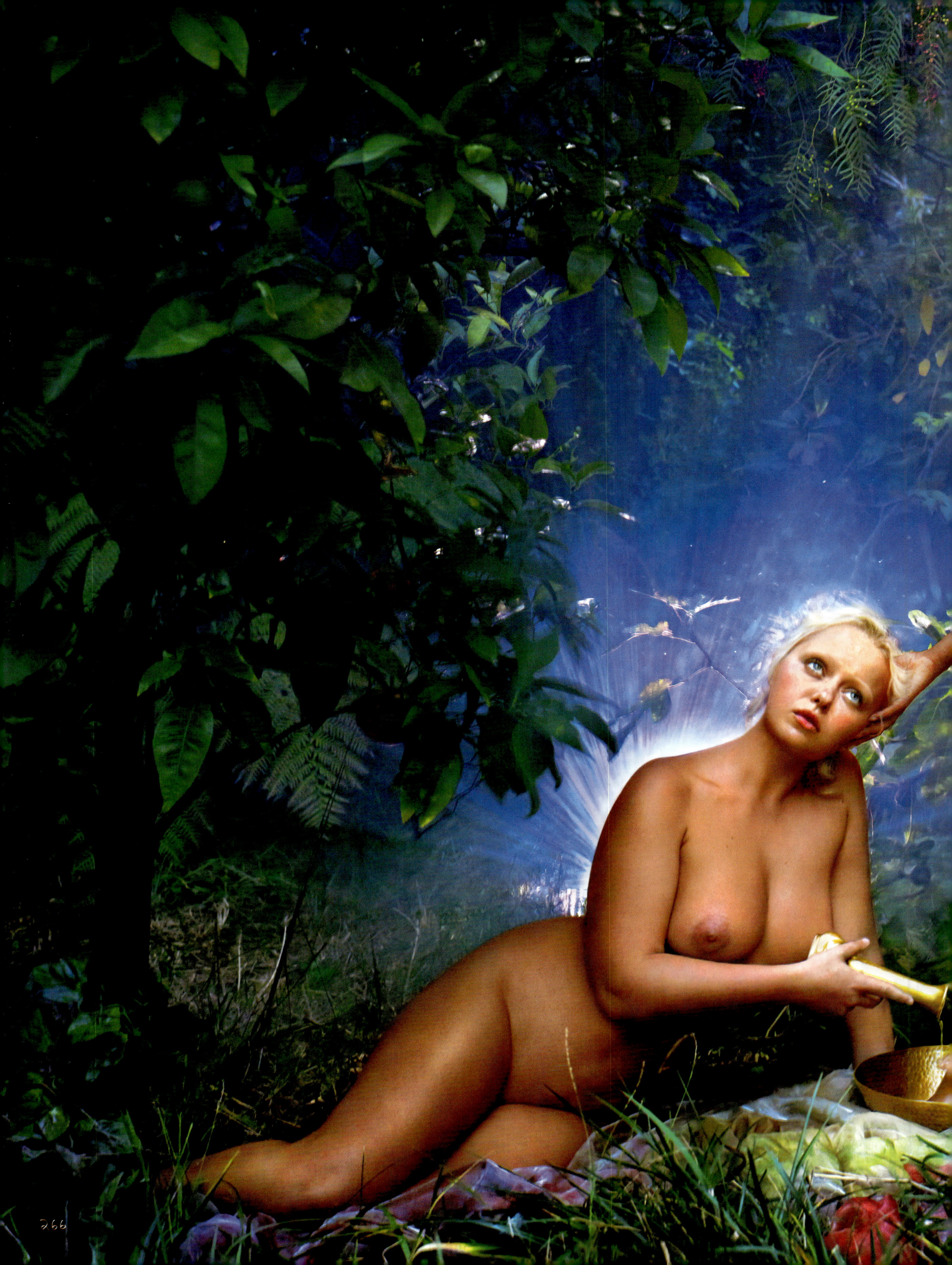

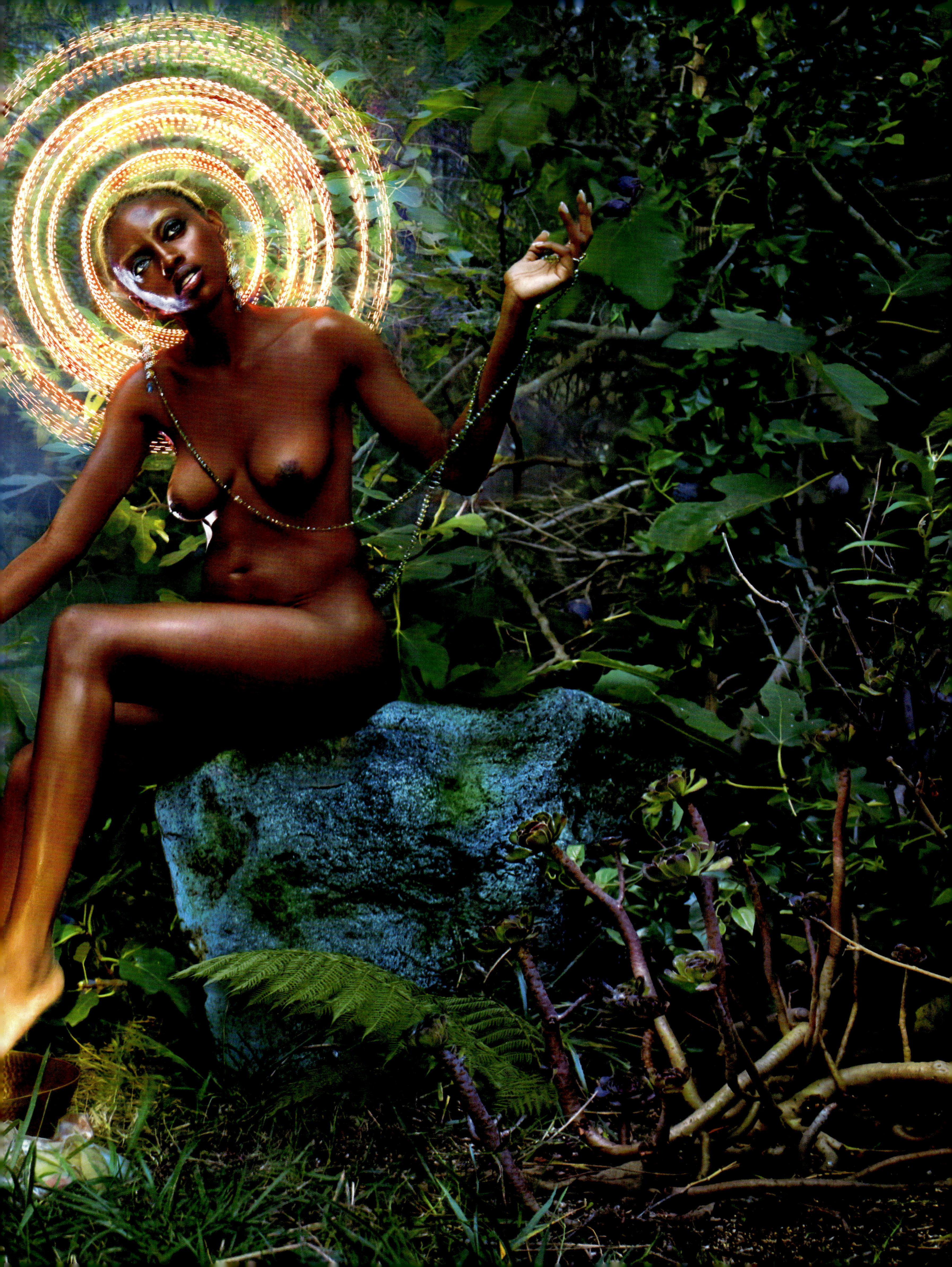

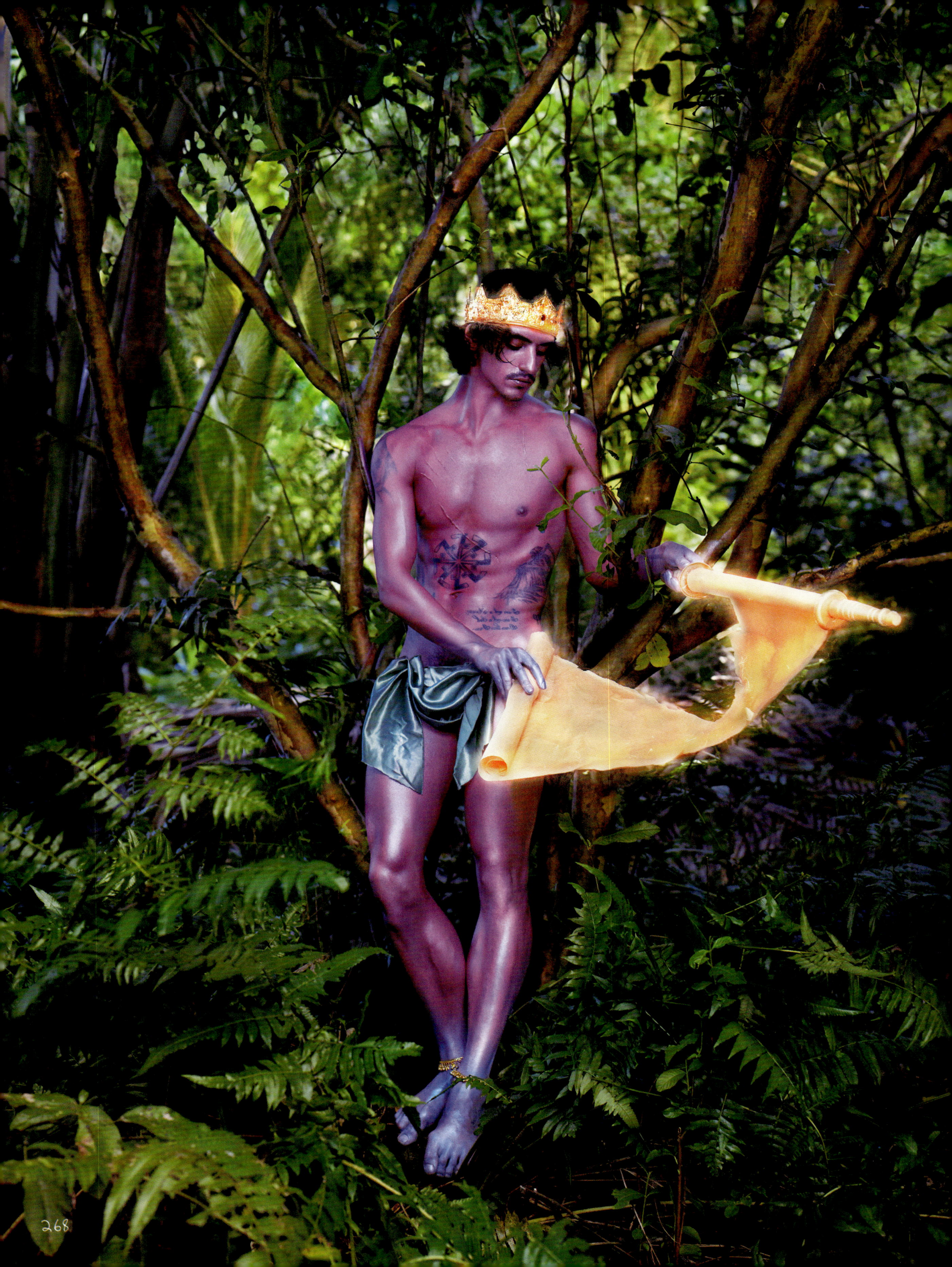

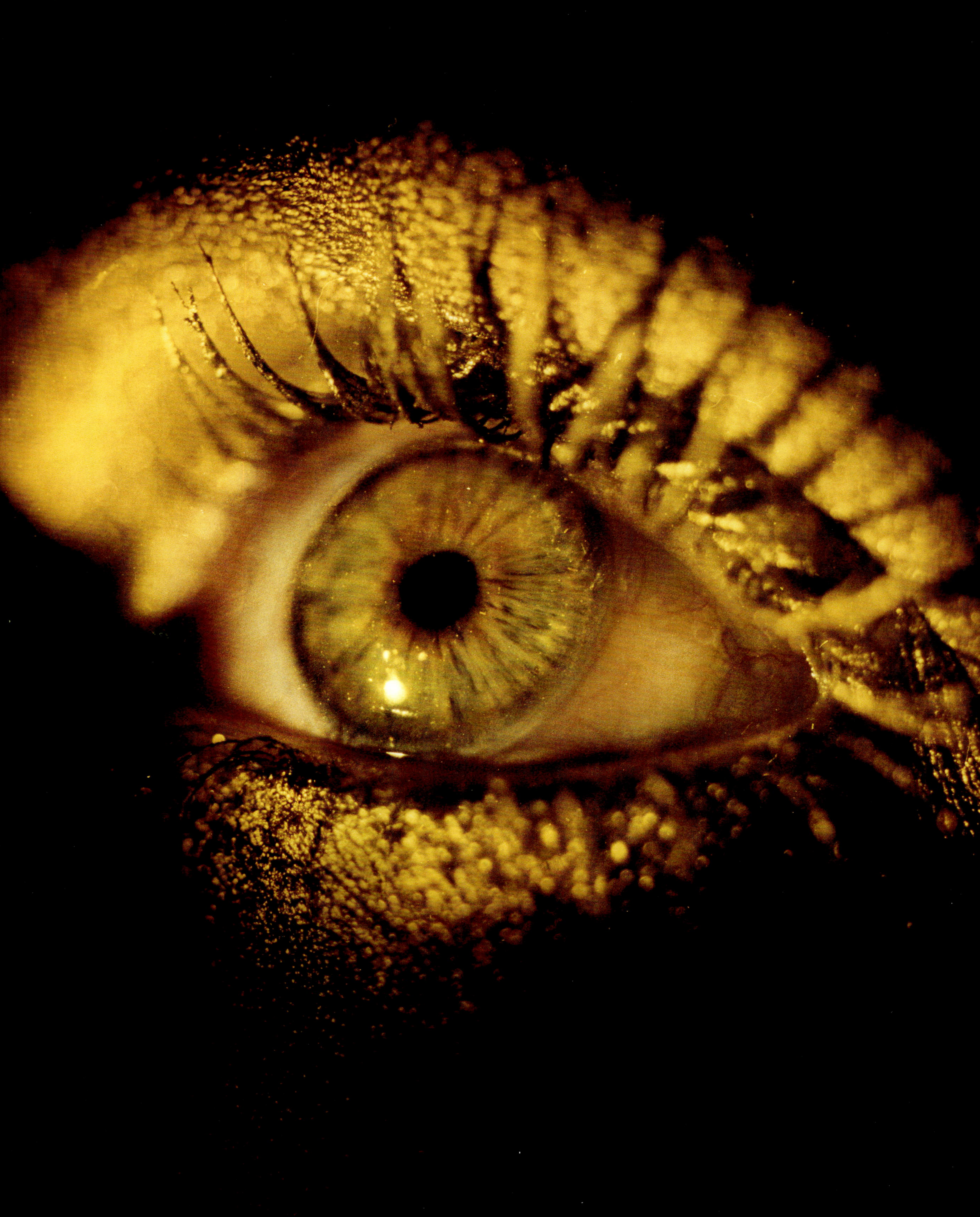

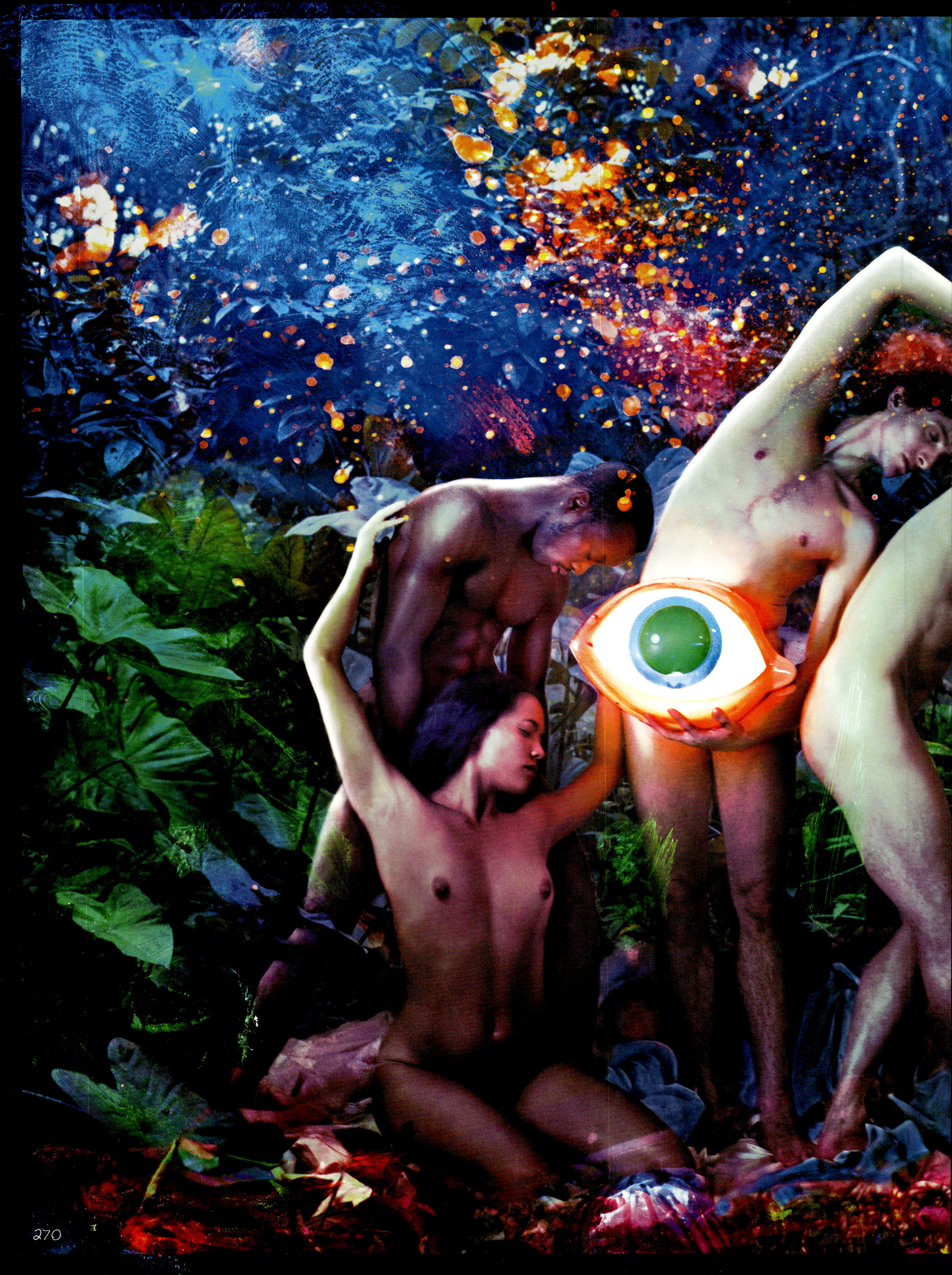

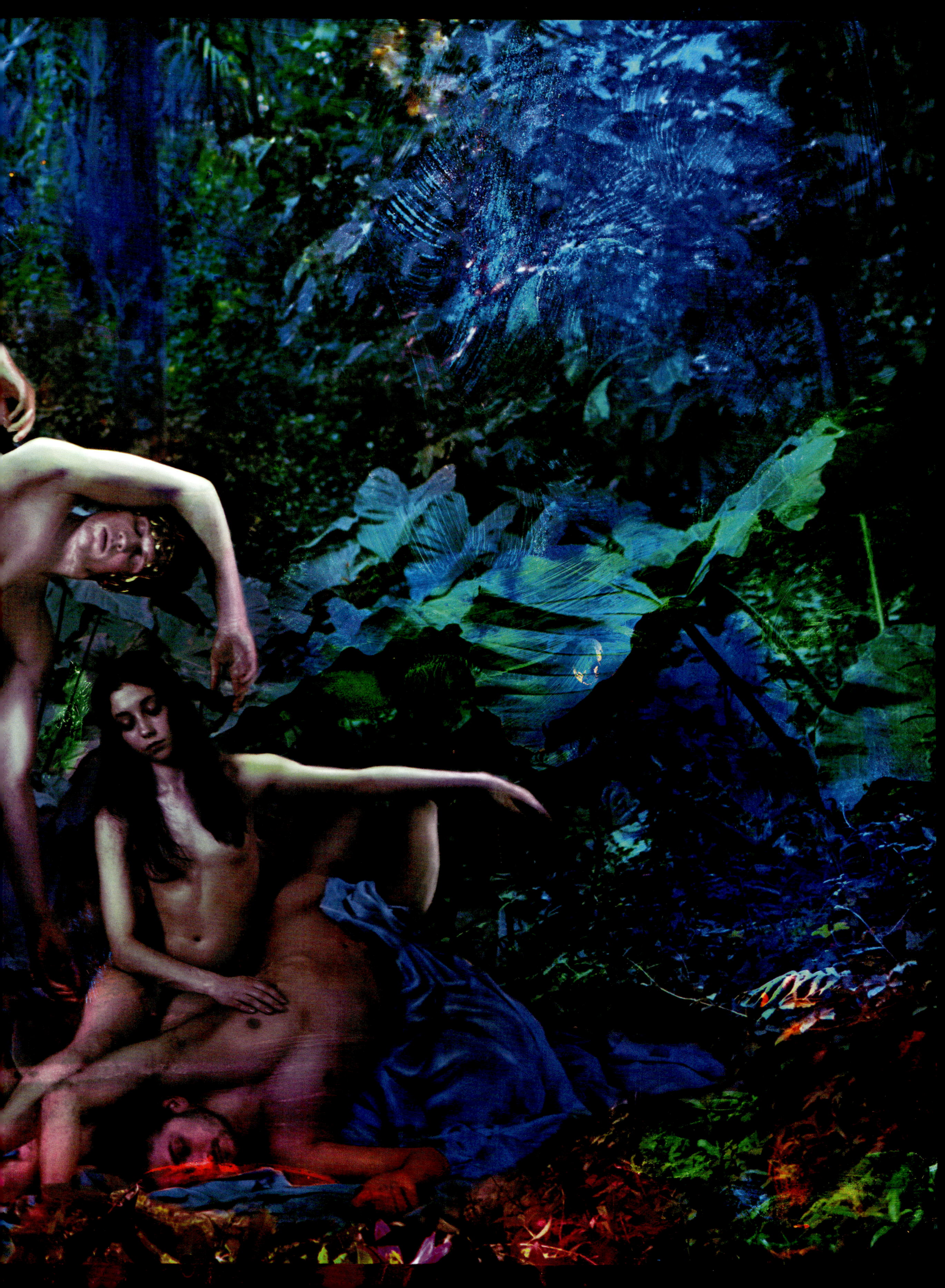

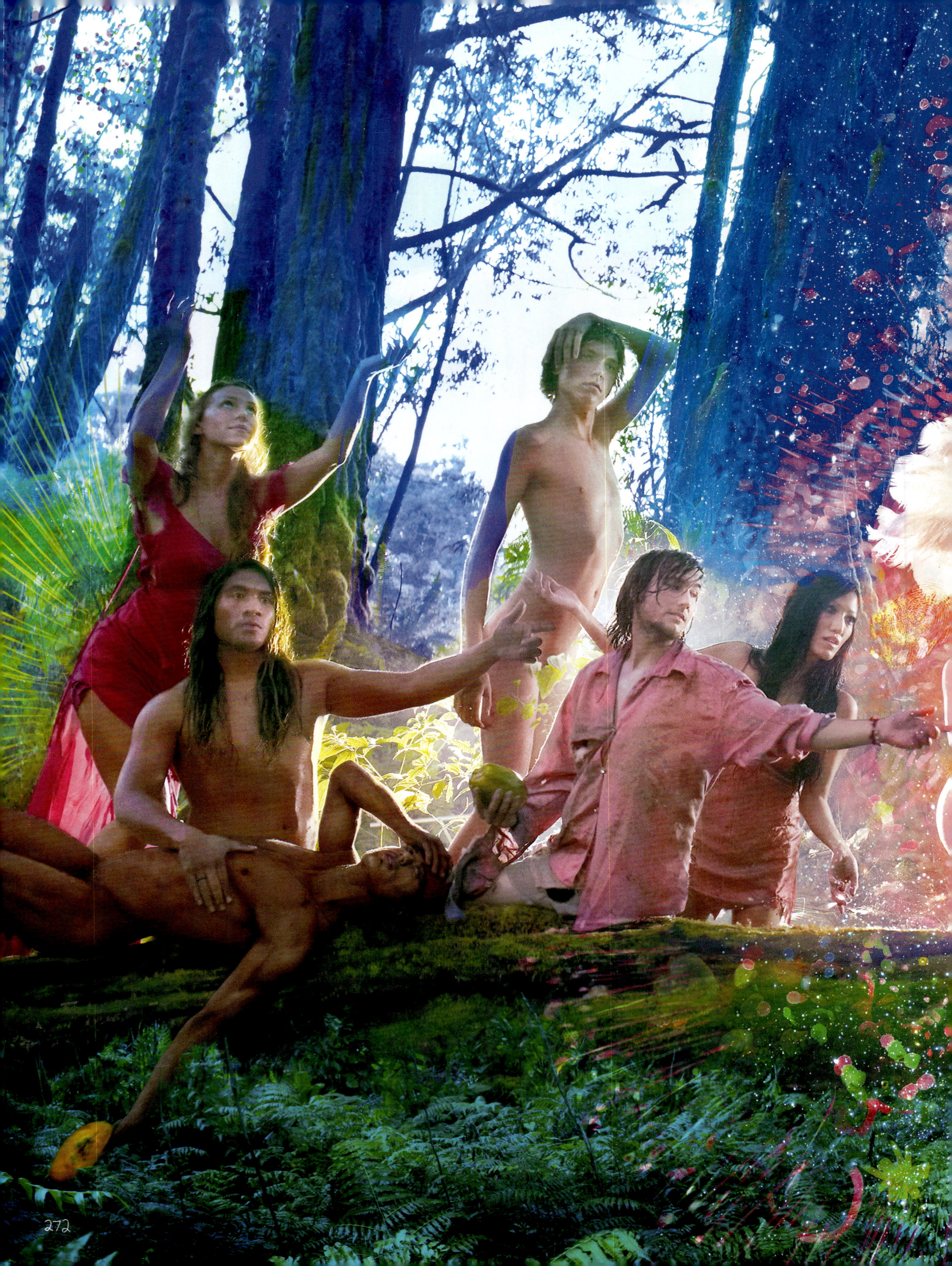

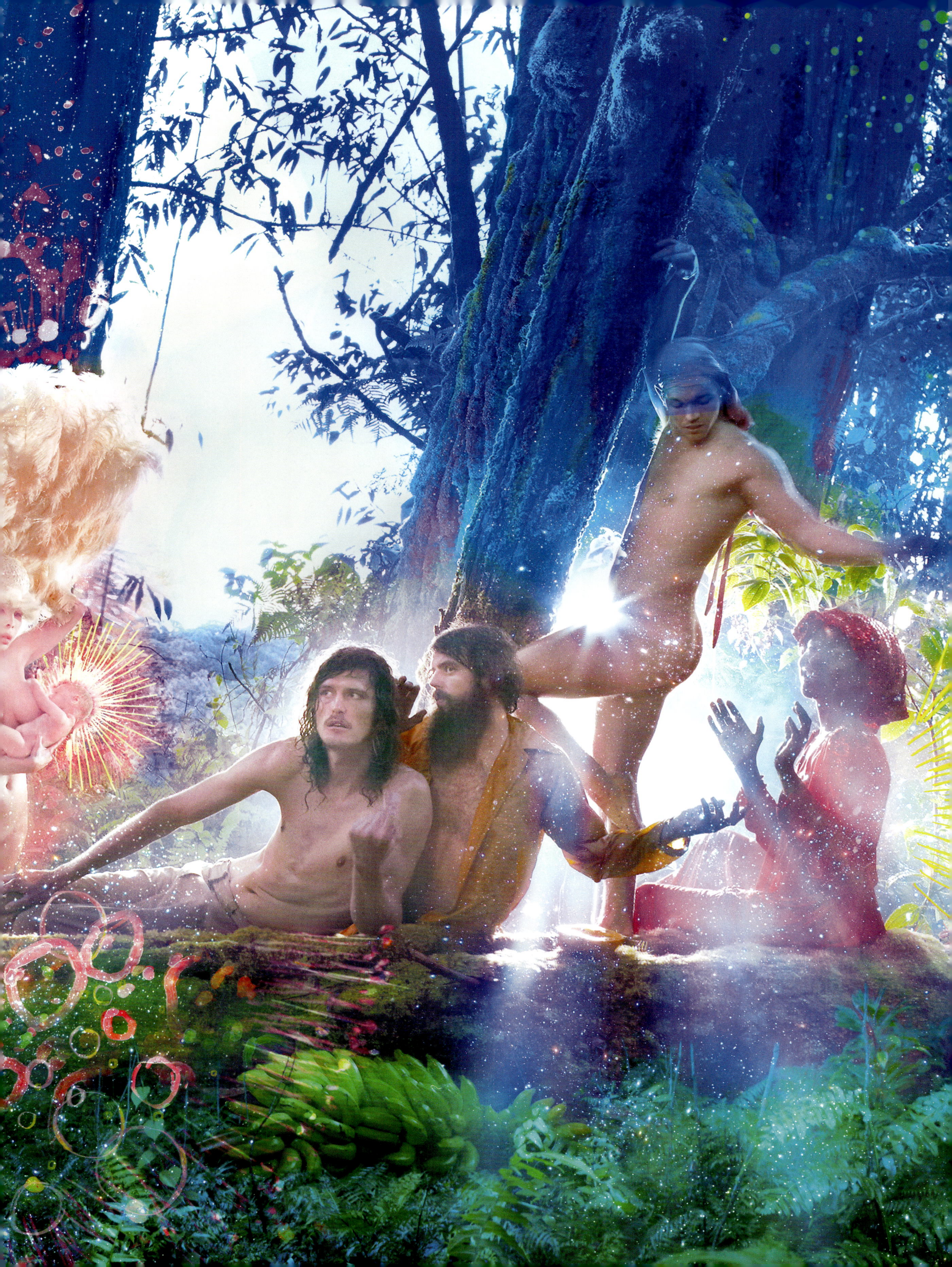

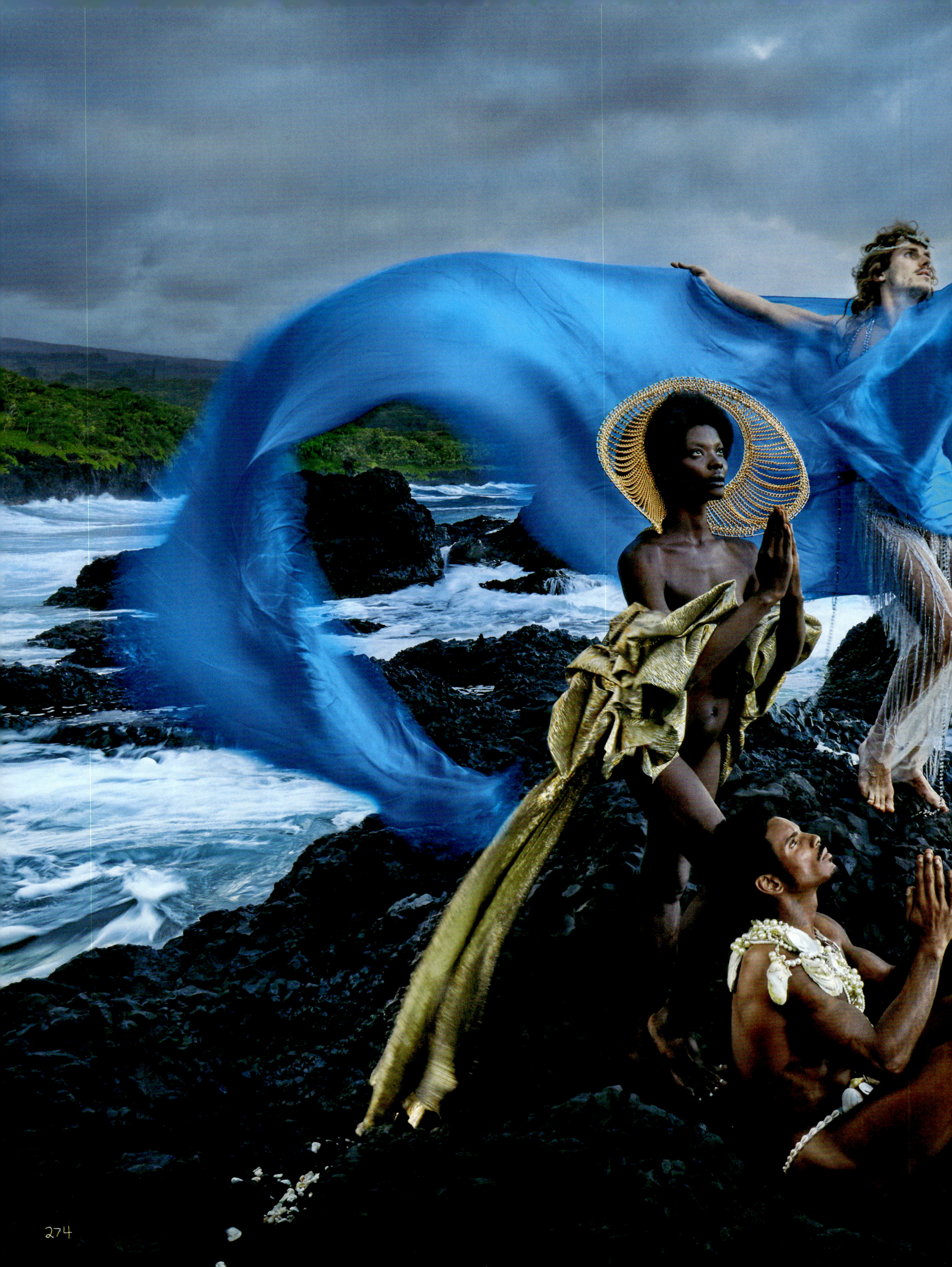

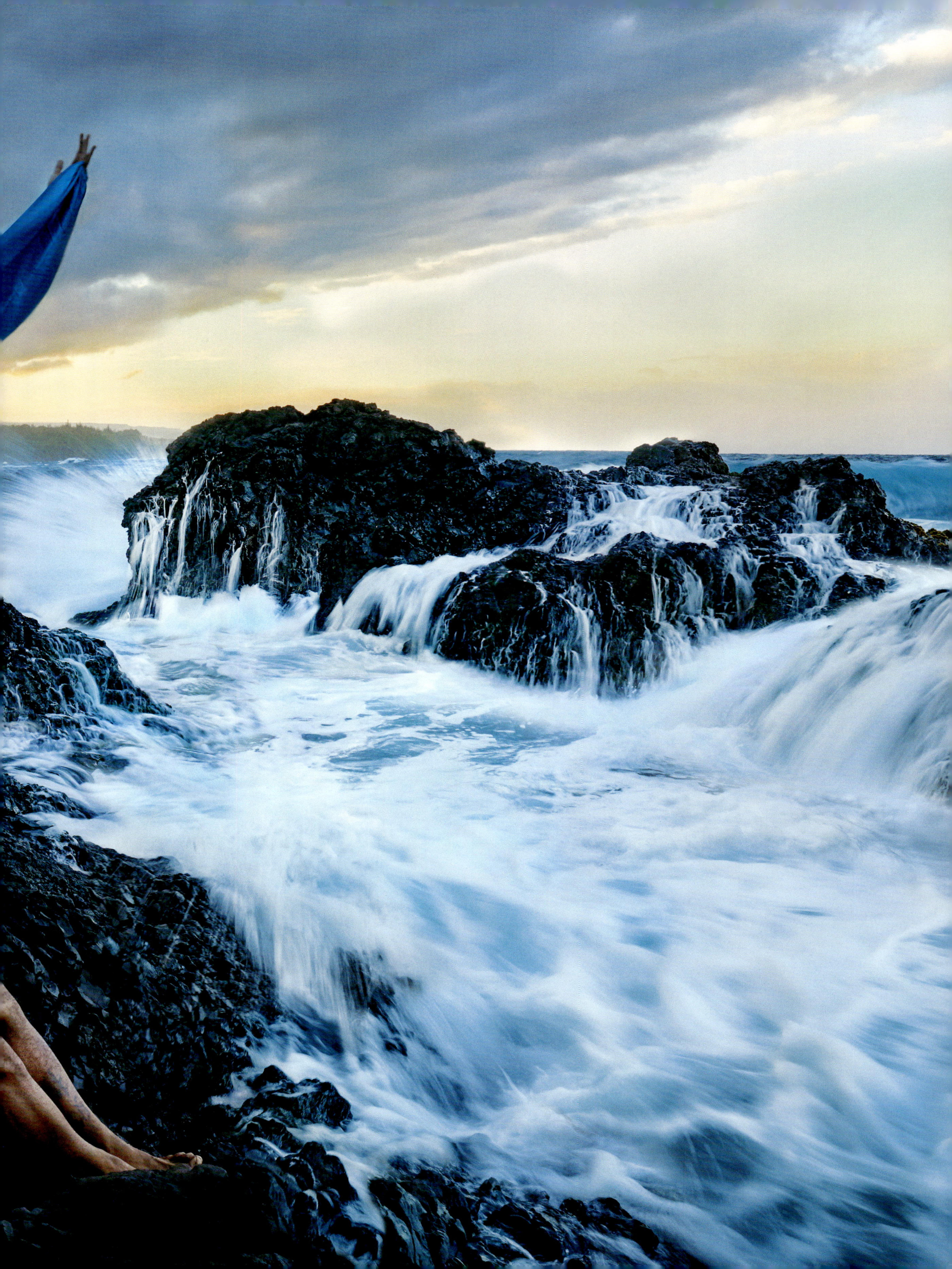

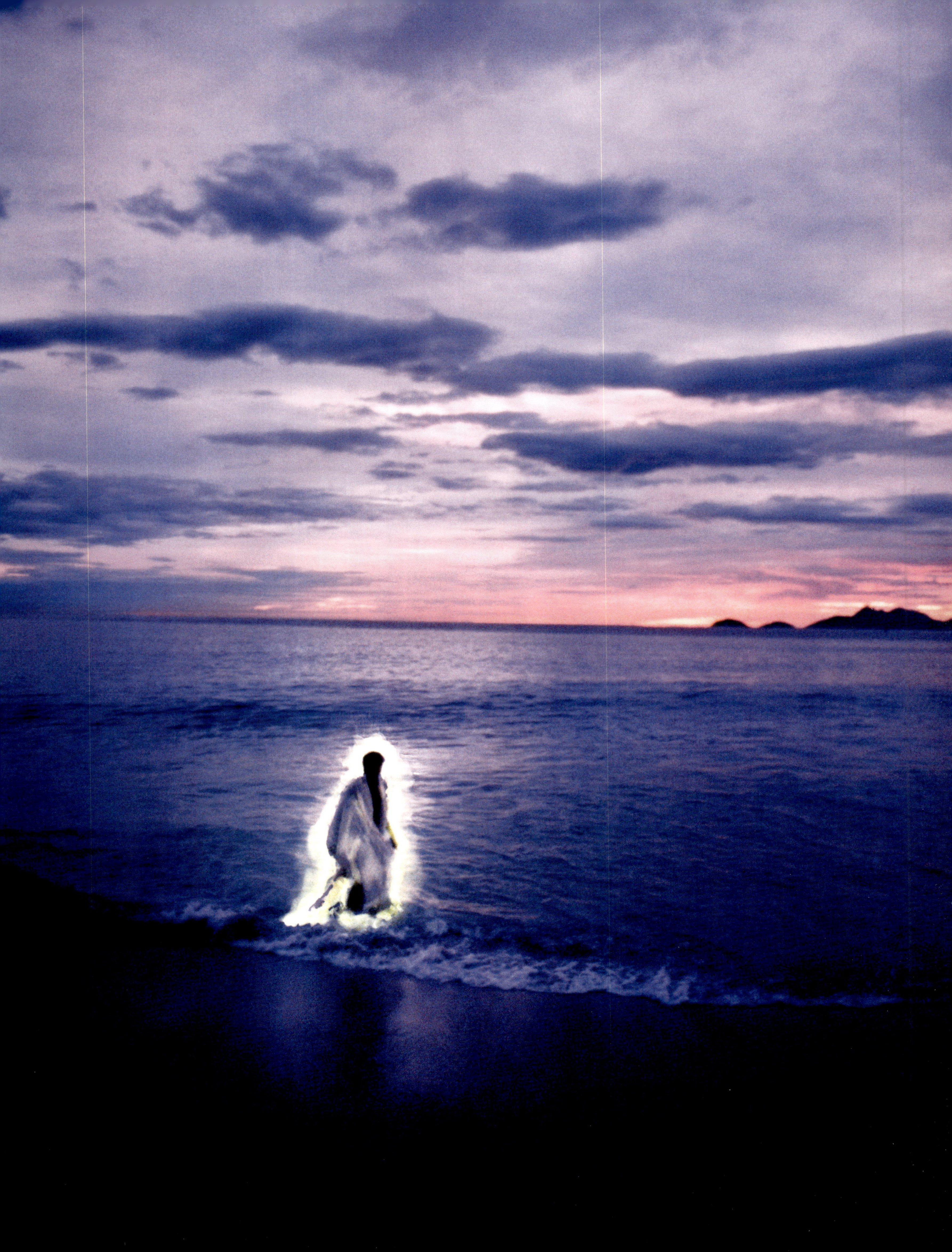

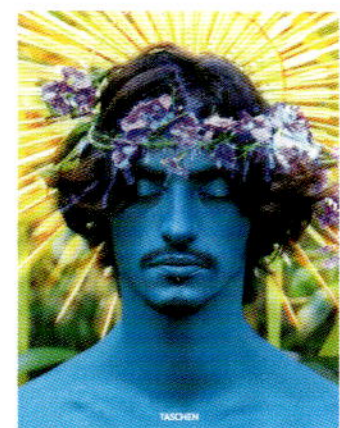

Sergei Polunin
Behold, 2016

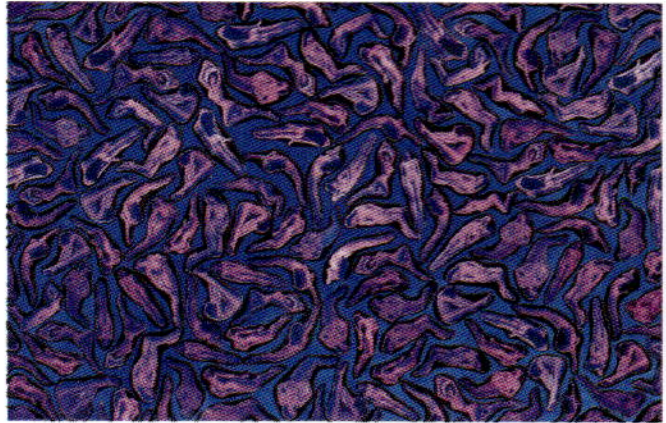

Eve Under a Microscope
"Everything you'll ever need to know is within you—The secrets of the universe are imprinted on the cells of your body." —Dan Millman

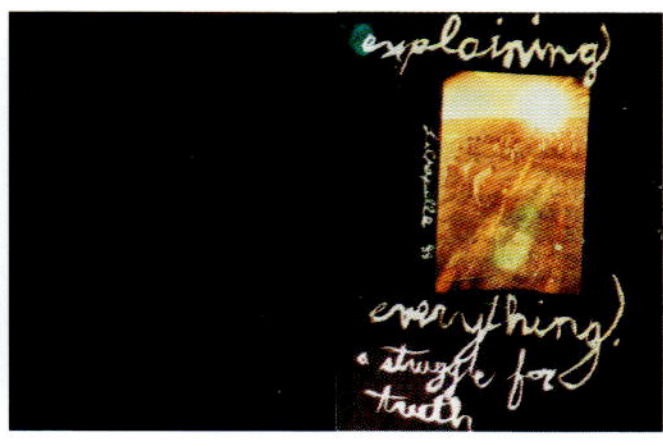

Explaining Everything.
A Struggle for Truth, 1988
Israel

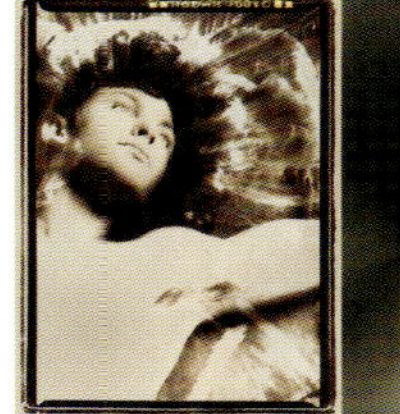

I Will Come To You, 1984
NYC

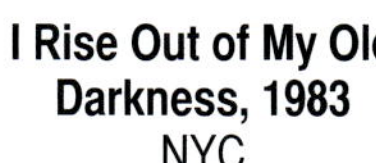

I Rise Out of My Old Darkness, 1983
NYC

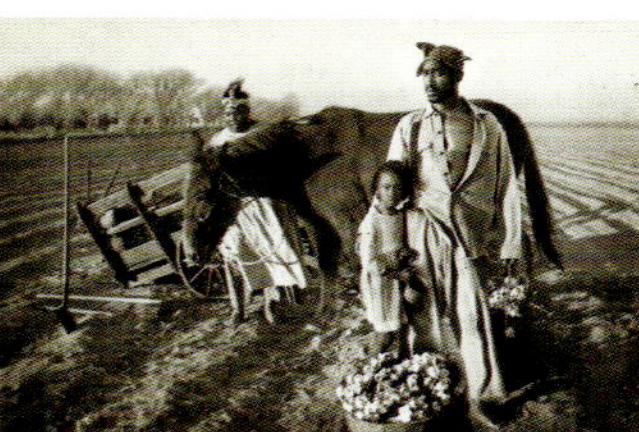

Tupac Shakur
Still I Rise, 1996
California

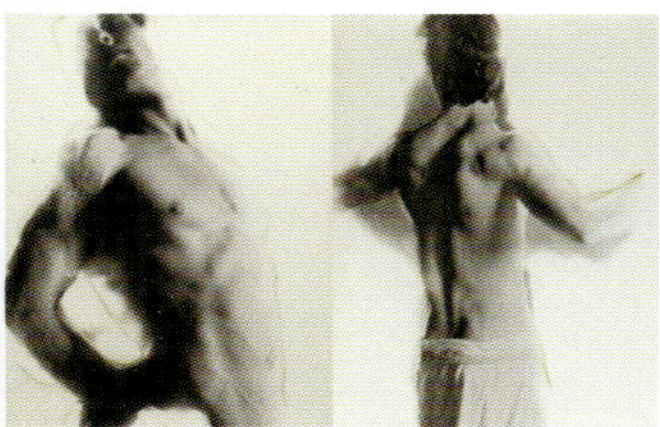

In That Place, 1983
NYC

Where Shadow Ceases, 1983
NYC

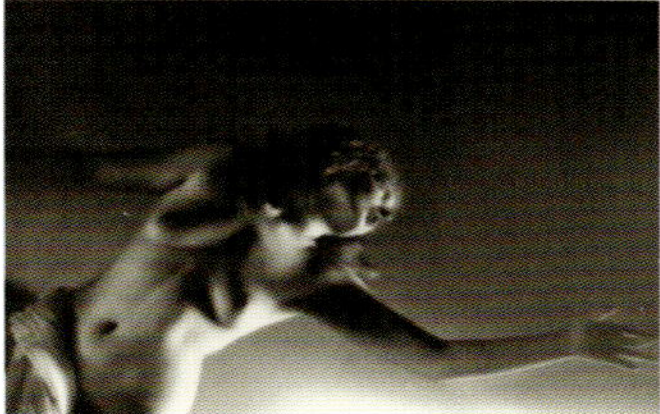

There Is a Light That Leads Us to All Goodness, 1983
NYC

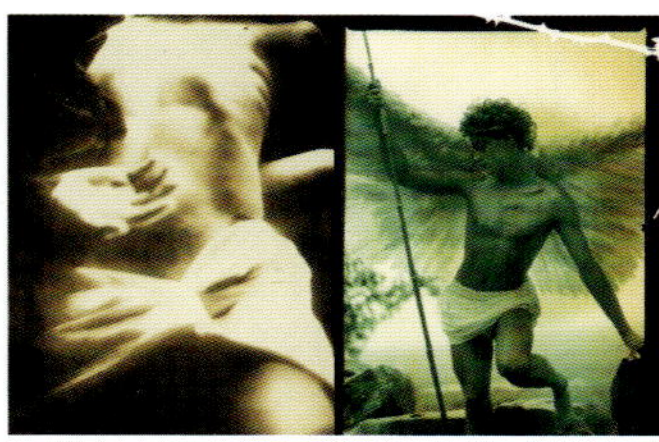

I Surrender, 1984
NYC

Divine Thoughts, 1986
Farmington, Connecticut

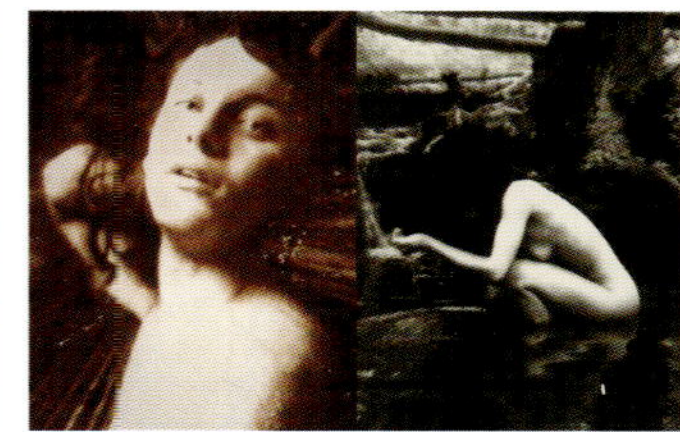

My Friend With Love in His Eyes, 1984
NYC

Create in Me a Clean Heart, 1984
Farmington, Connecticut

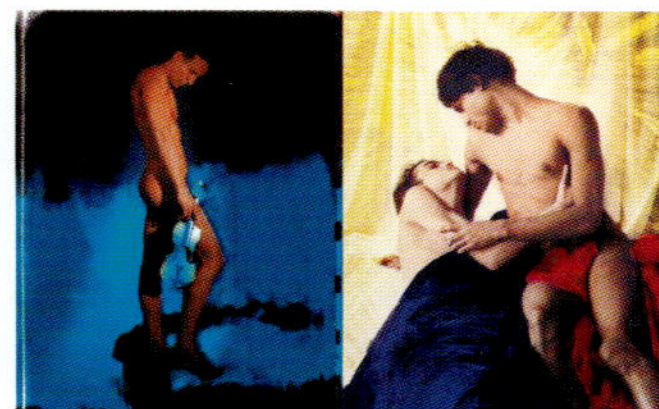

And the Band Played On…, 1986
NYC

But the Love Will Never Die, 1986
NYC

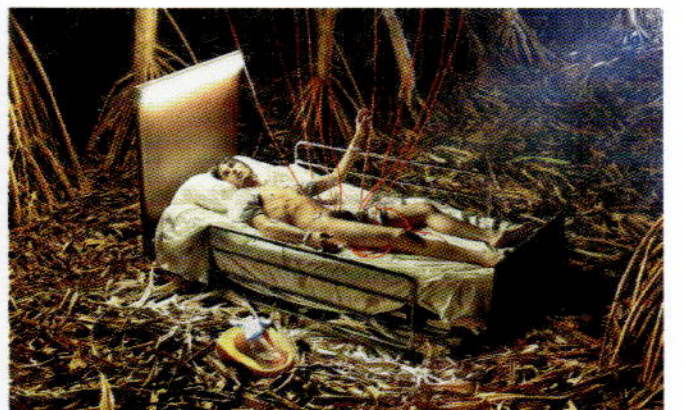

A Plague Came, 2008

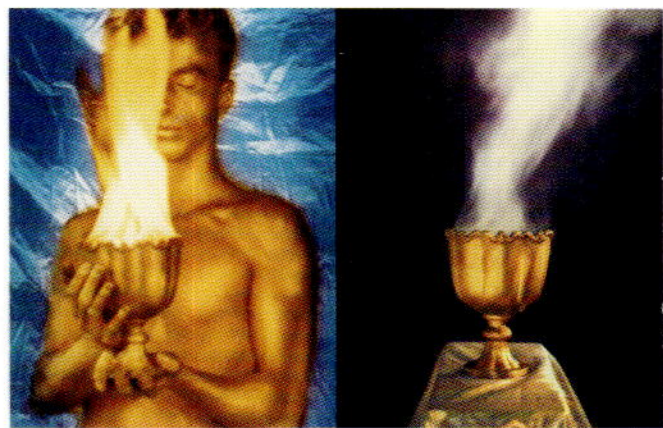

Before You Weren't Here, 1987
NYC

1987
NYC

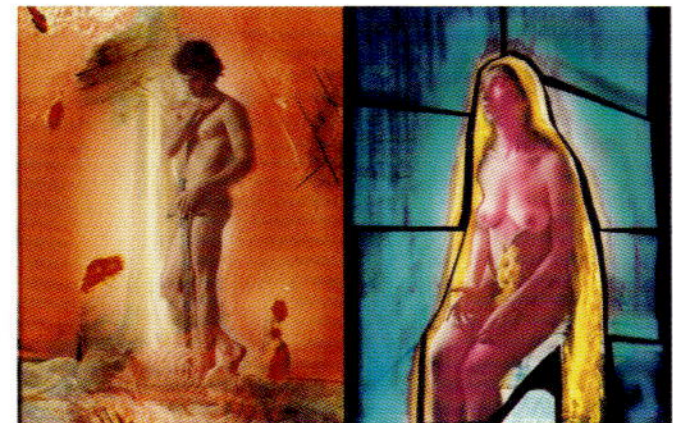

And Life Never Dies, 1989
NYC

Altar of Nature, 1989
NYC

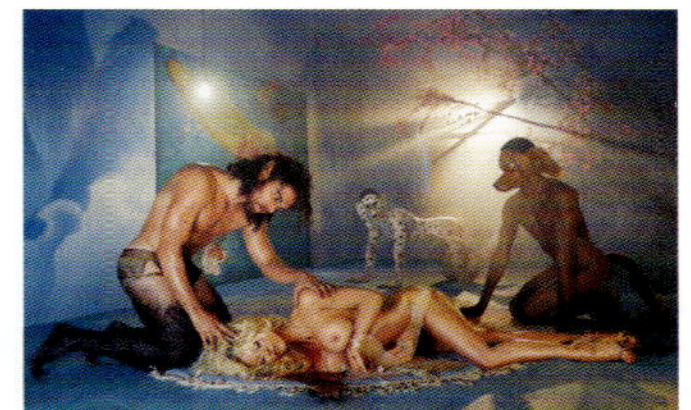

And Yet There Still Was Your Light, 2009
Los Angeles

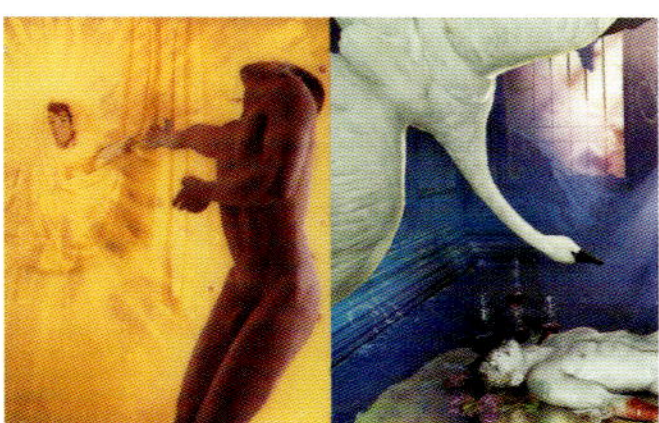

Reaching Towards the Sun, 1988
NYC

Dying Swan, 2013
Los Angeles

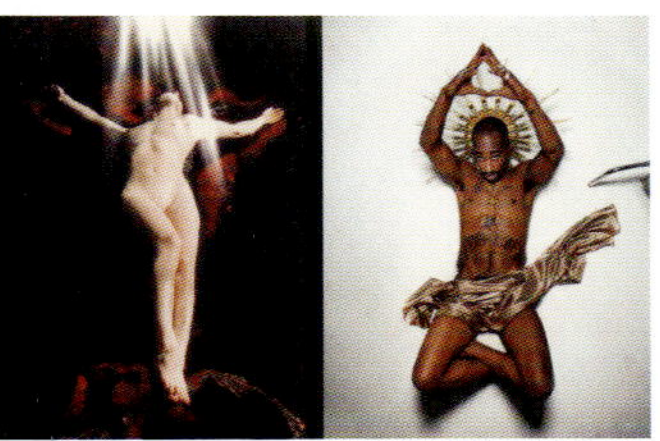

Good News of Great Joy!, 1984
Farmington, Connecticut

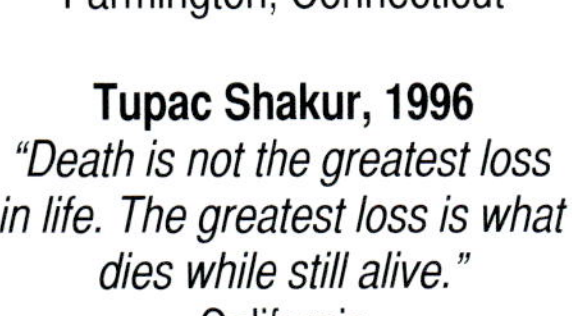

Tupac Shakur, 1996
"Death is not the greatest loss in life. The greatest loss is what dies while still alive."
California

American Jesus:
Hold Me Carry Me Boldly, 2007
Hawaii

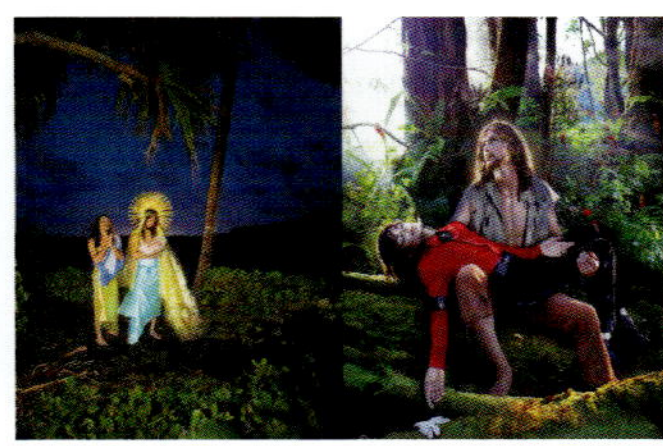

We Can Know the Ways of Heaven

In Jesus' Arms

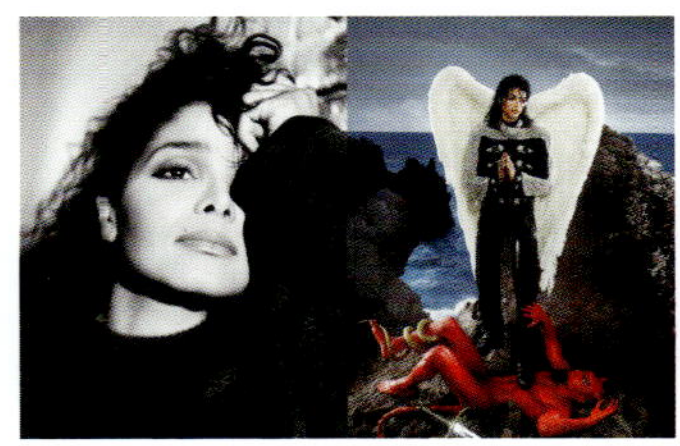

Janet Jackson, 1987
"Our love can be great."
Brooklyn, NYC

Archangel Michael, 1990
"And no message could have been any clearer."

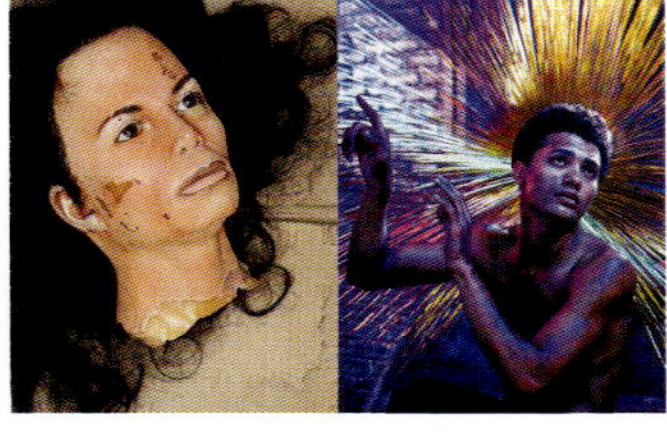

Still Life Series: Regarding the Pain of Others, 2010
Wax museum figure, Hollywood

The Joy Inside My Tears
From Stevie Wonder's *Songs in the Key of Life*. An album everyone must listen to—a most miraculous recording.

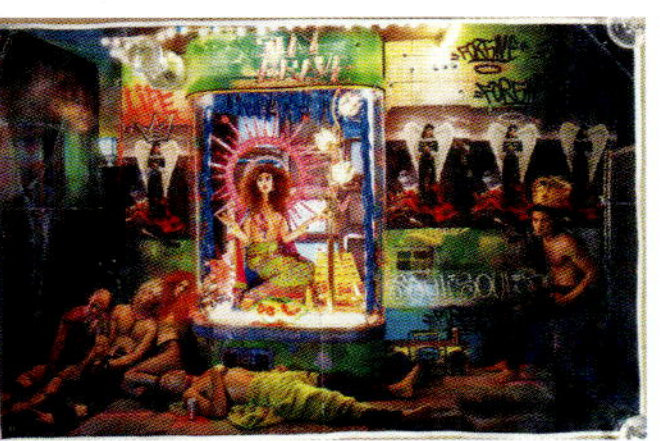

The Eyes of Men Are Closed, the Scared Have Locked Their Doors

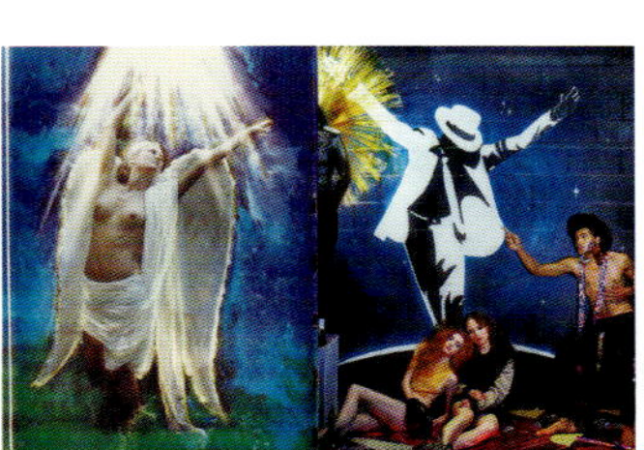

Stayed With Me Just Long Enough, to Rescue Me, 1988
Farmington, Connecticut

"Keep the Faith", 2016
Hollywood

Paris Jackson
What Her Father Taught Her—This Beautiful Daughter, 2017

Oh Happy Day!!, 2007
Hawaii

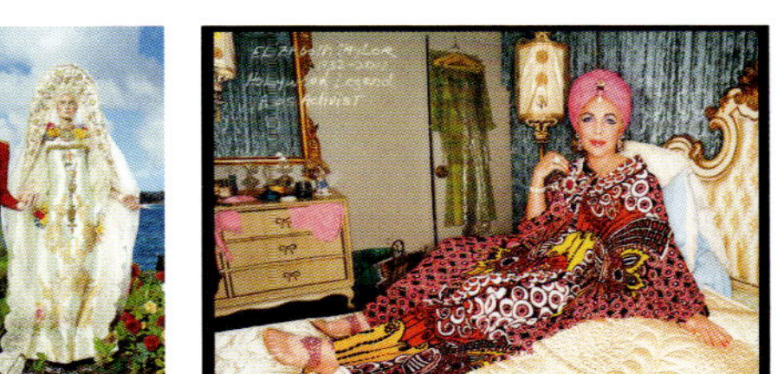

Elizabeth Taylor
She Stood by Him Till the End—His Loving Friend, 2002
Hollywood

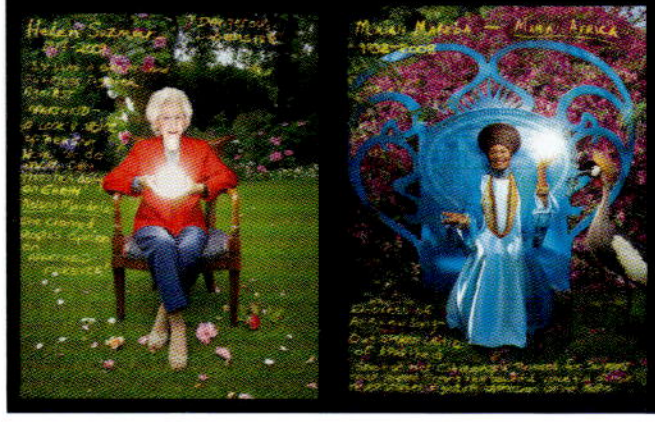

Helen Suzman (1917–2009)**, 2007**
Johannesburg, South Africa

Miriam Makeba (1932–2008)**, 2007**
Johannesburg, South Africa

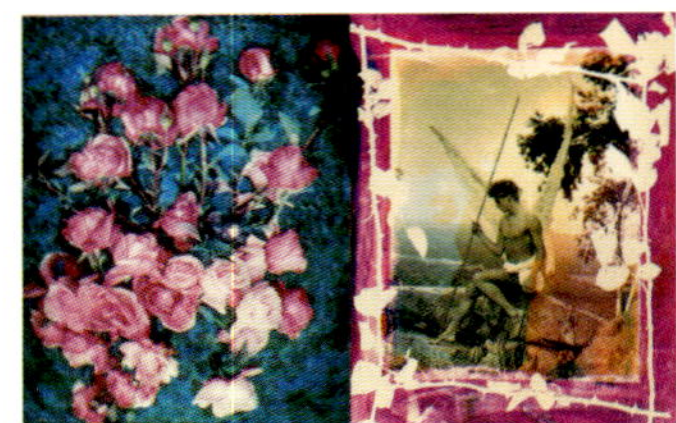

I Touch Roses, 1988
Farmington, Connecticut

Waiting Angel, 1988

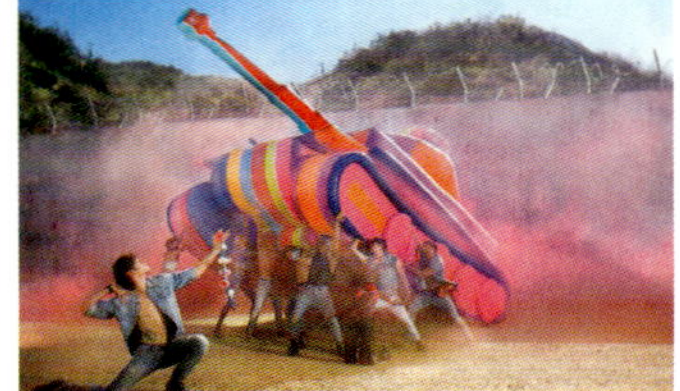

Make Love Not Walls, 2016
California

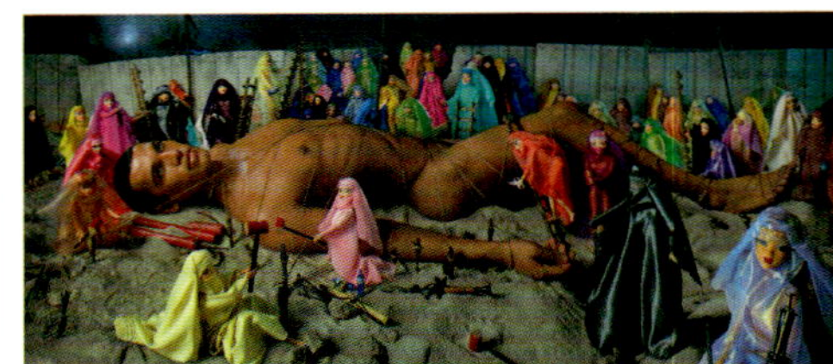

Seventytwo Virgins, 2008
Los Angeles

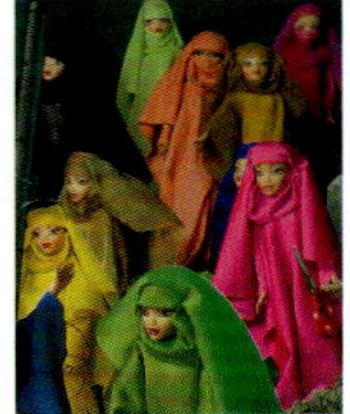

Seventytwo Virgins, 2008
Detail

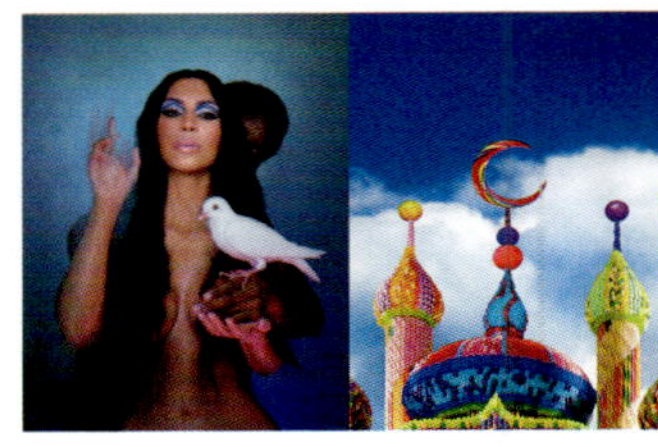

Mary Magdalene, 2018
"Trials are nothing else but the forge that purifies the soul of all its imperfections."

Candy Mosque, 2007
Detail

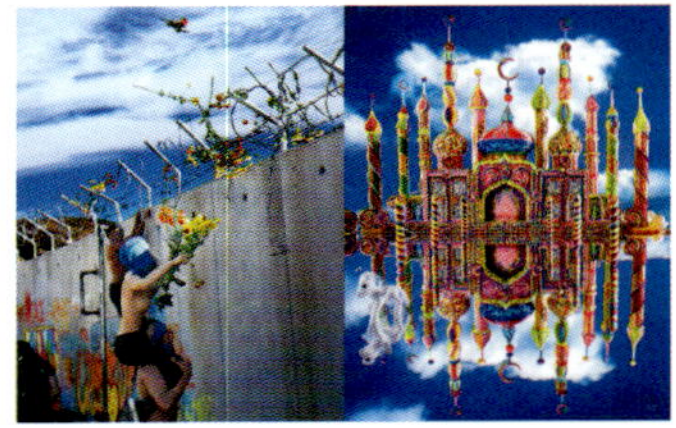

Pete Seeger, 2017
"Where have all the flowers gone?"

Candy Mosque, 2007
Los Angeles

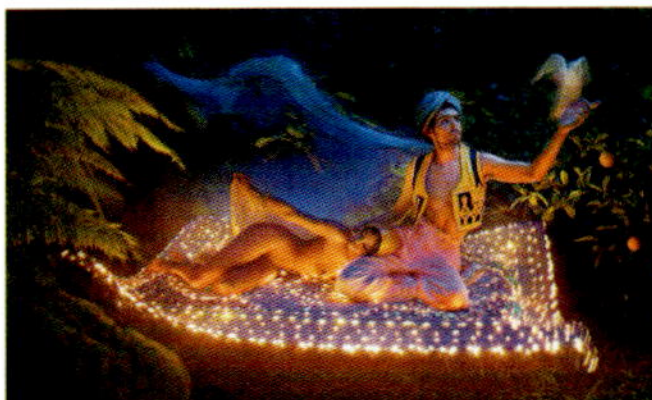

Omar From Baghdad in the Garden of Allah, 2017

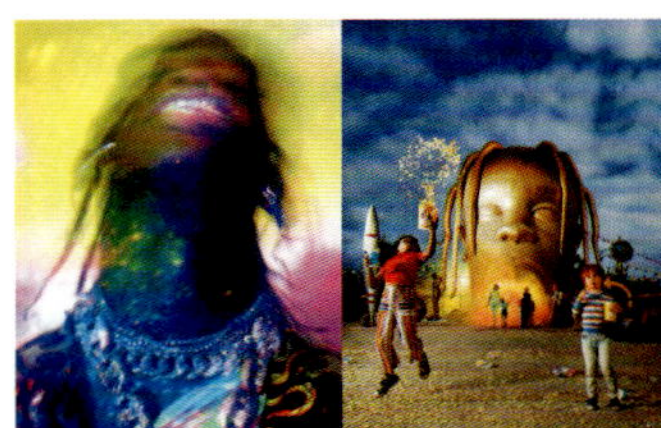

Butterfly Effect, 2019

Golden Idols 1, 2018
Astroworld

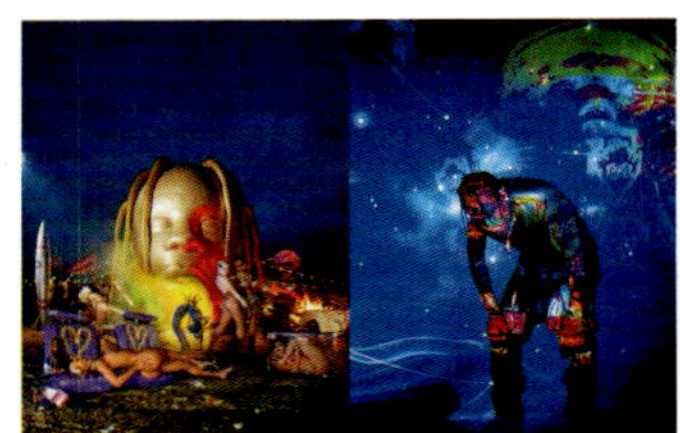

Golden Idols 2, 2018
Astroworld

Travis Scott L.A. Flame, 2019

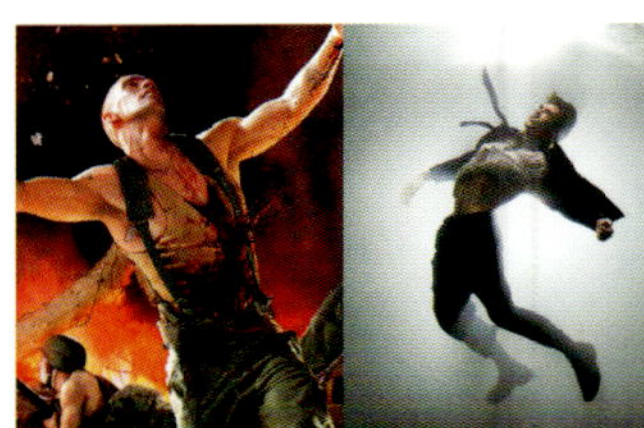

Holy War!—Lies— No War Could Ever Be Holy, 2008
Hollywood

Awakened Job, 2007
Los Angeles

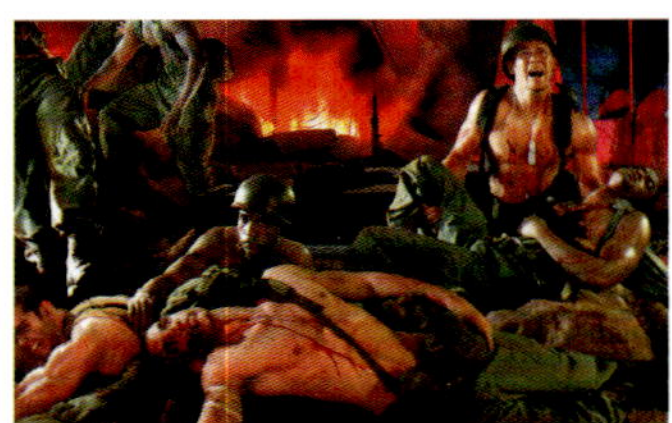

You Will Hear of Wars And Rumors of Wars... Matthew 24:6, 2008
Hollywood

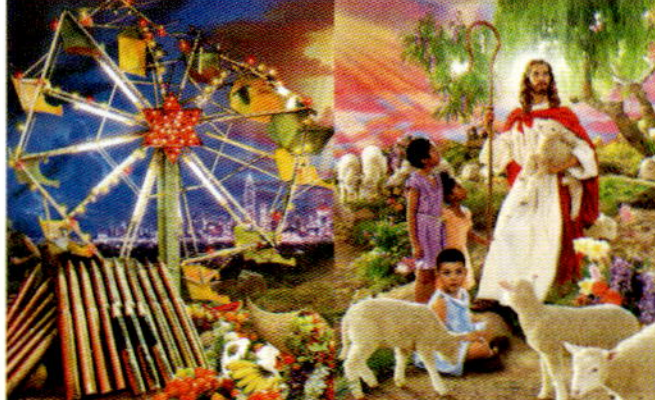

Holy Wars Lies— For No War Could Be Holy, 2008
Hollywood

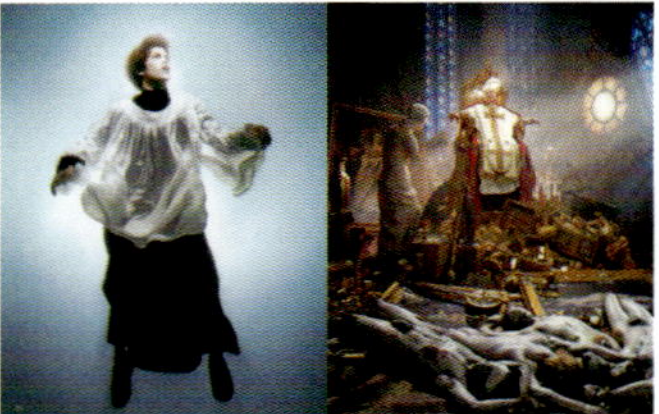

Awakened Altar Boy, 2007

God Help Us, 2009

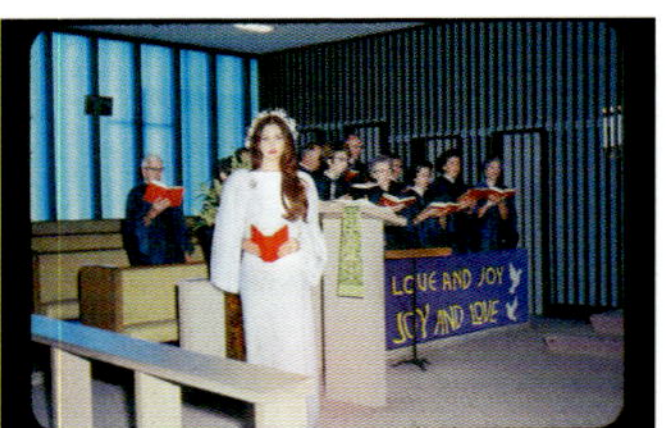

Lana Del Rey Let the Choir Sing, 2017
California

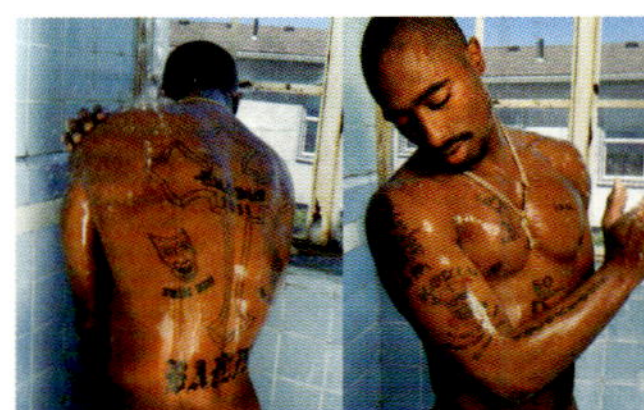

Tupac Shakur To Begin Again, 1996
California

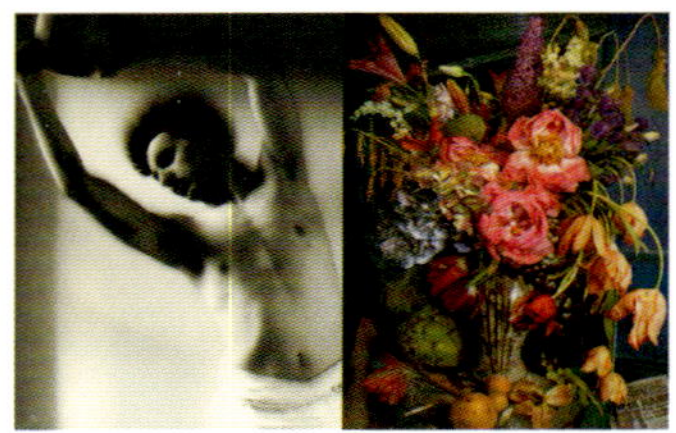

Body of Water, 1983
NYC

Earth Laughs in Flowers Wilting Gossip, 2008–2011
Hollywood

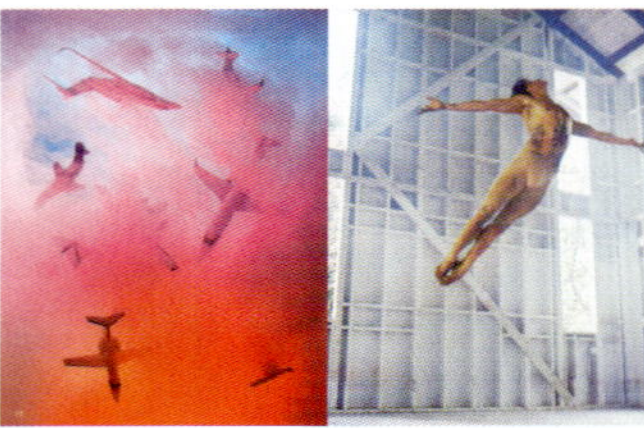

Airistocracy Clouded Minds, 2014

Sergei Polunin Take Me to Church, 2015
Hawaii

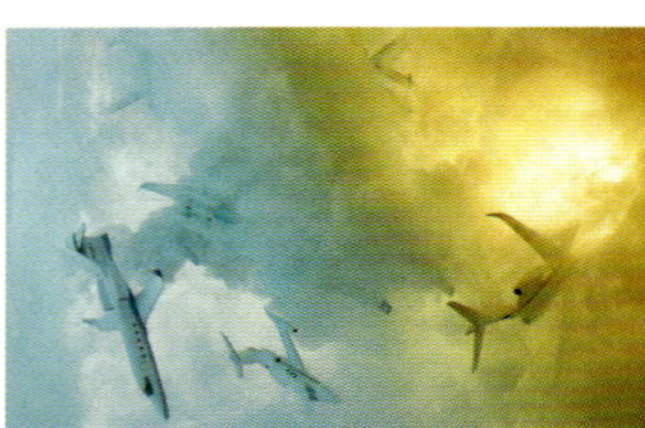

Airistocracy Endless Acquisitions and the Race to Nowwhere..., 2014

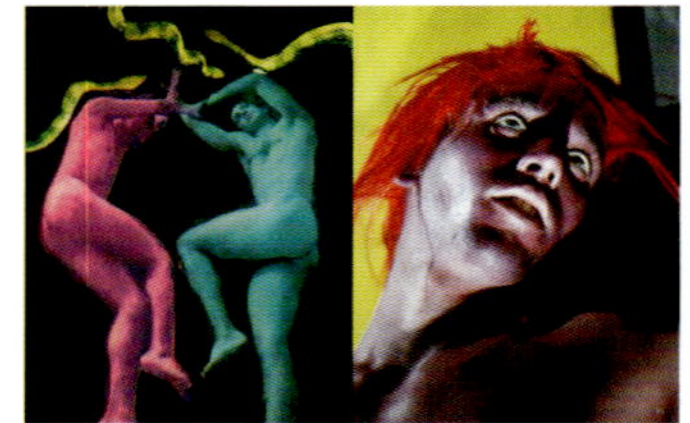

Cain and Abel, 1989
NYC

But Now I See, 1989

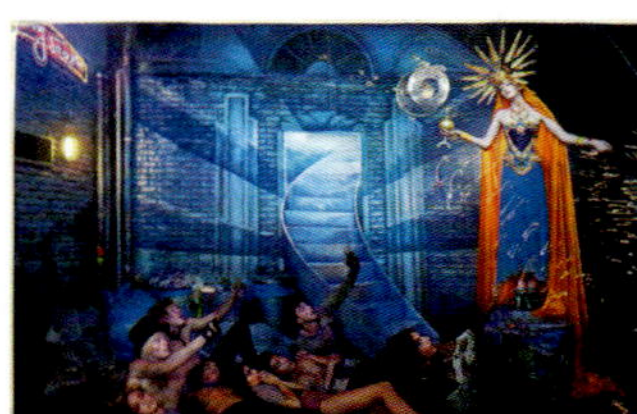

Quenching Every Thirst, 2015
Hollywood

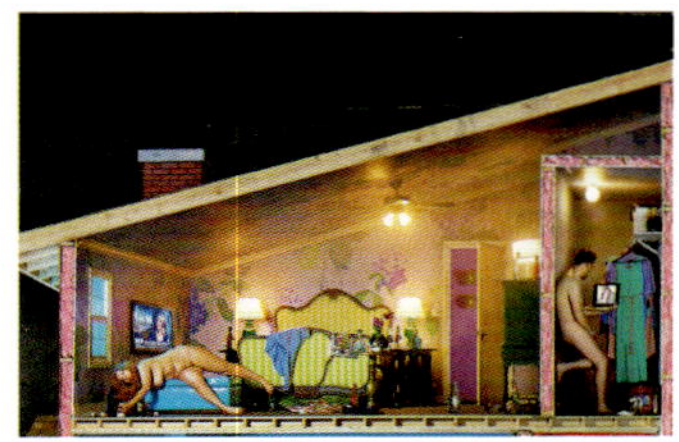

The Rooms I Dwell In, 2013
Hollywood

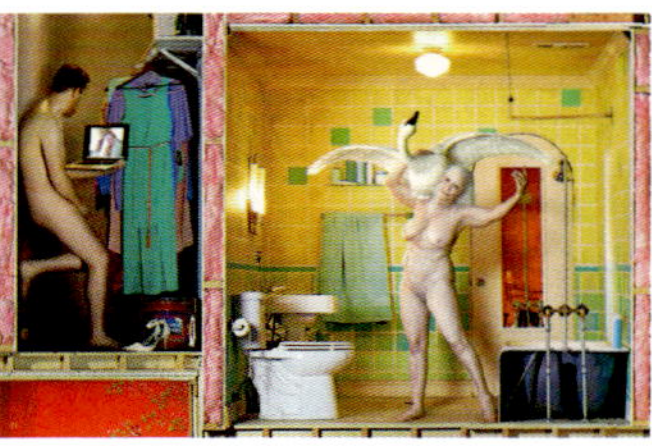

Lust, 2013
Hollywood

Wisdom and Aging, 2013
Hollywood

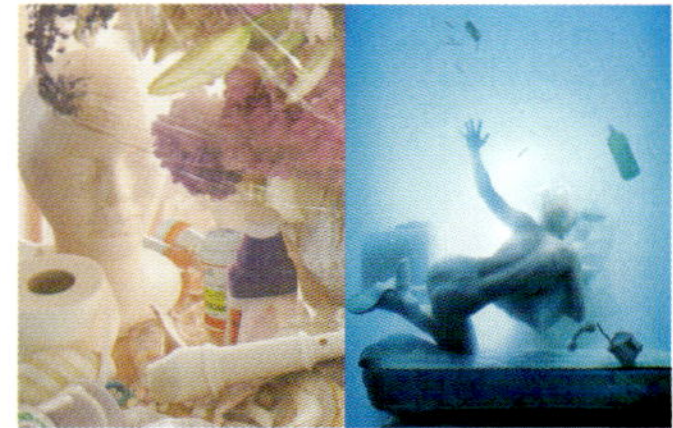

Earth Laughs in Flowers Deathless Winter, 2008–2011
Los Angeles

Silent Screaming, 2007

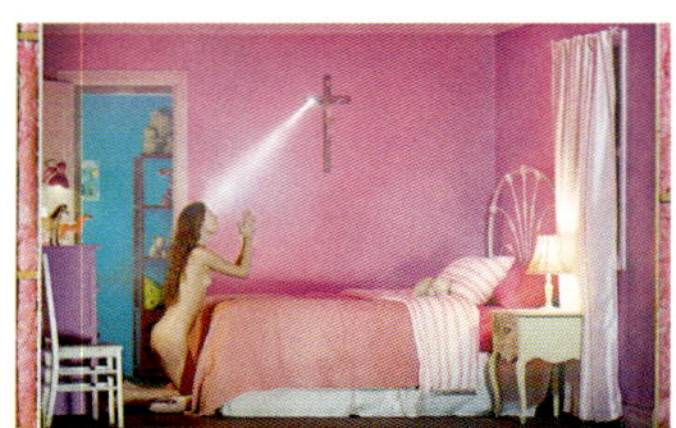

Prayer, 2013
Hollywood

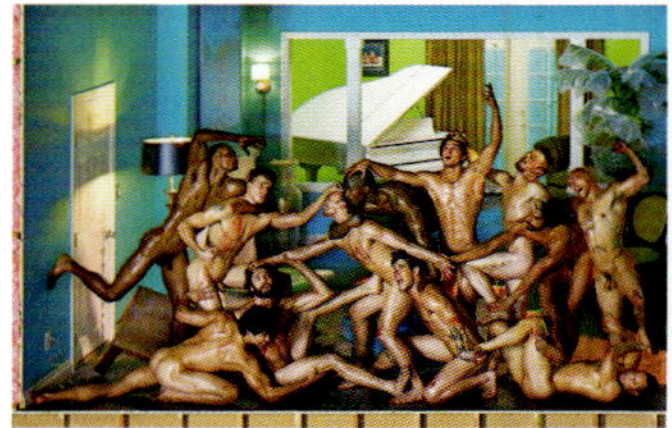

Anger, 2013
Hollywood

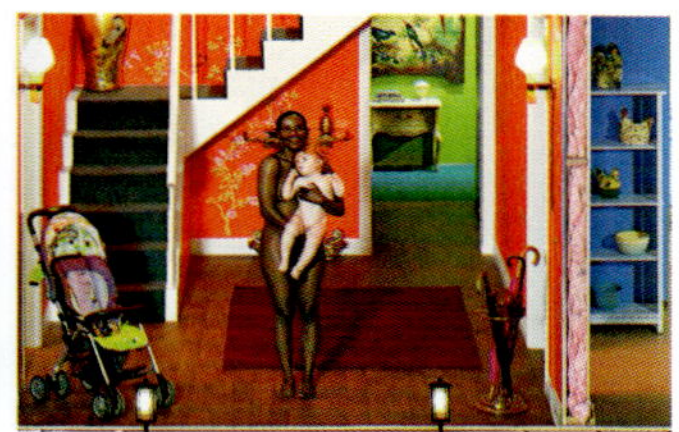
Unconditional Love, 2013
Hollywood

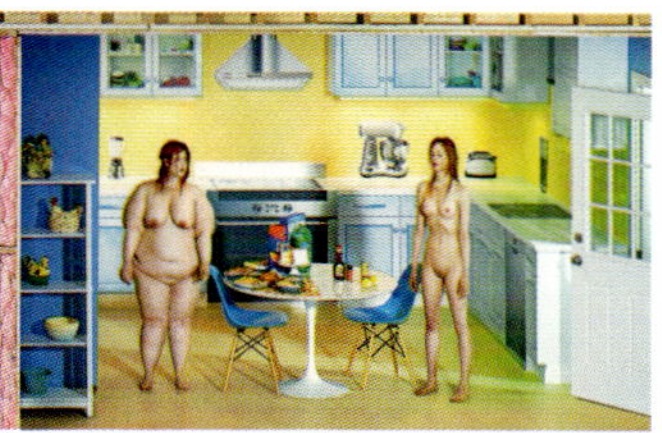
Dysmorphia, 2013
Hollywood

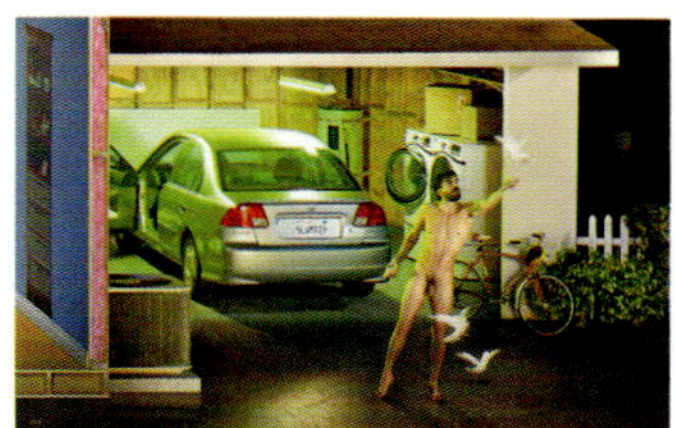
Spirit, 2013
Hollywood

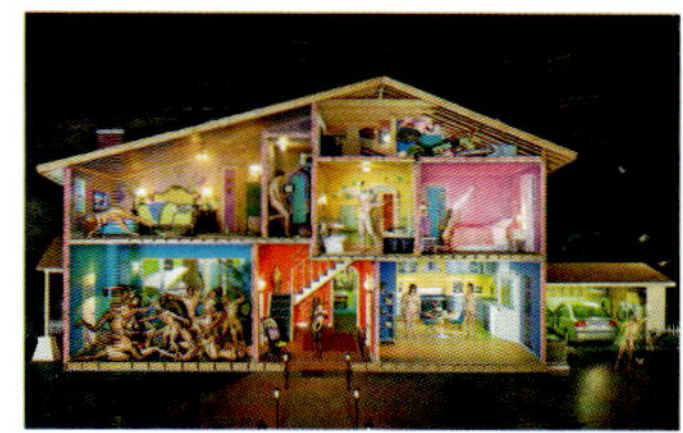
Self-Portrait as a House, 2013
Hollywood

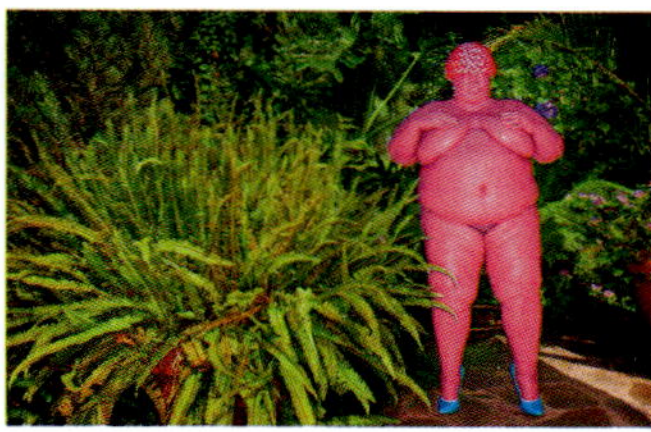
Venus of Willendorf, 2016
Hollywood

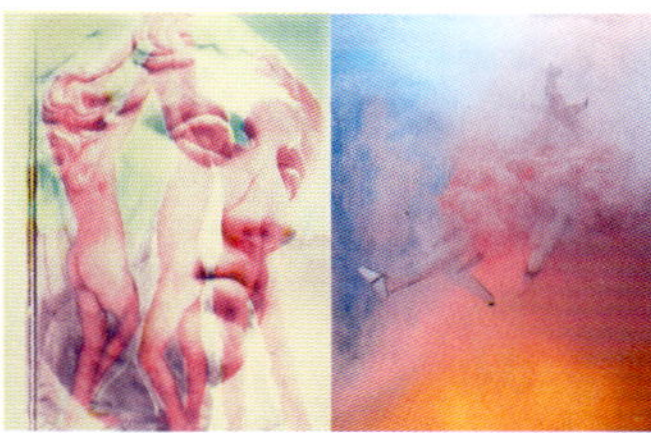
The Past Awoken, 1988
NYC

Airistocracy
Private Pirates, 2014
Los Angeles

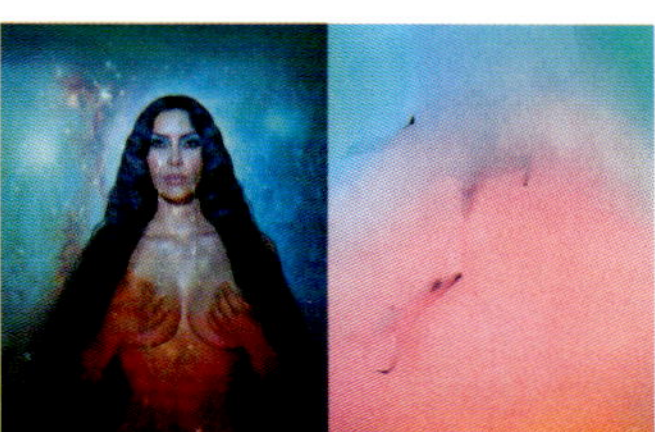
"When a star girl cries, she sheds not tears but light."
—Jerry Spinelli

Airistocracy
Earthly Wealth Is Confusion—Your Riches an Illusion, 2014

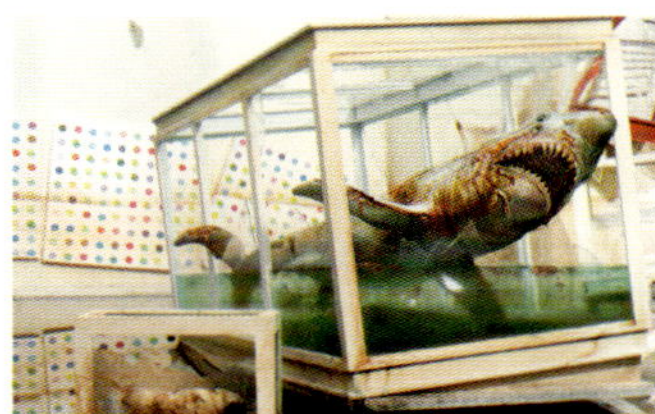
Your Trophy Is Dead, 2012
Hollywood

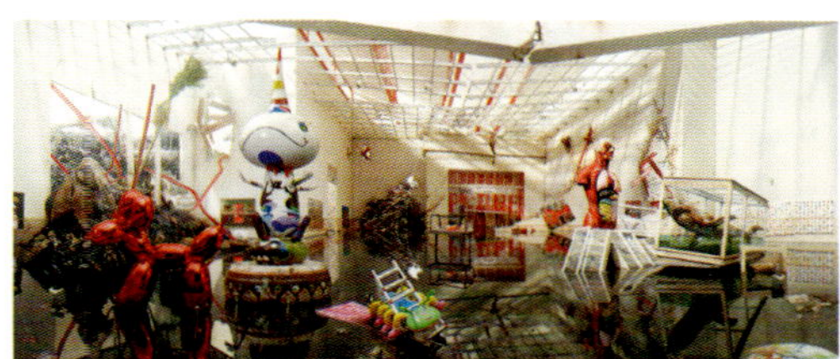
Seismic Shift, 2012

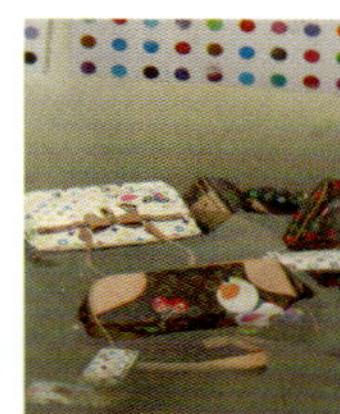
Hand Bags, 2012

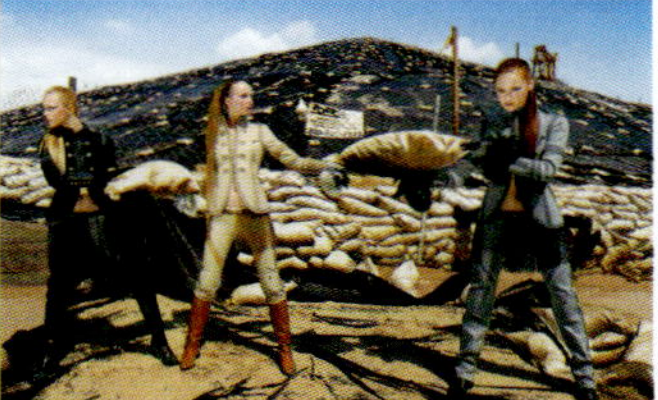
2 Sandbags, 2005
California

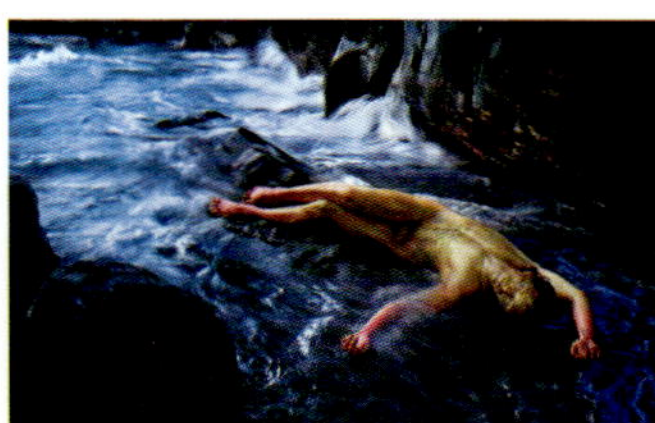
Wash Me Clean—Cleanse My Soul, 2016
Hawaii

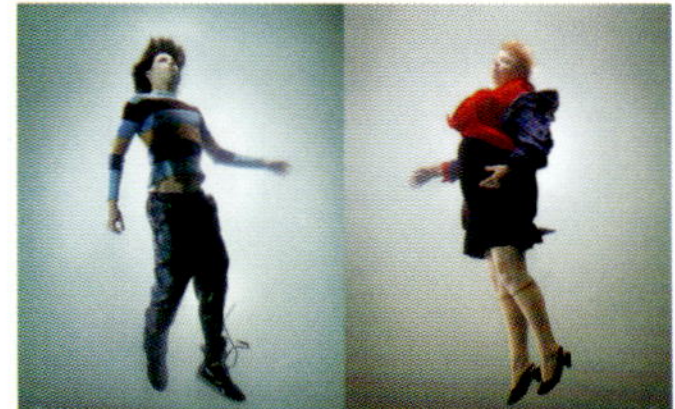
Awakened
Jonah, 2007
Los Angeles

Awakened
Ruth

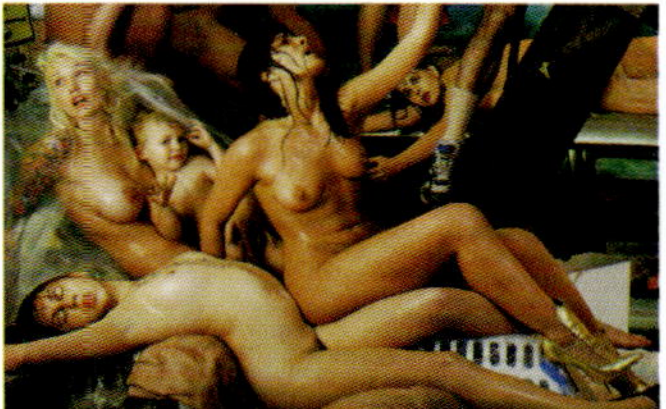
Deluge, 2006
Detail

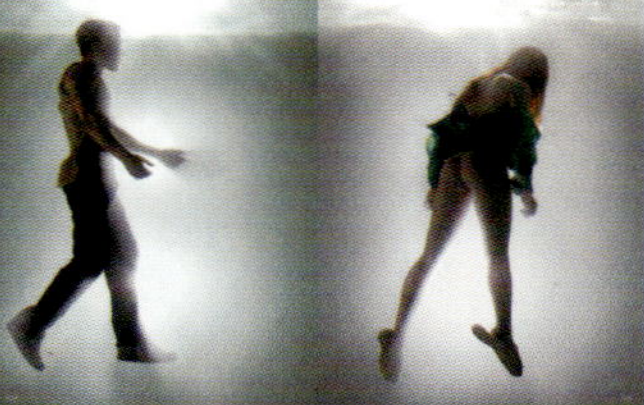
Awakened
Daniel, 2007

Awakened
Sarah

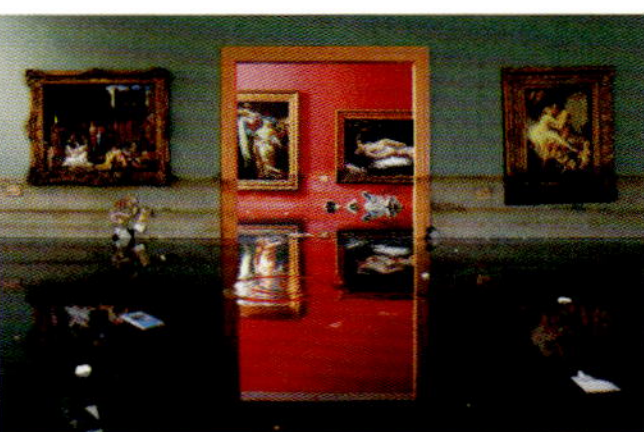
What Was Once Priceless Is So Again, 2007
Hollywood

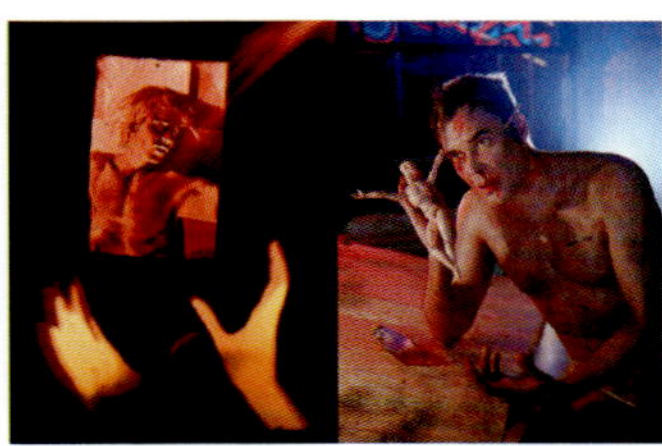
Drawn to Me, 1986
NYC

Premonition, 2009
Hollywood

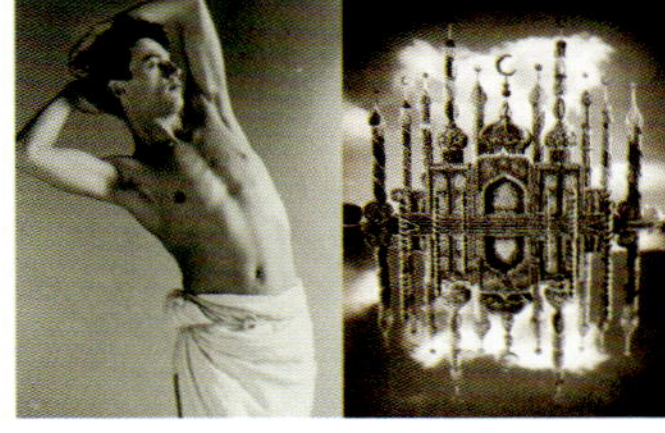
The Truth Lives Inside of Us, 1983
NYC

From Both Sides, 2007

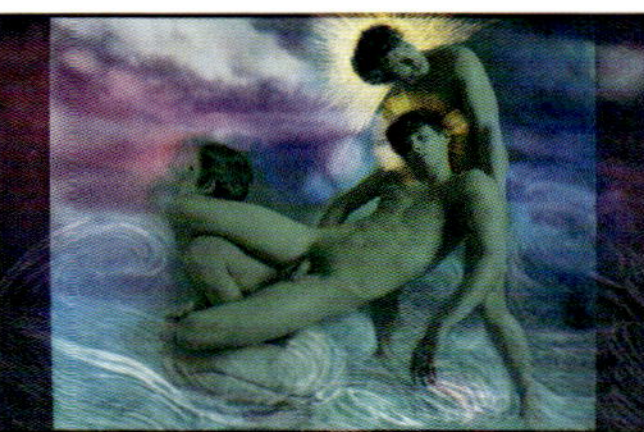
Life's Final Hour, 2012

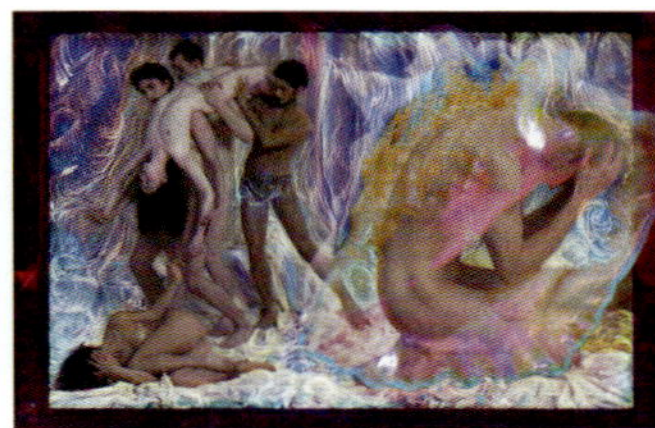
"I pass death with the dying and birth with the new born babe"
—Walt Whitman
London, 2017

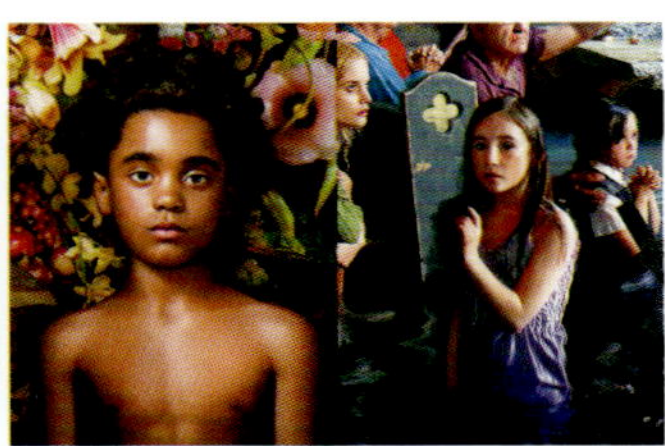
Innocence, 2007

That I May Know the Truth, 2007

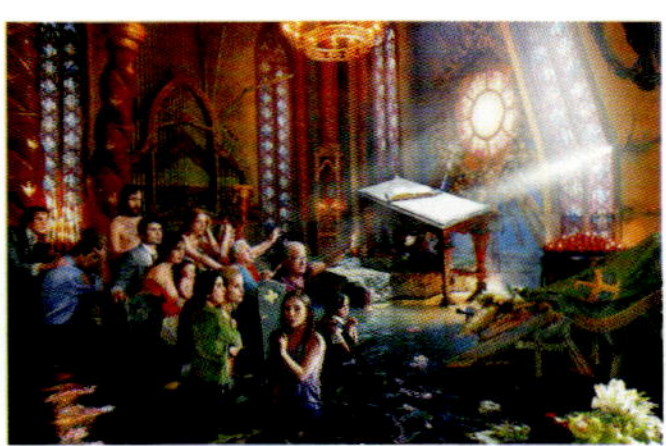
They Will Ask Where Is Your God?, 2007
Hollywood

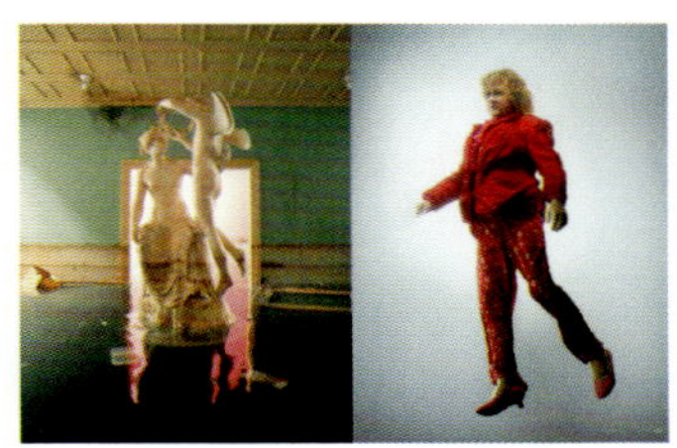
The End of All We Knew, 2007
Hollywood

Awakened
Rhoda, 2007

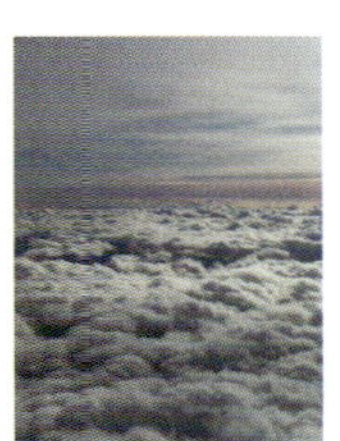
Renaissance Is My Hope
Renaissance = Rebirth or Awakening, 2006

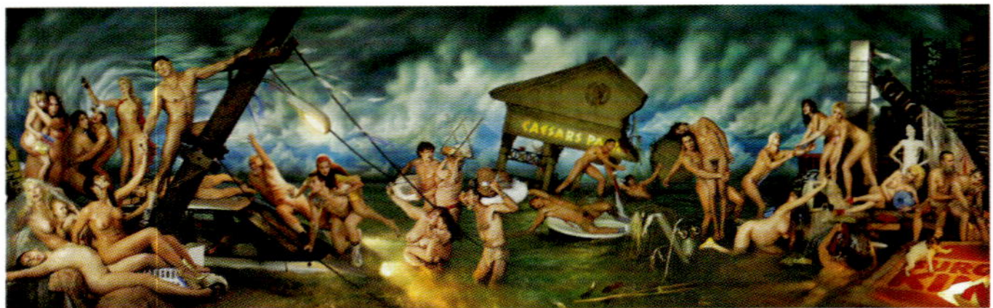

Deluge, 2006
Hollywood

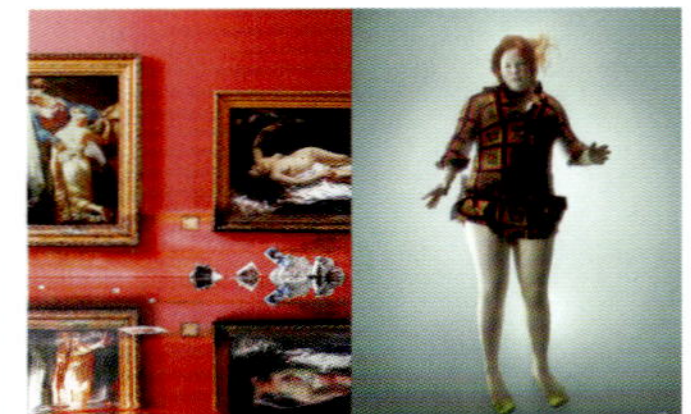

The World's Desire, 2007
Hollywood

Awakened
Hannah

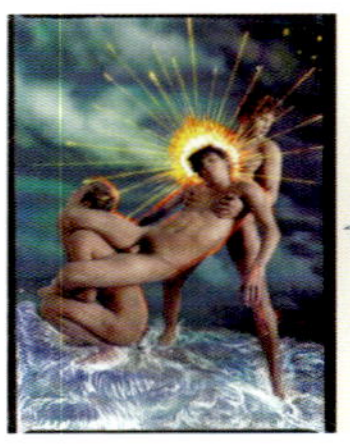

No More Fear, 2012
Hollywood

Revelations, 1987
Farmington, Connecticut

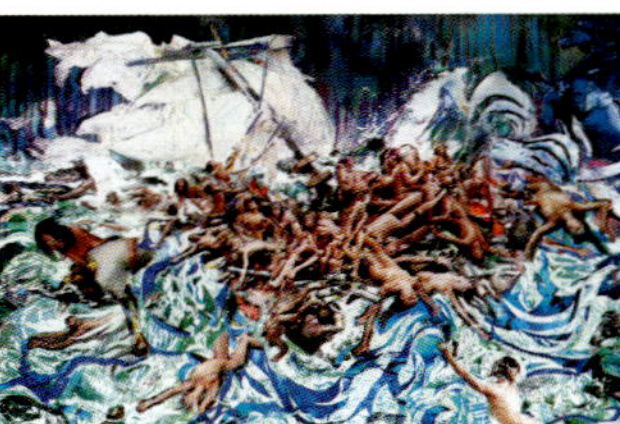

I Among the Lost, 2009
Hawaii

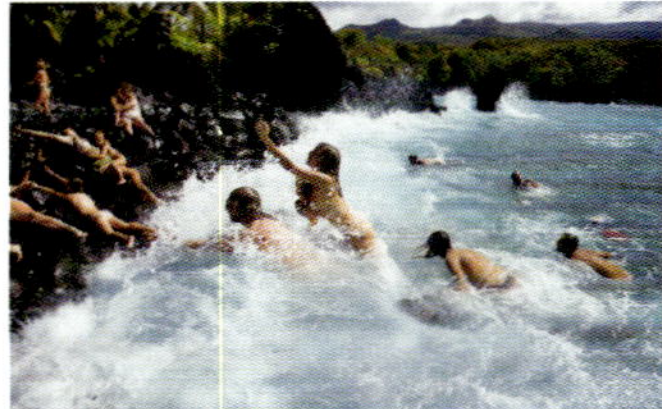

Now at the Shore!, 2009
Hawaii

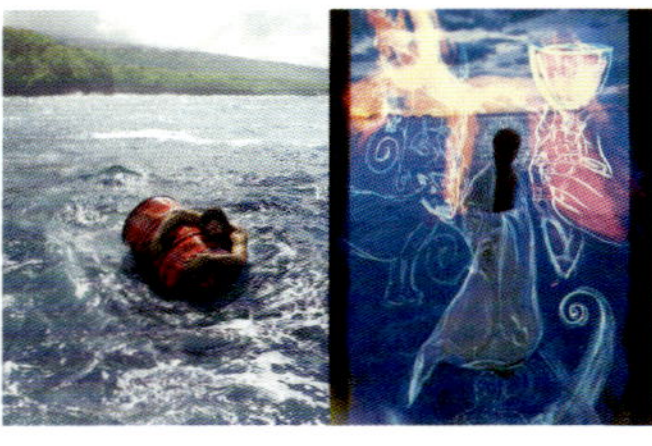

Then I Saw a New Heaven and a New Earth, for the First Heaven and the First Earth Had Passed Away, 2009 | 1986

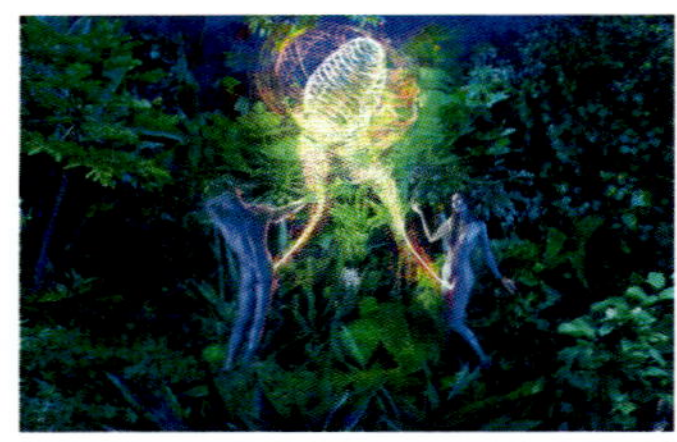

A New Adam
A New Eve, 2009

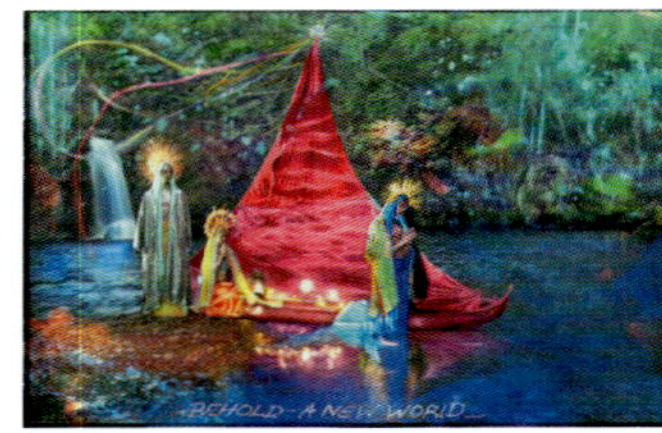

A New World, 2015

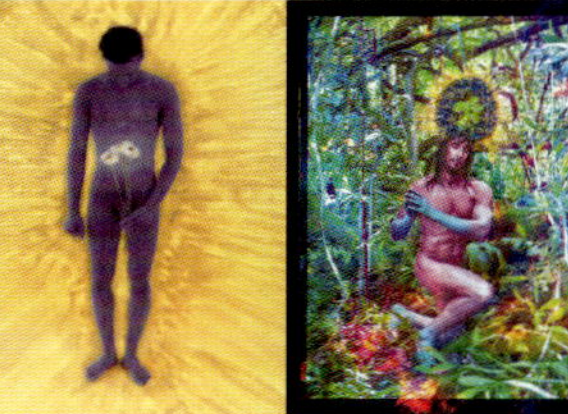

Please Forgive Me, 1986
NYC

Joy Ever More!
Hawaii

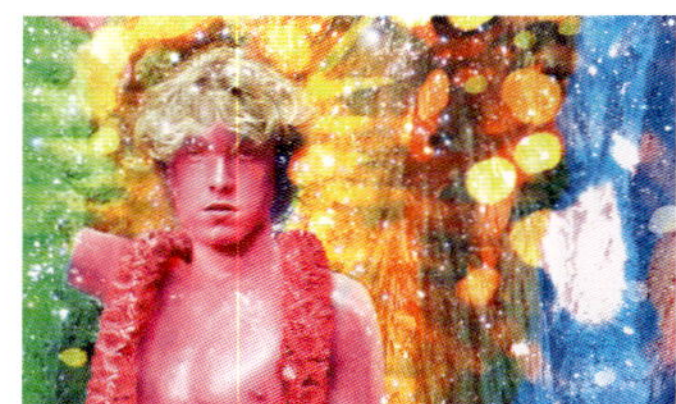

In Paradise, 2015

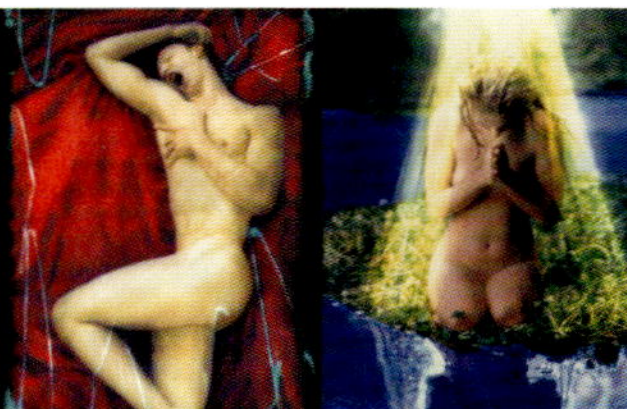

There Is No More Suffering, 1987
NYC

For This I Give Thanks, 1988

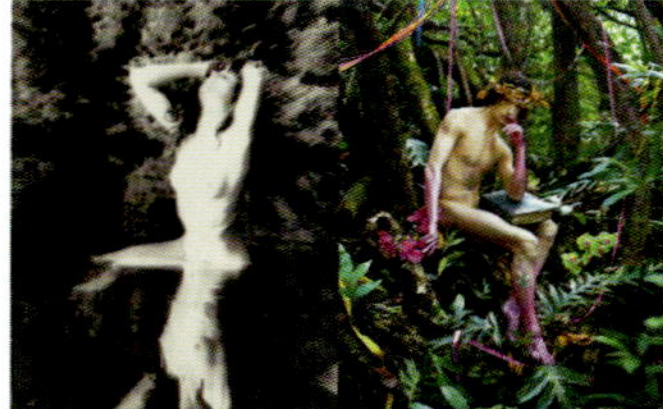

Still Waters, 1984
Farmington, Connecticut

The Prophets and Teachers
The Artists
You and I, 2015
Hawaii

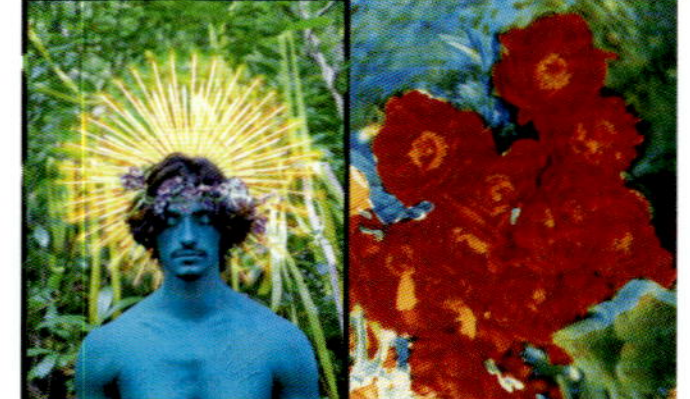

Blessed, 2015

Flowers Bloom, 1988
NYC

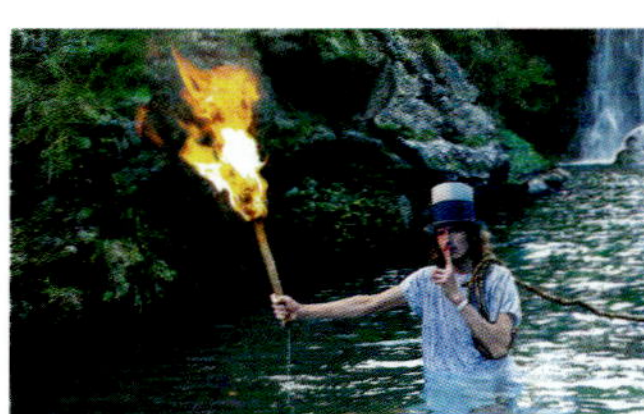

I Believe, 2015
Hawaii

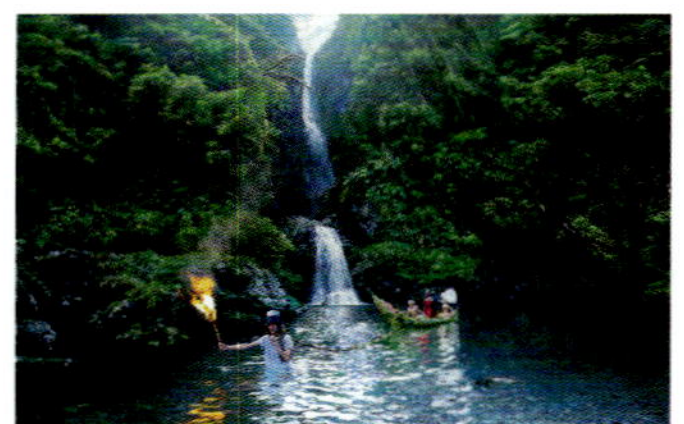

In Truth and Love, 2015
Hawaii
All religions are like guides for living—they are alike in many ways—rivers of truth leading to the same ocean.

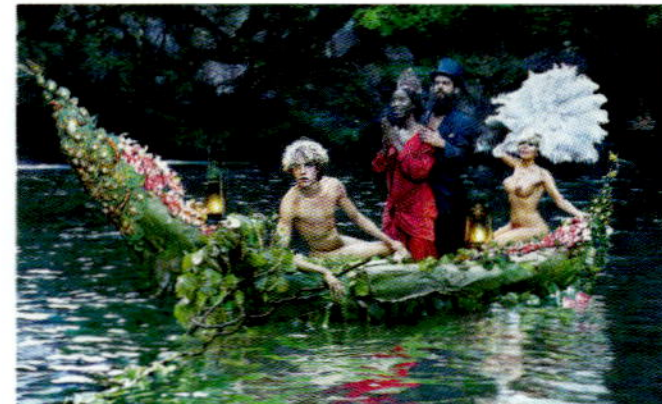

Forever

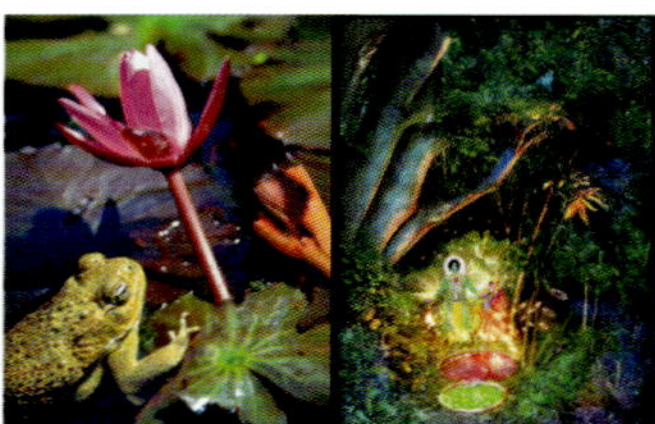

The Frog Protects the Flower, 2007

Under a Tree, 2015

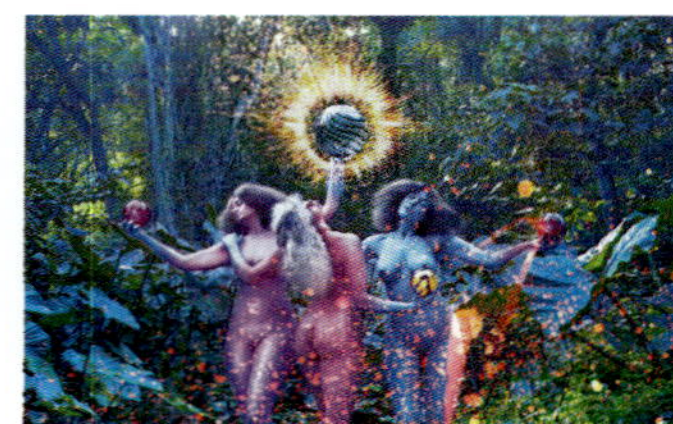

Praise Dance, 2009
We must be joyful.

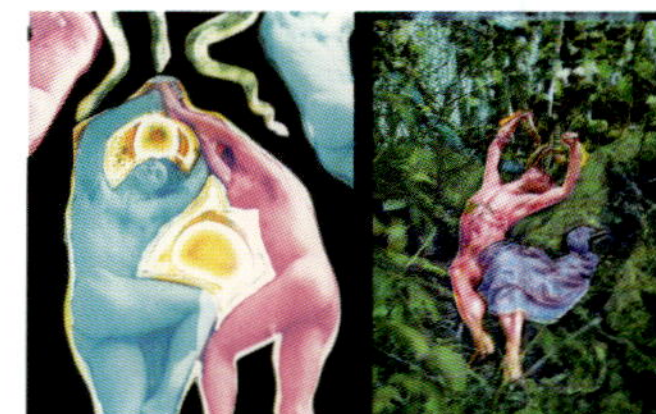

Abel Forgives Cain for Killing Him, 1989
NYC

Guilt Is a Serpent to Be Cast Out, 2015
Hawaii

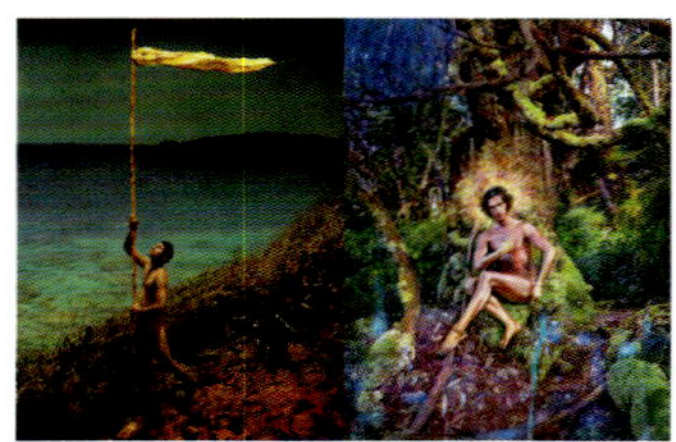

I Am Free Now!, 1986
Culebra, Puerto Rico

To Be Who I Really Am, 2016
Hawaii

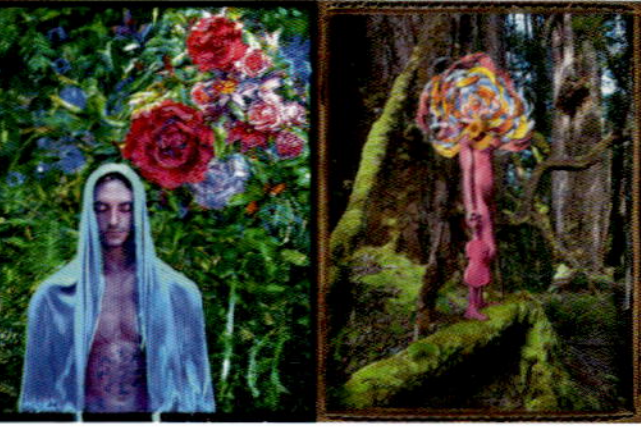

All I Need to Know

Songs in My Head, 2015
Hawaii

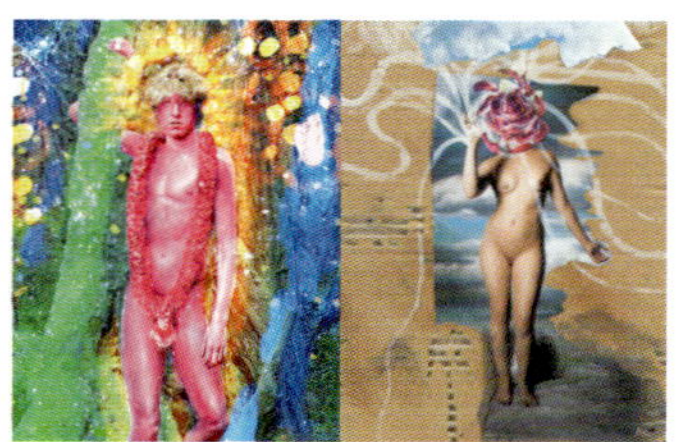

We Shine So Brightly, 2015

The Gift, 2010
Los Angeles

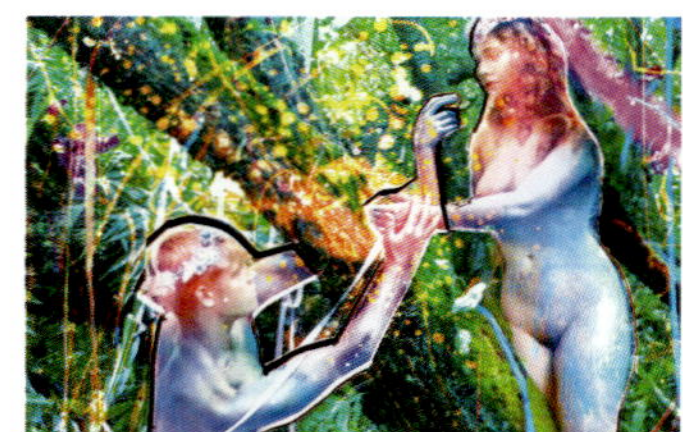

Found We, 2010
Hawaii

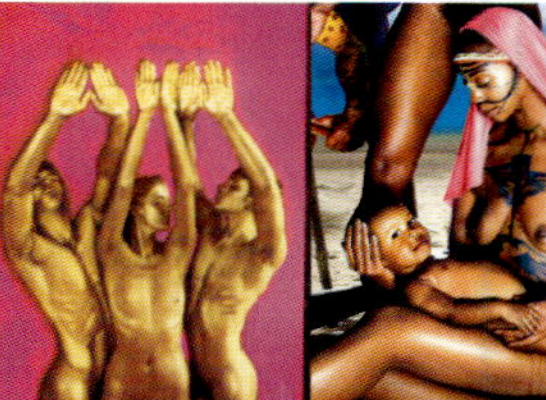

Glorify, 1986
NYC

Nativity, 2012
Hollywood

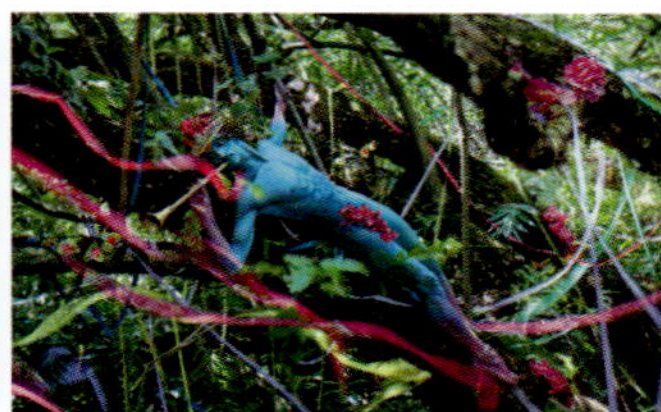

Make a Joyful Noise, 2015
Hawaii

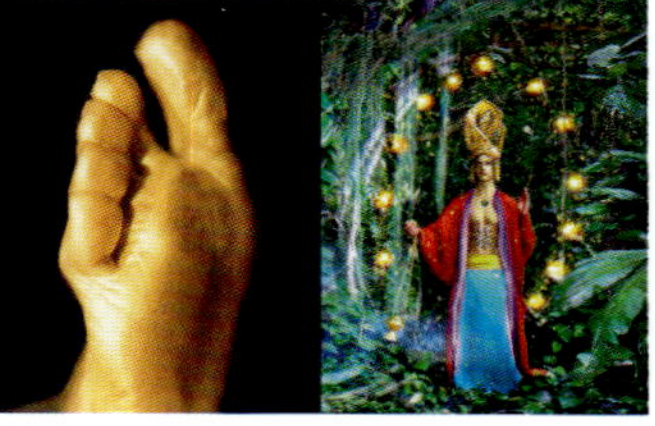

Pillar, 1985
NYC

Beautiful Rituals in Nature's Cathedral, 2015

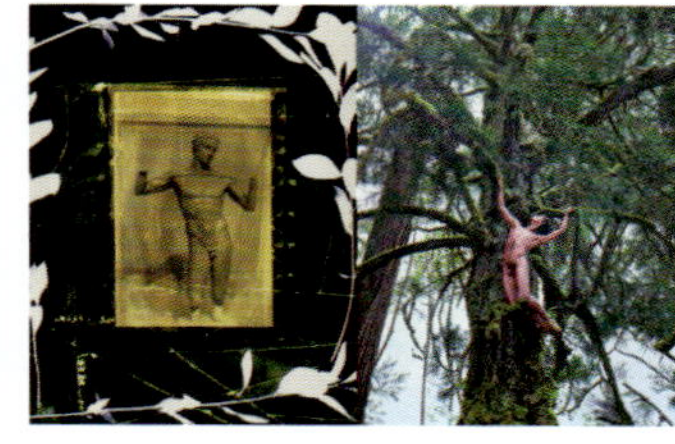

Be Brave, 1988
NYC
"The woods are lovely dark and deep—but I have promises to keep, and miles to go before I sleep… and miles to go before I sleep."
—Robert Frost

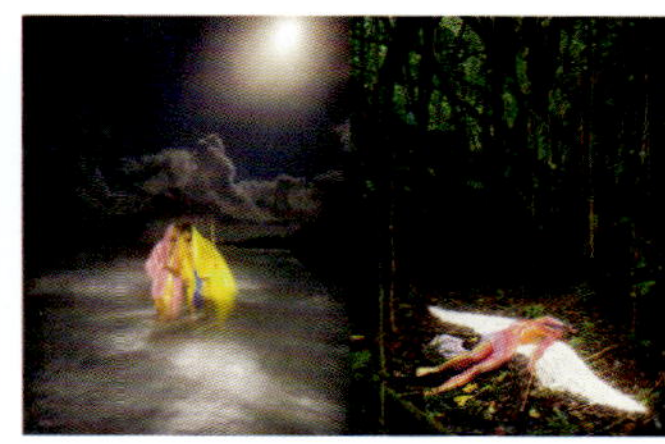

Good Friday, 2015

What Was Unseen, 2013
Hawaii

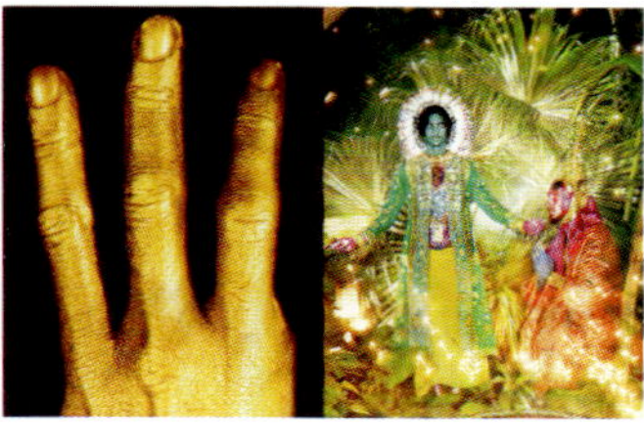

Touch, 1985
NYC

Holy Ones, 2015
We can live like this!

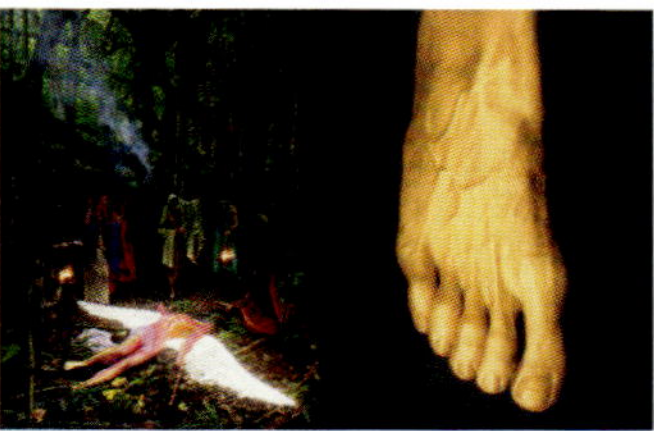

Is Now Discovered, 2013

Paces, 1985
NYC

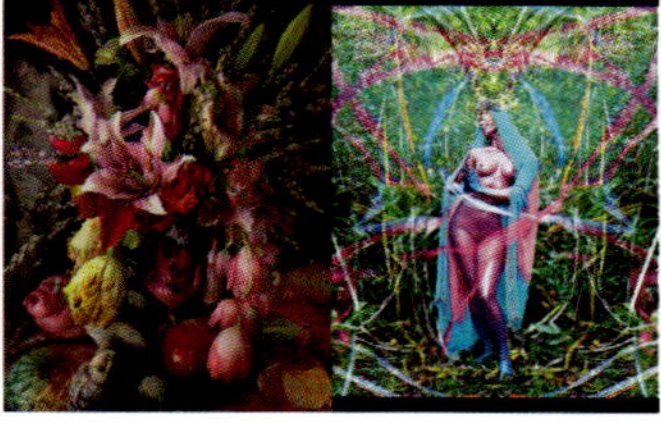

Earth Laughs in Flowers, 2008–2011

New Creation I Am, 2014

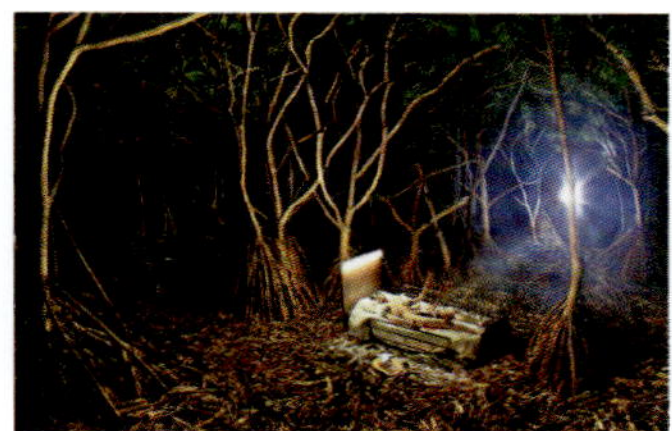

Reborn! Nature's Transfusion, 2009
Hawaii

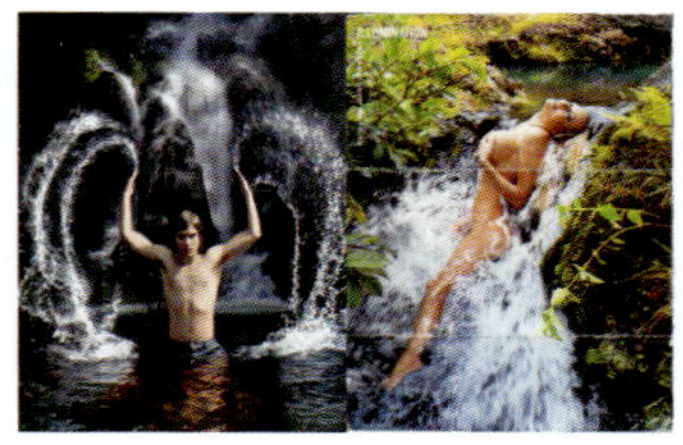

In Water We Let Go Of Everything, 2008 | 2010
Hawaii

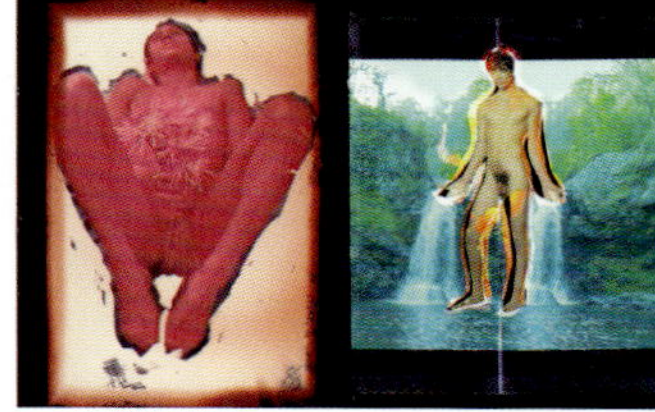

Flower Seed, 1987
NYC

Sorrow Falls Away, 2008
Hawaii

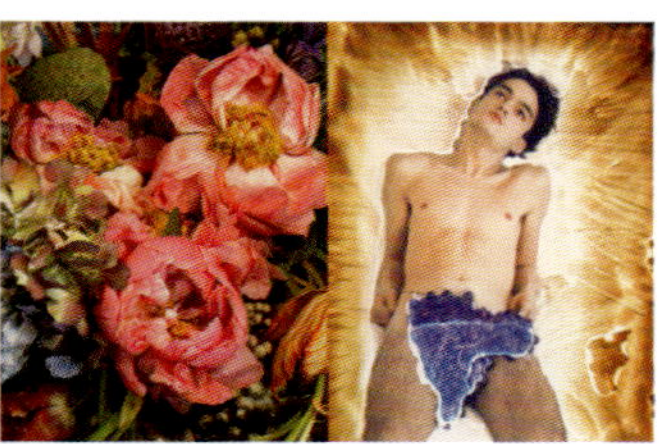

For You, 2008–2011
Los Angeles

Luis, 1988
NYC

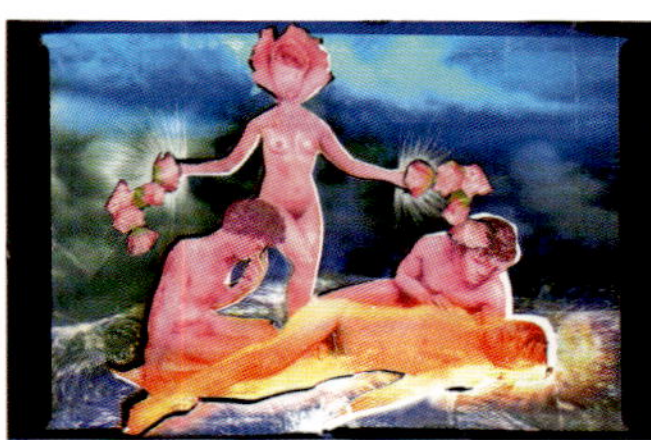

All the Flowers Decided to Glow, 2008
Los Angeles

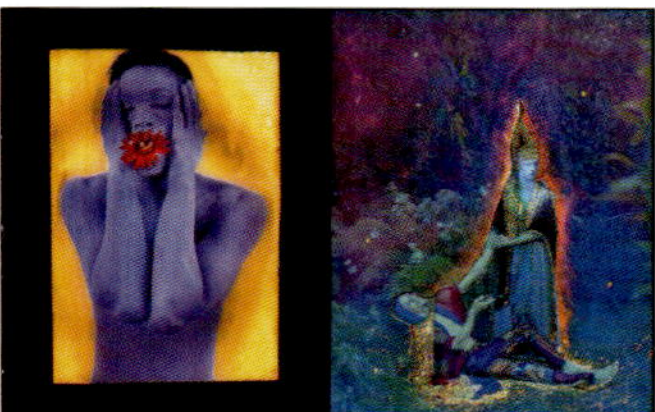

Song, 1986
NYC

When We Gather Together, 2014
Hawaii

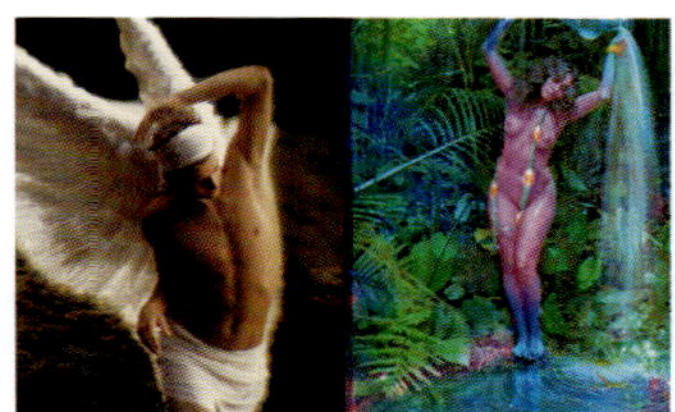

Adore, 1987
Farmington, Connecticut

Birth, 2013

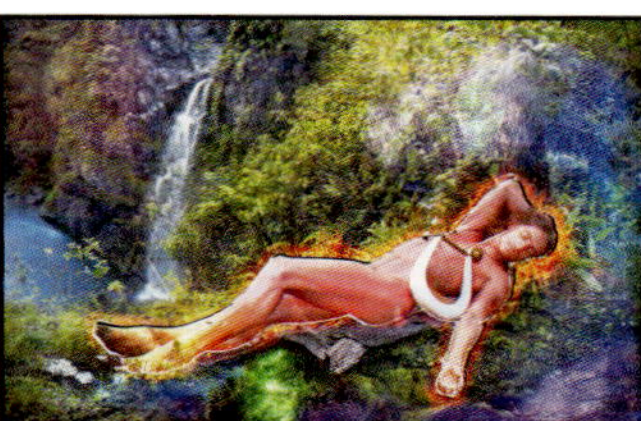

A Time to Rest, 2015
Hawaii

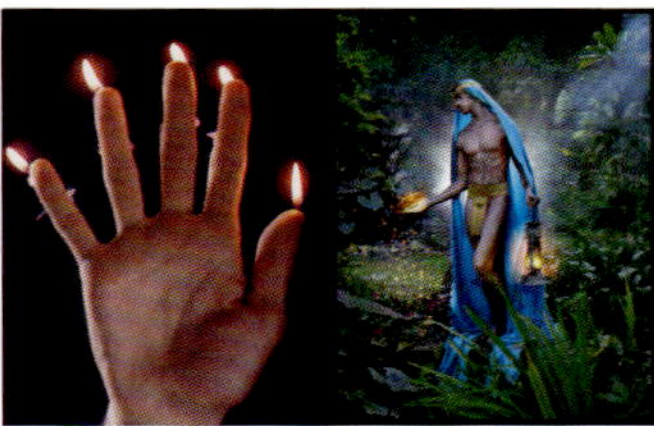

Touched by Fire, 1986
NYC

Sparks of Light, 2015

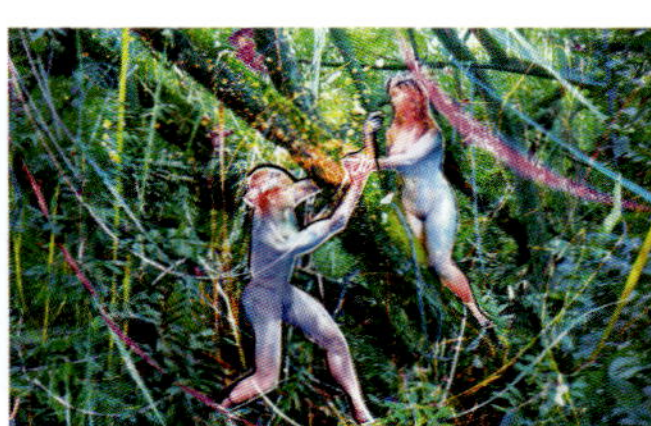

Here We Find Ourselves, 2015

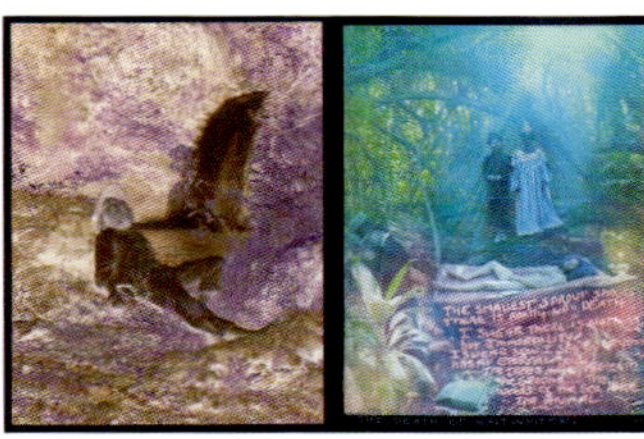

Walt Whitman, 2014

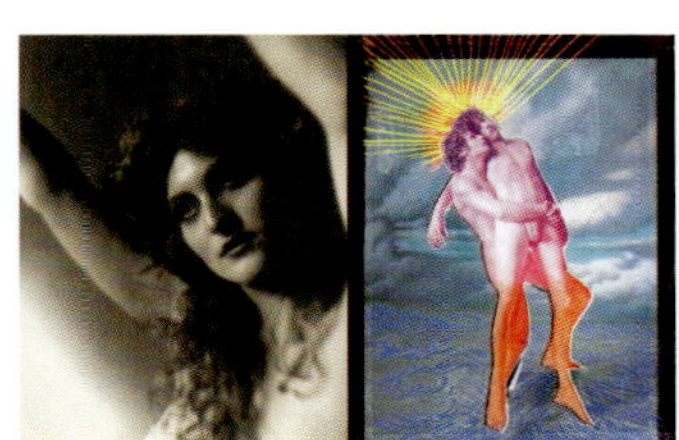

Songs of Myself, 1984
NYC

The Greatest Of These Is Love, 2007
Los Angeles

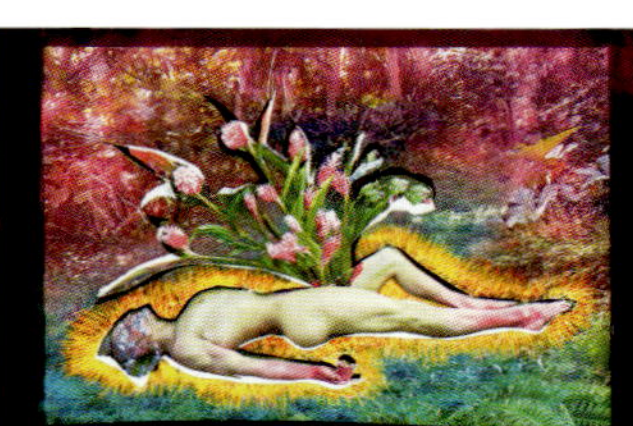

Flowers Grow
Hawaii

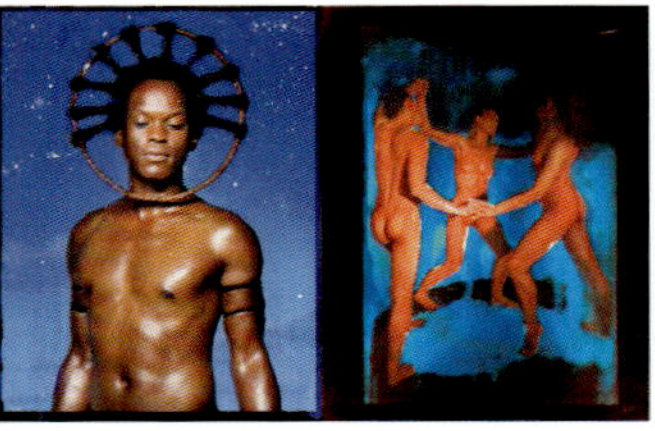

Joseph Zdiz
Hollywood

Dance, 1987
NYC
We must dance + sing! Our love must be demonstrated with joy!

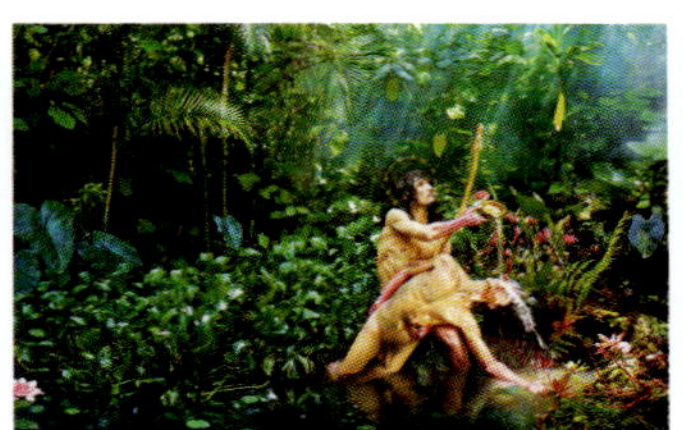

Water Flows, Eyes Closed, I Am New Again, 2015
Hawaii

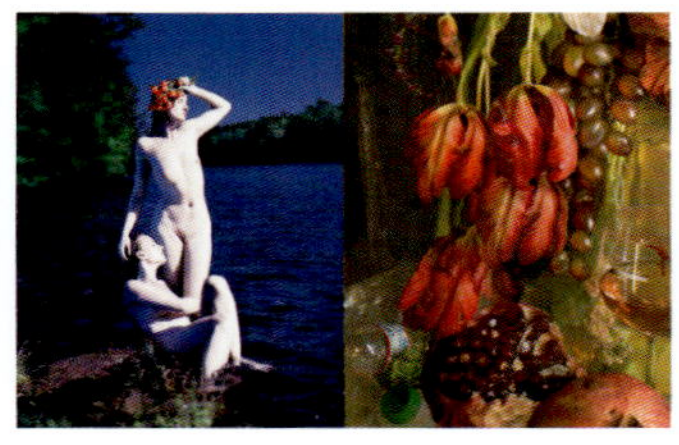

This Day Is Ours, 1985
Farmington, Connecticut

Earth Laughs in Flowers, 2008–2011
Los Angeles

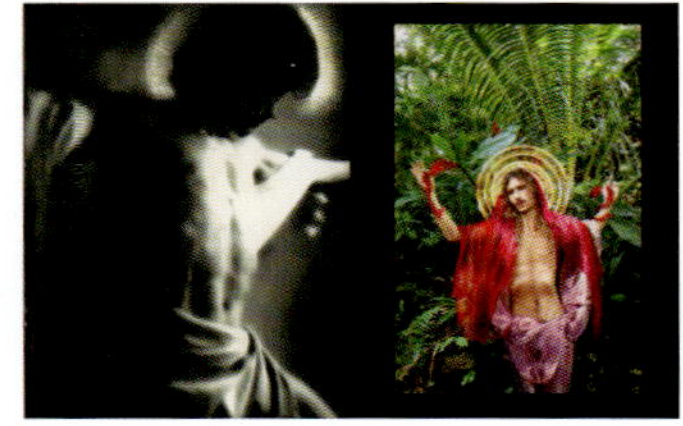

Friend, 1984
NYC

Passion of the Flowers, 2019
NYC

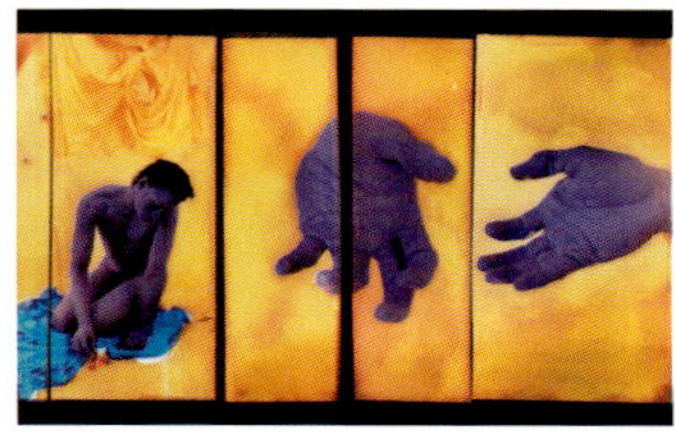

To Listen to Hear, 1987
NYC

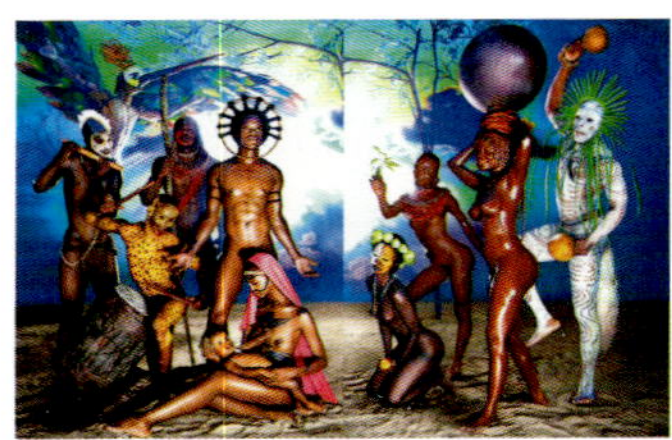

Nativity, 2012
Hollywood

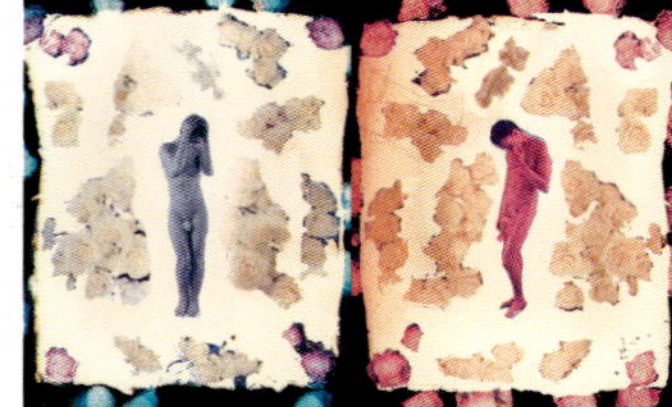

Here Lands the Female
Here Lands the Male, 1988
NYC

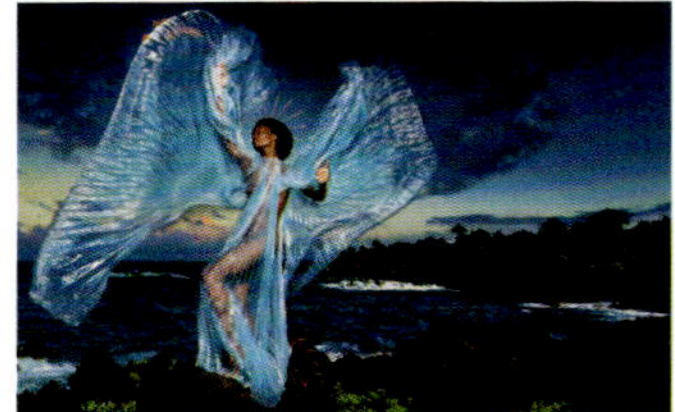

Sister Moon, 2019

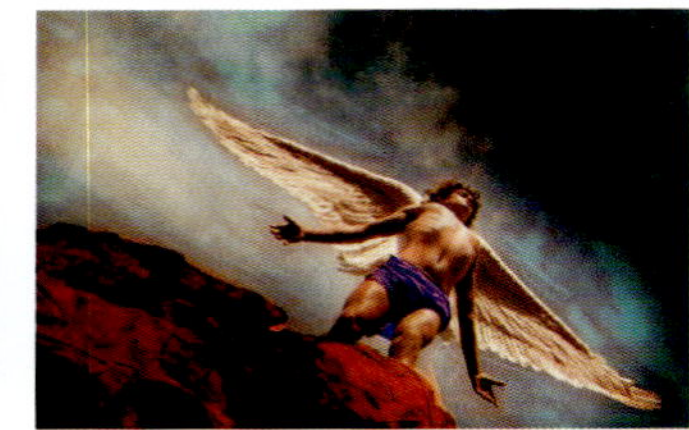

Fly on My Sweet Angel
Fly on to the Sky, 1988
Farmington, Connecticut

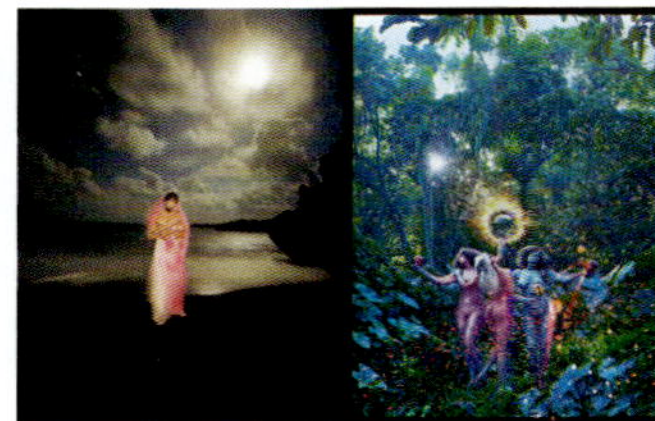

The Moon and the Sun, 2011

Praise!, 2009

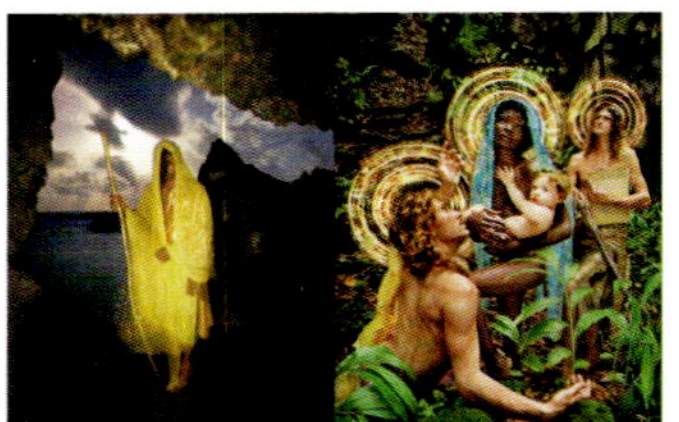

Each New Dawn, 2011
Hawaii

Holy Family with
Saint Francis, 2019

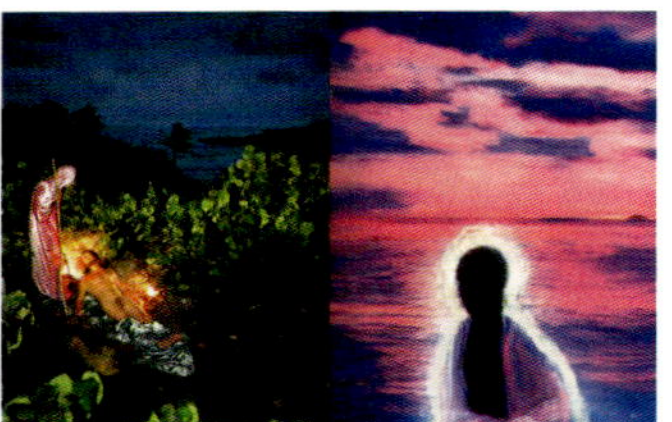

Arise, 2015

All is Illuminated, 1986
Brazil

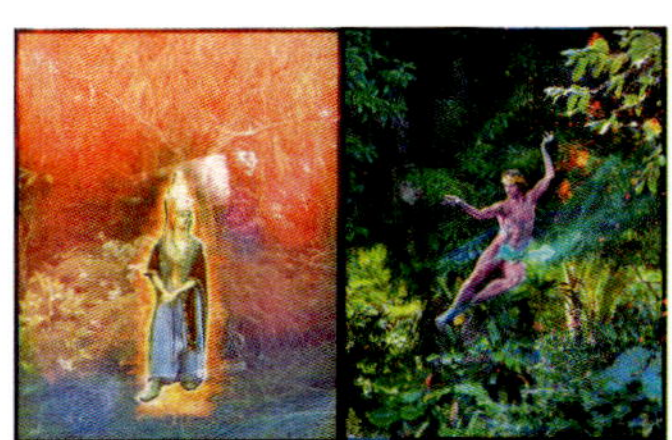

Buddha Under a Tree, 2015

In Awe You Glide
Floating Upward

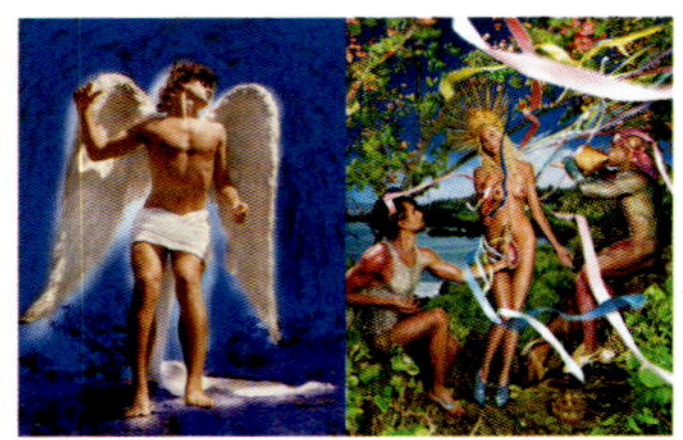

Gabriel Messenger, 1988
Farmington, Connecticut

Rebirth of Venus, 2015

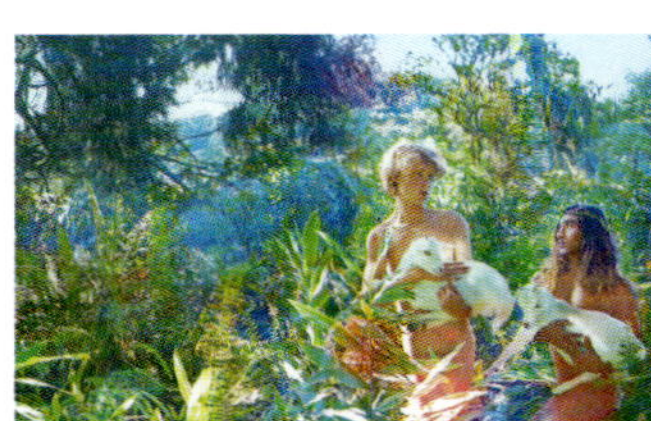

On Earth in Heaven as It Is, 2015

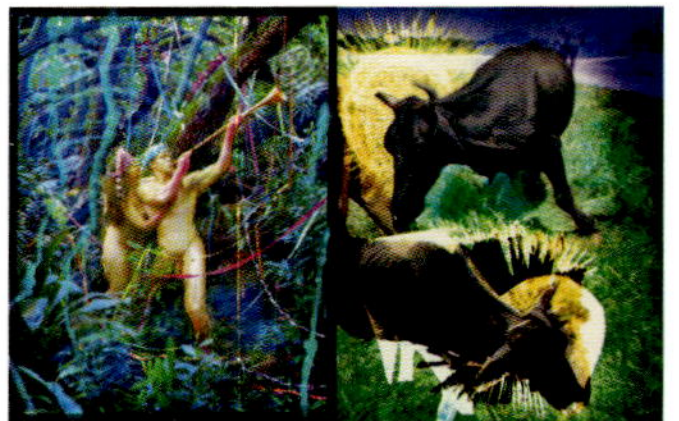

For All the World to Hear, 2013
Hawaii

Sacred Life, 1986
Brazil

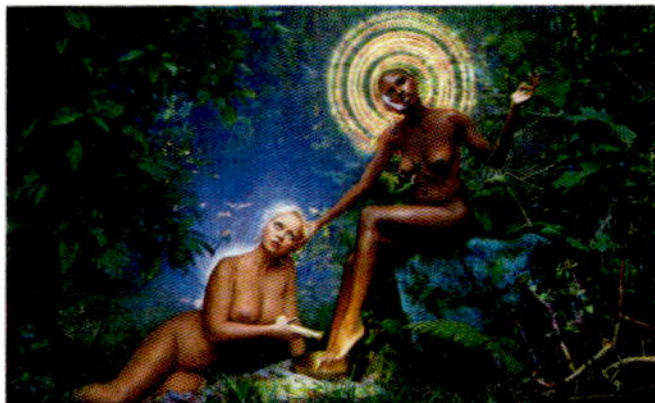

We Forgave Deeply Then Love
Flooded Our Hearts, 2017

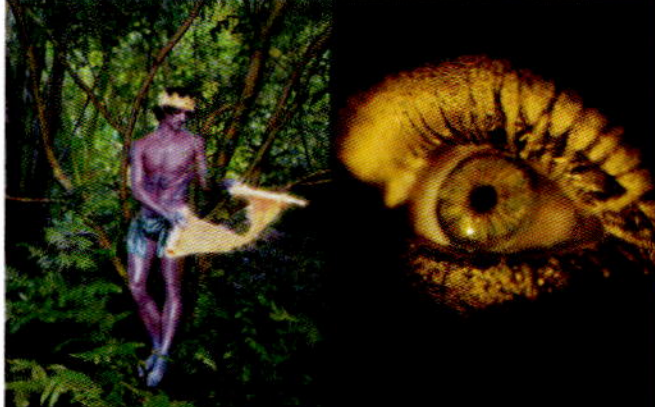

Seek the Truth, 2015
Hawaii

Now I See, 1985
NYC

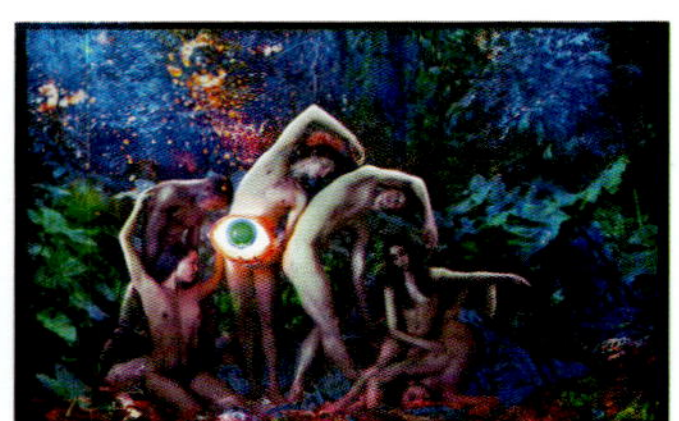

We are Blessed, 2017
Hawaii

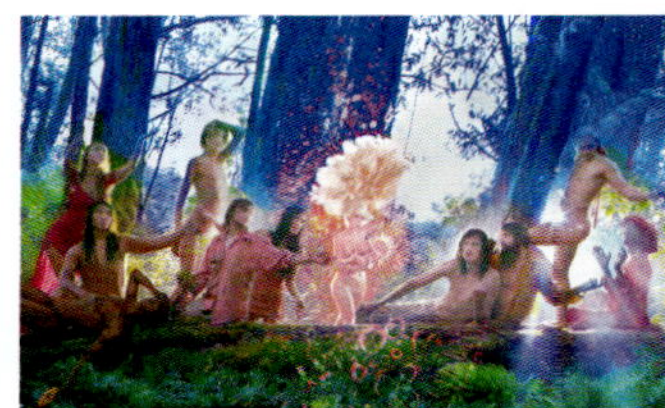

The First Supper, 2015

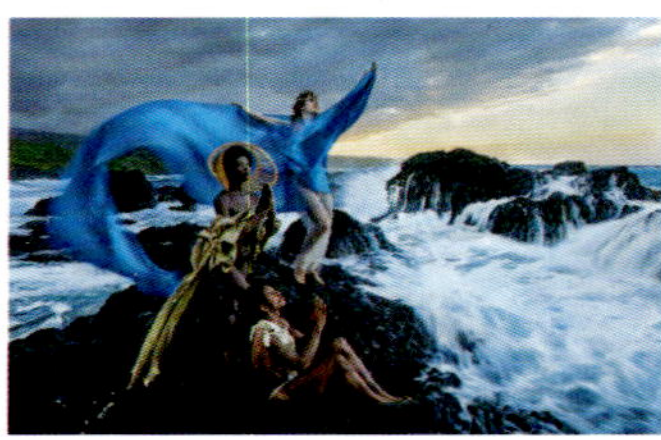

Eventide, 2019

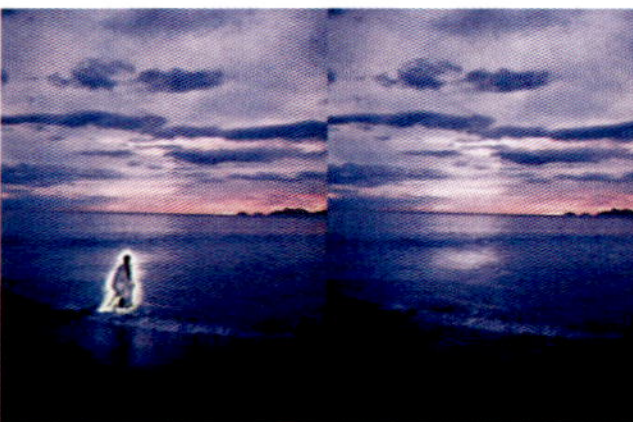

Fernando Meets Iemanjá, 1986
Brazil

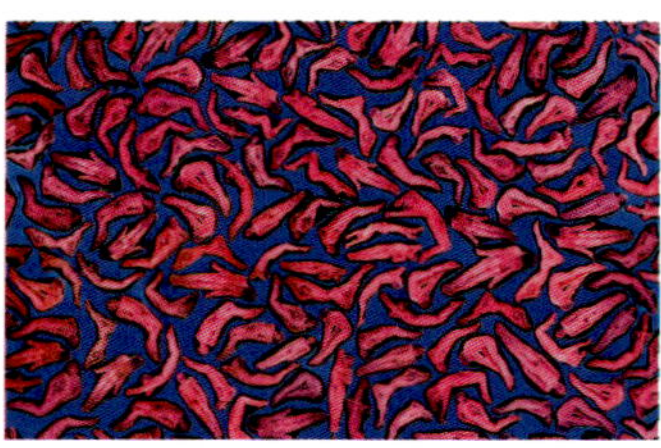

Adam Under a Microscope—
Theology and Science Align,
1990

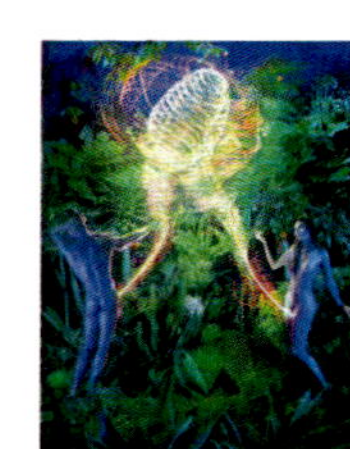

A New Adam
A New Eve, 2009
Detail

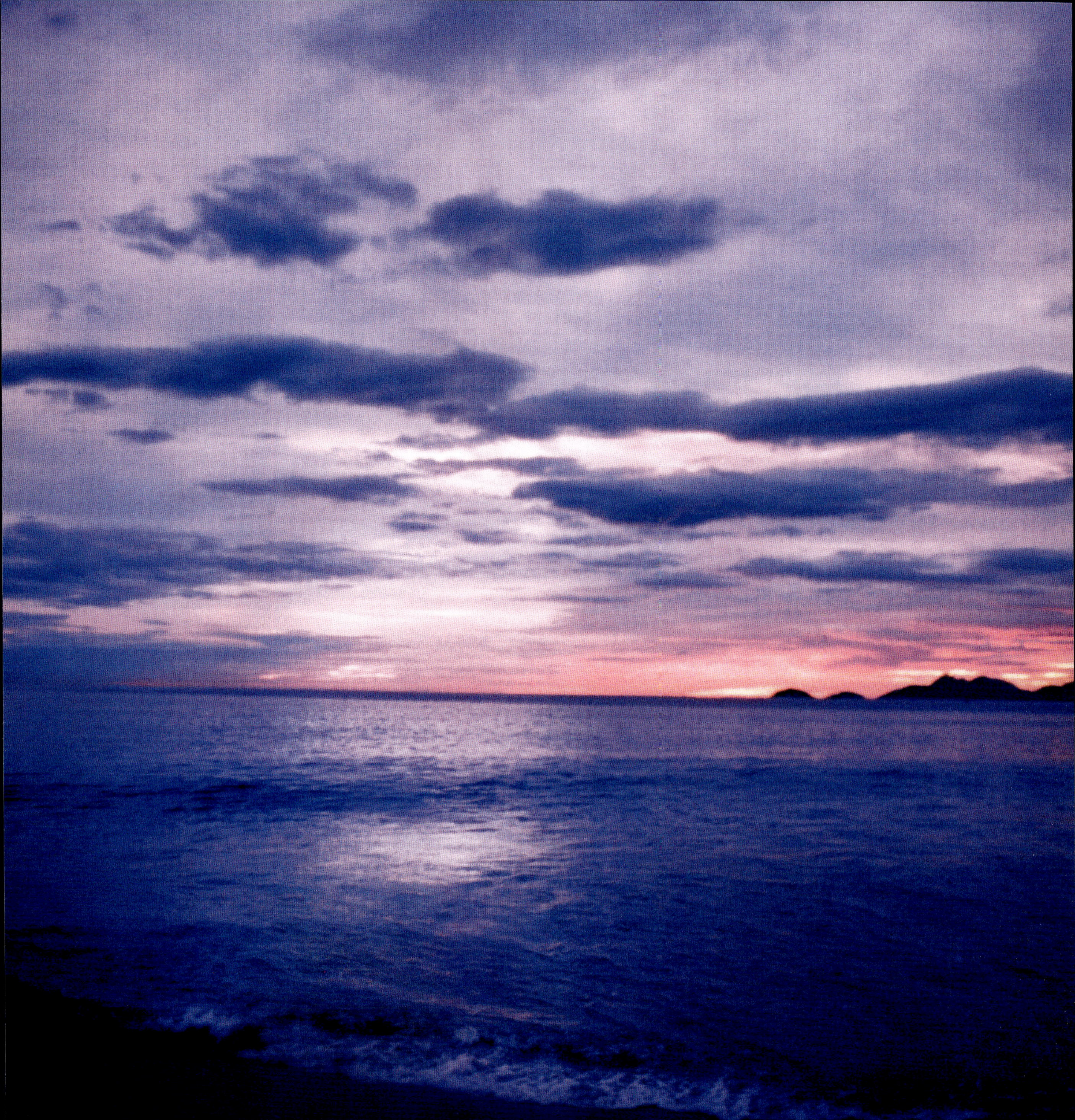

THESE TWO BOOKS, *LOST + FOUND* AND *GOOD NEWS* ARE FOR CHRISTOPHER,
MY DIAMOND IN THE WINDOW.

TO ALL OF THE ARTISTS WHOM I'VE HAD THE PRIVILEGE AND HONOR TO WORK WITH—
ALL OF THE PEOPLE WHO HAVE MADE THESE BOOKS POSSIBLE, BOTH BEHIND THE SCENES,
AND IN FRONT OF THE CAMERA—TO MY FAMILY, SONJA LACHAPELLE, HELGA & PHILLIP LACHAPELLE,
BAMBINI, KUMI, GHRETTA, AND MAMA MAKEUP—MY LOVE AND GRATITUDE.
DAVID LACHAPELLE

A PORTION OF THE AUTHOR'S PROFITS FROM THIS BOOK WILL BE DONATED TO SMILE TRAIN.

EACH AND EVERY TASCHEN BOOK PLANTS A SEED!
TASCHEN IS A CARBON NEUTRAL PUBLISHER. EACH YEAR, WE OFFSET OUR ANNUAL CARBON EMISSIONS WITH
CARBON CREDITS AT THE INSTITUTO TERRA, A REFORESTATION PROGRAM IN MINAS GERAIS, BRAZIL, FOUNDED
BY LÉLIA AND SEBASTIÃO SALGADO. TO FIND OUT MORE ABOUT THIS ECOLOGICAL PARTNERSHIP,
PLEASE CHECK: WWW.TASCHEN.COM/ZEROCARBON

TO STAY INFORMED ABOUT TASCHEN AND OUR UPCOMING TITLES, PLEASE SUBSCRIBE TO OUR FREE
MAGAZINE AT WWW.TASCHEN.COM/MAGAZINE, FOLLOW US ON INSTAGRAM AND FACEBOOK,
OR EMAIL YOUR QUESTIONS TO CONTACT@TASCHEN.COM.

HOHENZOLLERNRING 53, D-50672 KÖLN
WWW.TASCHEN.COM

EDITED AND DESIGNED BY DAVID LACHAPELLE AND NEMUEL DEPAULA, LOS ANGELES

PRINTED IN ITALY
ISBN 978-3-8365-9965-8

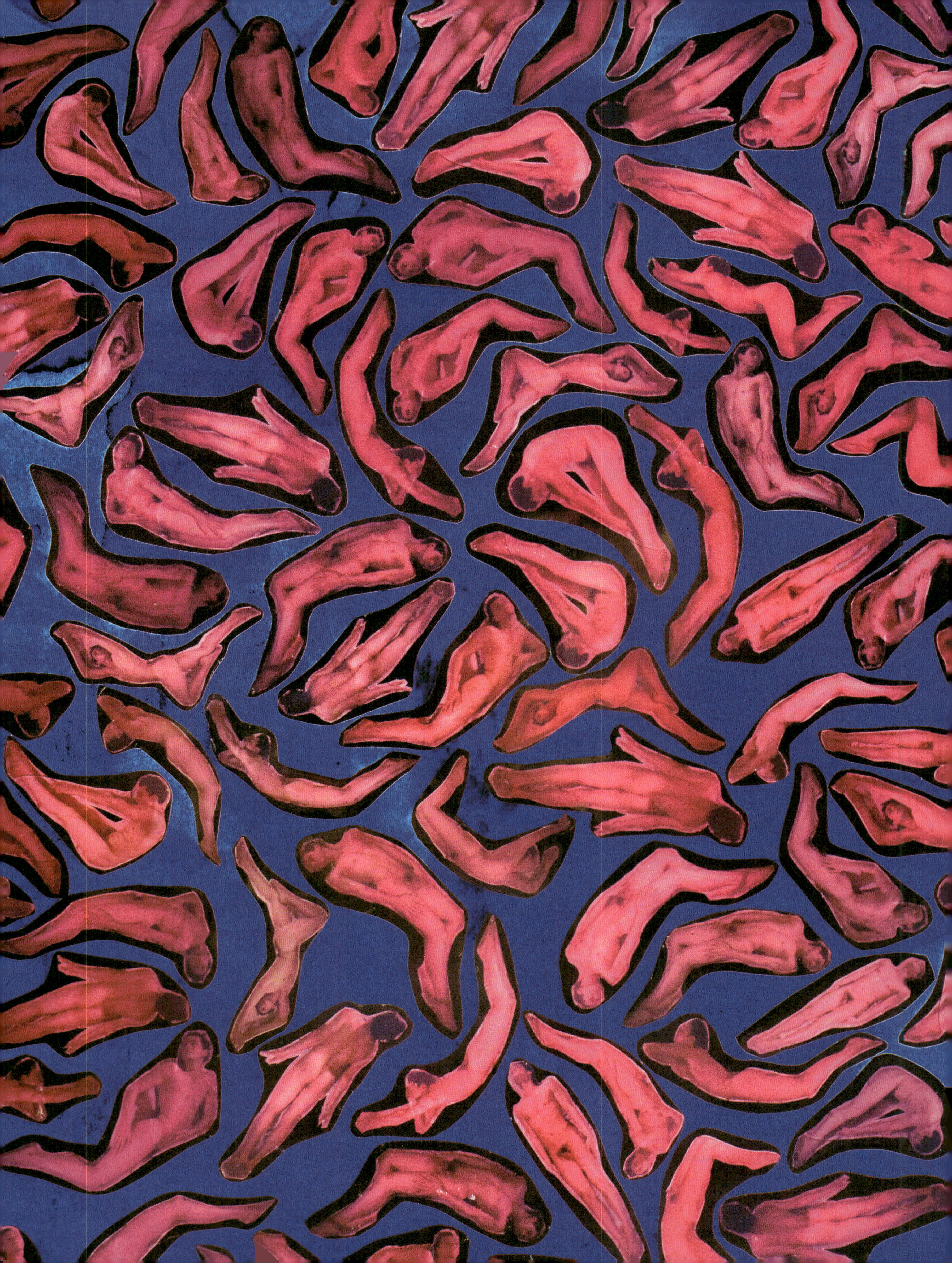